Francis Vinton Greene

The Russian Army and its Campaigns in Turkey in 1877-1878

Francis Vinton Greene

The Russian Army and its Campaigns in Turkey in 1877-1878

ISBN/EAN: 9783337168742

Printed in Europe, USA, Canada, Australia, Japan

Cover: Foto ©ninafisch / pixelio.de

More available books at **www.hansebooks.com**

THE
RUSSIAN ARMY

AND

ITS CAMPAIGNS IN TURKEY

IN

1877-1878.

BY

F. V. GREENE,

FIRST LIEUTENANT IN THE CORPS OF ENGINEERS, U. S. ARMY, AND LATELY MILITARY ATTACHÉ
TO THE UNITED STATES LEGATION AT ST. PETERSBURG.

NEW YORK:
D. APPLETON AND COMPANY,
549 AND 551 BROADWAY.
1879.

PREFACE.

Soon after the outbreak of the recent war between Russia and Turkey, I had the honor to be selected by the War Department to go abroad for the purpose of observing the military operations from the Russian side, and for this purpose was assigned to duty as Military Attaché to the United States Legation at St. Petersburg. I left New York on the 30th of June and reached St. Petersburg on the 18th of July, 1877, where the necessary formalities precedent to my joining the army, including the granting of the Emperor's permission, were speedily complied with, and I therefore proceeded without delay to the field, reaching the imperial headquarters on the 5th of August.

I remained with the army continuously throughout the rest of the campaign—reaching Constantinople with it in the following month of February—and until the month of July, 1878, when a definite peace was assured by the meeting of the Congress of Berlin. I then returned to St. Petersburg, resumed my post at the legation, and remained there until January, 1879, engaged in collecting and digesting the official reports of the war, as well as the data for a study of the Russian military system.

The following pages are a reprint, made with the permission

of the War Department, of my official report to the Government upon the subjects which I was sent abroad to report upon. This report aims to give, first, a concise but accurate description of the Russian Army; second, a narrative of the course of the campaigns in Europe and in Asia Minor; and third, a brief discussion of the use of temporary field fortifications in connection with the modern breech-loading musket.

The description of the Russian Army includes its laws of military service, its organization and strength in time of peace, and the development of which it is capable in time of war, the armament and equipment of its troops in the field, a synopsis of its system of military administration or Army Regulations, and some notes on its tactics. It is wholly based upon the data given in the following works:

1. "Spravotchnaia Kneeshka dlia Russkik Offizierof" ("Hand-Book of Information for Russian Officers"), by Major-General Makhotin, of the General Staff, 1875.
2. "Shtaty Russkik Regularnik Voisk," etc. ("Effective Strength of Russian Regular and Reserve Troops, Militia, and Military Departments and Establishments"), by Colonel Martianof, Russian General Staff, 1878.
3. "Zapisky Voiennoe Administratzie" ("Memoir on Russian Military Administration, for the use of Military Schools"), by Colonel Lobko, Russian General Staff, 1877.
4. "The New Law regulating Military Service in Russia," translated in the Intelligence Branch of the Quartermaster-General's Department, Horse Guards, London, 1875.
5. "The Armed Strength of Russia,"* translated at the Intelligence Branch of the Quartermaster-General's Department, Horse Guards, from a report published by the Austrian Staff in 1871.

The narrative of the campaign is based primarily upon the official reports of the Russian commanders, which were published in the Russian reviews and in the semi-official French paper at St. Petersburg. My own notes made during the cam-

* So many changes have taken place since this report was drawn up, that it is now useful only for the condition of the army in 1871.

paign, including reports made from time to time of the progress of events, were very numerous, and have been freely used. While with the troops at the front I usually received copies of the field orders for every movement, and these, combined with my observation of the actual results, afforded me a great many very valuable data. Personally I was present in the battles of Shipka, August 23d and 24th, 1877; Plevna, September 11, 1877; Taskossen, December 31, 1877; and Philippopolis, January 15–17, 1878, besides a few minor combats and skirmishes. I was also at the headquarters of the Cesarevitch in October, and rode along the line of his outposts and positions between the Lom and Yantra. I passed the Balkans with Gourko's column during the winter, and remained with it until it reached Adrianople; I then joined General Skobeleff, who commanded the advance guard, and arrived in front of Constantinople with him.

Of the operations which I thus personally witnessed, the official reports gave an extremely clear and faithful account, and I have therefore placed full reliance upon all the official reports. In the few rare cases where the statement of relative losses seemed exaggerated, an exception has been noted in the following pages.

Besides the official reports, I have consulted more or less the following works:

1. "Der Kampf um Plevna," von Thilo von Trotha, Berlin, 1878.
2. "Russisch-Türkische Krieg im Jahre 1877," von Carl Regenspursky, Wien, 1878.
3. "Rückblicke auf die Russische Taktik," von Norbert Spaleny, Gras, 1878.
4. "Die Armee-Operationen im Balkan-Feldzug," von Cardinal von Widdern, Berlin, 1878.
5. "Der Orientalische Krieg in den Jahren 1877 und 1878," von W. Rüstow, Zürich, 1878.
6. "Der Russisch-Türkische Krieg 1877 bis 1878," von Christian von Sarauw, Leipzig, 1878.
7. "Guerre d'Orient en 1876–1877," par Colonel Ferdinand Lecomte, Lausanne, 1878.

8. "La Fortification du Champ de Bataille," par Lieutenant-General A. Brialmont, Bruxelles, 1878.
9. "La Guerre d'Orient," par Amédée Le Faure, Paris, 1878.
10. War correspondence of the "Daily News," 1877-'78.

The "Daily News" Correspondence, as well as that of "The Times," is replete with the most interesting information on every subject connected with the war; and, in the absence of official Turkish reports, they form our principal source of information from that side. On the Russian side about seventy-five correspondents began the campaign, but only three followed it to its close. These three, viz., Messrs. J. A. MacGahan and F. D. Millet of the "Daily News," and Mr. E. M. Grant of "The Times," were all men of fine abilities and education, and although all three were foreigners (Americans) they were unusually well qualified to speak on the subjects of which they wrote, from previous experience in other wars and from long familiarity with the Eastern Question, no less than from their literary skill. The correspondence of Mr. Archibald Forbes, which attained such celebrity, is most graphic, but unfortunately it terminates early in the campaign, with the battle at Plevna in September, and the conclusions which he formed on returning to England are therefore founded on somewhat incomplete data.

Mr. MacGahan, as is well known, fell a victim at Constantinople to the typhus fever, which attacked his overworked brain and caused his death after a few days' illness. In him that large portion of the public which derives its information from the daily papers rather than from books lost one of its most valuable and faithful contributors, and America lost a son who had carried a reputation for pluck, energy, and fair statements throughout Europe and into the heart of Central Asia.

Of the political questions of the war no mention is made in the following pages except in so far as they had a direct immediate bearing upon the military operations. My sympathies, like those of a majority of my countrymen, were originally on the side of Russia, and my experience only served to confirm those sympathies; but this book only aims to give a strictly accurate account of the *military* steps in the process by which Russia crushed Turkey as a military power, and it was written without having any political views or aims in consideration.

Nor is there in the following pages anything referring to personal experiences, or to reminiscences of the principal commanders. It is, therefore, proper to state here that the Russian authorities extended to all the foreign officers who came properly accredited to them the most generous and open-hearted hospitality, and the most complete facilities for observing the course of events as they actually transpired. During the campaign there were present with the army military officers representing Germany, Austria, France, England, Denmark, Sweden, Switzerland, Japan, and the United States, as well as special delegates from Servia, Roumania, and Montenegro. In all we numbered at one time 18 officers. We were all presented to the Emperor on our arrival, and remained at his headquarters for several days, during which we were always his guests at table. We were then attached (nominally) to the Staff of the Grand Duke Nicholas, commanding the army, and there received the same hospitality as at the Emperor's. Those who desired to see the operations from a closer point of view than the general headquarters were invariably granted full permission to join whatever troops they chose, and there in turn, with one or two exceptions, the same hearty reception was accorded to them by the generals in command, so far as they had the means. By thus passing from one detachment of the troops to another and then returning to the general headquarters, a full opportunity was afforded of following the course of affairs and of judging of them in their general aspect as well as in their details.

At St. Petersburg the same official courtesy was extended to me by the Heads of Departments in the War Ministry, particularly the general staff, artillery, and engineers, in furnishing maps, plans, drawings, and information of every kind. I have endeavored to avoid any indiscretion in the use of this material, and in relation to the organization of the army have confined myself to extracts from Russian or other works already in print and which have long since found their way to the general staff of every army in Europe. The illustrations in the text and the maps composing the atlas are all based upon Russian information thus furnished, supplemented by a few sketches of my own.

F. V. G.

WASHINGTON, *April*, 1879.

CONTENTS.

PART I.

THE RUSSIAN ARMY.

	PAGE
CHAPTER I.—The Laws of Recruiting and Military Service..........	3
II.—Strength and Organization of the Land Forces	19
III.—Armament and Equipment............	52
IV.—Methods of Administration........................	82
V.—Tactics.................................	128

PART II.

THE CAMPAIGN IN BULGARIA.

INTRODUCTORY.—Declaration of War—The Theatre of Operations—Plan of Campaign............................. 139

CHAPTER I.—First Period of the War, April 24th to June 27th—The Concentration in Roumania and Passage of the Danube.. 147

II.—Operations of the Advance Guard under Gourko, July 12th to August 6th........................... 163

III.—Operations of the Right Wing, under Lieutenant-General Baron Krüdener......................... 185

IV.—General Condition of Affairs at the beginning of August—Battle of Shipka Pass, August 20th to 26th—Operations on the Lom in August and September.. 202

V.—Operations on the Right Flank in August and September—Battles of Lovtcha, September 3d, and Plevna, September 11th............................. 224

VI.—The Investment of Plevna—Battle of Gorni-Dubnik, October 24th, 1877............................ 262

VII.—Events on other portions of the Theatre of War from September to December, 1877—Shipka—The Lom—The Lower Danube—Gourko's Advance to Orkhanie 281

xiv   CONTENTS.

                                                                    PAGE
CHAPTER VIII.—The Fall of Plevna............................ 298
        IX.—The Passage of the Balkans near Sophia by Gourko's
              Column................. 321
         X.—Gourko's Advance to Philippopolis, and the Battles
              near that point, January 15th to 17th, 1878...... 338
        XI.—Capture of the Turkish Army at Shipka Pass 348
       XII.—The Advance to Constantinople—Remarks on the
              Winter Campaign........................... 358

                        PART III.

                THE CAMPAIGN IN ARMENIA.

CHAPTER I.—Progress of the Campaign from the Declaration of War
              to the Battle of Aladja Dagh, October 15th, 1877.. 377
       II.—Advance of the Russians to Erzeroum—The Storm of
              Kars, November 15th, 1877................ 397

                        PART IV.

    CONCLUSIONS—THE DEFENSE AND ATTACK OF FORTIFIED POSITIONS.

CHAPTER I.—General Remarks—Construction of the Turkish and
              Russian Fortifications, and their Defense 421
       II.—Attack of Fortified Positions...................... 440

INDEX TO PLATES.

REFERRED TO ON PAGES
No. 1. THE MILITARY CIRCUMSCRIPTIONS OF THE RUSSIAN EMPIRE..... 88
No. 2. THE THEATRE OF WAR IN EUROPE......... 142, 163, 176, 289, 338
No. 3. THE THEATRE OF WAR IN ASIA........................... 377
No. 4. PROGRESS MAP No. 1, APRIL 24TH TO JUNE 27TH.... 145, 150, 152
No. 5. PROGRESS MAP No. 2, JUNE 28TH TO DECEMBER 10TH......... 145
No. 6. PROGRESS MAP No. 3, DECEMBER 11TH TO MARCH 3D.... 145, 289, 324, 338
No. 7. CROSSING OF THE DANUBE AT GALATZ..................... 156
    CROSSING OF THE DANUBE AT ZIMNITZA-SISTOVA 158
No. 8. MAP OF THE VICINITY OF SISTOVA, NIKOPOLIS, AND PLEVNA, TO
    ILLUSTRATE THE MOVEMENTS OF THE RUSSIANS IMMEDIATELY
    AFTER THE PASSAGE OF THE DANUBE. 164, 185, 190, 225
No. 9. MAP OF THE BALKANS NEAR SHIPKA PASS, TO ILLUSTRATE
    GOURKO'S OPERATIONS IN JULY.................... 169, 176
No. 10. PLAN OF THE POSITIONS NEAR NIKOPOLIS............... 185, 186
No. 11. RELATIVE POSITIONS OF THE RUSSIAN AND TURKISH ARMIES,
    AUGUST 5TH.. 202
No. 12. PLEVNA, JULY 30TH 193, 195
No. 13. SHIPKA PASS 171, 207, 281
No. 14. COUNTRY BETWEEN THE LOM AND YANTRA RIVERS....... 215, 283
No. 15. BATTLE OF LOVTCHA..................................... 229
    BATTLE OF GORNI-DUBNIK................................. 273
    BATTLE OF METCHA-TRISTENIK............................. 285
No. 16. PLEVNA, SEPTEMBER 11TH........................ 236 *et seq.*
No. 17. THE INVESTMENT OF PLEVNA....... .... 262, 280
No. 18. PASSAGE OF THE BALKANS NEAR SOPHIA................ 292, 325
No. 19. PLEVNA, DECEMBER 10TH............................... 299
No. 20. THE BATTLES NEAR PHILIPPOPOLIS....................... 341
No. 21. MAP OF THE BALKANS NEAR SHIPKA PASS, TO ILLUSTRATE THE
    CAPTURE OF THE TURKISH ARMY....................... 348
No. 22. THE BATTLE OF ALADJA DAGH AND THE ASSAULT OF KARS ... 381, 390, 399
No. 23. TURKISH FORTIFICATIONS AT ADRIANOPLE 427
    TURKISH FORTIFICATIONS AT PLEVNA...................... 425
No. 24. TURKISH FORTIFICATIONS AT PLEVNA...................... 425
No. 25. RUSSIAN FORTIFICATIONS AT PLEVNA...................... 426
No. 26. FORTIFICATIONS AT SHIPKA PASS......................... 430
    INTRENCHING IMPLEMENTS..................... 429, 433, 437

PART I.

THE RUSSIAN ARMY.

THE RUSSIAN ARMY.

CHAPTER I.

LAWS OF RECRUITING AND MILITARY SERVICE.

THE military system of Russia, as it exists to-day, derives its authority from a ukase of the Emperor, dated January 1st (13th), 1874. Like that of every great nation on the continent of Europe, its fundamental principle is universal military service.

This principle is thus stated in the proclamation of the Emperor accompanying the ukase of that date:

"Having deemed it indispensable to reform the organization of the military forces of the Empire on the basis of the experience of the age, we ordered our Minister of War in 1870 to elaborate proposals for an improved system of recruitment for our armies, extending the obligation of military service to all classes of the population. . . .

"With a view to prepare a new regulation for military service on the general principles indicated in the foregoing, a special commission was appointed, composed of members from different branches of the administration, and other persons possessing special knowledge. The regulation elaborated by the Commission, and amended, after a careful examination, by the Council of the Empire, is in complete accord with our views. Adopting as a fundamental principle that the defense of the throne and of the country forms the sacred duty of every Russian subject, this regulation calls upon the entire male population to participate in military service, without exemption by purchase or by providing substitutes. The action of this new law will not be extended to the Cossack population, where military service is subject to special regulations, nor to certain foreign races in the Trans-Caucasus and other remote countries mentioned in the ukase to the governing Senate, and for whom special regulations will be promulgated. With these exceptions, and certain temporary exemptions stated in the aforesaid ukase, the male population of the Empire and of the kingdom of Poland, on attaining the age of 20 years, will be required to take part in a drawing by lot, which will determine once and for all those young men who must fulfill their obligations to active service, and those who are to remain exempt therefrom.

"Although a term of service of 15 years is fixed for those to be incorporated in the land forces, they will be dismissed to their homes at the end of 6 years, or sooner if possible, with the reservation that they join the colors at the summons of the Government, in case of urgent necessity.

"Special terms of service will be fixed for the Navy, and for those troops quartered in certain distant localities. Those young men who have been students in educational establishments, including even the primary schools, will have the duration of their service in the Army in time of peace notably reduced, according to the nature and degree of their instruction, while other important facilities are reserved to them."

The ukase of the Emperor prescribed that the Regulations drawn up by the above-mentioned commission, having received his approval, should be put into force in Russia and in Poland.* They constitute the fundamental military law of the Empire.

The essential features of these Regulations are given herewith (taken from a translation of them made by the Intelligence Branch of the Quartermaster's Department of the British Army):

"REGULATIONS RESPECTING MILITARY SERVICE IN THE RUSSIAN ARMY.†

"(*Confirmed by the Emperor, Jan.* 1, 1874.)

" CHAPTER I.—GENERAL REGULATIONS.

"Art. 1. The entire male population, without distinction of class, is liable to military service.

"2. Exemption by purchase, or by obtaining a substitute, is prohibited.

"3. No citizen of the male sex, who is upward of 15 years of age, can be relieved of his Russian nationality until he has com-

---

* The Grand Duchy of Finland furnishes a contingent of 5,000 men, under regulations drawn up by its own Government.
† The Regulations are contained in 224 articles, divided into 14 chapters.

LAWS OF RECRUITING AND MILITARY SERVICE. 5

pletely satisfied all obligations to military service, or has become exempted therefrom after taking part in the drawing.

"4. Persons upward of 15 years of age, who take up their residence in those parts of the Empire where military service is regulated by special provisions, are to be subject to the General Regulations in force in those particular districts.

"5. The armed force of the Empire consists of the Regular Forces and the Militia. The latter force is called out only when extraordinary events in time of war require its services.

"7. The Regular Land Army consists of—

"The Active Army, recruited by means of yearly levies taken throughout the Empire.

"The Reserve, to fill up the effective strength of the regiments, etc., composed of men allowed to remain on furlough until their term of service expires.

"The Cossacks.

"Regiments, etc., composed of foreigners.

"8. The Naval Forces consist of the Fleet and Reserve.

"9. The number of men required to complete the strength of the Army and the Fleet is fixed by the Legislature every year, on the recommendation of the Minister of War, and promulgated to the Senate by an Imperial Ukase.

"10. Admission to the service is determined by lot-drawing, in which every male person takes part once during lifetime. Those who are exempted from active service, by reason of having drawn a particular number, are enrolled in the Militia.

"11. One class only of the population is annually called upon to take part in the drawing, namely, that which comprises all the men who have reached the age of 20 years on the 1st of January of the year in which the recruiting takes place.

"12. It is lawful for those persons who have fulfilled the requisite stipulations respecting education, to relieve themselves from military service, without having recourse to the drawing, by enlisting as volunteers in accordance with the provisions contained in Chap. XII. of these Regulations.

"13. Any person who is deprived of all his civil rights, or only of such rights and prerogatives as belong to him individually, or by virtue of his condition, can not be admitted either to the drawing or to the service.

"14. The annual levy and the drawing for active service will take place from November 1st to December 15th, and in the case of Siberia from October 15th to December 31st. Should there be an application from the competent authorities (Art. 76–78), the Ministers for the Interior and for War may, by common consent, authorize a change in the normal term appointed for European Russia, but with the proviso that, when any change is sanctioned, the levy shall be completed by the 31st December at the latest.

"15. This article contains the regulations for recruiting the fleet.

. . . .

"CHAPTER II.—DURATION OF SERVICE IN THE ACTIVE ARMY AND IN THE RESERVE.

"17. In the case of recruits who have taken part in the drawing, the ordinary term of service in the land forces is fixed at 15 years, of which 6 years will be spent on active service, and 9 years in the reserve. An exception is made to this rule in the case of men who are called upon to serve in Corps belonging to the Military District of Turkestan, or in those quartered in the provinces of Semipalatinsk, the Transbaïkal, Yakootsk, Amoor, and the Maritime Provinces, in which the ordinary term of service is fixed at 10 years, of which 7 years are active, and 3 years reserve.

"18. In the naval forces, the ordinary term is 10 years, namely, 7 years' active service and 3 years in the reserve.

"19. The period of service for men who have taken part in the drawing will commence from the 1st of January of the year following the levy, in the event of their entering the service at the time of the levy, and from the 1st of the month following their entry into the service when it takes place at any other period of the year.

"20. The duration of service, as laid down in Arts. 17 and 18, applies only to times of peace; in the event of war, the men who constitute the land and sea forces must remain with the colors so long as the State requires their services.

"21. The Ministers of War and Marine are empowered to send to the reserve such men of the land and sea forces as are not non-commissioned officers, even if they have not completed their period of active service, according to Arts. 17 and 18. The naval and military authorities also reserve to themselves the right to grant during the entire period of service temporary furloughs, not exceeding one year, to men belonging to the land and sea forces who are not non-commissioned officers.

. . . .

"23. Men belonging to the Reserve will be called up for active service should it be found absolutely necessary to complete the strength of Regiments and Corps. This will be done by an Imperial Ukase to the Senate. During their service in the Reserve, the men can be called up for drill by the Minister of War or the Minister of Marine, but not oftener than twice during the whole of their reserve service, and for not more than six weeks at one time.

"24. Men who are employed by the State, or by any corporate body, and whose names are on a special list which has received the sanction of the authorities, are exempt from being called upon to serve in the Active Army.

. . . .

" CHAPTER IV.—SOLDIERS WHO BECOME INCAPACITATED FOR DUTY.

" 32 to 36. Men unfitted absolutely for the service, by reason of sickness or other infirmities, are granted their discharge from active service and also from the reserve, and receive an authenticated document stating that they have fulfilled all the necessary requirements. If they happen to be deficient in means, or not in a fit state to work, and have no relatives who can render them assistance, they receive from the Government a monthly allowance of three roubles, or are admitted into hospitals or other charitable institutions ; in default of this they are handed over to the care of persons of good character, who receive a monthly allowance not exceeding six roubles. The families of men who have been killed or have disappeared during time of war, or of men who have died of their wounds, are maintained according to special regulations. The families of reserve men who are called up for active service with the colors in time of war, are provided for by the zemstvos and urban or rural corporations where they reside.

" CHAPTER V.—THE MILITIA.

" 36 to 41. The Militia consists of all men, not forming part of the standing army, who are capable of bearing arms, and whose ages are between 20 and 40 years inclusive. The Militia includes also those men who have been released from the Reserve, either of the land or sea forces. All persons of more than 40 years of age are permitted to enroll themselves in the Militia should they desire to do so. The men belonging to the Militia are divided into two classes, of which the first consists of those who were enrolled in the Militia at the time the last four levies took place, and who would form part either of the mobilized Militia, or who would fill vacancies in the Regular Army, if required, or in the event of the number of reserves being insufficient. The Militia is mobilized by Imperial manifesto. The first ban may also be mobilized, if absolutely necessary for the reinforcement of the standing Army, by an Imperial Ukase to the Senate. The Militia is dismissed at the termination of a war, or previously should its services not be required. The families of men belonging to the Militia, who may be called out, will be provided for by the zemstvos and urban or rural corporations, in accordance with special regulations. Families of men of the Militia who may be killed in action or die of wounds received on a campaign, are provided for in a manner similar to that laid down for the families of men belonging to the Regular Army.

"CHAPTER VI.—EXEMPTIONS, POSTPONEMENTS, AND OTHER IMMUNITIES FROM MILITARY SERVICE.

"42 to 44. All men are exempt absolutely from military service who are unfit by reason of bodily defects or disease, except such as have injured themselves willfully, in which case they are compelled to serve in the Army. A detailed statement of the natural defects and maladies which debar young men from being admitted to the service, as well as instructions to the recruiting authorities regarding the examination of men drawn for the service, will shortly be published by the Minister of War, the Minister of the Interior, and the Director of the Ministry of Marine, after consultation with the Medical Council. Young men who are insufficiently developed, or are attacked with illness which is not of so aggravated a nature as to incapacitate them, or have not quite recovered from recent sickness, will be allowed one year before entering the service. If at the expiration of that period they are not fit to serve, another year will be allowed them; after which, should they still be unfit for the service, they will be finally discharged.

"45 to 51. These articles contain a statement of such exemptions as are allowed for family reasons. Of these there are three classes: The only son of a widowed mother, etc.

. . . .

"53 to 61. These articles relate to the periods for which recruits can postpone entering the service on the ground of education. Students in certain educational establishments (a list of which is annexed to these Regulations), who have reached the age appointed for entering the service, must attend the drawing like the rest;

LAWS OF RECRUITING AND MILITARY SERVICE. 9

should they express the wish, they are allowed to postpone taking part in the drawing in order to complete their education : firstly, until they are 22 years of age, in the case of " . . . . (certain educational establishments ; up to 24, 25, 27, and 28 years of age, for certain other educational establishments specified at length by name).

"54. Students belonging to the places of education named in the preceding article are permitted to declare, at least two months before the drawing takes place, that they wish to enter the service as enlisted volunteers, in which case they are relieved from the drawing and are allowed the periods above stated before being called upon to join.

"55. Those who have successfully finished their course of studies in the orthodox ecclesiastical seminaries and academies are granted a year's grace to allow of their entering the priesthood—a profession (according to Art. 62) which exempts them altogether from military service.

"56. Reduction in the period of obligatory service is made under the following circumstances :

"1. To 6 months in the Army and $14\frac{1}{2}$ years in the Reserve in the case of men who have completed their course of study at the universities and other educational establishments of the first class, or who have passed equivalent examinations.

"2. To 18 months in the Army and $13\frac{1}{2}$ years in the Reserve for men who have finished the course of six classes in the gymnasia or *real* schools, or of the second class in ecclesiastical seminaries, or the course in educational establishments of the second class, or who have passed examinations of the same scope.

"3. To 3 years in the Army and 12 years in the Reserve in the case of persons who have finished their course of study in educational establishments of the third class, or passed an examination equivalent to it.

"4. To 4 years in the Army and 11 years in the Reserve in the case of men who have received a certificate that they possess the knowledge demanded in the course of study of the primary schools, in accordance with the regulations of the 14th of July, 1864, or in that of educational establishments of the fourth class (except men enrolled in the military district of Turkestan, the Semipalatinsk, the Transbaïkal, the Yakootsk, the Amoor, and Maritime Provinces, or in the Fleet, in which cases the length of service is fixed at 6 years' active service and 4 years in the reserve).

. . . .

"59. The foregoing may (1) enter the Army immediately they

have completed their studies, or passed the necessary examinations, without waiting for the drawing, in which case their term of service is calculated according to the rules laid down in par. 2 of Art. 19 ; (2) be embodied in the branch of the service which they select, provided always the number in each branch does not exceed the regulated number fixed by the Minister of War.

". . . . . . ."

"62 to 65. These articles have reference to exemptions originating from the social condition or the occupations of recruits.

"62. The following are exempted from serving :

"1. The clergy of all Christian denominations.

"2. Singers in orthodox churches, who have completed their course of study at an ecclesiastical academy, seminary, or school.

". . . . . . ."

"63. Of the men who have become liable to military service by reason of the number which they have drawn, the following are exempt, in time of peace, from serving actively, and are at once enrolled in the Reserve, and remain in it for a period of 15 years :

"1. Doctors of medicine, surgeons, licentiates in the veterinary art or in pharmacy, and veterinary surgeons, unless they are liable to obligatory military service by the statutes of the establishments in which they were educated.

"2. Exhibitioners in the Imperial Fine Arts Academy who are sent abroad to complete their education.

"3. Persons who belong to establishments named in Art. 53 and to any other public educational establishments not there enumerated, and whose business it is to impart instruction in subjects the study of which is obligatory according to their statutes ; also tutors or their assistants in such establishments as are under Government authority, or whose statutes are under its sanction.

". . . . . . ."

"CHAPTER VII.—RECRUITING CIRCUMSCRIPTIONS.

"67. The Recruiting Subdivisions may include a portion of a district or an entire district.

"68. Every town which contains 10,000 male inhabitants, as a minimum, may form one distinct Recruiting Subdivision. Should the inhabitants desire it, towns containing a smaller number than the above may also be made distinct Recruiting Subdivisions, provided that their male population amounts to at least 5,000 souls.

"71. Rural subdivisions, and subdivisions containing a mixed population partly resident in villages and partly in towns, must consist of from 8,000 to 20,000 male inhabitants ; subdivisions

LAWS OF RECRUITING AND MILITARY SERVICE. 11

strictly urban, of from 5,000 to 40,000 males. Towns whose male population exceeds the latter figure may be split up into a number of subdivisions.

"72. The rural subdivisions in Siberia are formed either of separate bailiwicks, or by the union of two, or at most three, bailiwicks. Bailiwicks nearest to towns which contain less than 5,000 males are united to the towns to form Recruiting Subdivisions.

"73. A certain place is fixed upon in each subdivision, at which those who take part in the drawing are to present themselves, and at which the recruits are to be received.

"74. As a general rule, the distance of the rendezvous from the most distant villages in a subdivision should not exceed 50 versts (about 33 miles).

"75. If a rural subdivision has no place suitable for a rendezvous, the drawing must take place in the town or village which is nearest to the subdivision, provided that it is not farther than 50 versts from the most distant part of the subdivision.

"Articles 76 to 79 explain the method to be adopted in forming the districts into subdivisions, and in selecting the rendezvous for the drawing. The results arrived at are, according to Art. 80, to be communicated by the local authorities to the Ministers of the Interior and War. The list of the subdivisions will be published by the first-named Minister.

"CHAPTER VIII.—AUTHORITIES CHARGED WITH THE RECRUITING.

"81. In each Government or Province a Recruiting Commission is formed, presided over by the Governor or Head of the Province. This Commission consists of the Marshal of the Nobility in the Government, the President of the provincial delegates, and one of its members, the Military Chief of the Government or the officer who is performing the duties as such, and, lastly, the Procureur of the District Court of Judicature or his deputy.

. . . .

"84. In each district or subdistrict, a Recruiting Commission is formed, under the presidency of the Marshal of the local Nobility; this Commission consists of an officer appointed by the military authorities, the Commissary of Police of the District, or the official who performs similar duties, and one of the provincial delegates of the District chosen by that body.

. . . .

"87. At St. Petersburg, Moscow, Odessa, Riga, Kazan, Kharkof, Kief, Saratof, Vilna, Kischinef, Cronstadt, Nicolaief, and Sevastopol, separate Urban Commissions are formed for recruiting purposes. These Commissions are presided over by the Mayor, and consist of an officer selected by the military authorities, an official appointed by the Chief of Police, and two members of the Municipal Administration, selected by the latter. The Commission at Warsaw, presided over by the City President, consists of an officer selected by the military authorities, an official appointed by the police authorities, and two residents chosen by the representative of the Emperor.

. . . .

"89. The following duties devolve upon the Commission of a Government or Province:

"1. To superintend generally the proceedings connected with the drawings, and to make the necessary arrangements for receiving the recruits.

"2. To apportion the number of recruits which the Government or Province has to supply among the Subdivisions within its jurisdiction.

"3. To call up for a second examination, in cases referred to in the present Regulations, such men as are sent back after their first examination.

"4. To inquire into any complaints which are made against the District, Subdistrict, and Urban Commissions.

"5. To examine the reports from these Commissions and draw up a general report on the recruiting in each Government or Province.

"6. To pass judgment upon or to submit, in case of necessity, to the decision of superior authority, any errors that may occur in the proceedings of these Commissions.

"90. The District, Subdistrict, and Urban Commissions have the following duties to perform:

"1. To draw up special lists of those persons named in Art. 95 who are to take part in the drawing.

"2. To correct these lists.

"3. To forward to the proper authorities returns of the number of young men who are liable to take part in the drawing.

"4. To summon to the rendezvous the men who are to take part in the drawing.

"5. To settle the rightful claims of each man.

"6. To decide upon the men that are to be admitted into the service, and upon the order in which they are to be taken.

"7. To cause an examination to be made of the recruits drawn for the service, for the purpose of assuring themselves as to their eligibility for military duties.

" 8. To make arrangements for the reception of recruits.

" 9. To forward to the Commission of the Government or Province, at the conclusion of their duties in the Subdivisions, a detailed account of the drawing and of the proceedings connected with the admission of the men to the service.

" 91. To each Recruiting Commission two medical men are appointed (one by the civil, the other by the military authorities) and one officer, belonging either to the Army or Navy; the two former for examining, and the latter for receiving, men about to enter the service. Besides these, two medical men are appointed to the Commissions for the purpose of attending to the recruits when required.

. . . .

"CHAPTER IX.—ENROLLMENT IN THE RECRUITING SUBDIVISIONS AND METHOD OF ARRANGING THE DRAWING LISTS.

" This chapter is divided into four sections. The first section refers to the enrollment of young men in the Recruiting Subdivisions, and shows the manner in which the lists are to be prepared.

. . . .

" CHAPTER X.—THE DRAWING AND ADMISSION TO THE SERVICE.

"This chapter contains nine sections, the first of which treats of the preparatory arrangements (Arts. 127 to 130); the second relates to the distribution of the annual contingent.

" 131. The distribution among Governments and Provinces is made annually by the Minister of War; it is then communicated to the Recruiting Commissions with a view to its being made public.

" 132-3. The contingent is subsequently reapportioned by the Commissions among the Recruiting Subdivisions, which receive from them the definite distribution. This latter distribution is then published in the local gazettes.

" 134. The third section has reference to the drawing, for which arrangements are made in the various Subdivisions by the District, Subdistrict, and Urban Recruiting Commissions.

. . . .

" 140. The fifth section, consisting only of one article, relates to the verification, by the Recruiting Commissions, of the lists of the names of men who are to take part in the drawing. Every person present is allowed the right of taking objection to the enrollments on this list, which is read in public; and if the Commission deems these objections to be well founded, it has power to make the requisite alterations. This being completed, the drawing takes place in accordance with the regulations contained in the sixth section (Arts. 141 to 143).

"144. The seventh section relates to the examination and reception of the men who are to enter the service. The examination takes place in the presence of the Recruiting Commissions; the president has the power to authorize third persons to take part in it.

"145. Men who are provided with certificates from a doctor in the employment of the State, showing that their physique and general state of health are such as to offer no impediments to their entering the service, are not required to present themselves for examination.

. . . .

" CHAPTER XII.—VOLUNTARY ENLISTMENT.

"This chapter contains two sections (Arts. 171 to 197). The first section relates to voluntary enlistment in the land forces. Men who are willing to enter the service as enlisted volunteers can do so on the following conditions:

"1. They must be at least 17 years of age; if they are minors, they are required to prove that they have received the consent of their parents, tutors, or guardians.

"2. Their state of health and physique must be such as to fulfill all the necessary conditions required of men admitted to the service.

"3. They must be provided with a document showing that they have passed the examination after a complete course of study either at one of the first-class educational establishments named in the appendix to Art. 53 of these Regulations, or of six classes at the gymnasia or *real* schools, or of the second class in an ecclesiastical seminary, or that they have passed an examination according to a special scheme drawn up by the Ministers of War and Public Instruction conjointly.

"173. Enlisted volunteers are divided into three classes, according to the education which they have received; their service in the active army is as follows:

"1. For *three months*, if they have passed their examination at a first-class educational establishment.

"2. *Six months*, if at one of the second-class establishments mentioned in section 3, Art. 171.

"3. *Two years*, if they have merely passed the examination in accordance with the joint scheme specially drawn up by the Ministers of War and Public Instruction.

LAWS OF RECRUITING AND MILITARY SERVICE. 15

"At the expiration of the above periods an enlisted volunteer is permitted, in peace time, if he is not a non-commissioned or commissioned officer, either to remain on active service or to be passed into the reserve, where he will remain for 9 years. In time of war, the regulations contained in Art. 20 apply equally to enlisted volunteers.

"174. Enlisted volunteers are allowed to enter the service at any time of the year. The period of service commences on the 1st of the month following that in which they join their regiment or corps.

"175. Enlisted volunteers can enter as private soldiers only such combatant branches of the service as are allowed to receive them. They are permitted to choose the arm with which they prefer to serve, provided that the number does not exceed the regulated number of each arm fixed by the Minister of War. In time of war enlisted volunteers are sent at first to the local regiments. Nurses can enter the service on all occasions as military nurses.

"176. Enlisted volunteers who join the guard or cavalry must maintain themselves at their own expense. In other regiments or corps they are maintained by the State, unless they express a wish to defray their own expenses.

"177. Enlisted volunteers who defray their own expenses may lodge where they please, except while they are assembled in camps of instruction; the commanding officer has the power, however, of depriving them of this privilege if he thinks fit.

"178. Enlisted volunteers join the service as private soldiers just as if they had taken part in the drawing, and fulfill the same obligations, with certain mitigations which the Minister of War shall appoint.

"179. In order to distinguish between enlisted volunteers and men who have taken part in the drawing, the former wear a distinguishing badge on their uniform, which, however, carries no privilege with it.

"180. When enlisted volunteers have passed the prescribed examinations they may, with the approbation of their immediate commanding officers, be promoted:

"1. To be non-commissioned officers after two months' service, should they belong to the first class named in Art. 173; after four months, if they belong to the second class; and after one year's service, if to the third class.

"2. To the rank of officer, if they have served as non-commissioned officer for 3 months, in the case of those belonging to the first class; for 6 months, in the case of the second class; and for

3 years, if they belong to the third class. The rank of officer can not, however, be granted to any enlisted volunteer, even though he belong to the first class, unless he has served in camp during at least one period of exercise.

"181. Officers who (Art. 173) belonged to the third class of enlisted volunteers can only enjoy the personal and civil rights appertaining to their station, after a service of at least three years with the colors.

"182. Enlisted volunteers are eligible for four months' furlough. But such period of absence is deducted from their term of active service, as well as from the period required of them before they can become non-commissioned officers or officers.

"183. Students in the special classes of the Corps of Pages, and those belonging to Military Infantry Schools, the Nicholas Cavalry School, the Nicholas Engineer School, the Michael Artillery School, and the Military Topographical Schools, are considered as enlisted volunteers. The time spent at the above-named schools and in the special classes for Pages is reckoned as active service in the case of men who leave them either as officers or as soldiers. They are required to remain with the colors one year and a half for each year spent at the above-mentioned establishments. The general term of service in their case is reckoned from the 1st of the month succeeding that in which they left these establishments.

"184. Students belonging to the establishments detailed in Art. 183, who may have left before completing the entire course of one of the classes, are also required to remain one year and a half for each year that they spent at the school. In no case can they be promoted to the rank of officer until they have completed one year's service in the ranks.

"185. Students who are educated at the expense of the State in civil educational establishments can also enter the military service in the capacity of enlisted volunteers, but in no case can they discharge the obligatory civil duties to which they are bound until after the expiration of the period during which they are with the colors, as laid down by these Regulations.

. . . .

"CHAPTER XIII.—APPEALS AND COMPLAINTS WITH REFERENCE TO MILITARY SERVICE.

"This chapter (Arts. 197 to 211) lays down the course of procedure to be observed in deciding upon any questions which may arise.

LAWS OF RECRUITING AND MILITARY SERVICE. 17

"CHAPTER XIV.—PENALTIES FOR OFFENSES AGAINST THE LAWS RELATING TO MILITARY SERVICE."

This chapter (Arts. 212 to 224) prescribes the penalties for failing to comply with the law previously quoted, for fraud in endeavoring to evade military service, for malingery, etc., etc. The punishments vary, according to the offense, from a fine of 100 roubles ($74) to imprisonment for six years at hard labor.

The essential principles of the above law are as follows:

1. Every able-bodied man between the ages of 20 and 40 owes military service to the state.

2. The state, not having need of the services of all such men, exempts permanently those whose labor is specially necessary at their homes, as well as priests, artists, etc., and draws by lot to determine which of the others shall enter into service.

3. Those drafted into the service pass 6 years with the Colors and 9 years in the Reserve, and are then discharged permanently.

4. Those not drafted into active service are enrolled at once in the Militia.

5. Those who have received an education are allowed to reduce their service in the ranks ("enlisted volunteers") to a very short period, at the end of which they may become officers, or resume their civic employment—being, however, enrolled in the Reserve until the conclusion of 15 years.

6. The students of various military schools are considered as serving their time in the ranks ("enlisted volunteers") while at the school, and become officers at once upon their graduation.

The officers of the army are all derived from one of the two classes mentioned in 5 and 6.

The number of men annually attaining the age of 20 years in Russia (exclusive of Cossacks, etc.,) is about 700,000.

In October, 1874, the first drawing was made under the new law. The contingent called for by the Imperial Ukase (Art. 9) was 150,000 men. The total number of men liable for service was 693,736, of whom 12,554 belonged to the classes exempt under the law. Of this number—

24,450 did not present themselves for the drawing.

49,452 were discharged for physical incapacity.

18,034 were allowed to postpone their service to complete their education (Arts. 53 to 61).

3,833 were suspected of feigning sickness and placed in hospitals for further examination.

144,934 were incorporated into the army.

The rest, 450,000 or more, were inscribed on the rolls of the Militia.

For 1876 the contingent called for (Ukase of June 1, 1875) was 180,000 men.

For 1877, 195,000 men.

For 1878, 218,000 men.

For 1879, 218,000 men.

Of those incorporated in the army in 1874, 11.8 per cent. could read and write.

CHAPTER II.

STRENGTH AND ORGANIZATION OF LAND FORCES.

THE armed strength of the Russian Empire, as stated in Arts. 5 and 7 of the General Regulations previously quoted, consists of the Permanent Forces (*Postoiannaya Voiska*) and the Militia (*Gosudarstvennoe Opoltchenie*). The Permanent Force on land, i. e., the Army, consists of—

1. The Active Army, or the troops actually under arms with their regiments.

2. The Reserve, or the troops permanently on furlough, but liable at any moment to be called upon to join their old regiments or form new regiments.

3. The Cossacks, or irregular troops, principally horsemen, coming from the vicinity of the Don, the Volga, etc., and from the Trans-Caucasus and Central Asia.

The Active Army is again divided into—

A. Field Troops.

B. Local Troops.

The latter are again subdivided into—

a. Garrison Troops, for the fortresses of European Russia.

β. Regular Troops in Asia.

γ. Stationary Troops, Gendarmes, and other special troops for local purposes.

Upon mobilization a part of the Reserve goes to fill up the Active Troops to the War Footing, and the rest to form,

a. Ersatz Troops, i. e., the troops formed at depots for the purpose of replacing losses among those in the field.

b. Reserve Troops, i. e., newly formed regiments, etc., forming an independent or reserve army, for service wherever needed.

The Militia is divided into classes, and these classes are called out (by Ukase of the Emperor) in case there are not enough soldiers of the Reserve for the purposes mentioned above. They enter as individual recruits into the Ersatz, there receive their arms, clothing, and instruction, and are then forwarded to the respective regiments, etc., in the field, and incorporated with them.

These classifications of the troops will perhaps be made more clear by the following tabular statement:

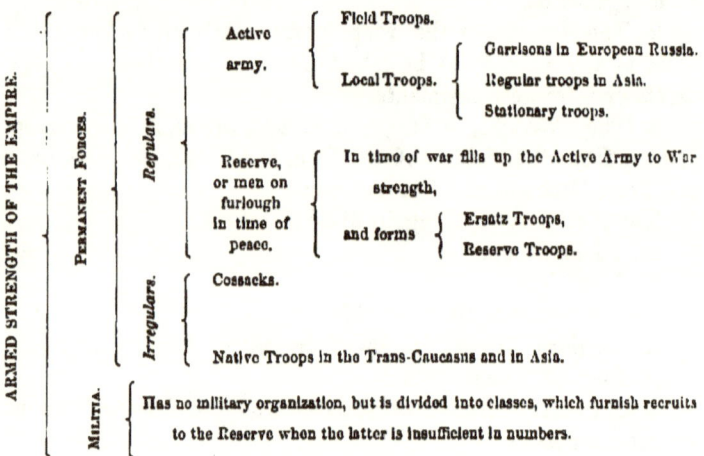

FIELD TROOPS.

The field troops of the Russian army consist of:
48 Divisions of Infantry,
8 Brigades of Rifles,
48 Brigades of Foot Artillery,
17 Divisions of Cavalry,
35 Batteries of Horse Artillery,
19 Battalions of Engineer Troops,
besides auxiliary organizations, such as Engineer and Artillery Parks, Hospitals, etc.

An Army Corps is composed of two (or three) Divisions of Infantry, two Brigades of Foot Artillery, and one Division of Cavalry with two horse batteries. The Rifles and Sappers are only temporarily attached to Army Corps.

In the Guard, and in the troops serving in the Caucasus (4th

STRENGTH AND ORGANIZATION OF LAND FORCES. 21

Division of Grenadiers, 19th, 20th, 21st, 38th, 39th, and 41st Divisions of the Line), the organization of the Infantry is as follows: 1 Division = 2 Brigades = 4 Regiments = 16 Battalions = 64 Companies.

In the rest of the army it is as follows: 1 Division = 2 Brigades = 4 Regiments = 12 Battalions = 60 Companies.

It is intended to apply the first organization to the whole army, but this has not yet been accomplished.

The organization of the Cavalry is as follows: 1 Division = 2 Brigades = 4 Regiments = 18 Squadrons (the Cossack regiment having 6 squadrons, the regular regiments 4 squadrons each).

In the Foot Artillery, 1 Brigade = 6 Batteries = 48 guns.

In the Horse Artillery, 1 Battery = 6 guns.

A Rifle Brigade is composed of 4 Battalions = 16 Companies.

An Engineer Brigade is composed of 1 Sapper Battalion and 1 Half Battalion of Pontoniers.

Infantry.

The 48 Infantry Divisions are composed of 3 Divisions of the Guard, 4 of Grenadiers, and 41 of the Line. They are numbered in each class, as 1st Division of the Guard, 1st Division of Grenadiers, 1st Division of the Line, etc. The Regiments are numbered in the same way, 1st to 12th of the Guard, 1st to 16th of Grenadiers, 1st to 164th of the Line. In addition, each regiment has its own name, which indicates, in the Grenadiers and in the Line, the locality from which the regiment comes; besides this, nearly all the regiments have honorary chiefs whose names they bear. The full titles of the regiments are therefore of the following nature: "The 1st Infantry Regiment, of Preobrazhensk, of the Guard"; "The 53d Infantry Regiment, of Volhynia, of His Imperial Highness the Grand Duke Field Marshal Nikolai Nikolaivitch"; "The 121st Infantry Regiment, of Penza, of Aide-de-Camp General Milutin," etc. In official reports these titles are given in full, but ordinarily the regiment is known simply by its name (not the number), as "The Preobrazhensky Regiment," "The Penzansky Regiment," etc. The battalions are numbered in each regiment from 1 to 4, and the companies from 1 to 16. The 4-battalion regiments have 3 battalions of the line and 1 of rifles or skirmishers, each battalion of 4 companies. In the 3-battalion regiments, each battalion is composed of 4 line companies and 1 rifle or skirmish company; these correspond to the old distinctions of heavy and light infantry, but, as there is now no difference whatever in the use of infantry, it is probable that these divisions will soon be done away with.

The 8 Rifle Brigades are as follows:
1 Rifle Brigade of the Guard,
5 Rifle Brigades of the Line,
1 Rifle Brigade of the Caucasus,
1 Rifle Brigade of Turkestan.

Strength of an Infantry Regiment.

		COMBATANTS.		NON-COMBATANTS.		Horses.	Wagons.
		Officers.	Men.	Officers.	Men.		
Of 4 Battalions.	War Footing	80	4057	7	226	186	44
	Peace Footing	64	1897	7	185	52	17
Of 3 Battalions.	War Footing	76	3061	6	186	174	41
	Increased Peace Footing	60	2363	6	185	185	41
	Peace Footing	60	1798	6	105	49	16

The Field and Staff of a 4-battalion regiment is composed of:
1 Regimental Commander (Major-General in the Guard, Colonel in the Line),
2 Field Officers, one of whom is in charge of the interior economy of the regiment, and the other is an assistant to the commander;

1 Regimental Adjutant,
1 Regimental Quartermaster,
1 Regimental Paymaster,
1 Regimental Instructor in Arms,
1 Officer commanding non-combatants.
} Of rank below Captain;

1 Secretary for the interior economy of the regiment,
1 Senior Surgeon,
4 Junior Surgeons,
1 Chaplain,
} Non-combatants.

The Guard and Grenadier regiments have each a Band, and also the first regiment of each division of the Line. It con-

STRENGTH AND ORGANIZATION OF LAND FORCES. 23

sists of 1 Band-Leader, 11 first-class musicians, and 28 second-class musicians. This increases the effective strength of these regiments by 40 men.

The non-combatants of a 4-battalion regiment are as follows:

	War footing.	Peace footing.
Sergeant Major of non-combatant company	1	1
Regimental Paymaster Sergeant	1	1
Regimental Quartermaster Sergeant	1	1
Regimental Ordnance Sergeant	1	1
Regimental clerk (writer)	1	1
Senior clerks "	4	4
Junior clerks "	5	5
Medical N. C. Officers. { Senior	1	1
Junior	4	4
Apothecary	1	1
Veterinary	1	1
Belonging to Companies	16	16
Apprentices	..	16
Inspector of sick	1	1
Hospital attendants	16	10
Leader of choir	1	1
Master armorer	1	1
Assistant master armorers	2	2
Armorers	5	4
Gunstock-makers	2	2
Carpenters	4	2
Turner	1	1
Wheelwright	1	1
Blacksmiths	4	2
Locksmiths	2	1
Harness-maker	1	1
Tailor (cutter)	1	1
Tailor (fitter)	1	1
Fitter of accoutrements	2	2
Teamsters { N. C. officers	2	2
Privates	49	20
Officers' servants { (2 each for field officers and senior surgeon, 1 each for company officers, junior surgeon, secretary, and chaplain)	95	79
Total	226	185

Strength of a Battalion of Infantry.

	FIELD AND STAFF.		COMPANY OFFICERS AND MEN.											TOTAL.	
	Officers.	Men.	Captains.	Second Captains.	Lieutenants.	Sub-Lieutenants.	Ensigns.	Sergeant-Majors.	Volunteers.	Storekeeper Sergeant.	Senior N. C. Officers.	Junior N. C. Officers.	Drummers.	Buglers.	Lance-Corporals.	Privates.	Officers.	Men.
Of 4 companies { War Footing	2	2	2	2	4	4	4	4	16	4	16	56	6	10	90	820	18	1014
Peace Footing	2	2	2	2	3	2	2	4	16	4	16	16	6	10	40	360	18	474
Of 5 companies { War Footing	2	2	2	2	3	5	5	5	5	5	20	60	12	17	100	800	22	1026
Increas'd Peace Foot'g	2	2	2	2	3	4	4	8	3	5	5	20	60	6	12	90	590	17	737
Peace Footing	2	2	2	2	3	4	3	3	5	5	20	40	6	12	60	420	17	597

The Field and Staff of a Battalion consists of:

1 Battalion Commander (Colonel in the Guard, Lieutenant-colonel in the Line).
1 Battalion Adjutant.
1 Drummer.
1 Bugler.

Strength of a Battalion of Rifles (Four Companies).

		FIELD AND STAFF.		COMPANY.			TOTAL COMBATANTS.		NON-COMBAT'S.		WAGONS.			
		Officers.	Men.	Officers.	N. C. Officers.	Privates.	Officers.	Men.	Officers.	Men.	Horses.	Ammunition.	Sanitary.	Provisions and others.	Total.
In Europe	War Footing	6	1	20	96	720	26	817	2	56	60	4	1	11	16
	Increased Peace Foot'g	6	1	16	88	544	22	633	2	56	47	4	1	11	16
	Peace Footing	6	1	16	60	400	22	461	2	42	12	...	...	6	6
In the Caucasus	War Footing	5	1	16	112	900	21	1018	3	50	76	4	1	13	18
	Peace Footing	5	1	12	72	400	17	473	3	40	12	...	...	4	4

The Field and Staff consists of:
1 Battalion Commander (Colonel or Lieutenant-colonel),
1 Field officer, charged with administration, etc.,
1 Battalion Adjutant,
1 Battalion Quartermaster,
1 Battalion Paymaster,   } (these offices are united in
1 Battalion Instructor in Arms, }   the Caucasus,)
1 Bugler.

The non-combatant staff consists of a Senior and a Junior Surgeon, with the addition of a Chaplain and a Secretary in the battalions of the Guard and of the Caucasus.

The battalions of the Guard have also a band, increasing their strength by 46 men.

The non-combatant company contains the same classes of workmen as in a regiment, but fewer in number.

Cavalry.

The 17 Cavalry Divisions are composed of 2 divisions of the Guard, 14 of the Line, and 1 of the Caucasus.

Each cavalry division of the Line is formed of:
1 Regiment of Dragoons,
1 Regiment of Lancers,
1 Regiment of Hussars,
1 Regiment of Don Cossacks.

STRENGTH AND ORGANIZATION OF LAND FORCES. 25

The Cavalry Divisions of the Guard have at present an exceptional organization.

The 1st Division consists of:
4 Regiments of Cuirassiers,
2 Regiments of Don Cossacks.

The 2d Division consists of:
2 Regiments of Dragoons,
2 Regiments of Lancers,
2 Regiments of Hussars.

It is proposed, however, to change this organization, so as to form 3 Divisions of the Guard, leaving the Cuirassiers in the 1st Division, and giving the 2d and 3d Divisions the same organization as in the Line. This has not yet been done.

The Caucasian Cavalry Division consists of 4 Regiments of Dragoons. The regiments are numbered according to the above classification, i. e., 1st to 14th Dragoons, 1st to 14th Lancers, etc. Each Regiment is also known by the locality from which it comes, as for instance "The Dragoons of Astrakhan," etc.; and the majority of the regiments bear the name of some prince or distinguished general, who is its honorary chief.

Strength of a Cavalry Regiment (Four Squadrons).

FIELD AND STAFF		SQUADRON OFFICERS AND MEN.														TOTAL COMBATANTS.		NON-COMBATANTS.		TRAIN.	
Officers.	Men.	Majors.	Captains.	Second Captains.	Lieutenants.	Cornets.	Sergeant-Majors.	Volunteers.	Sergeants.	Quarter-master Sergeants.	N. C. Officers.	Trumpeters.	Lance-Corporals.	Privates.		Officers.	Men.	Officers.	Men.	Horses.	Wagons.
8	1	4	4	5	4	8	4	16	16	4	41	24	16	604		33	728	593	0	141	64	16

The above strength is maintained, both in peace and war, except in the train, which is reduced to 15 horses and 9 wagons in time of peace.

The Regiments of the Guard have each a band, composed of 1 leader and 24 musicians.

The Field and Staff consists of:
1 Regimental Commander (Major-General in the Guard, Colonel in the Line),
2 Field Officers, one as aid to the commander and the other charged with administration, etc.,
1 Regimental Adjutant,
1 Regimental Quartermaster,
1 Regimental Paymaster,
1 Regimental Instructor in Arms,
1 Officer commanding non-combatants,
} below the rank of Captain;

1 Chief Trumpeter.

Of non-combatants:
1 Surgeon,
1 Assistant Surgeon,
1 Veterinary Surgeon,
1 Secretary,
1 Riding-Master,
1 Chaplain.

The non-combatants below the grade of officer are as follows:
1 Sergeant Major of non-combatant company,
1 Regimental Paymaster Sergeant,
1 Regimental Quartermaster Sergeant,
10 Clerks (writers) of different classes,
18 Medical N. C. officers of different classes, including veterinary surgeons,
1 Inspector of Sick,
8 Hospital Attendants,
1 Leader of Choir,
5 Armorers of different classes,
1 Locksmith,
2 Gunstock-makers,
2 Carpenters,
1 Wheelwright,
5 Blacksmiths,
5 Saddlers,
22 Tailors and Bootmakers,
10 Teamsters,
47 Officers' Servants.

STRENGTH AND ORGANIZATION OF LAND FORCES. 27

Artillery.

The 48 Artillery Brigades consist of 3 of the Guard, 4 of Grenadiers, and 41 of the Line. Each is commanded by a major-general, under the orders of the commander of the infantry division to which it is attached and of which it forms a part; it also has the same number as its division; e. g., "The 17th Artillery Brigade of the Line," i. e., the artillery brigade belonging to the 17th infantry division of the Line.

A Brigade of Foot Artillery consists of 6 batteries, the first three 9-pdrs., and the other three 4-pdrs.

The horse batteries are attached to the Cavalry, 2 batteries to a division, under the orders of the Division Commander. The mountain batteries are attached to special corps for special service. The mitrailleuse batteries were formerly attached to the Artillery Brigades, the 6th Battery in each being composed of mitrailleuses; but this organization has now been superseded, and but few mitrailleuse batteries remain, and they are attached for special purposes to special corps.

Strength of a Battery of Artillery.

		No. of Guns	OFFICERS.					N. C. OFFICERS.				PRIVATES.			TOTAL COMBATANTS.				NON-COMBATANTS.			
			Lt. Col. com'd'g.	Captains.	Lieutenants.	Sub-Lieutenants.	Ensigns.	Volunteers.	Sergeant-Majors.	Sergeants of Artillery.	Trumpeters.	Laboratory Bombardiers.	Bombardiers.	Gunners.	Officers.	Men.	Carriages.	Horses.	Officers.	Men.	Wagons.	Horses.
9-pdr. foot	War Footing	8	1	1	1	1	2	..	1	2	24	4	8	50	190	6	279	30	180	..	38	4	17
	Inc. Peace Footing	8	1	1	1	1	2	..	1	2	19	4	8	40	150	6	224	15	88	..	29	4	14
	Peace Footing	4	1	1	1	1	2	..	1	2	14	4	8	30	180	6	189	5	42	..	29	2	6
4-pdr. foot	War Footing	8	1	1	1	1	1	1	1	2	24	4	8	40	140	6	219	20	135	..	37	4	17
	Inc. Peace Footing	8	1	1	1	1	1	1	1	2	19	4	8	30	110	6	174	10	71	..	29	4	14
	Peace Footing	4	1	1	1	1	1	1	1	2	14	4	8	20	100	6	149	6	34	..	29	2	6
Mitr'l. leuse.	War Footing	8	1	1	1	1	1	1	1	2	24	4	8	30	110	6	179	..	107	..	37	4	17
	Inc. Peace Footing	8	1	1	1	1	1	1	1	2	19	4	8	20	90	6	144	..	71	..	29	4	14
	Peace Footing	4	1	1	1	1	1	1	1	2	14	4	8	20	80	6	129	..	34	..	20	2	6
4-pdr. horse.	War Footing	6	1	1	2	1	1	1	1	2	24	4	8	50	200	7	289	..	250	..	42	4	17
	Inc. Peace Footing	6	1	1	2	1	1	1	1	2	19	4	8	40	160	7	234	..	214	..	34	4	14
	Peace Footing	6	1	1	2	1	1	1	1	2	14	4	8	40	160	7	229	..	105	..	34	2	6
M'tain horse.	War Footing	8	1	1	2	1	1	1	1	4	24	4	8	30	135	7	206	..	243	..	61	..	..
	Inc. Peace Footing	..	..	..	..	..	..	..	..	..	..	..	..	..	..	..	..	..	..	..	..	..	..
	Peace Footing	..	..	..	..	..	..	..	..	..	..	..	..	..	..	..	..	..	..	..	..	..	..

The non-combatants of a 4-pdr. horse battery consist of 2 writers, 3 medical n. c. officers, 2 hospital attendants, 1 barber, 14 saddlers, harness-makers, carpenters, blacksmiths, etc., 12 teamsters, and 8 servants; and for other batteries nearly the same, the difference being in the number of saddlers, etc.

As the Don Cossacks form part of each Cavalry Division, in the proportion of 1 to 3 of regular cavalry, so the Don Cossack horse batteries form a part of the horse artillery in the same proportion; i. e., there are 21 horse batteries of regulars and 7 horse batteries of Don Cossacks, for the 28 batteries necessary for the 14 Divisions of Cavalry of the Line. Divisions 1 to 7 have both batteries of regulars; divisions 8 to 14 have one battery of regulars and one battery of Don Cossacks. There is, however, no difference between these batteries except in name.

The 2d Cavalry Division of the Guard has three horse batteries (instead of two, as in the other Cavalry Divisions).

Engineers.

The Engineer Troops consist of Sappers and Pontoniers. Of the former there are 15 battalions (1 Guard, 1 Grenadier, 10 Line and 3 Caucasus). Of the latter there are six Half-Battalions. In time of war there is also a Railroad Battalion.

Strength of a Sapper Battalion (Four Companies).

FOOTING.	FIELD AND STAFF.		COMPANY.											TOTAL COMBATANTS.		NON-COMBATANTS.		TRAIN.	
	Officers.	Men.	Captains.	Second Captain.	Lieutenants.	Sub-Lieutenants.	Ensigns.	Sergeant-Majors.	Volunteers.	Senior N. C. Officers.	Junior N. C. Officers.	Drummers.	Buglers.	First Class Privates.	Second Class Privates.	Third Class Privates.	Officers.	Men.	Officers.	Men.	Horses.	Wagons.
War......	7	2	2	2	4	6	7	4	4	20	56	12 12	100	800	500	28	1010	2	124	60	18
Peace.....	7	2	2	2	4	0	7	4	4	20	48	12,12	70	200	330	28	702	2	98	12	8

The Field and Staff consists of:
1 Battalion Commander (Major-General in the Guard, Colonel in the Line),
1 Field Officer, charged with administration, etc.,
1 Battalion Adjutant,
1 Battalion Paymaster,
1 Battalion Quartermaster,   } of rank below Captain;
1 Battalion Instructor in Arms,
1 Commander of non-combatants,
1 Drummer,
1 Bugler.

STRENGTH AND ORGANIZATION OF LAND FORCES. 29

Of non-combatants:
1 Senior Surgeon,
1 Junior Surgeon.
The non-combatants below the grade of officer consist of:
1 Battalion Storekeeper Sergeant,
10 Clerks (writers) of various classes,
5 Medical N. C. officers, including 1 veterinary,
1 Inspector of Sick,
6 Hospital Attendants (5 in time of peace),
4 Barbers,
7 Armorers of various classes,
3 Gunstock-makers,
3 Joiners,
1 Carpenter,
2 Turners,
1 Wheelwright,
4 Blacksmiths,
2 Locksmiths,
1 Harness-maker,
40 Teamsters (10 in time of peace),
33 Officers' Servants.

124

Strength of a Pontonier Half-Battalion (Two Companies).

FIELD AND STAFF.		COMPANY.											MOUNTED.		TOTAL COM- BAT'TS.		NON- COM- BAT'TS.		TRAIN.	
Officers.	Men.	Captains.	Second Captains.	Lieutenants.	Sub-Lieutenants.	Ensigns.	Sergeant-Majors.	Volunteers.	Storekeeper Sergeants.	Senior N. C. Officers.	Junior N. C. Officers.	Lance Corporals.	Privates.	Sergeants.	N. C. Officers.	Lance Corporals.	Privates.	Officers.	Men.	Officers.	Men.	Horses.	Wagons.
War footing..	3	2	2	2	8	1	2	8	2	6	32	4	32	286	4	3	16	116	12	520	3	68	81	9
Peace footing	3	2	2	2	2	1	2	8	2	6	16	4	32	218	..	..	..	...	12	292	2	51	6	3

The Field and Staff consists of:
1 Battalion Commander (Colonel),
1 Battalion Adjutant, } of rank below
1 Battalion Paymaster and Quartermaster, } Captain;
1 Drummer,
1 Trumpeter.

And of non-combatants:
1 Secretary,
2 Surgeons (1 in time of peace).

Strength of a Railroad Battalion (Four Companies).

FIELD AND STAFF.		COMPANY										TOTAL COMBATANTS.		NON-COMBATANTS.		TRAIN.	
Officers.	Men.	Captains.	Second Captains.	Lieutenants.	Sub-Lieutenants.	Ensigns.	Sergeant-Majors.	Storekeeper Sergeants.	Senior N. C. Officers.	Junior N. C. Officers.	Drummers.	Lance Corporals.	Privates.	Officers.	Men.	Officers.	Men.	Horses.	Wagons.
5	2	2	2	5	5	5	4	4	16	56	8	80	620	25	990	3	79	69	16

The Field and Staff consists of:
1 Battalion Commander (Colonel),
1 Field officer, charged with administration, etc.,
1 Battalion Adjutant,
1 Battalion Paymaster,
1 Battalion Quartermaster.
And of non-combatants:
1 Secretary,
2 Surgeons.
The Battalion exists only in time of war.

Staff of an Army Corps.

	Generals.	Other Officers.	Civilian Officials.	Enlisted Men.	Wagons.	Horses.
Commander, general or lieutenant-general	1	..	..	..	..	..
Personal aides-de-camp	..	3	..	..	..	..
Chief of Staff, major-general	1	..	..	..	..	..
Officers of the general staff	..	7	..	..	..	..
Chief of Artillery, major-general	1	..	..	..	..	..
Officers of artillery	..	3	..	..	..	..
Chief Intendant	..	..	1	..	..	..
Chief Surgeon	..	..	1	..	..	..
Writers and other men on special duty	..	..	..	19	..	..
Servants	..	..	..	27	..	..
Teamsters	..	..	..	6	..	..
Wagons and Horses	..	..	..	..	6	28
Total	3	13	2	52	6	28

In addition to the above, an engineer officer is detailed as Chief Engineer of the Corps if there is any need for his services; and a certain number of lieutenants, usually from 4 to 6, are

STRENGTH AND ORGANIZATION OF LAND FORCES. 31

temporarily detailed from the troops of the corps as "Orderly Officers," to carry messages, etc. An Independent Army Corps —being in fact a small army—has the same staff as an army, and only slightly inferior to it in numbers. As prescribed in the order of November, 1876, it numbers in all 6 Generals, 46 other officers, 122 officials, 169 enlisted men, 28 wagons, and 116 horses.

Staff of an Infantry Division.

	Generals.	Field officers.	Company officers.	Civilian officials.	Enlisted men.	Wagons.	Horses.
Commander, Lieutenant-General	1	..	..	..	..	..	..
Chief of staff, Colonel	..	1	..	..	..	..	..
Officers of general staff	..	..	2	..	..	..	..
Division Surgeon	..	..	..	1	..	..	..
Trumpeter	..	..	..	..	1	..	..
Writers	..	..	..	..	3	..	..
Teamsters	..	..	..	..	8	..	..
Servants	..	..	..	..	15	..	..
Train	..	..	..	..	..	3	14
Total	1	1	2	1	27	3	14

During the campaign there were in addition to the above a certain number (from 3 to 5) of company officers detailed for temporary duty as "Orderly officers," to carry orders, etc.

The Staff of a Brigade consists of the Major-General commanding, a Brigade Adjutant, 1 writer and 4 servants. The adjutant is chosen from among the company officers of the brigade, and is only temporarily detached from his regiment.

From what has preceded we are now able to compute the regulation strength of an army corps, composed of 3-battalion regiments, in time of war.

Strength of an Army Corps:

	ORGANIZATION.			COMBATANTS.				NON-COMBATANTS.			
	Battalions.	Batteries.	Squadrons.	Generals.	Officers.	Men.	Guns.	Horses.	Officials.	Men.	Wagons.	Horses.
1 Corps Staff	..	..	..	8	13	..	..	..	2	52	6	28
2 Divisions Infantry	24	..	..	6	614	24,648	..	..	50	1,162	342	1,456
2 Brigades Foot Artillery	..	12	..	2	76	2,788	96	1,944	6	486	48	204
1 Division Cavalry	..	..	18	3	123	3,057	..	2,652	20	520	71	288
2 Horse Batteries	..	2	..	..	14	578	12	578	..	84	8	84
Total	24	14	18	14	840	31,071	108	5,174	78	2,304	475	2,006

An Army Corps composed of 4-battalion regiments has 32 battalions, 872 officers and 38,879 men of combatants, and 86 officials and 3,024 men of non-combatants; otherwise as in the preceding table.

This completes the data of the fighting strength of the Field Troops. The figures have all been taken from the book of Colonel Martianof, mentioned in the Preface, and are correct according to the regulations in force at the end of the year 1878. From this data we are able to compute the total strength of the Field Army, as given in the following table:

Strength of the Russian Field Army.

			ORGANIZATION.				
	Divisions.	Brigades.	Regiments.	Battalions.	Squadrons.	Batteries.	Guns.
INFANTRY. Guard	2	6	12	48	..	..	....
Grenadiers	3	6	12	36	..	..	....
" (Caucasus)	1	2	4	16	..	..	....
Line	35	70	140	420	..	..	....
" (Caucasus)	6	12	24	96	..	..	....
RIFLES. { Guard	..	1	..	4	..	..	....
{ Line	..	6	..	24	..	..	....
{ " (Caucasus)	..	1	..	4	..	..	....
TOTAL INFANTRY	48	104	192	648	..	..	...
CAVALRY. Guard	2	6	12	..	52	..	....
Line	14	28	56	..	252	..	....
" (Caucasus)	1	2	4	..	16	..	....
TOTAL CAVALRY	17	36	72	..	320	..	...
ARTILLERY. FOOT { Guard	..	3	..	..	..	18	144
{ Grenadiers	..	4	..	..	..	24	192
{ Line	..	41	..	..	..	246	1,968
HORSE. { Guard	..	..	..	..	..	5	30
{ Line	..	..	..	..	..	30	180
TOTAL ARTILLERY	..	48	..	..	..	323	2,514
ENGINEERS. Guard	..	..	..	1	..	..	....
Grenadiers	..	..	..	1	..	..	....
Line	..	5	..	17	..	..	....
TOTAL ENGINEERS	..	5	..	19	..	..	...
H'DQ'RS STAFF. 20 Corps Staffs	..	..	..	..	..	..	....
64 Division Staffs	..	..	..	..	..	..	....
191 Brigade Staffs	..	..	..	..	..	..	....
TOTAL STAFF	..	..	..	..	..	..	..
TOTAL FIELD ARMY.	..	..	..	667	320	323	2,514

STRENGTH AND ORGANIZATION OF LAND FORCES. 33

Strength of the Russian Field Army—Continued.

		WAR FOOTING.							PEACE FOOTING.					
	Generals.	Officers.	Men.	Horses.	Ozdals.	Non-combatants Men.	Horses.	Wagons.	Generals.	Officers.	Combatants Men.	Horses.	Ozdals.	Non-combatants Men.	Horses.	Wagons.

	Generals	Officers	Men	Horses	Ozdals	Men	Horses	Wagons	Generals	Officers	Men	Horses	Ozdals	Men	Horses	Wagons
INFANTRY { Guard	18	948	49,164	....	94	2,712	2,232	528	12	768	28,244	....	84	2,320	624	204
Grenadiers	....	912	37,092	....	72	1,692	2,083	492	....	720	21,646	....	72	1,260	558	192
Line	....	380	18,263	....	28	604	744	176	....	256	7,698	....	25	740	208	68
" (Caucasus)	....	10,640	492,740	....	840	10,040	24,860	5,740	....	8,400	252,420	....	864	14,400	6,880	2,240
" (Caucasus)	....	1,920	97,606	....	168	5,424	4,464	1,058	....	1,536	45,763	....	168	4,440	1,243	408
RIFLES { Guard	....	104	3,552	....	12	223	240	64	....	88	2,109	....	12	172	43	24
Line	....	624	19,698	....	48	1,344	1,440	384	....	528	11,341	....	48	1,008	289	144
" (Caucasus)	....	64	4,056	....	12	900	804	72	....	68	1,802	....	12	160	43	16
TOTAL INFANTRY	12	15,559	660,084	....	1,264	31,484	35,872	5,612	12	12,364	366,240	....	508	24,700	9,912	3,296
CAV'LRY { Guard	12	494	9,442	7,052	68	1,710	768	192	12	406	8,693	6,899	68	1,690	180	108
Line	....	1,660	42,798	37,198	266	6,902	3,584	596	....	1,630	42,795	37,128	266	6,902	840	494
" (Caucasus)	....	182	2,918	2,912	24	664	264	64	....	182	2,912	2,912	24	654	60	36
TOTAL CAVALRY	12	2,236	55,152	47,592	358	9,176	4,616	1,152	12	2,216	54,408	46,848	359	9,086	1,080	638
ARTIL'Y { Foot { Guard	....	108	4,468	2,916	....	675	896	72	....	108	3,042	694	....	622	108	85
Grenadiers	....	144	5,970	8,858	....	900	408	66	....	144	4,056	912	....	696	144	43
Line	....	1,476	61,284	39,832	....	9,226	4,182	954	....	1,476	41,574	9,843	....	7,184	1,476	498
Horse { Guard	....	85	1,170	1,445	....	210	55	20	....	80	1,140	975	....	110	80	10
Line	....	210	7,920	8,670	....	1,260	510	120	....	210	6,370	5,850	....	1,020	180	60
TOTAL ARTILLERY	....	1,973	79,902	56,771	....	12,270	5,491	1,292	....	1,973	56,687	17,769	....	9,542	1,938	647
ENGINEERS { Guard	....	28	1,010	....	2	124	60	18	....	28	702	....	2	98	12	8
Grenadiers	....	28	1,070	....	2	124	60	18	....	28	702	....	2	98	12	....
Line	....	461	17,240	540	47	799	1,035	304	....	436	10,878	....	89	1,515	192	129
TOTAL ENGINEERS	....	517	19,260	540	51	1,047	1,155	340	....	492	12,282	....	42	1,701	216	138
STAFF { 20 Corps Staffs	60	260	....	....	40	1,040	560	120	60	200	....	....	40	1,040	560	120
64 Division Staffs	64	192	....	....	64	1,728	896	192	64	192	....	....	64	1,728	896	192
191 Brigade Staffs	191	....	....	....	....	1,537	1,528	882	191	....	....	....	....	1,537	1,528	882
TOTAL STAFF	315	452	....	....	104	4,305	2,984	694	315	452	....	....	104	4,305	2,984	694
TOTAL FIELD ARMY	339	20,730	814,398	105,903	1,777	58,282	50,118	11,990	339	17,499	489,617	64,617	1,012	49,331	16,130	5,413

3

Military Establishments.

Having now given the numbers of the troops who do the actual fighting, we come to that class who provide them with the means therefor, take part in special operations, or care for their wants in sickness and in health. A part of them might be classed as combatants and a part as non-combatants, but there is no great significance in this division; they are all troops destined for special duties. They are as follows:

Engineers.
 1. The Field Engineer Parks.
 2. The Siege Engineer Parks.
 3. The Field Telegraph Parks.

Artillery (Ordnance).
 4. The Field Ammunition Parks.
 5. The Siege Artillery Parks.
 6. The Mobile Artillery Workshops.
 7. The Mobile Laboratory Workshops.
 8. The Ammunition Depots.

Medical.
 9. The Field Hospitals.
 10. The Mobile Division Hospitals.
 11. The Mobile Dispensaries.

Intendance.—The Intendance Transport.

Engineer Parks.

There are in all 5 Field Engineer Parks (order of January 27 [February 8], 1877), 2 Siege Engineer Parks, and 9 Field Telegraph Parks (order of November 13 [25], 1876.) The first keep the Sapper Battalions supplied with the requisite tools for their special duties in the field; the second supply the engineer tools required in a siege; the third supply the material and perform the service of the field telegraph, each park having 100 kilometres (62·14 miles) of wire.

Strength of an Engineer Park.

		Combatants.		Non-Combatants.				Total.		Horses.		Wagons.	
		Field Officers.	Comp'y Officers.	Enlisted Men.	Engineer Functionaries.	Artificers, Writers, etc.	Teamsters.	Servants.	Officers.	Men.	Park Draught.	Train Draught.	Park.	Train.
Field Engineer Park...	War Footing......	3	11	125	3	19	69	18	17	281	240	16	54	4
	Peace Footing	3	2	42	1	5	6	7	6	60	....	3	....	....
Siege Engineer Park ..	War Footing....	2	5	220	4	36	4	12	11	272	370	17	112	4
	Peace Footing	2	2	66	1	9	2	6	5	88	....	4	....	....

STRENGTH AND ORGANIZATION OF LAND FORCES. 35

Strength of an Engineer Park—Continued.

		Field Officers.	Comp'y Officers.	Operators.	Mechanics.	N. C. Officers and Privates.	Clerks, etc.	Teamsters.	Servants.	TOTAL. Officers.	TOTAL. Men.	HORSES. Park.	HORSES. Train.	WAGONS. Park.	WAGONS. Train.
Field Telegraph Park...	War Footing......	1	7	24	6	255	7	66	9	8	367	174	14	30	3
	Peace Footing.....	1	6	24	6	37	1	1	8	7	77	....	....	....	....

Ammunition Parks.

The Ammunition Parks are charged with keeping the troops (Artillery, Infantry, and Cavalry) supplied with ammunition of all kinds. According to the new organization (March 22 [April 3], 1877,) there are:

17 Flying Parks for Cavalry Divisions,
7 Flying Parks for Rifle Brigades,
48 Flying Parks for Infantry Divisions (with 130 four-wheeled caissons, or 124 two-wheeled caissons),
48 Mobile Parks for Infantry Divisions,
8 Siege Artillery Parks.

Strength of Ammunition Parks.

			COMBATANTS.			NON-COMBATANTS.				TOTAL.		HORSES.		WAGONS.	
			Officers.	N. C. Officers.	Privates.	Officials.	Artificers, Clerks, etc.	Teamsters.	Servants.	Officers.	Men.	Park.	Train.	Park.	Train.
Cavalry and Rifle Flying Parks..	War Footing	Cavalry.	2	10	130	1	9	6	3	3	158	155	14	25	4
		Rifle ...	2	10	90	1	9	6	3	3	118	105	14	17	4
	Peace Footing		2	4	30	1	4	1	3	3	44	....	....	....	....
Division Flying Parks...	130 caissons	War Footing.	11	51	700	8	56	14	20	19	841	841	31	135	9
		Peace Foot'g.	8	8	45	1	18	2	5	4	73	....	....	....	....
	124 caissons	War Footing.	11	51	430	7	51	14	17	18	564	412	31	129	8
		Peace Foot'g.	8	8	45	1	18	2	5	4	73	....	....	....	....
Division Mobile Park—War Footing			8	10	200	1	15	10	3	8	233	206	18 Own	40	5
Siege Artillery Park (6 divisions)......	War Footing......		68	246	2010	36	214	540	111	104	3121	2766	1944	....	....
	Peace Footing.....		....	....	....	12	80	....	12	12	42	....	....	....	....

Hospitals.

There are in all 84 Field Hospitals and 64 Division Hospitals (one for each Division of Infantry and Cavalry).

Strength of a Hospital in Time of War.

	Director of the Hospital	MEDICAL STAFF.			ADMINISTRATIVE STAFF.			ATTENDANTS.			TRAIN.			COMPANY OF STRETCHER BEARERS.				Officers' Servants.	TOTAL.					ACCOMMODATION FOR	
		Surgeons.	Apothecaries.	Dressers.	Officials.	Chaplains.	Clerks.	N. C. Officers.	Sick Attendants.	Artificers.	Officers.	N. C. Officers.	Teamsters.	Officers.	N. C. Officers.	Privates.		Officers.	Men.	Ambulances.	Wagons.	Horses.	Officers.	Men.
Field Hospital......		10	4	24	6	2	12	11	138	36	..	9	54	..	..	..	..	..	..	..	..	..	..	..
	1	38			20			185			63			..		..		13	28	297	..	27	114	80	600
Division Hospital..	...	6	1	17	3	2	2	2	50	20	1	8	108	1		9	200	..	..	..	..	..	..	..
		26			7			72			117			210				14	16	440	30	26	228	6	160
Mobile Dispensary.	.....	3	8	..	..	..	9	..	..	..	..	2	28	..	..	..	..	..	3	42	..	28	115	..	..

Intendance Transport.

This has no existence in time of peace, and in time of war is provided for according to circumstances under the direction of the Chief Intendant of the Army. Ox carts or horse carts are usually hired for the service at so much a month. They are divided into divisions of 350 wagons each, and to each division are assigned a few subofficials, responsible for the property transported, and a squad of Cossacks as an escort, greater or less in size according to circumstances.

The Mobile Artillery Workshops, Ammunition Depots, etc., are formed in rear of the army, and have an organization and strength dependent upon the circumstances of the case. It is from them that the Parks receive their ammunition, implements, etc., etc.

LOCAL TROOPS.

Garrisons of Fortresses and Fortified Points.

The Garrison Troops consist in time of peace of,
24 Infantry Battalions,
55 Artillery Companies.

In time of war each Battalion may be increased to a Regiment of 4 battalions. Although these troops are primarily intended for the defense of the fortified points, yet they may be used elsewhere in case of emergency.

Strength and Distribution of Fortress Garrisons.

GOVERN-MENTS OF	FORTIFIED POINTS	Garrison Authorities		IN PEACE								IN WAR								
				Infantry		Artillery			Total			Infantry			Artillery			Total		
		Off.	Men.	Batt.	Off.	Men.	Comm.	Off.	Men.	Officers	Men.	Batt.	Officers	Men.	Comm.	Off.	Men.	Officers	Men.
St. Petersburg	St. Petersburg	8	26				2	10	569	18	604				2	12	910	20	946
	Cronstadt	25	70	3	78	3,042	8	40	2,272	143	5,354	13	287	12,174	13	78	5,915	840	18,159
	Sveaborg	8	36	8	78	3,042	8	15	652	101	8,930	12	287	12,174	6	86	2,780	251	11,940
	Vyborg	8	36	1	26	1,014	2	10	451	44	1,501	4	79	4,058	4	24	1,620	111	5,914
Finland	Dünamünde	4	25				1	5	284	9	899				3	19	1,365	29	1,890
Vilna	Dünaburg	8	36	2	52	2,028	8	15	552	75	2,916	8	158	8,116	5	20	2,245	191	10,307
	Bobruisk	8	36	1	26	1,014	5	15	889	89	1,359	4	79	4,058	4	10	568	97	4,992
Warsaw	Warsaw	8	36	1	26	1,014	5	15	852	49	1,902	4	79	4,058	4	15	1,347	102	5,441
	Novogeorgievsk	8	36	4	104	4,056	5	30	1,704	142	5,796	16	316	16,232	6	40	8,092	364	19,560
	Ivangorod	4	25	2	52	2,028	2	10	563	66	2,621	8	158	8,116	3	15	1,347	177	9,458
	Brest-Litevsky	8	36	8	78	3,042	2	10	552	101	3,990	12	237	12,174	8	25	2,245	270	14,455
Kief	Kief	8	36				2	10	508	18	604				2	10	678	38	2,780
Odessa	Bender	8	36	1	26	1,014	4	20	281	81	1,334	4	79	4,058	5	30	2,275	97	4,772
	Nikolaïef	9	36	det.	8	248	2	20	1,186	51	1,420	1	3	243	5	10	3,640	41	2,559
	Kertch	8	36	2	52	2,028	1	10	1,186	89	8,201	8	158	8,116	8	80	1,856	215	11,798
	Alexandropol	8	36	1	21	974	2	10	453	13	1,466	1	79	4,057	4	43	568	107	5,449
Caucasus	Tiflis	4	25				2	10	458	14	604				2	20	403	18	664
	Province of Terek	8	25				2	10	568	9	458				1	10	889	14	463
	" Daghestan	4	30				1	5	389	8	364				1	5	229	9	864
	" Kuban	8	20				1	5	229	8	249				1	5	229	8	249
East Siberia	Akhalzyk	11	51				1	5	284	16	385				1	5	254	16	335
	Nikolaïef (on the Amoor)	4	25				1	5	229	9	254				1	5	229	9	254
Turkestan	Tashkend	4	25				1	5	173	9	198				1	5	178	9	198
	Vyernoye	4	25				1	5	229	9	254				1	5	229	9	254
	Chinaz	3	20				1	5	173	6	108				1	5	173	5	198
	Fort Petrovski																			
Total		156	861	24	622	24,544	59	295	16,087	1,103	41,492	96	1,899	97,689	91	406	88,073	2,581	136,578

STRENGTH AND ORGANIZATION OF LAND FORCES. 37

Strength of Garrison Infantry.

		Officers.	N. C. Officers.	Volunteers.	Musicians.	Privates.	Total Enlisted.	NON-COMBATANTS.		
								Officials.	Men.	Servants.
In Europe	Garrison Battalion.........	26	80	16	18	900	1014	3	25	32
	Garrison Regiment.	79	820	64	74	3000	4038	6	51	93
In the Caucasus...	Garrison Battalion..........	21	40	16	18	900	974	2	32	25
	Garrison Regiment.........	79	820	64	78	3000	4057	6	67	93

The artillery companies are of various classes, according to locality, having 150, 200, 250, and 300 privates in time of peace, and 300 and 400 in time of war; the number of officers is 5 in time of peace and 6 in time of war, and the non-commissioned officers vary from 45 to 15 in the various classes. In time of war new companies may be formed, carrying the total number up to 91. It is proposed to have a new organization of 50 companies in time of peace, each of which in time of war should become a battalion; but this has not yet been accomplished.

Frontier Troops in Asia (Linia Bataliona).

These consist of
7 Battalions in the Caucasus,
2 " " Orenburg,
17 " " Turkestan,
4 " " West Siberia,
6 " " East Siberia.

They perform garrison or other service in those remote localities. The Battalions in the Caucasus have 4 companies each, and their strength and organization is the same as that of a battalion of 4 Companies in the field army (p. 23), with the addition of the Staff of the Battalion; i. e., it consists of 21 officers and 1,014 men in time of war, and 17 officers and 474 men in time of peace. The other Battalions have 5 Companies each, and the same organization as such a Battalion in the Field Army (p. 23). Their strength is 26 officers and 1,026 men in war, and 21 officers and 597 men in peace.

STRENGTH AND ORGANIZATION OF LAND FORCES. 39

Strength of Frontier Troops.

	Battalions.	IN WAR.			IN PEACE.		
		Officers.	Men.	Non-Combatants.	Officers.	Men.	Non-Combatants.
In the Caucasus	7	147	7,093	812	119	8,318	618
In Central Asia	29	754	25,754	2,610	609	17,113	2,320
Total	36	901	36,852	8,422	728	20,431	2,988

Stationary Troops (Maestnia Voiska).

These are, properly speaking, the local troops; i.e., they remain under all circumstances in the same locality. They comprise: *a*, troops remaining in localities whence the active troops have left for the field; *b*, police; *c*, guards and watchmen; *d*, *étappe* and escort troops; *e*, various detachments in Europe, in the remote provinces, on the frontiers to prevent smuggling, etc., etc. In other countries they would be considered rather as civil employees than as part of the army.

In all they comprise

9 Local Cadre Battalions, each of which in time of war may be raised to a regiment of 4 battalions; 8 of them in Europe and 1 in the Caucasus.

68 Local Battalions (of which 23 are in the Caucasus and Asia).

582 Local Detachments, of different strength and organization (of which 114 are in the Caucasus and Asia).

Without attempting to give the various organizations and location of these troops, it is enough to say that in time of peace they number 75,000 men, and in time of war may be increased to 133,000.

Special Corps.

Of the same nature as these troops just mentioned, i. e., not contributing to the real strength of the army, are the following special corps:

1. Palace Grenadiers.
2. Garrison Body-Guards.
3. Pensioners of the Guard.
4. Gendarmerie corps.

The Palace Grenadiers form a company consisting of 8 officers, 16 non-commissioned officers, 142 grenadiers, and 16 clerks, servants, etc. They perform guard duty at the Winter Palace in St. Petersburg, and at the Kremlin in Moscow.

The Garrison Body-Guards perform similar service at the various imperial buildings in St. Petersburg. The organization is that of a battalion, with 20 officers and 558 non-commissioned officers and men.

The Pensioners of the Guard consist of old soldiers of specially meritorious service; they are distributed among the various regiments of the guard, and perform nominal light duty as long as they are capable of it. In all, they number 31 officers and 1,132 non-commissioned officers and men. All three of these bodies are in fact pensioners, formed of old soldiers who have passed their lives in the army and performed exceptional service.

The Corps of Gendarmes, or military police, consists of 271 officers, 17 officials, and 4,163 men. The officers are chosen from the field and regimental officers of the army, of not less than 5 years of service. The men are chosen from soldiers of exceptional intelligence and good character, who have completed their 6 years of service with their regiments. The Corps is divided into various detachments stationed in different parts of the empire.

THE RESERVE.

The Reserve consists of those soldiers who have passed 6 years on duty with their regiments, and who have then been placed on furlough for the remaining 9 years of their military service. Up to the beginning of the war these men had no definite organization in time of peace, except a Cadre Battalion for the Reserve Regiment of the Guard; they were simply held liable to be called upon at any moment for active service in one of the following categories:

1. To fill up the Active Regiments to war strength.
2. To form Ersatz* Battalions.

---

* The German word *Ersatz* has now passed into all languages with a definite technical meaning; the Ersatz troops are those which fill up the vacancies caused by death or other causes among the troops at the front. The proper English word would be recruit; but recruits in English are generally understood to be raw untrained men, whereas the Ersatz troops are in great part old soldiers.

STRENGTH AND ORGANIZATION OF LAND FORCES. 41

3. To form Reserve * Battalions.

According to the original scheme under which the Russian army is organized, that of January 1st (13th), 1874, the reserve soldiers would in time of war, besides filling the whole army up to war strength, form

192 Infantry Battalions,
7 Rifle Battalions,
56 Squadrons,
48 Foot Batteries,
3 Horse Batteries,
5 Sapper Battalions,
} of Ersatz;

that is, in the proportion of 1 battalion for each regiment of Infantry or brigade of rifles or sappers, 1 squadron for each cavalry regiment, and 1 battery for each artillery brigade, in the field; and also

4 Battalions (1 Regiment) of Infantry of the Guard,
164 Infantry Battalions of the Line,
112 Squadrons,
44 Batteries,
5 Sapper companies,
} of Reserve;

which would be organized into Divisions and form an army in itself, equal in strength to one fourth of that already in the field (one half in the cavalry arm).

In order that this scheme should work itself out in all its details (i. e., that the Ersatz and Reserve should all be old soldiers), 9 years should have elapsed. The non-commissioned officers and privates of the Active Army number in time of peace, in round numbers, 540,000 men, in time of war 870,000. Disregarding, for the sake of simplicity, the local troops of all kinds, the annual contingent for the active army is something under 100,000 men. At the end of 9 years there would therefore be 6 contingents on duty with the colors, and 9 contingents at hand in the Reserve. Owing to deaths in the mean time, these latter may be considered as numbering 800,000 men. At the outbreak of war these 800,000 men would be disposed of as follows:

* Reserve troops have nothing to do with the troops at the front, but have their own organization, and are ready to take the field if necessary. In that case their losses would be supplied from the Ersatz.

1. To fill up the active army to war strength.............. 330,000
2. { 204 Battalions.... 210,000 }
   { 56 Squadrons.... 10,000 } Total Ersatz............. 235,000
   { 51 Batteries..... 15,000 }
3. { 167 Battalions.... 170,000 }
   { 112 Squadrons.... 18,000 } Total Reserve............ 200,000
   { 44 Batteries..... 12,000 }
        Total.. 765,000

That is to say, the Active Army would be filled up to its war strength of 870,000 men, it would have its Ersatz troops capable of supplying its losses to the extent of 25 per cent., and there would be another army of 200,000 men in reserve and ready for use wherever required.

Such is, in outline, the plan of the organization of 1874.

It is now interesting to see how this plan was put into practical operation in the last war.

The first call under the new system having been made in the autumn of 1874, only three contingents had been set free before the outbreak of the war, viz., those of January 1st, 1875, 1876, and 1877; there were therefore, at the most, 300,000 reserve soldiers disposable. But on the other hand all the Army was not mobilized. Up to July 1st, 1877, there had been mobilized much less than half of it, as follows:

In Europe ..... { 14 Infantry Divisions..
                  2 Rifle Brigades.....
                  7 Cavalry Divisions..
                  14 Artillery Brigades.. } Total.. { 244 Battalions,
In the Caucasus. { 4 Infantry Divisions..   100 Squadrons (exclusive
                   1 Rifle Brigade......   of Cossacks),
                   1 Cavalry Division...   108 Batteries.
                   4 Artillery Brigades.. }

To increase these troops from peace to war strength required...................................... 125,000 men, and at the same time it was necessary to form
61 Battalions, }
25 Squadrons, } of Ersatz, requiring.......... 70,000 "
18 Batteries, }
        Total....................................... 195,000 "
thus leaving about 105,000 men of the reserve still available. But in the month of August a further mobilization was made of

STRENGTH AND ORGANIZATION OF LAND FORCES. 43

The Guard ....
The Grenadiers ....
4 Divisions of the Line in Europe .....
3 Divisions of the Line in the Caucasus

Total..
184 Battalions,
28 Squadrons (exclusive of Cossacks),
78 Batteries;

and this mobilization necessitated the formation of
46 Battalions,
7 Squadrons, } of Ersatz.
13 Batteries,

To complete the war strength of the troops ordered to be mobilized required 100,000 men, and for the Ersatz about 55,000 men. This alone would more than absorb the rest of the reserve on hand.

But in addition to all this there were ordered to be formed
52 Battalions,
12 Batteries, } of Reserve,

which would require 55,000 men; and it was also in contemplation to order the formation of more battalions of reserve (as was in fact subsequently done).* As there were not enough reservists (i. e., old soldiers) to satisfy all these demands, recourse was had to the Militia, of which the first class (188,600 men) was called out by Imperial Ukase dated July 10th (22d), 1877, in accordance with art. 39 of the Regulations. These men, having never seen military service, were at once incorporated into the Ersatz for instruction, while the reserve battalions were formed of the old soldiers already in the Ersatz. Subsequently new reserve battalions were ordered to be formed, until at the conclusion of peace there were 96 battalions and 32 batteries, forming 8 divisions of reserves, with 8 artillery brigades of 4 batteries each. These troops were formed in part of the original contingents of reserves (old soldiers) and in part of the Militiamen after they had passed a certain time in the Ersatz. These reserve divisions were concentrated near the frontier, and three of them passed over into Roumania, for service along the line of communications of the army in Bulgaria, and also to be prepared for any emergency which might have arisen at that uncertain time.†

---

* The above figures make no pretense to exact accuracy, but are intended simply to illustrate the working of the reserve system as applied to the Field Troops. The same principles would obtain for the Local Troops.

† Had Austria declared war after the treaty of San Stefano, Russia could immediately have put into the field against her 10 divisions of the Active army and

Meanwhile the Ersatz depots began in the month of August, 1877, to send forward squads of men to replace the losses already incurred in Bulgaria. At first these were wholly reservists (old soldiers); but as soon as the militia men had been clothed, armed, and received their first instruction in drill at the depots, the reservists were retained to form reserve divisions and the militia men were sent forward to the field, and a steady stream of them kept arriving throughout the campaign, and in fact (for the troops of occupation) continues to this moment (December, 1878).

The practical results of this system were most excellent. Regiments were now and then almost annihilated in the bloody battles around Plevna, but a month or six weeks afterward they were again at their full strength; and there was always *the leaven of old soldiers*, who had survived the battles, to prevent the regiment from being a mere collection of raw recruits.

The Ersatz Troops and Depots are under the orders of the general commanding the military circumscription in which they are situated. When a division (or part of it) has lost men in a campaign, its chief makes a requisition upon the commander of the army for men to fill his division up to its normal strength; from the army commander this goes to the Minister of War, who orders the general commanding the circumscription from which the division comes to furnish the men. They are sent forward to the army commander, and by him sent to the division, where they are distributed to the regiments and so on. Should that particular circumscription have already furnished its full quota, then the demand is made upon another. The army commander always has the authority to distribute the men, on their arrival, where they are most needed; but in general an effort is made to assign the men to the regiments of the localities from which they come.

We thus see that up to the beginning of the recent war the Reserve had never been organized at all; that during the war a portion of it was formed with an organization of a division of

these 8 divisions of the Reserve army, which, with their artillery and cavalry, would have made a force of over 200,000 men, and could also have formed the remaining 8 Reserve divisions, or 100,000 more; and this without moving a man from Turkey or the Black Sea coast. To have found the money for their maintenance would, however, have required great sacrifices.

STRENGTH AND ORGANIZATION OF LAND FORCES. 45

12 battalions (not organized into regiments) and of 4 batteries. Eight such divisions were formed, but the organization was wholly temporary. During the months of June and July, 1878, 3 more reserve divisions were formed, but with an organization of 4 regiments, of 4 battalions each, to a division; and at the same time reserve divisions Nos. 5 to 8 had their organization changed from that of 12-battalion divisions to that of 4-regiment divisions. Reserve divisions Nos. 1 to 4 being in service near the armies (1, 2, and 4 in Bulgaria, and 3 in Armenia), their temporary organization remains up to the present time (December, 1878).

In the month of September, 1878, the definite plan for the organization of the Reserve was promulgated from the War Office. It prescribes that in time of peace there will exist 96 cadre battalions, of a strength of 13 officers and 464 men; each of these Battalions to consist of 5 companies; in time of war each company is to be developed into a battalion, 4 battalions forming a regiment for active service, and the 5th battalion remaining at home as Ersatz. These 96 regiments will form 24 divisions of 16 battalions each, or 384 battalions, and also the 96 battalions of Ersatz; i. e., in all, 480 battalions, or a half million of men. As the mobilization of the Active Army and the formation of its Ersatz require, as we have seen, 565,000 men, leaving only 235,000 available of the 9 annual contingents of Reserve, recourse would have to be made at once to the Militia in order to organize these Reserve Divisions and their Ersatz, if this scheme were fully carried out. But of course it never can be. In another war we should see the same thing happen as in the last—a portion of the Active Army mobilized, its Ersatz formed, and then a certain portion of the Reserve Army mobilized, or more properly speaking organized; and the number of these would depend upon the circumstances and requirements of the case. Russia has men for military service in almost unlimited numbers, but lack of money and lack of officers must always put a limit in practice to this organizing of men by the half million. The fundamental principles of the Reserve, however—i. e., the Ersatz to fill up the losses in the field, and the Reserve Divisions to form a second army, greater or less in size—will be put in practical application in every war; and in time of peace the permanent organization of the reserve will, in connection with the increasing facilities of communication by railways and other roads, allow a large portion of the local troops to be dispensed with, and thus introduce simplicity into the military system.

IRREGULAR TROOPS.

The Irregular Troops consist of the Cossacks, of the Tartars of the Crimea and of Bashkir, and of certain native militia in Daghestan and Georgia in the Caucasus. The term irregulars is somewhat misleading, for in point of fact, in a strictly military sense, there is very little difference between certain portions of the Cossacks—especially those of the Don—and the regular troops. As already stated, a Don Cossack Cavalry Regiment is an integral part of every Cavalry Division of the Active Army, in time of peace as well as in war.

Their military service is, however, based upon principles differing in detail from those affecting the service in the regular army.

According to the Regulations, approved by the Emperor April 29 (May 11), 1875, every Don Cossack is obliged to perform military service, and substitutes are not permitted. The only exceptions are priests, physicians, teachers, etc., and those who have suffered from fire, inundation, or other misfortunes, and can not be spared from their homes; also, of course, those who are physically incapable. On attaining his 19th year every male Cossack takes the oath of fidelity and is enrolled among the Cossacks; the total number of those so enrolled constitutes the Voissko (or army) of Cossacks of the Don. The Voissko is divided into 3 categories: those between the ages of 19 and 22, those between 22 and 34, and those between 34 and 39. The first class receive instruction and perform service in the interior; the second class are liable to active service away from their homes (ordinarily 4 years in active service and the remaining 8 years at home); and the third are permanently on furlough, and only called upon to fill up losses in time of war in the second category. On the same principle as in the regular army, a certain degree of education reduces the active service to 6 months, 1, 2, or 3 years.

The above is the outline of the rules for service of the tribe of Cossacks on the Don; for the other tribes it differs only in detail.

STRENGTH AND ORGANIZATION OF LAND FORCES. 47

The Cesarevitch is the Ataman (headman) of all the Cossacks, but each tribe has its own "Nakazny Ataman" (deputy headman), who manages all its affairs. Upon the recommendation of the Minister of War, the Emperor orders the Ataman to furnish the number of men required for any given year, and the Ataman takes all the measures necessary for that purpose.

In fact the general distinction between the Cossacks and the so-called regular troops may be said to consist in the fact that the Cossacks manage their own affairs, whereas in the regular regiments the Government manages everything for them. The Cossack populations pay no taxes, and in return render military service without pay. The Government furnishes a Cossack his arms and ammunition, but everything else he provides for himself when in service. The Government gives him an allowance in lieu of rations and forage, but his horse, his saddle, his uniform and his equipments are all his own property. As of course it often happens in war that there is nothing to be bought outside the army, then the Cossacks put their money in the hands of their Colonel, who purchases from the Intendance.

The Cossacks of the Don and of the Ural are fishermen and farmers in ordinary times. Their life is in a measure communistic, and the affairs of each village or community are directed by the headman of the village for the common good, each having the benefit of his own labor. They are fine horsemen, expert swimmers, good shots, and skillful boatmen. Those of the Caucasus are for the most part rather wild mountain tribes. They are extremely bold riders and accurate shots; they train their horses to lie down and keep quiet, while they fire over them, then to get up quickly and go off at a rapid galop. Like our Indians, they also train their horses to stand still and graze, while they dismount, walk off some distance, and fire; the horses do not need to be held or tied.

During the recent war, for the first time, Caucasian Cossacks were employed by Russia in Europe, one regiment of Kuban and one of Vladikavkas forming the Caucasian Cossack Brigade, of which frequent mention will be found in the following pages. Although well instructed in drill, their greatest usefulness was in following up a disorderly retreat, when they cut down the fugitives without mercy. After the battle of Lovtcha they followed the flying Turks and sabred 3,000 of them—nearly twice their own number. While Gourko was crossing the Balkans, just before the battle of Tashkossen, this brigade descended into the Sophia valley, captured a train of some 200 wagons, and sabred the last man of the two or three companies forming its escort. Again, after the dispersion of Sulciman Pasha's army at Philippopolis, they followed it into the mountains close upon its heels, and cut down every straggler. On the other hand, at the second battle of Plevna (July 30th), a half dozen sotnias of these Caucasians, under Skobeleff, fighting on foot, held their own all day against a brigade of Turkish infantry; and at the assault of Kars, some sotnias, arriving on foot about 1 A. M., decided the capture of Fort Kanly. But, as far as my experience with the brigade went, they are not naturally cruel; they are perfectly docile and honest with their friends, and completely subject to discipline. What distinguishes them principally from the ordinary Russian soldiers of the Line is their individuality. The infantry soldier expects to have everything arranged for him and to receive orders for everything in detail; left to his own resources, he is almost helpless. On the other hand, the Caucasian Cossack is never so well off or so useful as when thrown entirely upon his own resources, with only general instructions; he never fails to find food for himself and horse; he invariably has on his saddle a miscellaneous collection of odds and ends, comprising everything that is necessary for his personal comfort at all times; and he is unusually well trained in everything which goes with us by the name of "plains craft."

The Cossacks of the Don have these same qualities, but in a much less degree; and it is probable that their individuality has been somewhat injured by their assimilation to regular troops. They are at present simply light cavalry, and differ from the Lancers little but in name.

The Squadrons are known by the name of *sotnias* (signifying "a hundred"), and vary in strength from 100 to 200 men; the Don regiments have 6 sotnias, the others sometimes 6, and sometimes 4. The foot troops are all rifle battalions, known as *plastounes*. The organization of Cossacks and their total strength are given in the tables on the following page.

STRENGTH AND ORGANIZATION OF LAND FORCES.

Organization of Cossacks.

	COMBATANTS				NON-COMBATANTS		
	Officers	N. C. Officers	Musicians	Cossacks	Officials	Men	Servants
Cavalry.							
Don Cossack Regiment of the Guard { 6 sotnias in war	58	96	25	960	4	86	64
{ 4 sotnias in peace	39	64	25	640	4	57	43
Don Cossack Regiment of the Line, 6 sotnias	21	86	19	768	1	57	18
Kuban-Siberia-Ural-Cossack Regiment, 6 sotnias	21	56	19	798	1	29	..
Transbaikal-Astrakhan-Terek-Cossack Regiment, 4 sotnias	15	39	18	532	1	22	..
Orenburg Cossack Regiment, 6 sotnias	20	39	..	810	..	2	22
Semiriatchensk Cossack Regiment, 6 sotnias	20	50	18	798	1	2	..
Amoor Cossack Regiment, 4 sotnias	9	34	9	532	..	14	..
Ural Squadron of the Guard	7	18	4	180	..	2	8
Infantry.							
Kuban and Transbaikal Rifle Battalion, 5 sotnias	44	65	26	600	1	21	..
Amoor Rifle Battalion	12	82	20	920	..	16	..
Artillery.							
Don Cossack Battery (same as in Regular Army)	7	27	4	258	1	42	0
Kuban-Terek-Transbaikal Cossack Battery { War	7	25	4	256	1	87	0
{ Peace	7	11	4	86	1	81	9
Orenburg Cossack Battery	6	20	4	178	..	..	..

Total Strength of the Cossacks.

	MAXIMUM STRENGTH IN TIME OF WAR						ORDINARY STRENGTH IN TIME OF PEACE					
VOISSKO.	Battalions	Squadrons	Batteries	Officers	Men	Non-Combatants	Battalions	Squadrons	Batteries	Officers	Men	Non-Combatants
Of the Don {	..	372	..	1,366	55,542	4,563	..	124	..	673	18,189	1,620
	..	...	22	154	6,358	924	..	...	8	56	1,832	272
	6	...	..	264	4,146	132	2	...	..	88	1,382	44
Of Kuban (Caucasus) {	..	194	..	658	26,690	930	..	64	..	444	9,230	830
	..	...	5	35	1,435	235	..	...	5	35	505	205
Of the Terek (Caucasus) {	..	61	..	231	8,995	350	..	21	..	156	3,065	120
	..	...	2	14	570	94	..	...	2	14	202	82
Of Astrakhan (the Volga)	..	12	..	45	1,749	69	..	4	..	30	533	23
Of the Ural	..	55	..	194	8,007	275	..	19	..	132	2,769	95
Of Orenburg {	..	102	..	340	14,416	408	..	80	..	100	4,240	220
	..	...	8	43	1,616	....	..	...	4	24	606	....
Of Semiriatchensk	..	12	..	40	1,762	6	..	12	..	40	1,762	6
Of (West) Siberia	..	54	..	878	7,857	270	..	18	..	126	2,619	90
Of the Transbaikal (East Siberia) {	9	...	..	896	6,219	198	3	...	..	132	2,078	66
	..	24	..	90	3,498	189	..	8	..	60	1,168	46
	..	...	2	14	570	94	..	...	2	14	202	82
Of the Amoor {	2	...	..	24	2,044	82	2	...	..	24	2,044	82
	..	8	..	18	1,150	28	..	8	..	16	1,150	28
Total	17	884	39	4,309	152,514	8,751	7	308	21	2,371	53,621	3,861

In addition to the above there is the personal escort of the Emperor, consisting of 4 Squadrons, formed of detachments from each of the tribes of the Caucasus.

The Crimeans and Bashkirs form only one regiment altogether.

The native militia of the Caucasus forms a body of wholly irregular troops, furnishing their own arms, horses, etc., and wearing their own costumes. They are never employed except in the localities from which they come, and for the purpose of police duty and suppressing insurrections rather than with troops in war. They consist of—

The Daghestan Mounted Regiment, 6 sotnias;
The Kutais Mounted Regiment, 5 sotnias;
The Kuban Militia, 1 sotnia;
The Terek Militia, 11 sotnias;
The Daghestan Militia, 11 sotnias;
The Georgian Druhjina (Battalion), 4 sotnias;
The Gurian Foot sotnia, 1 sotnia.

RECAPITULATION.

The table on the following page gives a summary of the military forces of Russia on land. These forces comprise—

1. A *Field Army*, numbering 560,000 men in time of peace, which can readily be expanded to 900,000 men in time of war. This army forms a unit ready for offensive or defensive service in the field.

2. A force of *Local Troops*, numbering 150,000 men in time of peace, which can be expanded to 325,000 men in time of war. This force is used for home service, to garrison fortresses, frontiers, etc.

3. A force of *Cossacks*, or irregular horsemen, numbering 42,000 men in time of peace, which can be expanded to 143,000 men in time of war. They are used as auxiliaries to the field army.

4. A *Reserve of Trained Soldiers*, numbering something over 1,000,000 men, who are on furlough in time of peace, but are called upon in time of war—

First. To fill up the Active Army to its war strength.
Second. To fill up the Local Troops to war strength.
Third. To form the Reserve Army.
Fourth. To form Ersatz troops at the depots, whence they are sent as needed to the troops in the field to replace their losses in battle.

5. A *Militia*, comprising all members of the able-bodied

STRENGTH AND ORGANIZATION OF LAND FORCES. 51

male population, between twenty and forty years of age, who have not seen military service. These are drafted by classes, as required, into the Ersatz when the Reserve is not sufficient in numbers to meet the demands made upon it.

General Summary of the Land Forces of Russia.

				MAXIMUM STRENGTH IN TIME OF WAR.		ORDINARY STRENGTH IN TIME OF PEACE.	
				Combatants.	Non-Combatants.	Combatants.	Non-Combatants.
Regulars..	Active Army....	Field Troops.		835,500	60,000	507,500	50,500
		Local Troops	Fortress Garrisons......	130,000	5,000	42,500	4,000
			Frontier Troops.....	38,000	3,500	21,000	3,000
			Stationary Troops.....	183,000	4,500	75,000	4,000
	Reserve.........		Ersatz........	235,000	....	....	....
			Reserve Army	500,000	....	....	....
			Military Establishments...	.....	140,000	....	....
Irregulars.	Cossacks........			*143,000	8,000	*42,000	3,000
	Native Asiatics..			6,000	....	6,000	....
Total..				2,020,500	221,000	694,000	64,500

* 14,000 Cossacks of the Don (14 Regiments of Cavalry and 7 Batteries of Artillery) form part of the Field Army at all times, and are included in it in the above table. The total number of Cossacks is 157,000 in time of war, and 56,000 in time of peace.

CHAPTER III.

ARMAMENT AND EQUIPMENT.

ARMAMENT.—1. *Infantry.*

IN 1867 two projects were presented to the Russian Government for the conversion of the muzzle-loading rifles, model of 1856, which were then in service, into breech-loaders. The first of these was the invention of a Swede named Karle, who offered the same kind of mechanism as had been adopted in the Swedish army, viz., a sliding bolt and needle, in connection with a paper cartridge, after the fashion of the original Chassepot and needle-guns. Some 200,000 guns were altered on this system.

But not long afterward a second system was proposed by an Austrian armorer named Krenk, which, having the advantage of a metallic cartridge, immediately superseded that of Karle; the system was adopted, and over a million of guns were converted. With this Krenk-converted rifle all the troops of the Line in Europe were armed during the late war. The breech mechanism consists of a block (b, Fig. 1) turning to the left around an axis (c) parallel to that of the barrel; when closed the block rests against two shoulders, on the right and on the left, forming part of the breech-piece, which is screwed to the barrel; the recoil is taken up by these shoulders. This gun is shown in the following sketch.

FIG. 1.—Krenk Musket.

In 1868 General Berdan presented his first plan of breech-loader with small caliber, which was adopted as an experiment and 30,000 guns were ordered from the United States. A portion of these guns were in use by the rifle brigades of the Line in Europe during the late war. This gun is the one described in the Ordnance Report of 1873 as the "Russian Berdan"; it is known in Russia as the "Berdan first system." Its breech mechanism is a block opening to the front by turning round an axis perpendicular to that of the barrel; it is locked by a bolt projecting from the rear, and the recoil is taken up by the base of the breech-piece. The gun is shown in the following sketch.

FIG. 2.—Berdan, First System.

In 1870 the second system of Berdan was introduced, and 30,000 guns were ordered as an experiment. They were made at Birmingham in England, and the contract provided that all the machinery, tools, implements, etc., used in their manufacture should be furnished to the Russian Government after the guns were finished. This system has finally been adopted as the Infantry arm of the Russian Army, and their own factories have constructed machinery, modeled on that received from Birmingham, for their manufacture. The present capacity of the three factories (at Tula, Sestroryek, and Ishora) is 1,000 guns a day.

During the recent war this arm was in the hands only of the Guard and the troops in the Caucasus. At present nearly half of the Active Army is armed with it; and by the 1st of June, 1879, the whole of the Active Army, the Garrison troops, and "Linia" Battalions will be completely armed with this weapon, with depots of arms for the troops which may be called up on mobilization, i. e., there will be about 1,200,000 of them on hand.

The breech mechanism of the Krenk system is so extremely simple and convenient that it was at one time thought of adopting it for the new gun, in connection with a reduced caliber, smaller bullet, increased twist of rifling, etc., but the Commission to whom the subject was referred in 1874 reported in favor of the Berdan and against the Krenk, principally on the ground of the impossibility of devising a satisfactory extractor for the latter. The Krenk extractor consists of a simple lever, the end of which is moved by the breech-block as it is opened. By opening the breech-block suddenly it is possible to throw the empty cartridge clear of the breech, *if the gun is clean;* but if not, then the cartridge is withdrawn only the amount of movement of the end of the lever (about one tenth of an inch) and the ramrod must be used to push out the cartridge. This vital defect of the mechanism was plainly shown during the war, where the complaints of the total failure of the extractor were extremely numerous.

The Berdan Infantry Musket, as finally adopted, and its Essential Parts are shown on the accompanying plate, Figs. 3 to 16. The chamber (see Fig. 17) is at the rear of the barrel, and is bottle-shaped, of the same size as the cartridge. The other parts of the breech mechanism are, the *receiver, sliding bolt* and *tube, firing-pin* and *spring; nose-piece; extractor* and *spring; ejector; locking latch; sear; trigger; main spring* and *sear spring;* and the *pins* which hold them in place.

The *receiver,* Fig. 4, is of steel, and is screwed around the barrel in the usual manner; just behind the screw on the right-hand side is the slot in which the bolt is locked; behind this slot is a vertical cut through which the bolt slides; on the lower side is a cut through which the trigger and sear operate, and a projecting shoulder which transmits the recoil to the stock; at the rear is drilled a hole for the tang screw attaching the receiver (and with it the barrel) to the stock in the usual manner.

The *sliding bolt* is in two parts, the *bolt* proper, Fig. 5, and the *tube,* Fig. 6, in which it slides. The tube is bored out in the interior to allow the sliding movement of the bolt, and this latter is also bored out to allow the passage of the *firing-pin,* Fig. 7, which is firmly attached to the tube at its rear end. A *spiral spring,* Fig. 7, is contained in the bolt, one end of which rests against a shoulder of the bolt and the other against a shoulder of the firing-pin near its head. At the front end of the bolt is a *nose-piece,* Fig. 8, of hardened steel, against which the base of the cartridge rests, and which is perforated in the center to allow the passage of the point of the firing-pin. This nose-piece and the shoulder of the firing-pin are beveled in a peculiar manner, so that the firing-pin can not reach the cartridge unless the bolt is turned completely to the right and securely locked.

The *extractor*, Fig. 9, is contained in a longitudinal hole on the upper side of the bolt at its front end. The catch projects from this hole, rides over the rim of the cartridge when the bolt is closed and locked, and embraces the rim, being held in this position by springs.

The *ejector*, Fig. 10, is on the lower side of the receiver, fastened to the same pin as the sear; when the bolt is withdrawn, it pulls the empty cartridge with it, and at a certain point the ejector is disengaged by the bolt and strikes the lower side of the rim of the cartridge, and causes it to fly up and fall out of the receiver. A second notch on the ejector, engaging a similar notch on the lower side of the bolt, prevents the latter from being wholly withdrawn from the gun in loading. By pressing down this ejector, however, the bolt may be easily withdrawn for cleaning.

On the lower side of the tube are two notches, the safety-notch, which is hooked, and the full-cock notch, which is square; the point of the sear engages in these notches, of which the names explain the use. The arrangement of these parts of the breech mechanism in the gun is shown in Figs. 17, 18, and 19, on the following page.

To load the gun, the bolt is turned to the left on its axis by means of the projecting knob or handle; the bolt and tube are then withdrawn until stopped by the notch in the ejector; the motion of withdrawing the bolt throws out the empty cartridge; the new cartridge is placed in the receiver and the bolt pushed forward, the firing-pin spring and the stud on the upper side causing the tube to follow until it is stopped by the full-cock notch catching the sear; the tube then remaining stationary while the bolt is still pushed forward, the firing-pin spring is compressed; the bolt, being pushed home, is turned to the right on its axis, and locked against the shoulder on the right and rear of the receiver. The piece is now ready for firing; to let it down to half cock, the knob at the end of the rear bolt is held with one hand while the trigger is pulled with the other, and the tube allowed gently to move forward until the half-cock notch is caught by the sear. It is somewhat dangerous to try to let the piece down to half cock with the thumb and forefinger of one hand, as is done with guns having a hammer; at half cock, however, the firing-pin is not in contact with the cartridge. The *locking latch* shown in the following figures on the under side of the tube at the rear, and also in Fig. 11, prevents the bolt from turning on its axis when at the safety notch or half cock.

Berdan Musket Breech Apparatus.

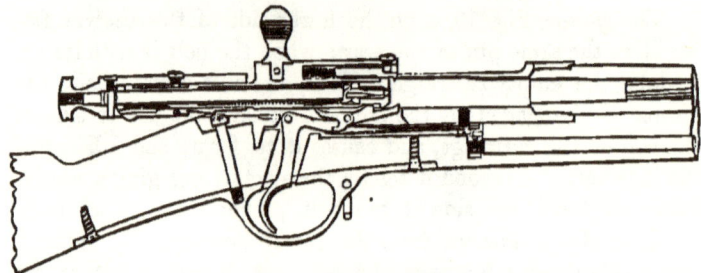

FIG. 17.—Ready for Loading.

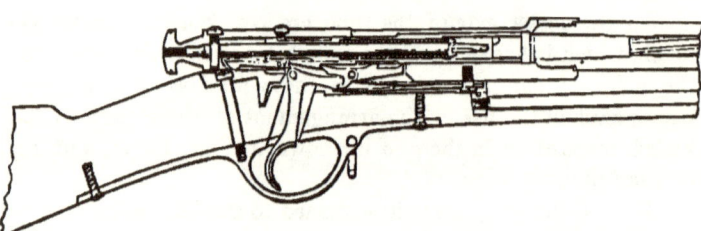

FIG. 18.—At Full Cock.

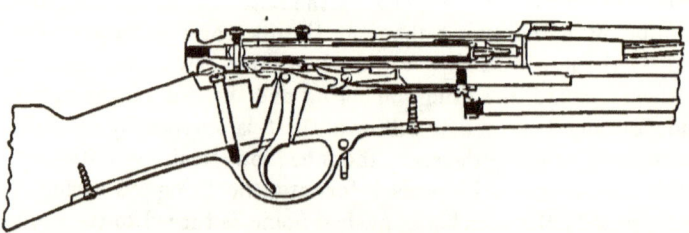

FIG. 19.—At Half-Cock.

The *rear sight*, Figs. 15 and 16, is of the ordinary leaf and slide pattern. The point-blank is 200 paces; steps on the sides

ARMAMENT AND EQUIPMENT. 57

of the sight give 300, 400, and 500 paces; beyond 500 the leaf is opened and the slide raised for 600 to 1,500 paces.

The *bayonet* weighs a pound, and is twenty inches long in the blade; its cross-section is an irregular quadrangular figure, shown in Fig. 20.

It is fastened on the gun by a *stud*, Fig. 14, on the right of the barrel, the blade of the bayonet being thus in the same plane as the axis of the barrel and ramrod; the *front sight* is fixed to a second stud just in rear of the shank of the bayonet. In place of tompion, a small leather hood is used, fastening over the muzzle of the gun.

Fig. 20.

Cartridges.

The cartridges both of the Krenk and Berdan systems are sufficiently explained in the following drawings, natural size, which show the bullet, the paper wrapper (in the Berdan), the lubricator, the charge, and the form of cup and primer at the base of the cartridge; the fire passes through the cup into the charge by three small equidistant holes in the Berdan and four in the Krenk.

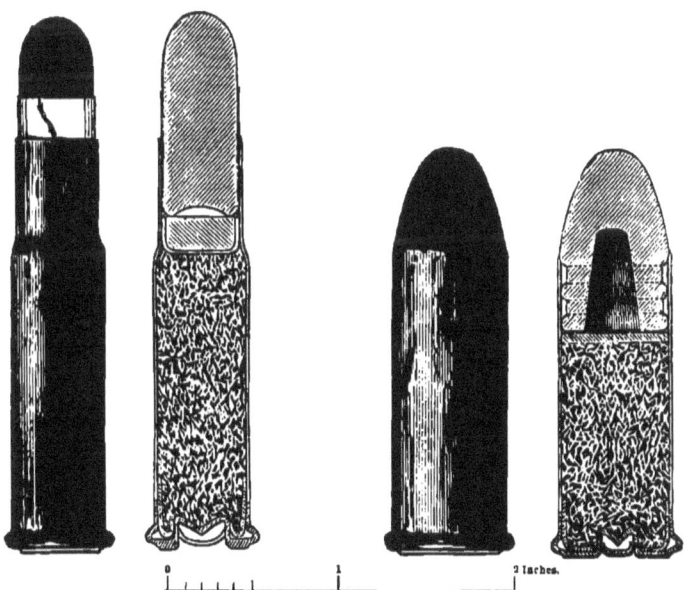

Fig. 21.—Berdan Cartridge.　　　Fig. 22.—Krenk Cartridge.

As the Karle and Krenk muskets were both altered from the old muzzle-loaders without changing the caliber, and as both had cartridges of the same weight, they were practically the same gun in range, penetration, etc., the difference between them being in the breech mechanism. Similarly, the two systems of Berdan, although widely different in mechanism, had the same caliber and nearly the same cartridge, and consequently about the same qualities of range, trajectory, etc. In the following table, therefore, only the Krenk and Berdan systems are considered; they may be considered as types of the breech-loaders of ten years ago and of to-day. This table shows in comparative form the principal features and performances of the two systems:

Dimensions, Range, etc., of Krenk and Berdan Muskets.

		KRENK.	BERDAN.
Caliber		0.60 ′	0·42″
Weight of bullet		556 grains.	372 grains.
" of charge		78 grains.	78 grains.
" of cartridge complete		541 grains.	608 grains.
Rifling.	Number of grooves	4	6
	Width of grooves	0.28″	0.15″
	Depth of grooves	0.015″	6.01″
	Width of lands	0.23″	0.07″
	Amount of twist	½ turn. (1 in 90 calibers).	1¼ turns. (1 in 50 calibers).
Length of barrel		37″ (61 calibers).	32·75″ 79 calibers.
Length of gun with bayonet		72·7″	78″
Length of gun without bayonet		53″	53″
Weight of gun with bayonet		10.84 lbs.	10·27 lbs.
Weight of gun without bayonet		9.91 lbs.	9·87 lbs.
Weight of 40 cartridges		5.77 lbs.	
Weight of 60 cartridges		....	5·19 lbs.
Initial velocity of bullet		1,082 ft. per sec.	1,450 ft. per sec.
Point-blank range		200 paces.	200 paces.
Extreme sight range		600 paces.	1,500 paces.
Extreme range (approximately)		1,200 paces.	2,000 paces.
Penetration in inch pine boards.	200 paces		8 inches.
	600 paces	5 inches.	....
	1,200 paces		3·5 inches.
Elevation	200 paces	0° 30′	0° 19′
	400 paces	1° 06′	0° 41′
	600 paces	1° 40′	1° 07′
	800 paces	2° 12′	1° 35′
	1,000 paces	2° 58′	2° 07′
	1,200 paces	3° 44′	2° 45′
	1,400 paces	....	3° 42′

2. Artillery.

The Russian artillery consists as follows:

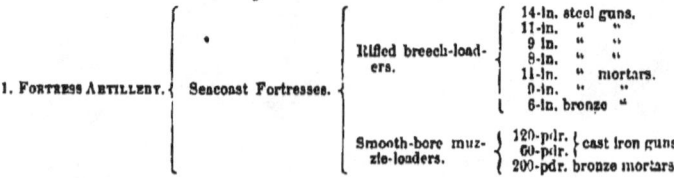

ARMAMENT AND EQUIPMENT. 59

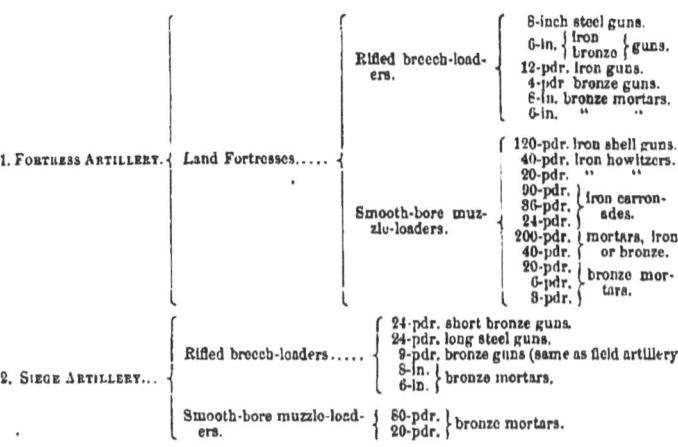

It is only with the field artillery that we are at present concerned. It is divided into foot artillery (that which accompanies infantry, and whose cannoneers are dismounted), and horse artillery (that which accompanies cavalry, and whose cannoneers are mounted). The foot artillery batteries have 8 guns each, and 6 batteries form a brigade, of which 3 are 9-pdr. and 3 4-pdr. batteries. One brigade is attached to each infantry division. The horse artillery batteries have 6 guns each, all 4-pdrs. Two batteries are attached to each cavalry division.

At the beginning of the war all the field artillery was of bronze, and it was with these guns that the war was fought. During the year 1877 it was determined to change the system from bronze to steel, and 1,500 guns were ordered from Krupp's factory; at the same time preparations were made to construct guns in Russia, at the Oboukhof factory, near St. Petersburg, of Russian iron, coal, etc., and with Russian workmen. The machinery was constructed during 1877 and 1878, and in the autumn of the latter year the manufacture was begun. It is intended to manufacture 1,800 guns at Oboukhof, which will give 3,300 steel guns in all, enough for the field artillery of the active army and of 12 divisions of the reserve army. The new artillery will be of three kinds, the infantry "heavy" gun (9-pdr.), the infantry "light" gun (4-pdr.), and the "horse" gun

(4-pdr.). The two latter have the same caliber and projectiles, and practically the same range; but the cavalry gun is 16 inches shorter and 180 lbs. lighter than the infantry light gun; this advantage is gained at the sacrifice of a smaller initial velocity, less accuracy, and a more curved trajectory.

The infantry "light" gun is shown in Fig. 23, which gives a view of the gun from the left side; the horse gun is shown in Figs. 24 and 25, which give respectively a horizontal section through the axis and a view from the top. Fig. 26 represents a section through the axis of the trunnions, and Fig. 27 a section of the rifling. The dimensions are all given in millimetres (0.03927").

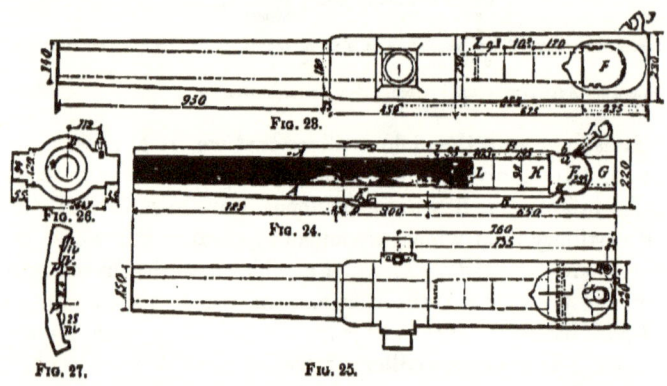

Fig. 23.
Fig. 26.
Fig. 24.
Fig. 27.
Fig. 25.

The relative qualities of the two systems will be best explained by the table on the following page.

The principal advantages of the new system arise from the improved quality of the metal, which permits the charge to be doubled, and the twist of the rifling to be greatly increased; and, from these changes in the form, the range and accuracy are nearly doubled, the initial velocity is greatly increased, and the angle of fall is diminished by one third, thus diminishing considerably the penetration of the projectile into the ground before exploding. More than 60 guns (bronze) out of 400 on the field were permanently disabled by "balloting" in the 4 days' bombardment of Plevna before the assaults of the 11th of September; with the steel guns this source of weakness will be almost wholly removed.

ARMAMENT AND EQUIPMENT.

Dimensions, Range, etc., of Bronze and Steel Systems of Field Artillery.

	BRONZE.		STEEL.	
	Nine-Pounder.	Four-Pounder.	Nine-Pounder.	Four-Pounder, Infantry.	Four-Pounder, Cavalry.
Caliber	4.2"	3.42"	4.25"	3.425"	3.425"
Length of gun	62.59"	63.50"	62.6"	82.6"	66.9"
Length of bore	17.83 calibers	17.44 calibers	17.15 calibers	21.42 calibers	16.55 calibers
Length of rifled part of bore	18.57 calibers	13.96 calibers	18.40 calibers	18.40 calibers	13.50 calibers
Distance between shoulders of trunnions	10.42"	9.0"	10.68"	10.47"	10.47"
Distance between exterior surfaces of trunnions			15.88"	14.75"	14.75"
Distance between axis of trunnions and base of breech			84.68"	84.45"	90.9"
Number of rifllngs	12	12	24	24	24
Depth of riflings			0.0493"	0.0493"	0.0498"
Twist (1 turn in)	50 calibers	4. calibers	86 calibers	40 calibers	86 calibers
Weight of gun, including breech apparatus	1,303 pounds	765 pounds	1,873 pounds	972 pounds	702 pounds
Weight of breech apparatus			116.9 pounds	82.8 pounds	62.8 pounds
Preponderance at base of breech	181.5 pounds	103.4 pounds	(*)	118.8 pounds	97.2 pounds
Initial velocity			27.54 pounds	1,430 feet	1,350 feet
Weight of shell (loaded)	24.80 pounds	12.6 pounds		15.12 pounds	15.12 pounds
Weight of shrapnel (loaded)	20.43 pounds	15.19 pounds		15.12 pounds	15.12 pounds
Weight of charge { shell	2.71 pounds	1.96 pound	0.99 pound	8.07 pounds	8.07 pounds
{ shrapnel	0.68 pound	0.42 pound		0.45 pound	0.45 pound
{ shell	0.38 pound	0.23 pound		0.15 pound	0.15 pound
Bursting charge { shrapnel					
Extreme range	3,000 yards	3,800 yards	(*)	7,000 yards	7,000 yards
				3,000 yards	3,000 yards
Cube of mean deviation	about	about			
Accuracy at 2,500 yards { Angle of elevation	16° x 10' x 18'	20" x 12' x 21'		62' x 4.8' x 6.7'	62' x 7.4' x 6.8'
{ Angle of fall	7° 45'	3° 41'		4° 06'	5° 25'
{ Time of flight	9° 88'	11° 15'		6° 09'	7° 52'
{ Terminal velocity	9½ seconds	11¼ seconds		6.7 seconds	7.3 seconds
	634 ft. per sec.	615 ft. per sec.		945 ft. per sec.	900 ft. per sec.
Cube of mean deviation	about				
Accuracy at 5,000 yards { Angle of elevation	300' x 80' x 120'			95' x 14' x 32'	117' x 81' x 46'
{ Angle of fall	19° 55'			18° 47'	15° 65'
{ Time of flight	32° 11'			19° 50'	21° 83'
{ Terminal velocity	25 seconds			16.4 seconds	18.2 seconds
	460 ft. per sec.			710 ft. per sec.	665 ft. per sec.

* That portion of the new Russian Artillery Manual which relates to the heavy (9-pounder) field gun not being yet (December, 1879) in print, I am unable to give the full data for that gun. The charge, however, will be about 8.6 lbs. of powder, and the range, accuracy, etc., of the gun will not differ greatly from those of the light (4-pounder) gun; the only great difference between the two guns is the heavier projectile thrown by the 9-pounder.

Breech Mechanism.

The breech mechanism of the old system of bronze guns is shown in the following drawings. Fig. 28, Profile, left side of breech. Fig. 29, Horizontal section through axis of gun.

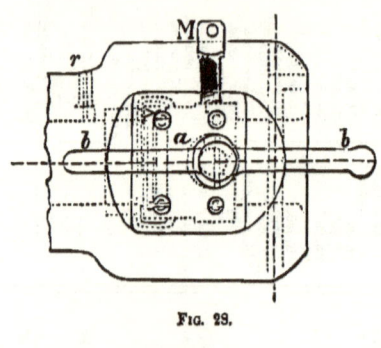

Fig. 28.

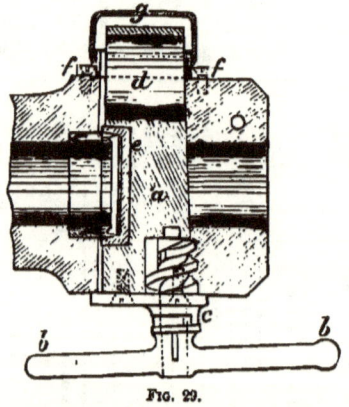

Fig. 29.

The breech-loading apparatus consisted of a solid bronze prismatic wedge, a; handle, b; plate, c; chamber, d; gas plate, e; ring, f; leather hood, g; and the stop, M. The wedge was of bronze. On its left face was solidly fastened the plate c, through which passed the axis of the screw; this screw worked in threads cut in the breech. By turning the handle to the left, this screw was turned, and the wedge freed from the breech; the wedge was then pulled out until arrested by the stop M. In this position the chamber was opposite the bore, and the mechanism ready for inserting the shell and the cartridge. The gas plate was of steel, fastened to the front side of the wedge, and in the front side of this plate was a circular gas check of the usual pattern. The bronze ring (f) was for the purpose of attaching the leather hood (g), which protected the end of the wedge from being injured in travel. The vent was in front of the breech mechanism (r); a priming wire was used with it in the ordinary manner.

In the new steel guns the breech mechanism is on the same general principles, but has many important modifications in details. These are shown in the accompanying plate, Figs. 31 to 37. Figs. 31 and 32 represent respectively a rear view, and a view from the left side, of the breech; Fig. 33, a longitudinal section through the axis of the vent; Fig. 34, a top view of the wedge; Fig. 35, the gas check; Fig. 36, the gas plate; and Fig. 37, the locking latch. The wedge is cylindro-prismatic in shape, and is made of steel; the locking screw is on the upper surface of the wedge, instead of in rear of it, and it is fastened by a small latch on the outside, to prevent the screw from turning when the piece is being moved. The gas plate is also of steel, and the gas check is a steel ring of the Broadwell pattern. The vent is diagonal in direction, and passes through the breech of the gun, the wedge, and the gas plate, and comes against the *rear* of the cartridge at its center. At its upper end the vent-piece terminates in a cup, pierced, in the direction of the vent, by a small hole, to allow the passage of the priming wire; the primer, however, is inserted inside the cup, which latter prevents the primer tube from flying when the piece is discharged. This vent-piece also acts as a "stop" in withdrawing the wedge; that portion of the vent-piece which is fixed in the breech fits in a groove of a certain length cut on top of the wedge; when the latter is withdrawn the length of this groove, the wedge is brought to a stop; the chamber of the wedge is then opposite that of the piece, and the gun is ready for loading.

Sights.

The front sight is of iron, painted black, and is fixed to the upper side of the shoulder of the right-hand trunnion (see Fig. 25). The rear sight, shown in Fig. 38, is of bronze,

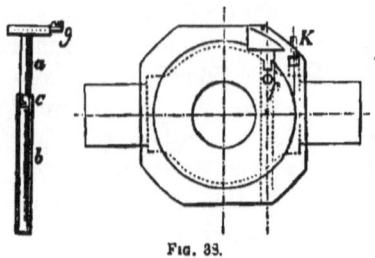

Fig. 33.

and rests in a socket in the breech near its base, in rear of the breech apparatus; it consists of two tubes moving in one another, and of a horizontal bar containing a tube capable of slight horizontal movement, to allow for deviation; the graduation is in lines (tenths of an inch), and the tables of fire are given with elevation and horizontal setting in lines for a given distance in sagenes (7 feet). When the sight is not in use, the socket is covered with a plug and leather cover.

Projectiles.

The old forms of projectiles for the bronze guns (shown in Fig. 39) were as follows: *ordinary shell*, A; *shell with spherical solid head*, B; *shell filled with bullets* (or shrapnel), C; *diaphragm-shrapnel*, D (introduced in 1876); and *canister*, E. All of these projectiles were provided with a casing of lead to take the rifling.

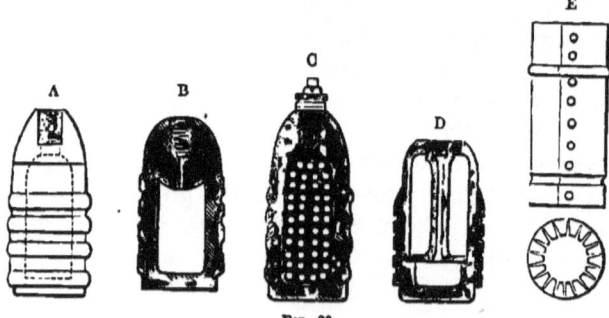

Fig. 39.

The projectiles for the new guns consist only of shells and shrapnel, and a very limited number of canister. The *shells* are all of the double-walled pattern, the outer wall being solid,

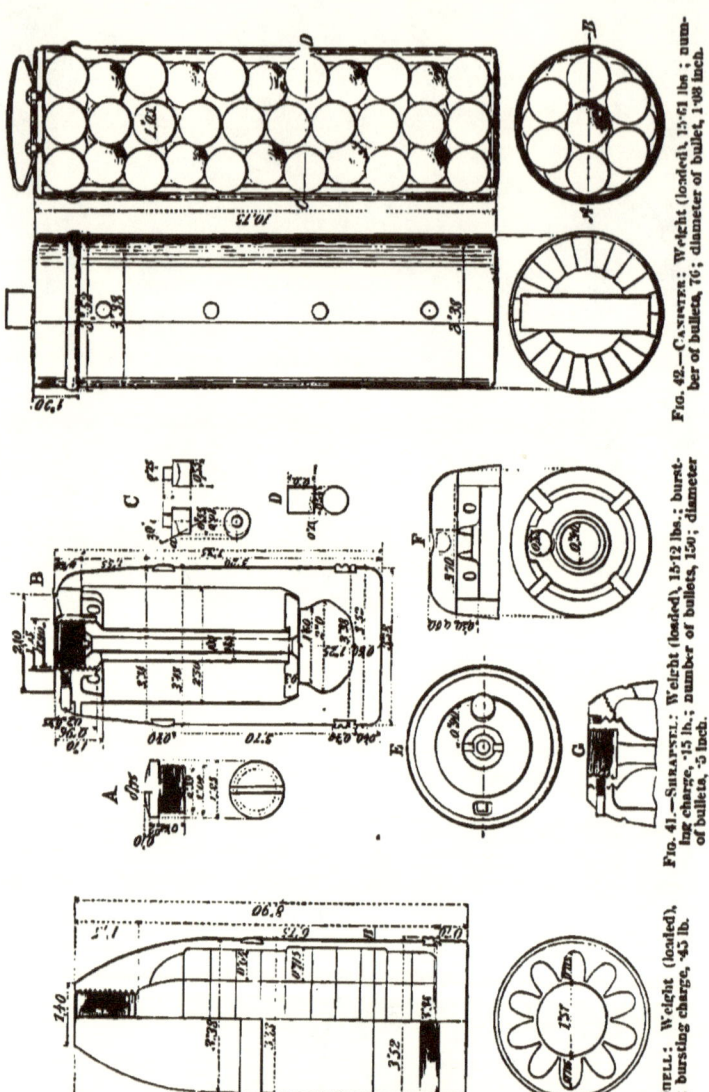

FIG. 40.—SHELL: Weight (loaded), 15·12 lbs.; bursting charge, ·43 lb.

FIG. 41.—SHRAPNEL: Weight (loaded), 15·12 lbs.; bursting charge, ·15 lb.; number of bullets, 150; diameter of bullets, ·5 inch.

Scale, ¼; dimensions in inches.

FIG. 42.—CANISTER: Weight (loaded), 15·61 lbs.; number of bullets, 76; diameter of bullet, 1·08 inch.

ARMAMENT AND EQUIPMENT. 65

and the inner one consisting of a series of layers of iron rings, placed one over another. The peculiar form of the inner side of this wall and the outer side of the rings, causing the projectile to fly into a great number of small pieces on explosion, is shown in the accompanying drawings, Fig. 40.

For both projectiles the arrangement for taking the rifling consists of two copper rings 0.4" broad, one near the base, projecting 0.07", and one in advance of the center of gravity, projecting 0.025" from the shell.

The *shrapnels* are all of the diaphragm pattern, shown in detail in Fig. 41. The essential feature is a chamber near the base of the projectile, in which the greater part of the bursting-charge is placed, and which is separated by a metallic diaphragm from the cylindrical portion, where the bullets are packed in tallow. The chamber is connected with the fuse by a metallic canal, which also is filled with powder. The original form of this shell (G, Fig. 41) had a solid head, but the later ones have a separate head which is inserted in the top of the shell, and held there by four screws perpendicular to the axis. In this head there is a hole through which the bullets and tallow are inserted, and which is then plugged up. The advantages of this new form of shrapnel are that the head is easily blown out, and the bullets are driven forward more than in the old form, where, with the charge in the middle of the projectile, the explosion was in a direction perpendicular to the line of trajectory; it is now more nearly parallel to it, and the bullets are driven forward along a cone of smaller angle.

The *canister* of the new system is shown in Fig. 42.

Fuses.

The fuses are of two kinds, *percussion* and *time fuses* (the latter are called *distance fuses* in Russian).

The *percussion fuse* is very similar to that in general use in all countries; its essential features are a fixed cap with fulminate, and a plunger carrying a sharp point, which explodes the cap when the motion of the shell is arrested.

The *time fuse* is shown in detail in Fig. 43. Its essential parts are the *barrel*, A, which is screwed into the head of the projectile; *time-piece*, B, carrying a train of powder, and movable around the barrel by means of the *setting-ring*, C, which

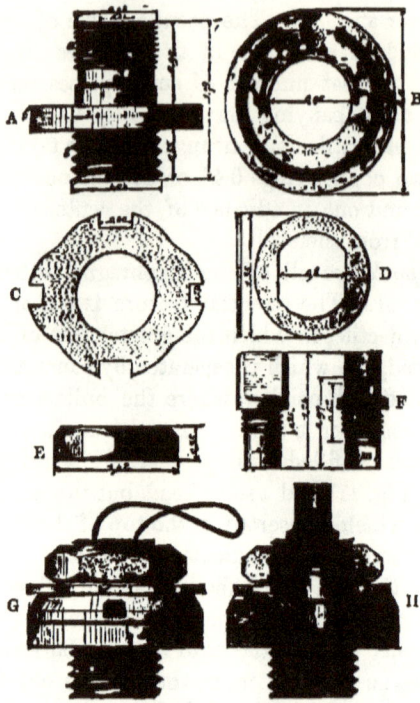

Fig. 48.—Time Fuse. (Scale ½; dimensions in inches.)

is fastened firmly to the time-piece by four projections on the latter, fitting into corresponding notches on the former; *washer*, D, which separates the time-piece from the nut; *nut*, E, which screws around the top of the barrel, and is used with a wrench to screw the whole fuse into the projectile; *fuse-plug*, F, which screws into the top of the barrel (being replaced up to the moment of loading by a common plug of cork), and carries the fulminate suspended by a fine wire. In the barrel is a channel, which is filled with powder, connecting the powder-train in the time-piece with the bursting-charge in the projectile; at the zero point of the time-piece is a lateral channel connecting the train with a small circular gutter, c, Fig. H, surrounding the barrel, and filled with powder; this latter gutter is in turn connected with the cavity in which the fulminates explode by three small transverse channels, d, Fig. H. The action of exploding is then as follows: On firing the gun the small wire sustaining the fulminate is broken; the latter falls, breaking through a small piece of paper at the bottom of its case, strikes the sharp stud, and explodes; the flame passes through the three channels, d, and ignites the powder in the small circular gutter, c; thence it passes through the lateral channel opposite the zero point into the train of the time-piece, thence along this, according to the setting, until it reaches the hole at the head of the channel in the barrel, and thence to the bursting-charge. As the zero point is moved farther away from the hole just mentioned, the interval of time before explosion is of course increased; this is done by moving the time-piece around the barrel by means of the setting-ring, the edge of which is cut away so as to be firmly held by the fingers. The time-piece is graduated on its outer edge to seconds and quarter seconds, and there is a pointer marked on the edge of the barrel, opposite this graduation.

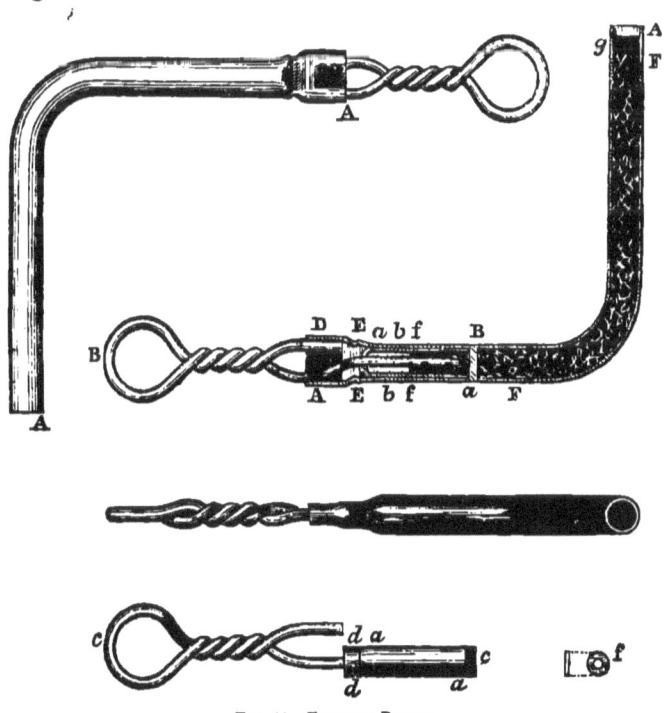

FIG. 44.—FRICTION PRIMER.

Friction Primers.

The *friction primers* of the old system were of the usual form, but the new ones are curved, as shown in the preceding drawing (Fig. 44).

Carriages.

The *gun-carriage* (Fig. 45) is of iron, consisting of two cheeks (¼ boiler-plate strengthened with angle irons), whose prolongation forms the trail; the cheeks are fastened to an iron axle, and to each other by three bolts placed at intervals along the trail and by the trail-plate; in place of a lunette, there is a circular hole in the trail-plate, through which the pintle is passed. The trunnion beds and plates are of bronze, of the usual form. The elevating-screw is a double screw, and acts on a lever, one end of which is fastened to a bolt connecting the cheeks, and the other supports the breech of the gun. The trail-handles and hand spike are of the usual form.

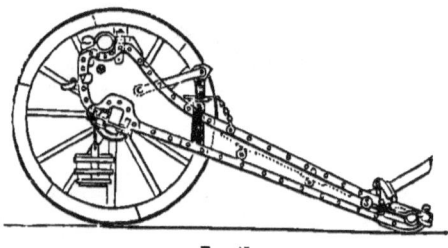

FIG. 45.

The carriages for 4- and 9-pdr. guns are the same in principle, and differ only in size and weight, as follows:

DETAILS.	9-pdr.	4-pdr.
Weight of carriage without wheels	712 lbs.	605 lbs.
Weight of each wheel (4½ feet diameter)	160 "	160 "
Total weight with gun	2,400 "	1,690 "
Pressure of trail (with gun) on pintle	244 "	217 "
Angles of elevation and depression	+ 20° to − 7°	+ 21° to − 7°

The *Limber* is shown in Fig. 46. Its principal feature, as differing from our own, is the pintle (*g*), which is an iron post, 18″ high, fixed to the rear end of the pole, which projects more than 2 feet behind the axle. This same arrangement is found in all of Krupp's guns, and will also be used in the new Russian

ARMAMENT AND EQUIPMENT.

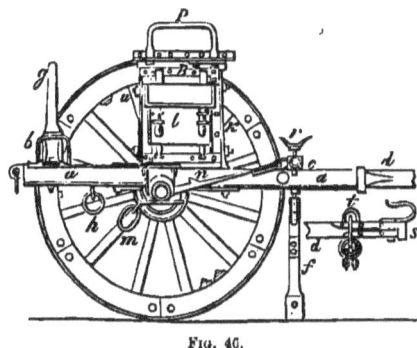

FIG. 46.

steel pieces. It affords more facility for limbering up, but causes a perpetual change of balance in the pole, the front end of which is sometimes on the level of the horses' necks and sometimes at their knees. The chest is placed somewhat in front of the axle, in order to counterbalance the pressure of the trail; but, as in the field a certain amount of forage and other things are always packed on the trail, and as the amount of ammunition in the chest varies according to circumstances, it is impossible to adjust these weights with such a long leverage of pintle. The chest is of wood in the bronze guns, but will be of sheet-iron in the new system. The pole-yoke and branches of our service do not exist in the Russian; the breech-strap passes from the collar to an ordinary iron ring, fastened to another ring, passing around the pole near its front end.

The pieces are drawn by six horses; the swing-trees are of iron, the traces of rope and the coupling extremely long, the distance between the couples of horses being over 5 ft. This, in conjunction with the proximity of the pole to the ground at times, frequently gives rise to a tangling of the traces in the horses' feet.

The weight of the limber, unloaded, including wheels, is 833 lbs.

Caissons.

The old system of caissons, Fig. 47, consisted of a chest, square in horizontal cross-section, 4 ft. 8 in. in exterior measurement, mounted on two wheels, and drawn by three horses abreast, the middle one in shafts, and the nigh one ridden by the driver. Three such caissons accompanied each piece in

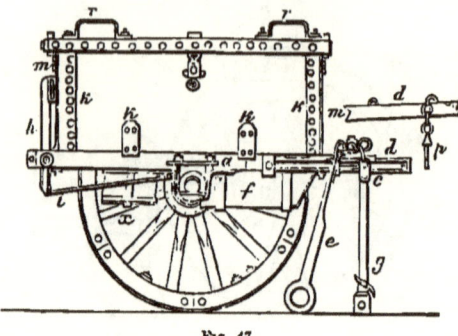

Fig. 47.

9-pdr. batteries, and two in 4-pdr. batteries. All artillery of the line in Europe had these caissons during the late war. They were very convenient for manœuvring and in making short turns, but very inconvenient in ascending and descending hills, and had the disadvantage of all two-wheeled vehicles in the weight which came on the back of the horse in the shafts. The chest opened from the right-hand side.

The new system of caissons, Fig. 48, with which only the Artillery of the Guard was furnished at the beginning of the late war, has four wheels, and is drawn by six horses; on the

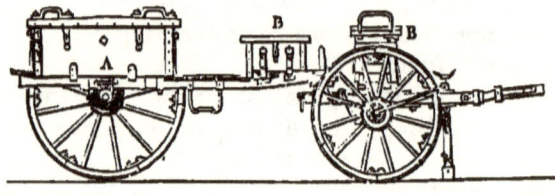

Fig. 48.

rear wheels is a large square ammunition chest, on the front wheels a small chest, similar to that of the limber, and on the stock a small box for tools, spare pieces of harness, etc., etc.

The *battery wagon*, Fig. 49, is similar in shape to the train wagons of the infantry and cavalry, and like them is drawn by four horses abreast, the driver sitting on the wagon. Its weight is 1,336 lbs., and load 2,528 lbs., or in all 3,864 lbs., a little less than 1,000 lbs. for each horse.

The *traveling forge* is shown in Fig. 50. Its weight, exclu-

ARMAMENT AND EQUIPMENT. 71

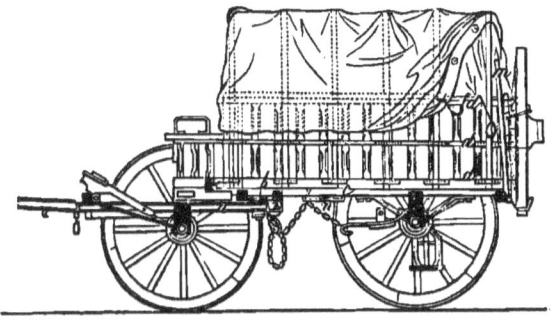

Fig. 49.

sive of tools, etc., in box (*d*), is 975 lbs., and it is drawn by one horse in shafts.

The ammunition carried with the battery (new system) is as follows:

KINDS.	"LIGHT" BATTERY, 6 GUNS.				HORSE BATTERY, 6 GUNS.			
	Total.	Each Gun Limber.	Each Caisson Limber.	Each Caisson Chest.	Total.	Each Gun Limber.	Each Caisson Limber.	Each Caisson Chest.
Shells............................	620	13	13	80	450	12	12	80
Shrapnel.........................	660	15	15	80	495	15	15	80
Canister.........................	40	2	2	..	45	8	8	..
Cartridges......................	1,320	30	30	60	990	30	30	60
Friction primers................	1,660	38	113	..	245	36	113	..
Percussion fuses................	680	..	...	..	..	..	...	..
" " plugs.............	756	22	43	..	552	20	46	..
" " stoppers...........	620	13	18	80	450	12	12	80
Time fuses.......................	672	..	..	..	504	..	...	..
" " primers..................	784	20	50	..	59	20	50	..
Signal rockets	4	..	...	..	3	..	...	..
Quick matches...................	4	..	...	..	3	..	...	..

The "Light" (4-pdr.) Batteries have 12, and the "Horse" (4-pdr.) Batteries 9 caissons; i. e., 3 caissons to 2 pieces. The

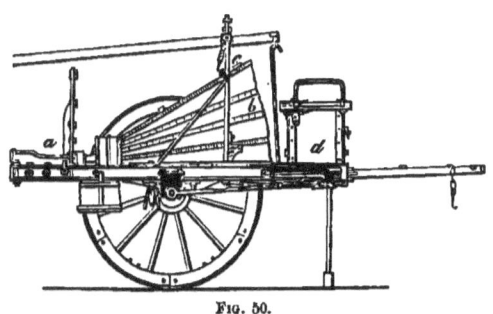

Fig. 50.

above table gives 165 rounds to each piece with the battery, and extra friction primers, fuses, etc.

The "Heavy" (9-pdr.) Batteries will have the same number of rounds per gun, which will require 16 caissons for the battery, or 2 for each piece.

3. *Cavalry.*

The arms of the Cavalry vary with the different branches of that service, as follows:

Heavy Cavalry.

Cuirassiers. — N. C. officers and musicians, revolver and broadsword; privates, revolver, broadsword, and lance.

Dragoons.—N. C. officers and musicians, revolver and saber; privates, saber and musket with bayonet.

Light Cavalry.

Lancers and Hussars.—N. C. officers and musicians, revolver and sabre; privates, front rank, saber, lance, and revolver; privates, rear rank, sabre, musket, and revolver.

Cossacks.—N. C. officers and musicians, revolver and "schaska"; privates, "schaska," lance, and musket.

The Cuirassier broadsword is straight, double-edged, 39 in. long, has a basket guard and steel scabbard, and weighs 2·8 lbs. without scabbard, and over 4 lbs. with it.

The Dragoon saber is curved, 3 ft. long, leather scabbard tipped with brass, guard of brass with single branch, weight 2 lbs. without scabbard, 2·7 lbs. with scabbard. The peculiar features of this saber (of which a drawing is given on p. 203 of McClellan's Report on the "Armies of Europe") are the bayonet scabbard on the outer side, extending from the upper band to about 5 in. below the lower band, and the peculiar manner in which it is worn; the rings are on the *convex* side of the scabbard, and the sabre is suspended from a small shoulder belt an inch wide, passing from one ring over the shoulder and back to the other ring. The two parts of the belt are fastened by a connecting piece about 6 in. long at the level of the waist or a little higher.

The Light Cavalry saber of the Lancers and Hussars resembles our own Cavalry saber so closely as to call for no special mention. It is worn suspended from the waist-belt in the usual manner.

The "*schaska*" of the Cossacks is a single-edged curved sword, about 35 in. long, handle of wood tipped with brass, without guard of any kind, scabbard of leather, weight a little less than the dragoon saber; worn with rings on the concave side of scabbard, suspended from a shoulder belt of similar style to that of dragoons, but made of leather three eighths of an inch wide, ornamented with pieces of enameled silver.

The Dragoon musket has the same caliber, cartridge, etc., as the Infantry musket (p. 54 to 57), but its barrel (27.75 in. long) is 5 in. shorter than the latter, the bayonet 1 in. shorter, and the weight (8.36 lbs. with bayonet) is nearly 2 lbs. less.

The Cossack carbine is the same as the Dragoon, except that it has no bayonet. Its weight is 7.4 lbs.

The Light Cavalry was formerly armed with a carbine having a barrel 17.5 in. long and weighing 6.2 lbs.; but this has now been superseded by the Cossack musket.

The muskets and carbines carried by mounted troops are all protected by a leather case, and are always worn slung over the shoulder from left to right, the muzzle up and projecting above the left shoulder, the butt behind the right thigh. This method of carrying the gun was adopted after competitive trials between it and the manner of hanging from a sling, muzzle down, in use in our service. It is also the manner in use from earliest traditions among the Cossack tribes, which probably influenced the decision in its favor. The sling-strap passes through cuts in the stock, one about 7 in. from the butt and the other near the upper band.

The lance is between 9 and 10 ft. long, 1½ in. in diameter, shod with iron, and weighs about 4½ lbs. At its base is a leather loop, through which the foot is passed before placing it in the stirrup, and which supports its weight. Opposite the arm is another and longer leather loop, through which the arm is inserted, to steady it.

The revolver is the Smith & Wesson, made in this country. It is carried in a yellow leather holster. Whenever the revolver is worn in the Russian service, it has a ring in the butt of the stock, through which passes a cord which is worn around the neck. This prevents it from dropping from the hand or being lost.

EQUIPMENTS.—1. *Infantry.*

The Infantry soldier carries a knapsack, haversack, canteen, waist belt, two cartridge boxes, bayonet scabbard, one stick, and one piece of a shelter tent; and the Guard and Grenadiers have in addition a short two-edged sword, about 20 in. long and weighing (with scabbard) nearly 3 lbs. The only use to which this antiquated weapon was put during the war was in hacking twigs and wood for camp fires, for which it is not adapted, and it will probably soon be abolished.

The knapsack is of black leather, with a wooden frame, the leather of the flap having the hair left on it. The contents of the knapsack are a change of underclothing, linen trousers, extra cartridges, and a Bible. An extra pair of boots is carried on top of it (the overcoat being worn in a roll over the shoulder, and the soldier having no blanket). The knapsack straps are similar to those in use in our service prior to 1873. On the back of the knapsack is fastened a copper kettle, an elliptical cylinder in shape, about 6×4 in. and 5 in. deep. This is the dish on which the soldier depends in time of war for all purposes; in it he receives his soup from the company boilers, makes his tea, brings water, etc. This and a wooden spoon comprise his personal mess outfit. The troops were often separated for long periods during the war from their knapsacks, but this kettle was guarded with great care at all times.

The canteen and haversack are similar to those in common use. A large proportion of them were lost during the campaign.

The bayonet scabbard is of leather, with brass tip, suspended from the waist belt. The regulations require the rifle battalions and skirmisher companies to carry the bayonet in the scabbard; but all other infantry troops invariably carry the bayonet on the gun during the march as well as in battle.

The waist belt is of plain black leather, with a brass buckle; two leather cartridge boxes, of very simple construction, are worn, one on each side of the buckle. They contain the cartridges in paper packages, two packages (24 cartridges "Krenk" or 30 cartridges "Berdan") in each. In December, 1878, it was decided to experiment with a modification of Metcalfe's cartridge-block attachment for the Berdan gun, and 250,000 were ordered for trial. The result of the trial is not yet known.

ARMAMENT AND EQUIPMENT. 75

The shelter tent is of linen, in three pieces, each about 4 ft. square, arranged with buttons. The ridge and upright poles are little sticks, an inch in diameter, jointed in two pieces. The joints were of cheap construction, and a number of them, as well as of the sticks, were broken before the troops had been long in the field. Three pieces formed a tent, protecting the men's heads and bodies, but leaving their feet exposed.

The winter campaign was made, as will be subsequently narrated, without tents of any kind.

The equipment of intrenching tools will be found discussed in Part IV.

Infantry officers wear a black glazed belt, and sword with steel scabbard, resembling that in use in our Artillery; they also carry a revolver in a glazed leather holster on their belt. Subaltern officers have a large shelter tent, formed of three pieces, each 7 ft. square, which, together with their baggage (40 lbs.), is carried in the wagons. They carry their overcoats and a small bag, filled with necessary articles, slung over the shoulder.

2. *Artillery.*

The gunners in the Artillery are equipped with a dragoon saber and a Smith & Wesson revolver. The drivers have no side arms.

The extra clothing, shelter tents, etc., of the men are carried in leather rolls on the cantles of the saddles of the Artillery horses.

The pouches, bags, etc., used in serving the pieces, are not essentially different from those of other armies. The saddle is the same as in the Cavalry.

3. *Cavalry.*

Saddle.—The Russian Cavalry saddle is a modification of the Hungarian saddle, described at length (pp. 324 *et seq.*) in McClellan's Report; the leather seat there represented does not exist in the modified form, which is wholly of wood, uncovered, and without flaps. The frame resembles somewhat the pattern of Artillery saddle in our service. The pommel and cantle are very high, and the whole affair is clumsy and heavy. The pad is a white blanket, folded twice one way and three times the other, and then attached by cords to a large piece of leather, which is worn under the saddle, completely covering the blanket, and protecting it from the rain; the blanket is, however, left folded with the saddle when the horse is unsaddled, instead of being unfolded and aired. There are three girths, each 1½ in. broad, fastened with buckles on the left side. The trooper's blanket is folded and placed on the saddle for a cover or cushion, and then strapped on with a surcingle. Over the whole, on parade, the schabraque is placed. It is of cloth, of different colors for different regiments, but usually dark, and it has the Emperor's cipher in the rear corners. Fastened to the cantle is a round leather valise, curved on the under side to the shape of the horse's back, in which the trooper's underclothes, etc., are carried. The copper soup-dish is circular, and it and the cover fit over the ends of the valise, being held in their places by straps. An extra pair of boots is strapped on top of the valise. The stirrups are large and of solid steel.

The headstall has two cheek-pieces, one for a snaffle-bit, fastening to it in the same manner that the watering-bits are fastened to the halter in our service, and the other for the curb-bit, which is fastened to it by two steel hooks, in which the bit terminates, which enter corresponding flat rings at the ends of the cheek-pieces. (See McClellan's "Armies of Europe," p. 201.) The curb is not unlike that in our service, but the branches have the convexity to the front instead of to the rear. The halter is usually tied up and attached to the saddle when the horse is bridled, but it can be used with the snaffle-bit as a watering-bridle.

The horses are picketed to a stout rope in camp in the usual manner. I do not remember to have seen any instances during the campaign of horses picketed out to graze, or any small picket-pins and lariats.

The Cossack saddle is also of wood, but shorter and much lighter than the regular Cavalry saddle. The pommel and cantle are nearly vertical, and the space between them is filled with a large hair cushion, covered with leather, and held in place by a surcingle. This makes the rider's seat nearly flat and from 6 to 8 inches above the horse's back; his feet are always above the line of the horse's belly; the stirrups are of brass, and the base of them is nearly circular. The bridle is very simple, without buckles, and the only bit is a snaffle.

ARMAMENT AND EQUIPMENT.

There is usually considerable ornamentation of enameled silver about the saddle and bridle. The Cossack horses carry their noses very high in the air, and have a general look of being badly set up and dressed; but they are the most serviceable animals for Cavalry in the world.

The equipments of the Cavalry soldier vary with the nature of his regiment. The Cuirassiers wear a steel cuirass, plated with brass, with front and back plates, the whole weighing from 17 to 20 lbs., according to size. They wear a white leather waist belt, from which the saber, holster, and sabretasche are suspended; the cartridge-box is attached by swivels to a belt passing over the left shoulder. Spurs are of steel, with straight shanks, and are permanently fastened to the heel of the boot by screws, for all mounted men.

The Dragoons and Cossacks carry their cartridges in two pouches on a waist belt, in the same manner as the infantry men. (The saber of these troops, as already noted, is suspended from the shoulder.)

The Lancers and Hussars wear a dark leather waist belt, from which the saber and pistol are suspended; the cartridge-box is slung from the shoulder. The Light Regiments in the Guard wear also the sabretasche.

UNIFORM.

The prevailing color of the Russian uniforms is a very dark olive-green. Some of the Cavalry regiments of the Guard have white coats as well as blue or red ones, but in general the uniform is dark, simple, and well adapted to use.

The overcoat is the only portion of the uniform which is common to all portions of the service. For officers it is gray, for men butternut; in shape a long sack, coming about 6 inches below the knee; gathered in at the back by a strap passing half way round the waist. The officers wear the undress shoulder-strap on the overcoat, as well as on the frock-coat, and there are certain facings on the collar, for both officers and men. In addition to this regulation overcoat ("paletot") for all seasons, the officers have an extra overcoat ("shuba" or pelisse), made very large and roomy, with cape coming to the waist, the skirts of the coat to the heels, and a high fur collar. This coat, as worn in the Guard, is padded with eider-down, and is at once the lightest and warmest garment that I have ever seen, and far superior in both respects to furs. With a handsome beaver collar, its cost varies from 300 to 600 roubles ($225 to $450), but the fur and eider-down last a lifetime. In summer a light waterproof cloak, of the same form, with cape, etc., replaces the "shuba."

In winter all troops wear a "bashlik" over the head; this is a sort of hood, with long, broad strings or ends, made of wool dyed drab color; the hood covers up the head and part of the face, and the ends are wrapped around the neck; it came originally from the Caucasus. All infantry troops have also black cloth mittens, and the cavalry have gloves. In winter all troops have also a "polushubok" (half pelisse), made of sheepskin, tanned with the wool, which is worn on the inside. For the infantry its length is sufficient to cover the knees, for the cavalry only a little below the hips; it is worn under the overcoat.

The undress cap ("foorazhka") is of two kinds. The Guard wear the ancient Russian national cap, whose shape is best known by photographs of German officers, the Prussian cap being only slightly modified from it; it is a cross, so to speak, between our style of policeman's cap and the sailor's cap in the navy. It has a small round visor of black glazed leather, and is made of cloth, without stiffening. Its only ornament is the small elliptical cockade of the Russian emperor, which is worn in front. The color of the cap is usually dark green, but there are also red, blue, black, and white, for different regiments and corps; the band and its piping vary in color for different divisions or arms of the service. The rest of the army wear the "képi" or French forage cap, of black cloth, with band varying in color according to the number of the regiment in the division.

The Guard cap is an admirable head cover, having the advantage of covering the back of the head, which the "képi" (like our own forage cap) does not. Its disadvantage is in the vizor, which is so small as to afford very little protection to the eyes.

All Russian soldiers, of every arm of the service, wear high boots, reaching nearly to the knee. In campaigns they are always worn outside of the trousers; in dress parades the trousers are worn outside, and, in the Cavalry, held down by straps.

In summer Infantry soldiers wear white linen blouses and trousers, and Cavalry and Artillery soldiers white linen blouses when on fatigue duty.

In place of socks, all soldiers wear a piece of linen in summer, and woolen cloth in winter, wrapped around the foot. This primitive affair has the great advantage of not wearing out, of being easily washed and aired, and (when properly put on) of never chafing the foot.

The undress cap, boots, and overcoat, as just described, are nearly the same for all parts of the army; the full-dress cap, coat, and trousers vary greatly, as follows:

Cap.—For the Infantry of the Grenadiers and the Line, the undress cap ("*képi*") of black cloth, with the addition of a short black horsehair plume; of the Guard, a black leather helmet, with brass spike, brass double eagle in front, and brass chin strap.

For the Artillery of the Grenadiers and the Line, the same cap as the infantry; of the Guard, the helmet with black horsehair plume.

For the Cavalry, as follows:

Cuirassiers—Brass helmet, with eagle.

Dragoons—Black leather helmet, with black horsehair plume.

Lancers—"Schapka," a black leather helmet, with square disk on top.

Hussars—Bearskin cap, with red cloth top and tassel falling to right side.

Cossacks—Black leather cap, about nine inches high, nearly cylindrical in shape.

Coat—For the Infantry and Artillery of the Grenadiers and Line, a black cloth tunic, single-breasted; of the Guard, dark olive-green tunic, double-breasted.

For the Cavalry, as follows:

Cuirassiers—Full dress, a white tunic without buttons, with brass shoulder scales; undress, a dark-green single-breasted tunic.

Dragoons—Dark-green tunic, shoulder scales.

Lancers—Blue tunic with brass epaulettes.

Hussars—Dark-blue Hussar jacket, with seven rows of yellow cord, three lines of frogs, and shoulder cords. The officers of the Hussars of the Guard have also a red and a white braided jacket, and a cloak hung from the shoulders by a cord.

Cossacks—Plain blue jacket, fitted to the body, without buttons or ornaments.

The buttons of all troops of the Guard, who wear them, have the Russian eagle; for other troops, plain.

Trousers.—For Infantry and Artillery of the Guard, of dark olive-green cloth, with a red welt; of the Grenadiers and the Line, of black cloth.

For the Cavalry, light blue, with the addition of parade trousers for the Guard, of black, with red stripe 1½ in. broad.

The distinguishing features of the uniform for different regiments, etc., are as follows:

Every soldier wears a cloth shoulder-strap 2 inches wide, extending from the collar to the point of the shoulder, on his tunic, a *paroli* or facing on the collar of his overcoat, and a cloth band around his cap. The cap band is red for the first Regiment of each Division, blue for the second, white for the third, and black for the fourth. In the Line the number of the regiment is also stamped or cut out of the band in front. The Division is distinguished by the color of the shoulder-strap or *paroli*, which is red for the 1st, blue for the 2d, and yellow for the 3d Division of the Guard, yellow (with a number) for the Grenadiers, red for the 1st Brigade and blue for the 2d Brigade of each Division of the Line, the number of the Division being stamped in large figures on the shoulder-strap.

The trimmings of the Rifle Brigades are crimson, with the number of the battalion stamped on the shoulder-strap.

The Artillery trimmings are uniformly red and black, with the number of the Division to which they belong stamped on the shoulder-strap. The Engineer trimmings are red with white piping.

The Cavalry uniforms are distinguished by their trimmings, on the same principles as the Infantry.

Officers' Uniforms.

These agree very nearly with the uniform of the men of the regiments or corps to which the officer belongs. Generals and General Staff Officers wear, for full dress, a single-breasted short frock coat, of dark green, with much gold embroidery on the collar and at the end of the sleeve, epaulettes, trousers of black with a broad red stripe, helmet with long white horse-hair plume. The Emperor's Aides-de-Camp wear aiguillettes of gold cord; the General Staff, of silver cord; Adjutants of regiments, white cord with black and orange threads intertwisted.

Their campaign dress is an olive-green double-breasted frock-coat, with red collar, skirts coming two thirds of the distance from the hip to the knee, shoulder-straps, light-blue trousers with red cord, and top boots. Aiguillettes are also worn on undress uniform by those entitled to them.

The epaulettes are of three classes: for Generals, with tassels $\frac{2}{3}$ inch in diameter; for Field Officers, with tassels $\frac{3}{16}$ inch in diameter; for Company Officers, without tassels.

The highest grade in each class (i. e., General, Colonel, Captain) has the body of the epaulette plain; the next grade (Lieutenant-General, Lieutenant-Colonel, Lieutenant) has three stars; the next (Major-General, Major, Sub-Lieutenant) has two stars; Cornets have one star.

Officers of the General Staff and of the *Chevalier Garde Regiment* have epaulettes plated with silver, other officers with gold.

The shoulder-strap, for undress uniform, is a flat piece of cloth and pasteboard, covered with gold (or silver) braid. Like the epaulette, it has three classes, plain for Generals, with two longitudinal stripes for Field officers, and with one longitudinal stripe for Company officers. The grades are distinguished by stars as on the epaulette.

CHAPTER IV.

METHODS OF ADMINISTRATION.

Commander-in-Chief.

THE Emperor is not only the fountain-head and source of all military authority, but he is also in fact the actual Commander-in-Chief of the Army. His organ for military affairs is the Minister of War, always a General of high rank, to whom all military authorities and affairs throughout the Empire are subject. The Emperor's orders are published by the Minister of War, and all military affairs requiring the Emperor's sanction are submitted to him by the same officer. The Minister of War is responsible for the condition of the Army in every respect, and makes such inspections in person or by his deputies as he sees fit. In matters of economy (accumulation and distribution of supplies, etc.) he has no personal authority except as President of the War Council.

CENTRAL ADMINISTRATION.*

This is the War Ministry, presided over by the Minister of War. The Ministry is composed of 2 Advisory Councils or Committees, 8 Administrative Sections or Bureaus, and 2 Special Sections, viz., the Emperor's Headquarters and the War Minister's office. The two great Committees are :

The War Council ;
The War Tribunal, or Military Supreme Court.

---

* In this chapter the word "Administration" is frequently used in the sense in which it is used in Continental Europe generally, meaning the body of men charged with the administrative business; the usual English word for this is "Staff," but the other word is used to avoid confusion with the general staff. The word "economy" is also used to mean all administrative business not of a purely military nature, e. g., the business of the Quartermaster's, Subsistence, and Pay Departments, and everything relating to money, property, or accounts.

METHODS OF ADMINISTRATION.

War Council.

This is the supreme body for examining and deciding affairs of a legislative or economical nature affecting the troops or military establishments. It is directly subordinate to the Emperor, responsible only to him, and subject to his orders alone. The members are appointed by the Emperor from among the Generals of the highest grade, and number 18 in all; the Minister of War is *ex-officio* President.

This body corresponds in military affairs to the "Directing Senate" of the Empire in civil affairs. Its functions are very extensive. In matters of legislation, all projects affecting in any way the strength or organization of the Army or its administration are examined by this Council, and submitted directly by its President to the Emperor for his approval; in matters of economy, it has the power of confirming or modifying all projects for the accumulation of military stores, approves the conditions of contracts for any amount, and generally supervises the military budget.

All legislative business and the more important affairs of economy are decided in full Council; but for acting upon minor affairs of economy, and for preliminary examination of legislative projects, there are 5 standing sub-committees, each composed of a President and 5 members, appointed by the Emperor from the members of the Council for one year. These sub-committees are as follows:

1. *Codifying Committee*, which codifies the military laws and orders, and which also makes a preliminary examination of projects of law before submission to the full Council.

2. *Organization Committee*, which examines all questions affecting the drill, equipment, armament, internal economy, and in general everything affecting the organization of the troops and their condition for fighting.

3. *Education Committee*, which examines all questions relating to military schools.

4. *Hospital Committee*, which examines all questions affecting hospitals and the medical service of the Army in general.

5. *Prison Committee*, which examines projects affecting military prisons, and has also a certain limited supervision over them.

From the above it will be seen that this Council is in money affairs (i. e., economy) a final board of control and management; but in purely military matters, although a part of the War Ministry, it has duties of a legislative and not of an executive nature, and corresponds to the Military Committees of the two Houses of Congress in our Government. The law in Russia is a collection of the Ukases of the Emperor; and the military law is drawn up by the above Council. Projects of changes in the law are submitted, by the special commission usually nominated for the purpose, or from whatever other source, to the Codifying Committee for a preliminary examination, then to the full Council, then to the Emperor for his approval; if not approved, they go back to the Council for amendment; if approved, they are returned to the Codifying Committee for register among the military laws of the Empire, where they stand until amended or revoked by subsequent laws framed in the same manner.

This system of framing military laws dates, in its general outlines, from Peter the Great, who was the first Tzar to form a regularly organized army. In successive reigns military commissions of high officers were formed to submit projects for modifying the military system in accordance with the requirements of the period. The Emperor Nicholas first caused the military laws to be codified—the code of 1838. The various changes in his reign multiplied the number of supplements and annexes to such an extent that early in the present reign a new code was edited—in 1859. But the radical reforms of the present Emperor necessitated another code, that of 1869, which, with its various supplements and annexes, forms the present military law of the Empire. It is comprised in 15 volumes, and divided into 6 parts, each part into articles, each article into chapters, each chapter into paragraphs; the whole is indexed alphabetically and into subjects, with references to the paragraphs, chapters, etc.

The contents are as follows:

Part I. (in 1 volume) *Military Administration*.
 Article 1. The War Ministry and its Bureaus.
  " 2. The Administration of Military Circumscriptions.
  " 3. Local Military Administrations.
  " 4. Administration of Troops in War.

Part II. (in 4 volumes) *Regular Troops.*
Article 5. Organization, Strength, and Methods of Administration of Regular Troops.
" 6. System of Mobilization.
" 7. Appointments, Promotions, etc.
" 8. Rewards, Pensions, etc.
Part III. (in 3 volumes) *Irregular Troops.*
Article 9. Organization, Strength, and Methods of Administration of Cossacks.
" 10. Laws of Service for Cossacks, their Rights, Duties, etc.
" 11. Internal Economy of Cossack Regiments.
Part IV. (in 2 volumes) *Military Departments.*
Article 12. Intendance or Supply Department.
" 13. Artillery "
" 14. Engineer "
" 15. Military Education "
" 16. Medical "
" '17. Prison "
Part V. (in 4 volumes) *Military Economy.*
Article 18. Depots of the Military Departments.
" 19. Supply of Troops.
" 20. Internal Economy of Regiments and Companies.
" 21. Accounts, Levies of Contributions on Inhabitants, Complaints under the same, etc.
Part VI. (in 1 volume) *Military Law.*
Article 22. Code of Punishments.
" 23. Code of Discipline.
" 24. Forms of Procedure in Military Tribunals.

Changes and modifications in the above code are made in the way previously stated, and are then published in orders by the Minister of War, and are edited from time to time by the Codifying Committee, forming supplements to the code. The fundamental law of military service of 1874 forms at present a special book by itself, but a complete new code in which this law will appear is now in process of editing.

The following orders of the War Minister are not included in the code:

1. Orders for the annual manœuvres, the location of troops, strength of garrisons, etc.

2. Orders prescribing the pay, the rations, and all provisions in kind, and the footing of the troops (war-footing or peace-footing), etc.

These orders are collected into special books.

The special orders of the General Staff, of the Chiefs of Circumscriptions, etc., etc., are also naturally excluded from the code.

War Tribunal (Military Supreme Court).

This is the supreme court of appeal for all military causes; it also examines projects of legislation affecting military justice. It is formed of members chosen by the Emperor, and its President is a General of the highest grade.

Decisions requiring the approval of the Emperor are submitted to him through the Minister of War.

Administrative Bureaus.

These are 8 in number, as follows:

1. General Staff Department;
2. Intendance (or Supply) Department;
3. Artillery "
4. Engineer "
5. Medical "
6. Military Education "
7. Military Justice "
8. Irregular Troops "

The above names sufficiently indicate the general nature of the functions of these Departments. At the head of each is a Chief, known as

Chief of the General Staff;
Intendant General;
Grand Master of the Artillery (Ordnance);
Inspector General of Engineers;
Inspector General of Military Medicine;
Chief of Military Educational Establishments;
Military Solicitor General;
Ataman of Irregular Troops.

These Chiefs have one or two Deputies at the head of their Departments. All the *personnel* of the Bureau is directly subordinate to the Chief, as well as also the Officers of the Corps or Department, in affairs of a technical nature affecting their specialty. Manufacturing establishments are under the direct orders of the Chief of the Department to which they belong. According to its amount of business, each Bureau is divided into two or more sections. The clerical force is under the Chief of Section, who has Chiefs of Sub-sections to assist him.

These principal departments have the general direction of affairs concerning their specialties throughout the whole Empire; the execution of the details is left to the corresponding departments at the headquarters of the Circumscriptions, as will be subsequently explained. The Chiefs are all members of the War Council, and are all directly subject to the orders of the Minister of War.

The Emperor's Headquarters.

The Minister of the Court, a General officer, is *ex officio* Commandant of the Emperor's Headquarters, but has two deputies for this special function. All Aide-de-camp Generals, all Major Generals of the Suite, all Aides-de-camp of the Emperor, and several other officers and officials specially attached, form nominally part of the Emperor's Headquarters; but, as the number of these is very great, and the larger part of them is employed in commanding troops in various localities, the number actually performing personal service to the Emperor is comparatively small. The principal duty of the Commandant of the Headquarters is to make all arrangements for the journeys of the Emperor, for the establishment and provisioning of the Headquarters, etc. If the Minister of War is not present with the Emperor in his travels, then all business of his ministry is submitted to the Emperor by the Commandant of the Headquarters. Attached to the Headquarters in travels, and under the orders of the Commandant, is the Military Chancery or office of the Emperor, which is charged with recording all correspondence requiring the Emperor's approval.

Office of the Minister of War.

In this chancery are concentrated all affairs of a general nature of the highest military importance requiring the special personal attention of the Minister. Here is also the secretariat and correspondence of the War Council.

The Inspector General of Cavalry and the Inspector General of Infantry and Rifles have also each a chancery or office at St. Petersburg, and are under the direct orders of the Minister of War, but their offices are not bureaus of the ministry.

MILITARY CIRCUMSCRIPTIONS.

The extent of the Russian Empire is so vast, its army so large, the means of communication (even including the 15,000 miles of railway existing at present) so limited, that it would be impossible to direct the whole administration of the Army from one point. The Empire is therefore divided into districts known as Military Circumscriptions, in each of which the military affairs are directed by an administration similar to that of the War Ministry on a smaller scale. There are 14 such Military Circumscriptions, known as those of St. Petersburg, Vilna, Finland, Warsaw, Kief, Odessa, Kharkof, Moscow, Kazan, the Caucasus, Orenburg, Turkestan, West Siberia, and East Siberia. Plate No. 1 of the atlas shows their position and size (except those of Siberia and Turkestan), the number of troops in each, and the railway system by means of which the troops may be concentrated on any point of the frontier. Each circumscription is under the orders of a Chief, a general of high grade, chosen directly by the Emperor and announced in a ukase to the Governing Senate. He commands everything military within the limits of his circumscription; in distant provinces he is also usually the Civil Governor of the province; in the three largest circumscriptions, St. Petersburg, Warsaw, and the Caucasus, he has a deputy.

The administration of the circumscription is composed as follows:

1. Council;
2. Chief of the General Staff;
3. Chief of the Intendance;
4. Chief of Artillery;
5. Chief of Engineers;
6. Chief Medical Inspector;
7. Chief Hospital Inspector.

In the Caucasus there is in addition a bureau having charge of the affairs of the mountain tribes.

1. *Council.*—This is composed of the Chief of the Circum-

METHODS OF ADMINISTRATION. 89

scription, who is the President, the Chiefs of Bureaus above named, and one delegate of the Minister of War—in all, a President and eight members. It is the supreme administrative body, for affairs of military economy in the circumscription. Questions are decided by a majority vote, the President casting the decisive vote in case of a tie; if there is a wide difference of opinion, the affair is referred to the War Council at the War Ministry. If the President differs greatly in opinion from the decisions of the majority, he has the right to hold the affair in suspense and refer it to the War Council with his own opinion, and, even while awaiting their decision, to order his own ideas to be carried out; but he is personally responsible and liable for the consequences of such action if it is not approved. On the other hand, the decision of the majority relieves him from all responsibility.

2. *General Staff.*—This is the organ for all orders, instruction, correspondence, and all purely military affairs, between the Chief of the Circumscription and all troops under his orders. The Chief of Staff has usually a deputy, and his office is divided into three sections: *a*. The Military section, concerned with the stations, movements, service, etc., of the troops; *b*. The Inspection section, concerned with the number of troops, their effective strength, etc.; *c*. The Economy section, concerned with correspondence affecting supplies, depots, etc.

There is also the chancery, or clerical office proper of the Chief of Staff, and the section in charge of records and archives. The chiefs of these sections are the senior officers of the General Staff at the headquarters of the Circumscription; the chiefs of the chancery and the archives are civilian officials.

3. *Intendance Department.*—This is charged with supplying the troops and hospitals with everything in the way of subsistence stores, forage, clothing, camp and garrison equipage, and pay and money allowances of every kind. It is divided into three sections. Each year the Chief Intendant makes estimates for the next year in form of a budget, and a plan of accumulation, stating in writing the estimate of money required, the places, dates, and prices, where supplies can be bought and accumulated, means of hired transport available, etc., etc. These estimates are examined by the Council, and then sent to the central War Council for approval, which examines the estimates

of all the circumscriptions, and determines where supplies shall be bought, etc., etc. The execution of all this business is the work of the Intendance Department of the Circumscription, as also the issue of supplies to the regiments from the depots, which are all under their control.

4. *Artillery Department.*—This has under its supervision—*a*, all troops of the artillery; *b*, all establishments pertaining to its branch of the service; and it is charged with supplying fortresses and troops with artillery and ordnance material of every kind. Thus everything in the Circumscription pertaining to artillery, its troops, armament, ordnance stores, establishments, institutions, etc., are under the direction of the Chief of Artillery of the Circumscription.

5. *Engineer Department.*—This has charge of all fortresses, military buildings, and constructions of all kinds, special engineer commands, establishments and workshops, and inspection of railways for certain military purposes. Field Engineer troops form part of the Line, and are commanded in the same manner as troops of Infantry, but are not under the orders of the Chief Engineer of the Circumscription; nor has he any direction of the construction of fortresses, which is carried on by officers specially detailed and under the orders of the Board of Fortifications at the central Engineer Department in St. Petersburg.

6. *Medical Department.*—This supervises the hygiene and military police affecting the troops, is responsible that troops are properly cared for in medical matters, distributes medical supplies, supervises veterinary service, etc.

7. *Hospital Department.*—This supervises the administration of the *permanent* military hospitals of the Circumscription. The chief of this Department is also usually Chief of the Local Troops in the Circumscription. He is charged with the accumulation of hospital stores, equipage, furniture, etc., for his whole circumscription, but the management of the hospital depends upon its chief.

In addition to the above branches of the staff, there is in each Circumscription a permanent Military Tribunal, charged with the trial of more important military causes; its powers are determined by the Code of Military Justice (Part VI. of the Military Code).

The chiefs of the Departments named above are responsible

to the Council of which they are members, and through it to the War Council and the Minister of War. The general administration of their departments is determined by this Council, in accordance with general laws and regulations; they are subject to the orders of the Chief the Circumscription, but he can override the decisions of the Council only at his own peril in case his action should not be approved.

In all affairs concerning their own specialties the chiefs of these departments in the Circumscriptions correspond directly with their respective chiefs at the Central Administration. For instance, the Chief Engineer reports directly to the Inspector General of Engineers any repairs necessary in fortresses or public buildings, with estimates for the cost of repair; the Chief of Artillery reports directly to the Grand Master of Artillery concerning the efficiency of the artillery, its requirements, etc.; the Chief Intendant corresponds directly with the Intendant General concerning the quality of stores, etc., etc.

Local Administrations.

As all parts of the Government, civil and military, take part in a mobilization, it is necessary to have central organs to supervise everything relating to mobilization. These organs are known as Local Military Administrations. They are of three classes, viz., those of the circumscription, of the province, and of the district (sub-province). Their business is to manage all affairs relating to the reserves in time of peace—the men and the material necessary to prepare the army for war; in time of war they are charged with all the details of mobilization.

The Chiefs of Local Troops in the sub-provinces are merely executives to carry out the orders of their chiefs. They keep registers and accounts of recruits, reserve soldiers, and the militia; they call out the reserve soldiers for exercise at certain periods, guard all reserve material, and take steps for organizing the reserves and ersatz on mobilization.

The Chief of Local Troops of a province keeps a register of all officers and ex-officers, and a general account of the number of reserves in his province. The Chief of Local Troops of a Circumscription has the general supervision and direction of all affairs of the reserve, its men, material, muster rolls, etc., and also commands all fortress and other local troops in the Circumscription; in time of war he commands also the reserves until their own commander is named. He and all his subordinates and bureaux are under the orders of the Chief of Circumscription.

Commandant de place.

At garrisoned points, whether fortresses or towns, there is a bureau consisting of a Commandant de place, Major de place, and Aide-de-Camp de place, besides their clerks and assistants. Their duties are similar to those of Provost Marshals in our service; they have charge of all sentinels, guard-houses, and everything relating to military police; they are responsible that order is kept in the fortresses and for the tranquillity of the garrison and inhabitants; they must be informed of the arrival and departure of every one in the garrison, and all persons are required to present their papers to them and explain their business on arrival. In time of war all persons in the garrison, civil and military, are directly subordinate to the orders of the Commandant, and his rights and duties are then greatly increased. In a garrison he is directly under the orders of the Commanding General or Officer; at a headquarters he is under the Chief of Staff. In towns where there is no Commandant de place, his duties are performed by the Chief of Local Troops of the subprovince.

Corps, Divisions, and Brigades.

The chiefs of Corps and Divisions are appointed directly by the Emperor. The administration of a Corps in time of peace is made up of (*a*) Chief of Staff, (*b*) Chief of Artillery, (*c*) Chief Surgeon, and their assistants, and two aides-de-camp of the Commanding General. The latter is responsible for the condition, military instruction, discipline, drill, etc., of the men under his command, but in matters of economy has only a supervision, to see that the troops are properly supplied. The Chief of Staff conducts all correspondence; the Chiefs of Artillery and Medicine transact the business of their special branches. The administration of a Division consists simply of a Chief of Staff and his assistants, and two aides-de-camp for the Commanding General.

The Chief of a Brigade has hardly any administrative functions, and he has about him only an Adjutant and one Writer. As a rule a Corps is commanded by a General, a Division by a Lieutenant-General, a Brigade by a Major-General, a Regiment by a Colonel. The Chiefs of Staff and of Artillery of the Corps are Major-Generals, and the Chief of Staff of a Division is a Colonel. (For the full military hierarchy, see pay table, p. 109.)

Regiments.

The Regiment is the military community whose affairs are managed in common, and of which the Companies are the families. The battalion is the tactical unit, but has no administrative business at all.

The Colonel not only commands all troops in his regiment, but he manages all their affairs according to certain general regulations, and has a wide range of responsibility and great liberty of action as compared with our service. He is chosen by the Emperor from the army at large, including the general staff, upon recommendation of division, corps, and circumscription Commanders. His rank is Major-General in the Guard and Colonel in the Line. His prerogatives are as follows:

To appoint all non-commissioned officers;

To augment the pay of an enlisted man from ordinary to increased pay;

To accept non-commissioned officers for a second term of service;

To relieve enlisted men from the "black list";

To confirm battalion adjutants;

To recommend officers for promotion and rewards;

To give leaves of absence to officers for two months;

To give furloughs to enlisted men, according to his judgment, for any period, to transfer them to the reserve, and to discharge them altogether;

To permit enlisted men of all grades to marry, according to certain regulations.

The Regimental Commander also controls all affairs of economy of the regiment. These affairs are all confided to the special charge of a field officer, under his direct orders, known as the Administrator of Economy.*

The Colonel also makes quarterly inspections of the companies or squadrons of his regiment. He issues regimental orders to the Chiefs of Battalions or Administrator, and is pecuniarily responsible for loss of money in the regimental chest if the loss results from his orders.

The Regimental Administration consists of—
1. Administrator of Economy;
2. Adjutant;
3. Secretary;
4. Paymaster (Cashier);
5. Quartermaster;
6. Ordnance Officer;
7. Commander of Non-Combatant Company;
8. Chief of Hospital;
9. President and Secretary of Regimental Court.
10. Chief Surgeon;
11. Chaplain.

The Administrator, the Adjutant, the President of the Court, the Chief Surgeon, and the Chaplain communicate directly with the Colonel; the others through the Administrator.

The Administrator of Economy is a field officer chosen by the Colonel, and confirmed by the Corps Commander. His duties are, in general terms, to supervise all the administrative business of the regiment; he is charged with the accumulation of provisions and stores of every description, their preservation in the storehouse, the employment of regimental funds, the distribution to the men of what is due to them, etc. He submits annual estimates of what is required for the next year, and is responsible for under- or over-estimates. He is always present at the disbursement of money from the chest. All officers in the regiment responsible for money or property are subject to his orders concerning the money or property. To assist him in his duties, he has under his direct orders the Secretary, Paymaster, Quartermaster, Ordnance Officer, and Commander of Non-combatant Company. The Secretary is chief of the chancery, or chief clerk, for all administrative business, and conducts

---

* Literally translated, the "man who manages the housekeeping.

METHODS OF ADMINISTRATION. 95

its correspondence, etc. The Paymaster* receives, keeps, and disburses, under orders from the Administrator, all money, property, material, clothing, etc., for the regiment, and has charge of the storehouses. The Quartermaster receives, keeps, and distributes all subsistence property and forage, and all effects pertaining to barracks and quarters. The Ordnance Officer receives and distributes arms and ammunition, watches over the proper use of arms and instruction in target practice, has charge of the master armorers, etc. The Commander of Non-combatant Company commands this company (see p. 23), and has charge of the regimental train, wagons, horses and harness, and of all regimental shops.

The Adjutant has charge of the purely military business of the regiment, as distinguished from that of an administrative nature. His duties are the composition of reports on the strength of the regiment, reports on battles, actions, etc., periodical reports and returns, and special reports. He has charge of the conduct rolls for all men of the regiment, and of the correspondence concerning nominations, appointments, leaves, discharges, and rewards, for officers and men; makes out the regimental orders, rosters, details for service, etc. He commands, with the rights of a Company Commander, the writers and musicians; and he keeps the regimental seal.

The Chief of the Hospital is an officer specially detailed to attend to the economy of the hospital, keep its accounts, supervise the issue of rations to sick and attendants, etc.

The President and Secretary of the Regimental Court rank as civilian officials; their duties are prescribed in the Code of Military Justice.

The Chief Surgeon looks after the medical condition of the Regiment, treats the sick and wounded, makes medical inspections of barracks and lodgings, and of the men and food, attends to the hygiene and cleanliness, prevents the spread of contagious diseases, etc. He has under his orders the Battalion Surgeons, the Medical Non-commissioned Officers and Apprentices, and the Hospital Stewards and attendants. He reports directly to the Colonel, and for medical affairs to the Chief Surgeon of the Division.

---

* In Russian, *Kaznatchey*, i. e., " the man in charge of the chest."

The Chaplain is charged with the register of births, marriages, and deaths; he reports directly to the Colonel, and, in ecclesiastical matters, to the Chief Chaplain of the Army or Circumscription.

The Non-combatant Staff (Medical and Ecclesiastical) are appointed by their own Departments. The Adjutant, Paymaster, Quartermaster, Secretary, and Commander of Non-combatant Company, are chosen by the Colonel from among the Lieutenants of the Regiment; but the Secretary may be, and usually is, a civilian official.

Companies.

The Company Commander is chosen by the Colonel, and confirmed by the Division Commander, from among the Captains, 2d Captains, or Lieutenants of the Regiment. He is responsible for the military proficiency, discipline, etc., of his company, as well as for its internal administration in matters of economy. The subaltern officers are usually two to a company in time of peace; for their education they are required to write theses in tactics on maps and plans, to play *Kriegspiel*, to have practical exercises in tactics at the autumn manœuvres, etc. Every Regiment has a society or club, with a lecture hall, library, billiard-room, fencing-room, checkers, and certain other games. On certain evenings of every month there are lectures, reading of papers, etc., by officers; on other evenings there are dances. The Government gives $900 a year to each Infantry regiment, and $450 to each Cavalry regiment, to aid in this purpose; of which sum 50 per cent. goes to house expenses, dinners, etc., 25 per cent. to the library, and 25 per cent. to the "officers' fund." There are also contributions from the officers to support the society.

The non-commissioned officers of an Infantry Company are:
1 Sergeant Major;
1 Storekeeper Sergeant (*Kapitanarmus*);
4 Senior Non-commissioned Officers;
8 Junior Non-commissioned Officers (12 in time of war);
16 (Lance) Corporals (20 in time of war).

The Sergeant Major is chosen among the non-commissioned officers of the company by the Captain, and confirmed by the Colonel. His duties are to execute the orders of the

Captain, make the details, supervise the economy, and keep all the company books, registers, and accounts of soldiers. He is responsible for the discipline, and makes a morning report of the strength and condition of the company; at evening he reads the orders of the day, calls the rolls, and makes the details for next day (so many men to each platoon, leaving the choice of men to the sub-officer of the platoon).

The Storekeeper Sergeant has charge of the company storehouse, receives the fuel, lights, etc., of the company, keeps books of the same, etc.

The Non-commissioned Officers are aids to the Sergeant Major. Each Infantry company is divided into 2 half companies, 4 platoons, 8 sections; each platoon has a Senior non-commissioned officer, called the sub-officer of the platoon; each section a Junior non-commissioned officer. While the Sergeant Major keeps all the books of the company, and is responsible for the discipline of the whole of it, yet the sub-officers of platoons have much of the responsibility pertaining to 1st Sergeants of companies in our service. This arises from the great size of the companies (200 men in time of war).

The best privates are chosen as Lance Corporals, one to every 10 men, and 1 additional to every section.

ARMY ADMINISTRATION IN TIME OF WAR.

At the time of the mobilization of the army destined to act in Bulgaria, i. e., in November, 1876, an Imperial order was issued defining the powers of a Commander-in-Chief, and fixing the organization, duties, etc., of the various administrations in time of war. The powers given to the Commander-in-Chief by this document are very extensive. He is appointed by the Emperor, and announced in a Ukase to the Senate. He commands every one in the army, including such members of the imperial family as may be serving in it; he has supreme command of all the Military Circumscriptions within the range of the theatre of operations, and of all provinces declared to be in a state of siege; he organizes temporary governments in conquered districts; his orders are everywhere to be obeyed as those of the Emperor himself; he acts according to his own will, conforming only in general terms to the plan of campaign approved by the Emperor. He has full power to conclude and to terminate armistices, but must have the Emperor's authority before opening negotiations for peace. He appoints the Regimental Commanders, Chiefs of Detachments, Military Governors, and Provost Marshals; rewards officers and soldiers with decorations of a certain degree; has authority to remove any officer from his post and functions, to send him to the rear, and bring him to trial; he can pardon criminals, mitigate sentences of courts-martial, and no death sentence can be executed without his approval; he has the right to inflict summary punishment of the highest degree possible under the law. In administrative business he has the right to confirm contracts for any amount, to reject any or all bids and call for new ones, and to employ all sums of money confided to him as he judges proper; his order for the disbursement of money relieves the disbursing officer of all personal liability. He can make requisitions and forced contributions on the inhabitants, and can increase the soldier's ration or change its component parts.

His headquarters administration is modeled on that of a Circumscription, with certain necessary additions. It consists of—

A. *Principal Sections.*

1. General Staff,
2. Intendance,
3. Artillery,
4. Engineer,
5. Communications (*Etappen*),

each subject directly to the Commander-in-Chief.

B. *Secondary Sections.*

1. Provost Marshal (Commandant),
2. Hospitals,
3. Medical,
4. Post-Office,
5. Chaplains,

each subordinate to the Chief of Staff.

The chiefs of all sections except the General Staff have limited duties and responsibilities, and have no right to interfere in any section but their own. The Chief of Staff, on the other hand, has no special restricted branch, no direct authority in matters of economy, no personal liability, and commands no troops; but he is the direct Deputy of the Commander-in-Chief in all matters of every nature whatsoever; he is his right-hand man, knows all his plans and ideas, issues all his orders, and is in general the means of communication between the Commander-in-Chief and all persons, administrative or combatant, under his orders.

The General Staff, like that of a circumscription, is divided into three sections—for correspondence, inspections, and economy—each under its chief of section, and all under the Deputy Chief of Staff. The latter is also charged with all the interior business of the Staff, i. e., its secretariat, the keeping of books and records, information concerning position of troops, the orders issued to them, reconnaissances, choice of positions, examination of roads, of guards, of outposts, etc. He also, under the Chief of Staff, has charge of the general office or chancery of the Staff, of the sections of military topography, of guides, of spies, etc. All propositions of the Intendance, Artillery, or other departments of the administration must be submitted to the Commander-in-Chief, either by the Chief of Staff or in his presence.

The Intendance, Artillery, and Medical Departments are similar to those of a Circumscription.

The Department of Communications keeps up communications between the army and its base, and has complete control of all roads, telegraphs, railroads, and water routes, and is responsible for their condition, as well as for everything connected with the transport of men, horses, supplies, sick and wounded, material, etc.; and in short has control of everything that takes place in the rear of the army. When the theatre of war is on Russian soil, then the local administrations are charged with the execution of everything necessary to facilitate the supply, etc., of an army; when the frontier of Russia is passed and a secondary base is established, then a new local administration is formed, which acts in fact as forwarders of everything connected with the army. If in the enemy's country, the chief of this administration is also Governor-General of the conquered territory; if in an allied state, he acts according to a special convention, and in conjunction with a commissioner named by the head of the allied state.

For instance, during the war in Bulgaria, the Military Circumscription of Odessa was declared in a state of siege, and all its troops and resources were subject to the orders of the Grand Duke Nicholas, Commander-in-Chief of the Active Army. At the outbreak of war a convention was at once concluded with Roumania, prescribing the conditions of the passage of the troops, etc. When the Danube was crossed, a local administration was established at Bucharest, under the orders of Aide-de-camp General Drenteln, who was subject only to the orders of the Commander-in-Chief, and who had control of everything military—troops, railroads, supplies, etc.—between the Pruth and the Danube. South of the Danube, between it and the army itself, all roads, routes, telegraphs, and posts were under control of the Communications Section of the Staff at Army Headquarters.

The Administration (or Staff) of an Army Corps in time of war differs from that previously given for time of peace in the addition of an Intendant, Provost Marshal, Chief of Train, and (if necessary) an Engineer Officer. If the Corps is independent (for which a special Ukase of the Emperor is necessary), its administration is precisely similar to that of an Army in the field, though slightly smaller in numbers.

DISCIPLINE.

Only the more serious cases of breach of military law are brought for trial before Courts-Martial, of which there are three grades, all permanent courts, viz.: the Supreme Court or War Tribunal at the War Ministry, the Circumscription Court, and the Regimental Court. These are all composed of army officers serving on the court for stated periods, and during that time liable to no other duties. To each court there are one or more Judge Advocates or Solicitors selected from the Corps of Judge Advocates. The findings and sentences of the court are in every case decided by a majority, but the forms of procedure and the punishments for different degrees of crime are specified with great minuteness in the Military Code. Appeals can be taken up as high as the Supreme Court. Pardons, in time of peace, can only be granted by the Emperor.

All minor offenses both of officers and men are punished summarily, the powers of each officer for this purpose being defined with great exactness, and a record of all punishments being made in a book kept under charge of the Adjutant, which can be called for at any time by inspecting officers.

METHODS OF ADMINISTRATION.

The scale of summary punishments is as follows:

For Officers.

1. Reprimand, verbal or written.
2. Reprimand in public orders.
3. Reprimand in presence of officers specially assembled for the purpose.
4. Extra tours of duty.
5. Arrest, simple or under guard, for one month. (Generals and Regimental Commanders can not be arrested except by order of the Emperor.)
6. Loss of regular promotion.
7. Deprivation of office or command.
8. Dismissal from service.

For Enlisted Men.

1. Confinement to limits of garrison.
2. Details for hard labor, not more than 8 days.
3. Extra duty, not more than 8 days.
4. Simple arrest, not more than one month.
5. Severe arrest, not more than 20 days.
6. Confinement in dark prison, not more than 8 days.
7. Reduction of pay for lance corporals.

Non-commissioned officers can not be put to hard labor or in dark prison, and the Sergeant Major can not be put in "severe" arrest. Non-commissioned officers can be reprimanded, have extra duty as privates, be deprived of chance of promotion, lowered in grade, or reduced altogether to privates.

Bad cases, on whom the above punishments have no effect, can be tried by court-martial and put on the "black list," and can then be flogged, not more than fifty lashes. In campaigns, or when arrest is impossible, private soldiers may be punished by extra hard work, loaded with weights for certain hours, etc. In the cavalry the men can be made to walk behind the wagons, wearing all their accouterments.

The powers of various grades of officers are as follows:

The Minister of War, or Commander of an Army or of a Circumscription, can inflict any and all of the summary punishishments in the above lists.

The Commander of a Division can inflict all the summary

punishments upon subaltern officers except dismissal from service, which is reserved to the Commander of the Circumscription.

The periods of arrest vary for field officers and subalterns from 3 days, for a subaltern by a Colonel, to 20 days, for a field officer by the Corps Commander. Company commanders can only inflict upon subaltern officers reprimands, arrest for 24 hours, and 2 tours of extra duty.

For enlisted men, the Regimental Commander has the right to inflict any and all of the above punishments except degradation and loss of the chance of promotion, which is reserved to the Commander of a Division.

The commander of a battalion can inflict confinement to limits of garrison for 3 months, "severe" arrest 10 days, dark prison 4 days, "black list" 25 lashes.

The commander of a company can inflict confinement to limits of garrison for 1 month, extra service 8 tours, simple and "severe" arrest 5 days, dark prison 2 days, "black list" 15 lashes.

Subaltern officers can inflict confinement to garrison for 4 days, extra service 4 tours, simple arrest 2 days.

Sergeant Major—confinement to garrison for 4 days, extra service 3 tours, simple arrest 1 day.

Platoon sub-officer—confinement to garrison for 2 days, extra service 2 tours.

Lance Corporals—confinement to garrison for 1 day, extra service 1 tour.

In general, officers can only inflict punishment on those under their own orders, but all officers must compel salutes from inferiors, and repress disorders at all times.

Flogging is always administered under the personal supervision of the company commander and in front of the company formed in line, and after the cause, time, and place have been published in orders.

To be put on the "black list" requires trial by the Circumscription Court, in case of non-commissioned officers and soldiers having decorations and service chevrons; for other soldiers, a trial by the Regimental Court. While on the "black list," soldiers lose all grades, decorations, extra pay, privilege of guards of honor, orderlies, etc., and can have no more liberty.

METHODS OF ADMINISTRATION. 103

After a year's service on the "black list," soldiers whose conduct has been good can be restored to good standing by the Regimental Commander; before a year has expired they can only be restored by the Commander of the Circumscription or Army, for bravery in combat or other extraordinary service.

Every punishment of officer or soldier is registered in a book subject to inspection by authorized officers. These books are part of the regimental records under charge of the Adjutant; they show the conduct of each officer and man; but (unless called for by order of the Emperor) only the following punishments are recorded in the "record" which each man takes with him on leaving the regiment:

For officers—Deprivation of command,
           Loss of rank or position,
           Dismissal.

For men—Loss of rank,
          Loss of pay,
          Time on "black list" recorded at length.

In addition to the regular tribunals, there exists in each regiment an extra-official board, or sort of Court of Honor, known as the Officers' Court. Officers who are not positively subject to trial by Court-Martial, but who lack the qualities of an officer and gentleman, either in battle or in the ordinary affairs of life, are judged by this board, which also examines quarrels between officers. The Regimental Commander decides whether the affair is worth submitting to this board. It is composed of seven members chosen from among the regimental officers above the grade of Lieutenant. They are elected each year by the officers of the regiment, the seven receiving the highest ballots being permanent members, and the next two being substitutes.

The Board begins by a preliminary examination, either on motion of the Regimental Commander or upon the receipt of letters from any of the officers. As the result of that preliminary examination, the President reports to the Regimental Commander whether the affair should be tried or not. If the trial is proceeded with, the officer is heard in justification of himself; but the whole trial is oral, and the only written record is the decision, which is made by a majority of votes. The result of the decision is—(a) to acquit the officer, (b) to recommend that he be admonished or brought to trial, or (c) to request him to resign. The decision is signed by the members, and is immediately communicated to the accused and submitted to the Regimental Commander. There is no appeal from this Court, but the accused may within three days ask for a rehearing of the case on the ground of error; if the Regimental Commander finds this request plausible, he can reconvene the Court.

Of course, the decision of this Court has no binding official authority; but, if the accused refused to resign in obedience to its request, there would probably be grounds enough for his trial by Court-Martial, or for his summary dismissal by the Commander of the Circumscription. In case of such a resignation or dismissal, if the officer has served the full time of obligatory service, he leaves the army altogether; otherwise he is enrolled in the reserve.

Good order about the barracks and quarters is kept by certain officers and non-commissioned officers, who are "on service" for the day, like our Officers of the Day, and of the Guard. These officers are:

For each Regiment, one company commander;
For each Battalion, one subaltern officer;
For each Company, one non-commissioned officer;
For each Platoon, one lance corporal.

These officers are always at their posts during the twenty-four hours, and are responsible for the behavior of the men and the cleanliness, ventilation, and general good order of their barracks. The regimental officer inspects the food of the men. All the officers and men "on service" are assembled at 6 A. M. to receive orders from the regimental officer, and at 8 P. M. to report upon the condition of things. Any extraordinary matter, such as fire, riot, etc., is reported at once. Soldiers on liberty report their arrival and departure to the regimental or battalion officer, and he is also responsible for all watchmen, guards, etc.

PAY AND ALLOWANCES.

The pay of officers is intended to feed, clothe, and support them; the pay of enlisted men—which is extremely small in amount—is only pocket-money, all their real wants being supplied in kind by the Government. The pay and allowances of officers are complicated and of various kinds, as follows:

METHODS OF ADMINISTRATION. 105

1. Salary;
2. Table money;
3. Extra pay;
4. Extra allowances;
5. Lodging allowances;
6. Forage allowances;
7. Servants' allowances.

1. *Salary.*

Salary is of two kinds, ordinary and increased; the latter is about 50 per cent. more than the former, and is given to all troops in time of war, and to those serving in the Caucasus, Turkestan, and Siberia in time of peace. All officers' salary has a permanent stoppage of $2\frac{1}{2}$ per cent. for the hospital and medical attendance fund, and 6 per cent. for the officers' fund; there are also temporary stoppages upon receiving decorations, promotions, etc., which go to pay for insignia, commissions, etc.

2. *Table Money.*

This pertains to the position held by the officer and not to his grade; it can be drawn only while the position is actually filled and its duties performed.

3. *Extra Pay.*

This is a fixed annual sum also given to the position and not to the grade, and is drawn under the same conditions as the above.

4. *Extra Allowances.*

These are of various kinds. They are given to officers as follows: *a. Travel Pay.* In case of movement of detached troops of more than three days in duration, generals receive $1.87, field officers $1.15, and company officers 67 cts., a day. *b. Camp Pay.* In the summer camps, of not less than 6 battalions, field officers receive 45 cts., and company officers 23 cents a day; in the grand manœuvres they receive the same as the travel pay just mentioned. These accounts are presented to the Intendant of the Circumscription, and paid by him at the end of every 15 days. In time of war this travel pay is replaced by a war allowance of $6 for corps commanders, $4.50 for division commanders, $3 for regimental commanders, $1.50 for field officers, 75 cts. for company commanders, and 40 cts. for subaltern officers. The above is the daily allowance for troops at the front; those on the line of communications receive one half of this. If provisions can not be bought, then officers may draw soldiers' rations in kind. In garrisons, field officers receive 45 cts. and company officers 23 cts. extra for each day that they are on guard. Officers serving in the recruiting commissions and in procuring cavalry remounts are also paid extra.

Extra pay is given to soldiers for fatigue work, for reviews, special services in saving life, etc. All regiments of which the Emperor is chief receive on his birthday (April 17th) special presents of money.

Officers having a good record, when ordered to Turkestan, receive a present of two years' salary if they have families, and one year's if unmarried; similarly, for East Siberia one year's extra salary, and for West Siberia half a year's. Officers who have accepted these presents are obliged to serve three years in those localities.

Upon the outbreak of war all officers receive an indemnity for their outfit. For general officers and regimental commanders (who can receive this present but once), the amount of this is enough to buy the extra saddle-horses required in war, and the draught-horses and wagon or carriage for their private baggage; for field officers and company commanders the amount is $112, for subaltern officers $75.

When traveling on duty without troops, all officers have their actual expenses paid; if traveling beyond the reach of railroads, they receive orders for post-horses, the number depending on their grade.

5. *Lodging Allowances.*

Every officer is entitled to quarters, fuel, lights, and plain furniture; this is either furnished in kind in government buildings or barracks, or its equivalent is paid in money. A General officer is considered entitled to 9 rooms, a regimental commander to 7, a field officer to 4, and a company officer to $1\frac{1}{4}$. The money paid in lieu of quarters varies in different localities for different grades; the cities of the Empire are divided into five classes, each of which has its designated allowance for lodging, etc. The three great cities St. Petersburg, Moscow, and

Odessa make up the first class; in the second are Vilna, Kief, etc.; in the other classes smaller cities and towns. At Warsaw, and in the Caucasus and other distant localities, there is a special distinct lodging allowance. Soldiers are quartered in barracks or other government buildings, in hired buildings, or on the inhabitants in special cases, under very carefully defined laws. Each soldier is entitled to 1,157 cubic feet of space (10½ feet cube), which may be reduced in extreme cases to 343 feet (7 feet cube). Fuel, lights, beds, etc., are furnished in kind to the companies for use in the barracks.

6. *Forage Allowance.*

The daily allowance of forage is as follows:

	Oats.	Hay.	Straw.
Cavalry horses { Guard...............	15 lbs.	10 lbs.	4 lbs.
Cavalry horses { Line.................	12 "	10 "	4 "
Train horses.......................	10 "	10 "	......

Each mounted officer receives forage in kind or money equivalent for 1 horse in time of peace, and also a money allowance for his keep. In time of war the number of horses is greatly increased, and varies for different regiments and arms of the service. The Commander-in-Chief, for instance, receives forage for 40 horses and $3 a day for their care; a regimental commander has forage in kind for 3 saddle- and 4 baggage-horses, and 77 cts. a day extra for the expenses attending their care; a sub-lieutenant, 2 saddle-horses and 1 pack-horse, and 4½ cts. a day for their care. The money value of one daily allowance of forage is about 20 cts.

7. *Servants' Allowance.*

General Officers are allowed 3 servants, Field Officers 2, and Company Officers 1 servant, chosen from the enlisted men (married officers, 1 servant additional). These men follow the officers everywhere, but receive their pay and allowances from the Government, and are carried on the company rolls of their regiments. Officers who do not wish to use the servants allowed them, receive $75 a year for each servant in lieu thereof.

From the above it is evident that it would be difficult to make a simple pay-table, showing the pay and allowances of each grade of officers, since every officer's pay varies with the nature of his duties and the amount of allowances drawn in kind or in money. The actual salary (corresponding to the old "pay proper" in our service) also varies for the different arms of the service, the Guard receiving more than the Line, the Artillery and Engineers more than the Infantry and Cavalry, etc. The table on p. 109, compiled from the "Spravotchnaya Kneeshka," gives an approximation (to the nearest $5) of the pay of the Young Guard, Engineers, and Artillery, which is a medium between that of the "Old Guard" and the Infantry of the Line. The figures are exclusive of the 8½ per cent. stoppages previously explained.

Officers receive their pay at the end of every month, the men at the end of every quarter. There are separate muster- and pay-rolls in duplicate for officers and for the men, which pass through the headquarters of the regiment and division, to those of the circumscription, where they are approved; one copy is kept by the Intendant and the other returned to the regiment. Each officer is named separately in the pay-roll, but the men simply in a lump, so many of each grade. Of the copy returned to the regiment, the stub is retained there, and the body sent to the nearest money depository for payment to the Cashier or Paymaster of the Regiment; the money is then distributed, each officer signing a receipt, and each company commander signing for his whole company. After 15 days for officers and 45 days for men, these receipts are sent to the Department of Control.

Regimental Money in General.

This is of two kinds; 1. Government Money; 2. Regimental Funds.

1. The Government Money is of two kinds: *a.* The pay, table, and other allowances of officers, money given in lieu of rations to the men, etc., etc. This money merely passes through the regimental chest as through a bank, and must be disbursed exactly according to regulations and without any discretion in the regiment, and the balances always rigidly accounted for. *b.* The money for clothing, camp and garrison equipage, men's quarters, forage, remounts, etc., all of which forms one sum, disbursed for any or all of the purposes indicated, according to the discretion of the Council of Administration of the Regi-

Annual Pay and Allowances in the Russian Army.

GRADE.	Salary. Ordinary.	Salary. Increased (1).	Table Money (3).	Extra Pay (4).		Extra Allowances. (5)	Lodging Allowances.	Forage Allowances. Sad-dle.	Forage Allowances. Baggage.	Forage Allowances. Money for Care.	Servants' Allowances.	Approximate Total (7).
General.............................	$1,270	$1,900	Class A... $2,250	A..	$1,900	$2,190	$375 to $1,500	8	16	$990	$225	$11,050
Lieutenant-General.................	1,015	1,520	Class B... 1,900	R..	1,125	1,560	900 to 1,125	6	12	525	225	6,010
Major-General......................	755	1,145	Class C... 1,575	C..	900	1,200	225 to 750	5	7	460	225	6,380
			Class D... 1,350	D..	675							
			Class E... 1,125	E..	450							
Colonel.............................	515	775	Class F... 900	F..	225	1,100	175 to 600	3	4	250	150	4,890
			Class G... 675									
Lieutenant-Colonel..................	400	600	Class H... 450			550	110 to 375	3	3	150	150	2,650
Major...............................	370	550	Class I... 315			500	110 to 375	3	3	100	150	2,250
Captain.............................	330	495	Class K... 270	G..	90	275	75 to 225	3	2	60	75	1,600
Second Captain.....................	275	410	Class L... 225			275	75 to 225	3	2	50	75	1,190
Lieutenant..........................	255	380				146	52 to 150	3	2	50	75	940
Sub-Lieutenant.....................	235	350				146	52 to 150	2	1	20	75	880
Ensign..............................	220	330			72 (8)	146	52 to 150	2	1	20	75	550
Sergeant-Major { Artillery and Engineers...	$27 00	$40 50 (2)										
{ Infantry and Cavalry.......	18 00	27 00										
{ Artillery and Engineers...	18 00	27 00										
Senior N. C. Officer { Infantry and Cavalry.......	18 50	19 75										
{ Artillery and Engineers...	6 75	13 03										
Junior N. C. Officer { Infantry and Cavalry.......	8 35	5 64										
{ First class..................	18 00	27 00										
Musicians { Second class................	3 60	7 00										
{ Drummers and Buglers......	8 35	5 63										
First class Private, Engineers and Artillery.....	4 78	9 11										
Second " " "	3 82	7 43										
Third " " "	2 81	5 40										
Lance Corporal, Infantry............	2 14	4 16										
Private, Infantry....................	2 05	3 94										

L. Commander of a company or squadron, Junior Field Officers of a Regiment, etc. Classes M to S relate to positions in distant parts of the Empire.
(4) Extra-pay classes: A. Corps Commander. B. Division Commander. C. Commander of a Regiment or of an Artillery Brigade. D. Chief of Staff of a Corps, Commander of a Rifle, Sapper, Infantry or Cavalry Brigade, of a Regiment of Fortress Artillery, etc. E. Commander of a Battery, Rifle Battalion, etc. F. Commander of a Fortress Battalion, Pontonier Battalion, etc. Q. Company Commander, etc.
(5) Subaltern officers on active duty, and not holding positions entitling them to table-money or extra pay, receive $72 a year in lieu thereof.
(6) Extra Allowances are as for subsistence in travelling with troops, for manœuvres, for subsistence in time of war, and special presents and rewards from the Emperor. They vary of course with the service performed; the figures given in the above table are simply for the allowance in time of war.
(7) Since an officer's pay varies so greatly with the nature of the service upon which he is employed, it is only possible to give a mere approximation of the total value of all his allowances, etc. In the above table the two column of total is derived from the increased salary, the highest table money and manœuvre allowance, presents, etc., etc., are all omitted. The pay is liberal in the higher grades, and insufficient in the lower ones. No one can enter as a subaltern the Guard or other troops stationed in the large cities without a private income independent of his pay. The above table is for the ordinary officer existing at all times; for a commander-in-chief, chief of staff, etc., of an army in time of war, or for extraordinary and distinguished services, the Emperor makes a special order giving a handsome income for life.

(1) Increased salary is given to troops serving in war and in distant Asiatic portions of the Empire. Officers on waiting orders or supernumerary receive the ordinary salary without allowances of any kind, and retired officers receive about 75 per cent. of the ordinary salary and no allowances.
(2) The pay of mechanics, medical apprentices, and other non-combatants varies from $392 a year for the medical N. C. officer to $70 for junior carpenters, etc.
(3) Table-money classes: A. Corps commander. B. Division Commander, Chief of Local Troops, Chief of Artillery of a Corps, Commander of a Sapper Brigade, etc. C. Commander of a Rifle Brigade. D. Chief of Staff of a Corps, Commander of an Infantry or Cavalry Brigade, etc. E. Commander of a Regiment or of an Artillery Brigade, of a Fortress of the first class, Chief of Staff of a Division, etc. F. Commander of a Fortress of the second class. G. Commander of an Independent Battalion, Administrator of Economy of a Regiment, officer in charge of remounts in cavalry and artillery regiments, etc. H. Commander of a Battery of Artillery, etc. II. Commander of a Battalion forming part of a Regiment, Administrator of Economy of a Battalion of fortress artillery, of a local detachment, artillery regiments, etc. I. Commander of a company or of fortress artillery. Junior staff officers at Corps Headquarters, etc. K. Commander of a company of fortress artillery.

ment, and whose balances are not accounted for to the Crown, but disbursed by the Council for the good of the regiment. The accounts are, of course, subject to inspection by the proper officers.

2. The Regimental Funds. These are derived from voluntary contributions or similar sources, and are kept in the chest by the Regimental Paymaster; they consist of—*a*. Officers' Fund, formed by voluntary stoppages, used to make loans to officers at rates not exceeding 6 per cent., and also as a savings bank. An officer, on leaving the regiment, receives all his deposits and the legal interest. *b*. Library Fund, derived also from voluntary stoppages. (The libraries of some of the older regiments number over 25,000 volumes.) The Government helps these two funds by 25 per cent. of the 6 per cent. stoppages made against all officers. *c*. Church Funds, formed by sales of tapers, and by contributions of the regimental parish; disbursed by the chaplain, under direction of the colonel, for images, etc. *d*. Soldiers' Deposits, kept in the chest for safety by the paymaster.

The general administrative economy of the regiment, including all these funds, is under direction of a Board of Officers or Council, appointed for one year. Their estimates, accounts, etc., are subject to the examination of the Colonel and Chief of the Division, the latter's approval being final.

The books of the regiment are the Day Book, kept by the paymaster, debited with the pay, money allowances, etc., received, and credited with the disbursements; the Book of Economy, kept by the secretary, containing a register of all transactions in this department; the Register of Soldiers' Letters containing money; and the Miscellaneous Book, containing the account of the Officers', Library, and other Funds. All money is kept on deposit in the regimental chest, the inner keys of which are kept by the chief of economy and the outer by the paymaster, both of whom must be present whenever the chest is opened. The Regimental and Company Funds are kept in separate compartments.

Rations.

In general only the farinaceous portion of the ration is issued in kind, the rest being given in money, known as "Soup-money"

(Preevarzheny Dengy), which is disbursed in each company, under direction of the Captain, by an enlisted man, having good talent as a marketer, and elected by the whole company.

The farinaceous ration, in time of war, is hard black biscuit, 2 lbs. per man per day; in time of peace, it is wheat or barley flour and a buckwheat gruel much esteemed by the Russian peasants. The ration of flour is 2·04 lbs.; of gruel (in the grain) 0·31 lb. for the Line, and 0·42 lb. for the Guard. The bread is usually baked by the men in company bakeries.

The Soup-money is intended to buy meat, vegetables, salt, vinegar, tea, sugar, spirits, beer, and other articles of food and drink. The amount of this money is determined by the price of meat, which is fixed each year by the Chief Intendant (with the approval of the Commander of the Circumscription); if greater than the last year's price, the question must be referred to the War Council for its approval. The other portions of the Soup-money are constant and invariable, and the whole sum is calculated to give the men $\frac{1}{2}$ lb. of meat about 4 times a week (196 days in the year, the rest of the year being fast days), and a certain amount of vegetables, tea, spirits, etc., etc. The allowance is in three grades: the ordinary grade for soldiers having a mess in common and no garden; the diminished (50 per cent.) for those having a mess and a garden; and the increased (150 per cent.) for those soldiers on detached service at Headquarters as clerks, etc. When troops are quartered on the inhabitants, the latter are obliged to feed them, and receive in return all the soldier's rations and allowances. Troops on the march carry 8 days' biscuit (5 days' in wagons and 3 days' on the person), and buy the meat in villages, or drive cattle along with them. There is no salt meat used in the Russian service.

Requisitions for rations in kind are made on company returns, consolidated into a regimental return, and sent to the nearest depot, whence they are issued to the regimental quartermaster. They are made for 30, 15, or 10 days. Requisitions for Soup-money are made for 4 months in advance on the chief intendant of the circumscription, who sends the money to the paymaster of the regiment in the same way as salaries, etc.

Complaints as to quality are made to the regimental commander with samples, and from him, if he and the field officers find the complaint well founded, to the division commander, and thence to circumscription headquarters. The rations are transported from the depot to the regiment in wagons hired by the intendance, if the distance is more than 18 miles; if less, by the wagons of the regimental train.

Clothing, Camp and Garrison Equipage.

The clothing issues consist of woolen cloth, skins, and linen.

The underclothing is issued to the men, and becomes their personal property. The annual allowance is 3 shirts (2 linen shirts made up, and 19 cts. for the 3d), 2 pairs drawers, leather cut out for 1 pair high boots and for refooting, 1 cravat, 1 pair linen summer pantaloons, and 1 gymnasium shirt. An annual allowance is made to each man of 40 cts., for sewing his boots, cleaning materials, a square piece of cloth (linen in summer, woolen in winter), which the Russian peasants wear in place of socks, for gloves, suspenders, etc.

The uniform is not at first the property of the soldier, but of the Government. The uniform coat lasts 2 years, winter pantaloons 2 years in the Line and 1 year in the Guard, overcoat 3 years in the Line and 2 years in the Guard, cap 2 years, and *bashlik* or ear-muffler 6 years. The administrator of economy of the regiment receives all the cloth for uniforms and the money to have it made up, according to tables fixing the price of each article, in the tailor shops of the regiment or company. The coat, pantaloons, and cap, during their first two years, are called "first term uniforms," kept in the regimental storehouse, and only issued to the men for parades and inspections. During their third and fourth years they are known as "second term uniforms," and are constantly worn by the men. After this they become the property of the men. Recruits are furnished with a complete outfit, which at the end of one year becomes a "second term uniform." They usually bring a little money to buy old uniforms from their comrades for every-day wear; otherwise they have great difficulty in keeping their clothes in order.

The accouterments are required to last a certain length of time, are always government property, and can only be condemned after inspection. The pompon lasts 5 years; the belt, cartridge-box, and knapsack straps, 12 years; the knapsack, 10 years; the cavalry valise (worn on the cantle of the saddle), 4 years; cavalry cartridge-box and holster, 8 years. These articles are issued ready-made. Certain varieties of equipments, such as harness, spades, wagons, etc., are issued but once, and then an annual allowance of money is made to repair or replace them.

In place of cloth and other effects in kind, the regimental commander may sometimes receive the money value thereof, and clothe and equip his regiment himself, being responsible to the division commander for the condition of his regiment and the material on hand. Requisitions for clothing and camp and garrison equipage are made out in the regiments and forwarded to the chief intendant of the circumscription so as to reach him by the 1st of September of each year. When approved by the commander of the circumscription, the intendant orders the nearest depot to issue and transport the goods to the regiment. They are there received by the paymaster in presence of the colonel and the administrator. Each bale, bearing the stamp of the "Depot Inspection Committee," is received and a receipt given to the forwarder. The regimental and company commanders then open and examine quantities and qualities. Any complaints must be made within two weeks by the regimental commander, and the depot must at once replace any shortages. Goods bad in quality are kept in store until the annual inspection of the division commander (which occurs about this same season of the year); and, if he finds them bad, then a special board of survey is convened, consisting of a representative of the intendance department and one of the officers of the Line. The finding of this board is sent to the council of the circumscription, which has final decision in the matter. If the complaint is not sustained, the regiment must accept the goods; if it is sustained, then the inspection committee is pecuniarily liable for the loss. This committee at each depot is composed of a president appointed by the Minister of War, the depot inspector, who is an employee of the intendance, a secretary who is a specialist in the trade represented by the goods, and two military officers chosen from the troops in the circumscription by its commander.

Uniforms are made up in the tailor shops of the regiment, and must be finished before spring.

The number of shops for each regiment of infantry or cav-

114   THE RUSSIAN ARMY.

alry, or brigade of artillery, is defined in orders. They consist of shops for tailors, blacksmiths, carpenters, armorers, locksmiths, and saddlers (in the cavalry and artillery). Before the late war tailor shops were organized at the depots to make up clothing and keep it stored ready for immediate use in the field —a certain portion of this ready-made clothing to be issued each year to the troops, to prevent its deterioration.

Soldiers on leaving their regiments to pass into the reserve receive a year's underclothing and pay, the "second term uniform," their knapsack, overcoat, and a sheepskin pelisse bought from the company fund.

Ordnance Property.

Arms are issued once, and an annual allowance is made for their repair and preservation. The company commanders are responsible for their condition. The regimental ordnance officer makes such inspections as the colonel orders, and once a year an officer of the artillery department also inspects them. Certain repairs are made in the regimental shops; others require the arm to be sent to the circumscription armories. The ordnance officer, assisted by the head master-armorer, has charge of the shop, and keeps in a book a register of each gun sent for repairs, the nature of repairs, etc. On the 1st of March of each year the division commander forwards to the headquarters of the circumscription a report upon all the arms of the troops under his command. Disabled arms are replaced at once on the basis of this report.

The number of small-arm cartridges required by the Regulations to accompany the troops is as follows:

		On the men.	In the wagon.
Infantry	Krenk	60 { 48 in cartridge-boxes	72
	Berdan	60 { 12 in knapsack	60
Dragoons	Krenk	24	48
	Berdan	40	50
Light Cavalry	Berdan carbine	20	80

Target practice is conducted partly with ready-made cartridges and partly with refilled cartridges. The requisitions for all ordnance property are made by the regimental commander through the division commander on the chief of artillery of the circumscription, who designates the arsenal to furnish them.

METHODS OF ADMINISTRATION. 115

Transport.

The Regimental Train for a 3-battalion regiment consists of 41 wagons, and for a 4-battalion regiment of 44 wagons, as follows: 15 for ammunition, 16 for rations, 4 for sick, 1 for implements of various kinds, 1 for the Paymaster's papers, 1 for the chest, 1 apothecary cart, 1 for hospital effects, and 1 for the pharmacy; for 4-battalion regiments 1 additional wagon each for ammunition, for rations, and for the sick. All the wagons are for 4 horses except the apothecary cart, which has 1 horse. A cavalry regiment has 2 ammunition and 5 ration wagons. The number of horses maintained in peace is only enough to give 3 horses each to the ration wagons, which do all the usual work required about the regiments. The wagons, horses, harness, etc., are issued but once, and each year an allowance of money is made for their repair or replacement, equal to one twelfth the cost price for wagons, and one tenth for horses.

The Private Train consists of the officers' carriages and baggage wagons, and the company soup wagons. In peace, officers may have as many equipages as they wish at their own expense; in war, they are limited to 2 officers' wagons for a battalion of infantry or two squadrons of cavalry—field officer's baggage to 80, and company officer's to 40 lbs.

Each Company and Squadron has a small four-wheeled cart for one horse, carrying an immense soup kettle, and all the kitchen apparatus. During the war some companies had the patent iron kitchen on wheels, somewhat like a portable forge, but it did not give much satisfaction.

Country carts are impressed into service by the Intendance Department, at rates of compensation and under restrictions defined with great minuteness in the military laws.

CAVALRY AND ARTILLERY REMOUNTS.

Horses for Cavalry remounts must fulfill the following conditions:

1. Age—For the Guard, 4 to 7 years; for the Line, 4 to 6 years.

2. Size—For the Cuirassiers of the Guard, from $15\frac{5}{16}$ to $16\frac{1}{16}$ hands; for the Light Cavalry of the Guard, from $14\frac{11}{16}$ to $15\frac{5}{16}$ hands; for the Line, from $14\frac{11}{16}$ to $15\frac{5}{16}$.

3. Color—Must be the same in each regiment of the Guard;

for the Line indifferent, arranged in the regiment by squadrons according to color as nearly as possible. Trumpeters always ride white horses.

4. Qualities—For the Guard, beauty as well as strength and fitness; for the Line, the usual characteristics of a good cavalry horse, without regard to beauty.

5. Breed—For the Guard, in the renowned stables and stud-farms, particularly those of the south of Russia; for the Line, principally in herds of hardy steppe horses, or in the stables on the steppe in the provinces of Pultowa, Kharkof, Kherson, Voronezh, and the Don Cossack country. However, Remount Officers may buy where they choose, provided the horse answers all the conditions.

The term of service of a cavalry horse is 9 years; the remount is therefore each year one ninth of the effective strength.

Stallions are not permitted, and of mares not more than one-third of the whole number of horses.

Remount Officers.—In each Regiment of the Guard and each Brigade of the Line, there is an officer appointed by the Regimental Commander, and confirmed by the Division Commander, known as the Remount Officer, whose sole duty it is to attend to everything connected with the remounts, and who has an officer detailed as his assistant, and a detachment of soldiers, who assist him in caring for the young horses and bringing them to the regiments. He receives $450 a year table money, and $520 travel allowance, and his assistant $240 and $400, in addition to their other pay and allowances. Each of these officers has his remount depot, designated by the Circumscription Commander, where the detachment remains, and where the horses are assembled and kept, previous to being sent to the regiment.

The Remount Officer receives in advance from the Government for each horse of the Cuirassiers, $225, of the Light Cavalry of the Guard, $140 to $152, of the Line, $94; for conducting the horses to the depots, $3 each for the Guard, and $2.25 for the Line. Having received this money and been notified of the number of horses required the next autumn, the Remount Officer undertakes the business precisely as if he were a contractor, buying at whatever age and whatever price he chooses—subject always to have his horses thrown back on his hands if not accepted, and to the pecuniary loss therefrom.

The new horses are received at the Regiment by a Commission, composed, in the Guard, of the Cavalry Division Commanders and of officers named by the Commanding General of the Guard, and the Inspector-General of Cavalry; in the Line, of a General officer appointed by the Inspector-General of Cavalry, a Cavalry Division Commander serving in the Circumscription, and the Brigade Commander in which the horses are to be received. The decision as to acceptance or rejection is made by a majority of votes. The young horses then pass a year in the Reserve or Depot Squadrons, and are there broken. The following autumn they are taken into the regiments, and distributed by the Division Commander to the squadrons.

The condemnation of horses already in service is made in the following manner: Each year, after the summer manœuvres, the horses are put out to grass for a month. When they are returned to the stables, the Regimental Commander designates the horses subject to condemnation, and they are then examined by a special Commission, composed of the Division, Brigade, and Regimental Commanders; all horses which have served 12 years are positively condemned, no matter in what condition they may be; the horses unfit for service from disease or other cause, and those which have served 11, 10, and 9 years, are examined by the Commission, which decides as to their fitness for service. The condemned horses are sold by auction, and the money turned at once into the Treasury.

Each horse receives a name upon being accepted in the regiment, the remount of each year all having names beginning with the same letter; and his history is kept in a Register in which his description, breed, etc., form the first entry.

The Regimental and Squadron Commanders are alone responsible for the condition and treatment of horses. In the stables each horse must have a space of at least 5 by 9 feet, and a passage between the lines of horses of at least $4\frac{1}{2}$ feet. Horses to be separated by partitions or swinging poles.

Officers are required absolutely to provide their own horses, but are allowed, under certain very limited and carefully defined restrictions, to buy once in 5 years a horse from the squadron, paying his cost price, transportation, and $15 extra. In each Regiment there is a Remount Fund, similar to the Officers' Fund previously described, which lends money at 4 per cent. to young officers to buy horses, to be repaid by stoppages from their pay in 3 years or less. When this fund exceeds $1,200, it is allowed to buy from it, by vote of the Regiment, a horse as a present to an officer of good record without fortune, who has lost his horse by some accident beyond his control.

Officers of the Guard are required to have horses of the color of their Regiment. As a matter of fact, the wealthier Regiments average 3 or 4 horses to each officer, thorough-breds, (English, Arab, and cross breeds), each horse worth on an average from $800 to $1,200.

EDUCATION.

The Military Schools in Russia are very numerous, varying from the primary schools, which take a boy in hand at 10 or 11 years of age, up to the higher schools for officers, which complete his professional education. They consist of three classes, as follows:

1. Military Gymnasia (Preparatory Schools);
2. Military Schools for the education of Junkers or Cadets to be Officers;
3. Military Academies for the higher professional education of Officers.

These constitute the regular course, but there are also Normal or Training Schools for education in special branches.

1. *Military Gymnasia.*

These are of two classes: the Gymnasia and the Progymnasia.

The *Progymnasia* take boys, of about 12 years of age, who have mastered the rudiments of reading, writing, and arithmetic, and educate them for the Military Schools for Junkers found in each Circumscription. The course is for 4 years, and the annual cost for each pupil is about $125. There are 10 of these schools, 4 of which are in Asia, and all of which, except one in St. Petersburg, are east of Moscow. The total number of pupils is 2,600, graduating about 500 each year.

The *Gymnasia* take boys at the same age, but restricted to the sons of the privileged classes, and educate them for the Military Schools for Cadets. The course is for three years, and comprises Mathematics to include Plane Trigonometry, the elements of Natural Philosophy and Physical Geography, of Natural History and Physiology, Geography, History, Languages (French and German), Russian Composition, Drawing, and instruction in Drill, Gymnastics, Fencing, etc., etc. Certain pupils, selected by the Minister of War, are admitted free, and the others pay about $200 a year.

In both the Gymnasia and Progymnasia the pupils all wear military uniform, have arms furnished by the Government, and are formed into companies and a battalion for military drill.

There are 14 Gymnasia, of which 2 are in Asia, 3 at St. Petersburg, 3 at Moscow, and 1 each in cities in other parts of the Empire in Europe. They contain 4,200 pupils, of whom about 1,200 or more graduate each year; they then pass into the Cadet Schools, or, if not physically qualified to be Officers, can pass to the lowest grade of Civilian Officials, or into business or other civil employment.

2. *Military Schools.*

These are the schools which furnish Officers of the Army. They are of several varieties—

a. Junker Schools.—These are under the direction of the Circumscription Commander, and take only the graduates of the Progymnasia or the non-commissioned Officers serving in the Circumscription. There are 11 schools for Infantry, 2 for Cavalry, and 2 for Cossacks. Of the Infantry schools, 5 are for 400 Junkers each, 5 for 300, and 1 for 200; the Cavalry schools are 1 for 300 and 1 for 150; and the Cossack schools are each for 120; giving a total of 4,390 Junkers under instruction. The course is for two years, and nearly 1,500 graduate each year, and form the great body of Officers of the Line of the Army. The time of service at these schools counts as service in the ranks, as already explained (p. 16). The theoretical course lasts seven months, examinations one month, practical instruction in the field (sketching, reconnaissances, etc.) one month, and the remaining three months are passed with the troops—the non-commissioned officers returning to their own Regiments, and the rest of the Junkers forming a battalion or company, and joining the troops in the manœuvres.

The whole course is in general education about equal to that of the Gymnasia, but has additional professional studies. The first year's studies comprise the Russian Language, Arithmetic, Geography and History, and the Army Regulations; the second year's course continues the Russian Language, and Algebra, Plane Geometry, Tactics and Military Science, Field Fortification, Drawing, and the Army Regulations, Methods of Administration, etc. , Drill, Gymnastics, etc., in each year.

The education of the majority of Officers of the Infantry and Cavalry is, therefore, seen to be not very profound or comprehensive.

b. The Cadet Schools.—These take boys from the Gymnasia and educate them to be Officers of Cavalry or Infantry of the Guard, the pupils being sons of the nobility. The most aristocratic of these institutions is the *Imperial Corps of Pages* at St. Petersburg, admission to which is obtained only by direct order of the Emperor. Those whose families are wealthy pay about $560 a year; others are educated free of expense. The pupils are divided into a preparatory class, 4 general classes, and 2 special classes; the preparatory class takes pupils as early as 12 years of age, and from it they pass into the general class; but the general or special classes can also be entered (the latter only between 16 and 18 years of age) by passing examinations about equal to the Gymnasium course. A portion of the pupils perform service as pages of the bed-chamber to the Emperor; they all receive military instruction in drill, etc. The two special classes (two years' course) are specially intended for those destined to be Officers of the Army; on graduating they become at once Sub-lieutenants or Ensigns, according to their proficiency, in the Guard, or, if they choose, in the Line.

The other schools of this class comprise three schools for Infantry, known as the *Paul, Constantine,* and *Alexander Schools*, and one for Cavalry, known as the *Nicholas School*—all situated at St. Petersburg, except the Alexander School, which is at Moscow; and also the Finland Cadet Corps, differing but little from the others, but situated at Helsingfors, and devoted to the education of Finnish Officers.

The Infantry Schools accommodate 300 Cadets each, and the Cavalry School 200, or 1,100 in all, and furnish annually about 400 Officers to the Infantry, and 80 or 90 to the Cavalry —the course being two years. Certain pupils, designated by the Minister of War, are free; the others pay about $300 a year.

METHODS OF ADMINISTRATION. 121

Each School forms a battalion of 4 companies—the Cavalry School 2 squadrons—for purposes of instruction in drill, etc., and in this capacity passes three months of the year in camp, taking part in the annual manœuvres. Candidates are admitted who have passed the Military Gymnasia (or Civil Gymnasia of equal grade), or who can pass an examination of the same degree. The course comprises instruction in the Russian, French, and German Languages, Natural Philosophy and Chemistry, History, Geography, and Statistical Information, Tactics, Military Science, Fortification, Drawing, Military Law and Methods of Administration, Drill, Gymnastics, etc.

These Schools furnish the body of Officers of the Guard, the graduates becoming Ensigns at once, and the course is seen to be more advanced than that of the Junker Schools. After a few years' service in the Guard, the more ambitious and intelligent Officers seek active service and advancement in Asia, or pass through the Staff Academy, and then return into the Guard or the Line, according to the amount of success they have achieved. The majority of Officers of the Guard, however, remain in their own Regiments until eligible to command a Regiment, when they have, as a rule, to pass into the Line in order to receive one.

c. The Artillery and Engineer Schools.—Cadets destined to the Artillery or Engineers are educated in separate schools—the Michael Artillery School, accommodating 160 pupils, and the Nicholas Engineer School, accommodating 120, both at St. Petersburg. Admission is limited to the more distinguished scholars of the Gymnasia, or to boys over sixteen years of age who can pass an equal examination. The course in each school is three years, and on graduation the cadets having the highest proficiency become at once sub-lieutenants in the Artillery or Engineers; the others are commissioned in the Infantry or Cavalry.

The Artillery course comprises instruction in Analytical Geometry, Differential and Integral Calculus, Mechanics, Natural Philosophy and Chemistry, History, and Military Geography, Russian, French, and German Languages, Tactics, Artillery, Fortification, Drawing, Military Law, and Methods of Administration. In summer they take part in the manœuvres as a battery of artillery.

The Engineer course is—Analytical Geometry, Natural Philosophy and Chemistry, Field and Permanent Fortification, including mining and the attack and defense of fortified places, Architecture, Russian, French, German, and English Languages, Drawing, Artillery.

In all Military Gymnasia and Schools the first and daily subject of instruction is Religion, and all pupils are members of the Russian Greek Church. The Gymnasia, Junker and Cadet Schools for Infantry and Cavalry, are under the direction of the Military Education Bureau of the War Ministry. The Artillery and Engineer Schools, as well as the Academies for officers, are each under the charge of their own Departments (Artillery, Engineers, or General Staff).

3. *Military Academies.*

These complete the professional education of officers who have already served for a few years with their regiments. There are four of these Academies, all at St. Petersburg, viz.: the Nicholas General Staff Academy, for 50 officers; the Michael Artillery Academy, for 30 officers; the Nicholas Engineer Academy, for 35 officers; the Military Law Academy, for 25 officers.

The *Staff Academy* is open to all officers up to the grade of Major in the Army or 2d Captain in the Guard, who have served for four years as officers, two of which with troops. They are required to pass an entrance examination, about equal to the course at the Military Schools, and those highest on the list are relieved from duty with their regiments and admitted to the Academy; the others are returned to their regiments, but can have another trial the next year if they wish. Certain lectures are, however, open to all officers present in St. Petersburg, as far as the capacity of the lecture hall will permit. Officers are quartered or receive lodging allowance in St. Petersburg, and attend the lectures, recitations, or examinations in the Academy at fixed hours. The course of study is for two years, and its principal subjects are Tactics, Strategy, Military History, Administration and Statistics, Geodesy, and Topography; the minor subjects are the Russian, French, and German Languages, Fortification, Artillery, and General History.

Officers who are not making satisfactory progress are at once returned to their regiments. At the final examination the highest officers receive one step in promotion if below the rank of Major, and a year's pay if of that grade, receive the gold badge of graduates of the Academy, and are at once assigned to duty in the General Staff; officers of less proficiency receive the silver badge of graduates, and are assigned to duty in the General Staff or returned to their regiments, according to the vacancies open at the time.

Attached to the General Staff Academy is a *Geodetical Section* for ten officers, for which the preliminary examination is the same as for the Academy, with the addition of Analytical Geometry and the Calculus. The course of instruction lasts two years, and the principal subjects are Astronomy, Physical Geography, Geodesy, Cartography, and Military Statistics; the minor subjects are Military Administration, Tactics, and Languages. At the end of their theoretical course they go to the Pulkova Observatory and have a two years' practical course in Astronomy and Geodesy, at the end of which, if proficient, they become Geodesists of the Topographical Corps, and receive one step in promotion and the badge of their scholarship.

The course at the Staff Academy, including the Geodetic Section, begins on the 1st of October and lasts a whole year.

The *Artillery* and *Engineer Academies* are open to all officers of any branch of the service, up to the grade of 2d Captain in the Army or Lieutenant in the Guard, who have served for three years as officers, two of which actually with troops, and who can pass an entrance examination equal to the graduating examination at the Artillery and Engineer Schools. The course in each is for two years; its principal subjects are, for the Artillery, Ballistics and Applied Mechanics, the History of Artillery, its organization, administration, and tactics; for the Engineers, the Science of Fortification and its History, Applied Mechanics, and the Theory of Building and Architecture, and engineering constructions of all kinds; the minor subjects are Higher Mathematics, Chemistry and Mineralogy, Drawing, etc.

On graduating, the officers, if proficient, wear the badge of the Academy, are assigned for a year to the batteries or sapper battalions of the Guard, and are then assigned to batteries or sapper battalions in the Line, or to engineer duty on fortifications.

The *Military Law Academy* is open to all officers who have served three years, and who can pass an examination showing an elementary knowledge of law, and a natural capacity for it. The course lasts two years, and its principal subjects are the different branches of military and international law and forms of procedure in the Russian and other services, and its minor branches are criminal, police, and civil law, and the principles of Military Administration. Officers on graduating receive the badge of the Academy, and are appointed permanently in the judicial branch of the Army when vacancies arise.

4. *Special Schools.*

There is (*a*) at Moscow a school for 75 students, designed to educate teachers for the Military Gymnasia; (*b*) at St. Petersburg a Pyrotechnical school for 100 students, designed to educate foremen and laboratory men for the artillery workshops; (*c*) at St. Petersburg a Drawing School for 200 students, designed to educate draughtsmen and subordinate topographers for the army; (*d*) at St. Petersburg a Topographical School for 40 pupils, designed to educate topographical officers and officials, chosen from among non-commissioned officers and civilians who pass a certain examination; (*e*) a Military Law School for 100 students, designed to educate subordinate officials for the Law Department; (*f*) a Riding-Master's School for 40 students, designed to educate the regimental riding-masters in riding, hippology, and veterinary science; (*g*) three surgical schools at St. Petersburg, Moscow, and Kief, accommodating 300 pupils in all, destined to educate Hospital Stewards and Surgical Assistants; and finally, (*h*) the Medico-Chirurgical Academy at St. Petersburg for 280 medical and 20 veterinary students, designed to furnish a well-educated body of Army Surgeons. The course is for five years, after which the graduates pass two years in the military hospitals, and then return to pass their examination for the degree of M. D. The six highest students are allowed $750 a year, and sent abroad at public expense to complete their education. Surgeons educated at the public expense are required to serve thirteen years in the Army, and two years additional for each year passed abroad.

The lack of a generally educated middle class in Russia, upon which to draw for the various classes of specialists required in an army, has compelled the Government to found all the special schools just named, most of which date from the reign of Nicholas, or of the present Emperor. Since the abolition of serfage, and particularly since the law of universal military service was passed, thorough schools for enlisted men have been established in every company in the Army, and non-commissioned officers' schools in every regiment, each under direction of an officer, and subject to rigid inspection. But active service and other causes have somewhat interfered with this, and the proportion of soldiers who could read and write was reported at 115 in 1,000 in 1870, and is estimated under 200 at present. This is a long way behind the German service, whose statistics give 965 out of every 1,000 men at large in the army as possessing a rudimentary knowledge of arithmetic as well as reading and writing.

RECAPITULATION.

The fundamental principles of Russian Military Administration may be summed up as follows:

1. The Emperor is Commander-in-Chief, and his organ for military affairs is the Minister of War, to whom all military persons and officers are subject.

2. The Ministry of War is composed of several bureaux for the administration of the military business of various kinds, these bureaux being subject to the Minister of War alone.

3. Owing to the vast extent of the Empire, it is divided into 14 districts called Military Circumscriptions, at the head of each of which is a small Ministry of War.

4. The Commander of one of these Circumscriptions has the rights of military command over every military person in it; but in affairs of property, supply, etc., he is only the President of a Council, the majority of whose votes decides all questions.

5. The Administration of one of these Circumscriptions consists, besides the Commander, only of—1. The General Staff, having the duties of the Adjutant-General's and Inspector-General's Department in our service; 2. The Intendance, charged with everything in the way of supplies, whether in money or in kind, and of all business not of a technical military nature, i. e., the business of the Quartermaster, Subsistence, and Pay Departments of our service; 3. The Artillery Department,

charged with a supervision of the condition of artillery troops, and with the supply of everything known as ordnance and ordnance property in our service; 4. The Engineer Department, charged with a supervision of the condition of fortifications, roads, etc.; 5. The Medical Department, charged with the care of the health of the troops. This makes up what we would call the *Staff* of the Circumscription. There is, also, at each Circumscription Headquarters a permanent Court-Martial, formed of officers detailed for a term of years.

6. The General Staff, being a purely military branch, draws its officers from the Line, and sends them back to it. For instance, a Lieutenant of four years' service goes to the Staff Academy and graduates after two years, then becoming a Captain of the General Staff, and attached to the Headquarters of a Corps; after a few years' service, depending on his efficiency, he becomes a Colonel of the General Staff, and Chief of Staff of a Division; he is then, after a few years, according to his merit, eligible either to receive command of a regiment, or be promoted to Major-General and Chief of Staff of a Corps; subsequently he receives command of a Brigade, or of a Division, becoming a Lieutenant-General; he then may be chosen Chief of Staff of an Army, with the rank of full General, and after that be appointed to the command of an Army, or Chief of the Corps of General Staff. Constant interchange between service in command of troops and service as Chief of Staff is the essential principle.

7. The Officers of the Intendance or Supply Department are chosen, usually but not always, from officers of the Army. Once appointed in the Intendance, they remain there, but they are not rated as officers, but as Military officials of a certain grade in the Hierarchy or "Tchin." For instance, the Intendant of a Corps is an official of the 6th grade, ranking with a Colonel; the Intendant General, Chief of the Intendance Bureau of the War Ministry, is of the 3d grade, ranking with a full General. The permanent Law Officers are chosen and rated and promoted in the same way; the Medical Officers also in the same way, except that they are taken from graduates of the Medical Academy, and not from officers of the Army.

8. The Engineer and Artillery officers alternate in service between duty with troops of their own arm and duty in con-

struction or in administration in their own specialties. Those showing special aptitude in construction are usually retained for great lengths of time, or even permanently, on that duty. The highest offices are those of Chief of the Department, or Chief of Artillery or Engineer at Headquarters of a large body of troops. For example, the Chief of Artillery of a Circumscription is a Lieutenant-General, and is chosen from officers who have served on construction duty as well as in command of Brigades of Artillery. After having been Chief of a Department, the only position they are eligible to is to command a Circumscription or an Active Army, e. g., General Todleben; if not appointed to this, they must be retired.

9. The Administration of a regiment is made up of a Colonel in command, an Adjutant for military business, a Surgeon for medical affairs, and an officer (usually next to the Colonel in rank) who has charge of all business not of a technical nature. He is known as the Administrator of Economy, and has a certain number of Lieutenants detailed to assist him as Paymaster, Quartermaster, Commander of Non-Combatants, Secretary, etc.

10. Promotion is by seniority up to the grade of Company Commander; after that by selection, due regard being paid to the officer's capacity as well as his length of service. Regimental Commanders and Generals are appointed and assigned to command by the Emperor, on the Recommendation of the Minister of War. Battalion and Company Commanders are appointed by the Circumscription Commander, on the recommendation of the Commanders of Divisions and Regiments.

CHAPTER V.

TACTICS.*

1. *Infantry Tactics.*

THE Company is formed in two ranks, the men ranged according to size from right to left. Each Company, which consists of 2 or more files, is divided into 2 platoons, each platoon into 2 half-platoons, and each half-platoon into 2 sections.

The length of pace in the ordinary march is 1 arshin (28 inches), and the number of paces 112 to 116 to a minute.

The formations of the Company are:
The Deployed Line,
The Columns,
The Square.

In the deployed line (*razvernuti front*) the half-platoons are placed one beside the other, according to their numbers, from right to left.

The columns are those of Platoons, Half-Platoons, and Sections, according to the front; columns at full distance, half distance, and close column, according to their depth, the last having a distance of 5 paces.

Files (column of twos) and double files (column of fours) are formed by facing to the right or left.

The Square is formed from the column when as many as two half-platoons are present; a single half-platoon can not form

---

* The following chapter is merely a brief summary of the Tactics prescribed in the Russian Regulations, as given in the "Spravotchnaya Knoczhka," edition of 1875. In Part IV. will be found some discussion of the tactics as practiced and developed during the campaign.

a square. The sections formed into square fire by volleys or by file. The Russian Square is in reality a shallow rectangle, and is formed from the close column of platoons by the two files on both flanks of each platoon simply facing outward and filling up the gap of 5 paces between the two platoons.

For an attack the dispersed order is employed. The company deploys a half-platoon in front as skirmishers, and the rest follow, 300 paces behind, assembled as a reserve. The skirmishers consist of groups of 4 men each, under command of the oldest soldier of the group. To strengthen or weaken the line, the intervals are diminished or increased.

When the skirmishers advance under fire, they will spring forward from one cover to another at distances of 25 to 50 paces; this will be accomplished upright and running quickly; bending over is regarded as demoralizing.

If the ground affords cover for the whole line, it will run forward together from 50 to 100 paces; the order for this will be given by the officer commanding the skirmish line by trumpet signal.

For the charge, the signal charge ("*Attak*") will be beaten or sounded at 100 paces from the enemy; at 50 paces the officer signals to drop the bayonet, and at 30 paces commands "*Hurrah*," at which the men take the gun "in the balance," and, yelling "Hurrah," throw themselves upon the enemy.

Should the signal "Attack" be sounded for the reserve, the skirmish line will move to the flanks to allow the reserve to pass, and will pour in a fire upon the enemy, advancing on the flanks of the reserve should the attack succeed.

In case of an attack by cavalry, the groups of fours rally on the nearest officer and non-commissioned officers, and form squads. The reserve (half-platoon or section) remains in deployed line, opens fire by volleys against the advancing cavalry at about 300 paces, and at the same time begins to approach the skirmish groups.

When a battalion is assembled, a whole company acts as skirmishers.

The Battalion consists of from 2 to 5 Companies. The first four companies are known as Line companies, and the fifth as the Rifle company.

The formations are the Deployed Line, the Columns, the

Order of Battle by Companies (Company Column), and the Square.

In the Deployed Line the four line companies are drawn up in line, with intervals of one pace from one to another, from right to left, according to their numbers. The rifle company is drawn up in Column of Platoons, 50 paces behind the center of the battalion.

The battalion columns are those of Double-platoon, Platoon, Half-platoon, Section, and File, according to the front; right in front, left in front, or on the center, according to the leading platoon or section; at full distance, half distance, or close-column, according to the distance. These names sufficiently explain the formations.

In the double column by platoons on the center, the left platoon of the 2d company and the right platoon of the 3d company are in front, the other platoons follow them, those of the 2d and 1st companies forming the right of the double column, and those of the 3d and 4th the left; the rifle company takes its place in rear, the 1st platoon in the right column, the second in the left. The distance is 5 paces.

In the column of half-platoons on the center, the head of column is formed by the 4th half-platoon of the 2d company and the 1st half-platoon of the 3d company; the half-platoons of the 2d and 1st companies form the right of the double column, and those of the 3d and 4th companies the left. The rifle company is broken into half-platoons, of which Nos. 1 and 2 take their places at the rear of the right column, and 3 and 4 at the rear of the left column.

To form column of double files on the center, the 1st and 2d companies face to the left and file to the right, the 3d and 4th companies face to the right and file to the left; the skirmish companies follow, at a distance of 5 paces, in column of sections.

In the Company Column, the line companies may be formed in one or in two lines; the Battalion Commander designates the number of companies for each line. The companies of the first line are either in line or in column, those of the second line in column of platoons or half-platoons. If two companies are in one line, the interval between them must be not less than 4 platoon fronts; if three companies, not less than 1 platoon front; if four companies, not less than 1 pace. At the command of the Battalion Commander these intervals, which leave room for the full deployment of the battalion, may be extended. The second line follows the first at a distance of 200 to 400 paces.

To receive a cavalry attack, square is formed by those companies only which are on the threatened flank, and only in case the ground affords no cover.

In the Battalion square the companies are grouped as in Battalion columns on the center. The line companies form each a company square (all the platoons facing to the front), and the rifle company remains in line facing to the rear. The Square formation is only employed in those rare cases in which the Battalion has not time to deploy at least a part of itself into line in the direction from which the attack is threatened.

The Battalion is formed in dispersed order, with skirmish line, and reserves (supports) on the same principles as explained for the company; only the skirmish line must always be of sufficient length to cover the whole front of the battalion. The strengthening of the skirmish line, the advance, and the attack with the bayonet, are conducted in the same manner as in the company.

If the battalion is in line and the signal "Deploy" is given, each line company deploys a half-platoon as skirmishers; but if the battalion be formed in the order of battle by companies in platoon column, then at the above signal the half-platoons at the head of each column in the first line are deployed as skirmishers. The Battalion Commander may, however, if he sees fit, order a platoon or a whole company into the skirmish line.

If a battalion deployed in line is unable to arrest the advance of the enemy by its fire, when the latter comes within 50 paces, the last volley is delivered, and the Battalion Commander cries "Hurrah," whereupon the line companies rush forward, with the same shout, upon the enemy with the bayonet. The rifle company will hold itself in readiness to support one of the wings or the center of the battalion, or to cover the retreat.

Two or more battalions united are formed either alongside of one another, forming a battalion-line, or behind one another, forming a general column. From both formations echelons may be formed. In battalion line, the battalions may be formed either in line or in column, or in the order by companies, or finally in square. The general column may also be formed from battalion columns.

Of the different battalion columns, those on the center by platoons or half platoons are exclusively used in manœuvres previous to engagements.

In battalion line with deployed battalions, the intervals are 40 to 50 paces; with the battalions in the order by companies, the intervals are 40 to 50 paces if the companies are in one line, and 80 to 100 if in two lines. If several battalions are drawn up in two lines, the distance between the lines is from 400 to 500 paces; the battalions are then formed in columns on the center, and those of the rear line are covered by those of the front.

Echelons are formed by successive forward or backward marching of one of the two wings or of the center. The strength of the echelons and their distances are fixed by the commanders; if not so fixed, the distance is taken at the number of paces in a battalion front.

2. *Artillery.*

Two guns, with their limbers and caissons, form a platoon, two platoons a division, and two divisions a battery. In the deployed line of a battery the guns are at intervals of 6, 12, or 24 paces. Firing is by piece, by platoon, by division, or by battery.

3. *Cavalry.*

The squadron is drawn up in two ranks and divided into 4 platoons; the chiefs of platoons are posted in front of their platoons.

The formations of the squadron are the deployed line and the columns. The latter are either by half-squadrons or by platoons; in the former case at full distance, in the latter at half distance. The column of platoons is considered the most convenient formation for all exercises. There are also columns by file, of twos, of threes, and of sixes.

The charge is made in close and in dispersed order, from rest or in motion. In the latter case the squadron moves forward first at a walk, then at a trot, finally at a gallop, and at 80 to 150 paces from the enemy the command "*Marsch—marsch*" is given. In the former case (from at rest) the command "*Marsch—marsch*" is given, and the squadron commanders execute the "*Shock.*"

The attack in dispersed order is made only by a half-squadron, the other half following at about 150 to 200 paces in close order as reserve.

The Regiment consists of four squadrons, and two squadrons form a division.

The formations of the Regiment are the Deployed Line, the Line of Columns, the Close-Column Line ("*Mass*"), and the Regimental Columns.

In the Deployed Line the squadron intervals are one platoon front.

In the Line of Columns the squadrons are in column at deploying intervals.

In the Close-Column Line the squadrons are in column with intervals of one pace.

In the Regimental Columns the squadrons follow each other either in deployed lines or in columns of half-squadrons, or platoons, or files. The column of platoons is always at full distance; that of half-squadrons or squadrons may be at full or at half distance.

Echelons may be formed by squadrons or half-squadrons, in the same manner as in the infantry. The strength of the echelons and their distance are determined by the Regimental Commander.

The charge in close or dispersed order is executed in the same manner as in the squadron. In dispersed order the deployed half-squadrons are commanded by a Division Commander.

For fighting on foot, the Dragoons are all furnished with the musket and bayonet; Nos. 1 and 3 dismount, and No. 2 remains mounted, holding the horses of the men on either side of him. All the Cossacks are furnished with muskets and fight on foot in the same way as the Dragoons. In the Lancers and Hussars only the rear rank is armed with muskets.

4. *Tactics of Large Bodies of Troops.*

When in reserve large bodies of troops are formed as follows: Infantry in battalion double columns on the center of half-platoons at half distance, in one or two lines, with intervals of 50 paces between battalions. The artillery, in columns of half-batteries on the center, is posted in rear.

For parade, the infantry is formed in one or two lines in battalion double columns on the center of platoons at half distance, the artillery in rear of the infantry; and the cavalry in rear of all.

For action, the formation is in three lines: in the first line, battalions of infantry in line or in Company Columns, the artillery on the flanks or in the center, detachments of cavalry on the extreme flanks; in the second line, battalions of infantry in the order of Company Columns, with artillery as in the first line—the distance between the two lines not to exceed 400 paces; in the third line, the reserve formed in battalion columns as just above mentioned, with the artillery massed. The strength of the reserve is from one third to one fourth of the whole force, and it is placed out of range, at a distance depending on circumstances and the nature of the ground.

The batteries are supported by detachments from the nearest battalions, and these detachments send out skirmishers to keep off those of the enemy and protect the batteries. The main body of the cavalry is, at the beginning of the action, with the reserve.

5. *Bivouacs.*

Infantry Battalions bivouac in battalion columns on the center of platoons at half distance. The arms are stacked in this position, and if the bivouac is for a single night, the men pitch their shelter-tents and sleep in line behind the stacks; if for a longer period, the men move out on either flank clear of the stacks, and pitch their tents or build huts in lines of platoons. The Regiment is bivouacked with the battalions as above, in one line for three-battalion regiments, and two lines for four-battalion regiments. The Division is bivouacked with the Regiments in one or two lines.

Batteries bivouac in deployed line between Regiments.

Cavalry Regiments bivouac in Regimental columns of squadrons in line, the front rank of each squadron pitch their tents in one line, and the rear rank in another; the two lines are separated by a distance of 12 paces, in which the horses are picketed in line with their heads together.

All camps have the usual camp guards in addition to the outposts.

6. *Outposts.*

If the enemy is over two days' march distant, he is observed by detachments of cavalry sent forward in reconnaissance. These go forward 7 to 10 miles in the direction of the enemy, post squads or pickets on all lines of approach and other important points, these pickets being not more than 1 verst (two thirds of a mile) apart, keep the rest of the force in reserve behind the line of pickets, and send out scouting patrols to observe the enemy.

If the enemy is at closer distance, he is watched by an outpost in three lines, the pickets in the first line, supports in the second, and main body in the third. If composed of foot troops, the pickets are from 100 to 150, or in very open country 300 paces apart; the supports are at cross-roads or other points about 500 paces behind them; and the main body, in a ravine or otherwise out of sight if possible, about 1,000 paces behind the supports. If composed of cavalry, the pickets are from 300 to 500 paces apart, the supports 1,000 paces behind them, and the main body 1,500 paces behind the supports. The main body consists of two thirds of the whole outpost, the remaining third being in the pickets or supports; the infantry are not allowed to leave the vicinity of the stacks of arms, the guns are horsed, and the cavalry horses are saddled and one third of the troopers ready to mount. The supports consist of 8 to 12 men each, and are posted at convenient points to give assistance quickly to the pickets; one half of the men are on duty, the other half resting. The pickets consist of 4 men (6 in the Cossacks); 2 men are resting, grazing their horses, etc., under cover if possible, and the other 2 form the picket, one of whom is always mounted and in observation, and the other under cover if possible, but ready to replace the first if he is hit, or to carry messages, etc.

A squadron of cavalry can watch a front of about 3,000 to 4,000 paces, a company of infantry from 1,000 to 1,500 paces.

7. *Marches.*

All troops marching in the neighborhood of the enemy are formed into an advance guard, main body, and rear guard. The advance guard is about one sixth to one quarter of the whole force, the rear guard one twentieth or less. If the advance guard consists of one or more regiments of infantry, it is accompanied by artillery. The main body follows the advance guard, at a distance at least equal to the length of column of the latter, and in one column if not stronger than a division, or if stronger in two or three columns, according to the nature of the roads and halting places. The advance guard sends advance and flanking detachments, of cavalry if the command contains any, in which case they move out a mile and a half from the bulk of the advance guard; and the flanking detachments send out patrols of 10 or 15 men to a further distance of two thirds of a mile. If the command contains no cavalry, these advance and flanking detachments are formed of infantry, which must not be separated by more than 300 to 400 paces from the bulk of the advance guard. The rear guard marches in rear of and as guard to the wagon train immediately accompanying the troops.

The rates of march, under good conditions of weather and roads, are as follows, per hour:

For infantry	$2\frac{3}{4}$ miles.
For foot artillery	$3\frac{1}{8}$ "
For cavalry and horse artillery, at a walk	$3\frac{1}{4}$ "
For cavalry and horse artillery, alternately at walk and trot	$4\frac{3}{8}$ "
Horse train	$2\frac{3}{8}$ "
Ox train	2 "

The length of a division of infantry on the march, in column of double files or sections, is from 3,000 to 4,000 paces; and including its wagon train, from 9,000 to 12,000 paces. The length of a cavalry division on the march, in column of threes, is from 4,000 to 5,000 paces, and including its train, from 9,000 to 10,000 paces.

PART II.

THE CAMPAIGN IN BULGARIA.

THE CAMPAIGN IN BULGARIA.

INTRODUCTORY.

DECLARATION OF WAR.—THE THEATRE OF OPERATIONS.—PLAN OF CAMPAIGN.

ON the 24th of April, 1877, the Emperor of Russia promulgated at Kishineff his manifesto, reciting his warm interest in the welfare of the oppressed Christian races in Turkey and his desire to ameliorate their condition, which desire was shared by the whole Russian people, and stating that for two years—ever since the disturbances in Bosnia—he had constantly striven, in concert with the other European powers, by peaceful negotiations, to induce the Porte to introduce those reforms to which it was solemnly bound by previous engagements, and by which alone the Christians in Turkey could be protected from local exaction and extortion; that these negotiations had all failed through the obstinacy of the Porte; and now, all peaceful methods being exhausted, the moment had arrived for him to act independently and impose his will on the Turks by force; and therefore the order had been given to his army to cross the Turkish frontier.

In the previous month of November the six army corps (VII., VIII., IX., X., XI., and XII.), occupying the districts nearest the Roumanian frontier, had been mobilized, and four of them had been concentrated in the vicinity of Kishineff, the other two remaining near Odessa and in the Crimea. Later in the winter the IV., XIII., and XIV. Corps had also been mobilized, but had remained in their respective districts in the interior, at a distance by rail of from 400 to 800 miles.

The "Army of the South," under the command of the Grand Duke Nicholas, which was ordered to cross the frontier on the 24th of April, consisted of the four corps at Kishineff and two rifle brigades. A few days later (May 8) the IV., XIII., and XIV. Corps were also placed under his orders, and moved forward to the frontier by rail. The organization of the Russian army corps has been previously explained (p. 31) to consist of two divisions (24 battalions) of infantry, two brigades (96 guns) of artillery, and one division (18 squadrons) of cavalry, with two batteries (12 guns). With seven army corps and two rifle brigades, therefore, the force which was thought sufficient for the invasion of Turkey consisted of about 180 battalions, 200 squadrons, and 800 guns—in all, about 200,000 men, which the usual casualties in the way of sickness, detachments, etc., at the beginning of a campaign, would reduce to 180,000 effectives by the time they reached the Danube. From this great defect of insufficiency of numbers more than from any other cause came the checks and reverses which Russia met with after crossing the Danube.

The exact number of troops which Turkey had under arms in Europe at the outbreak of the war it is not possible to state; but in round numbers she had about 360 battalions, 85 squadrons, and 450 guns—an effective force of about 250,000 men of regular troops (*nizam* and *redif*), distributed as follows:

In the western provinces from Bosnia to Thessaly, including the army operating against Montenegro.	85,000
On the Upper Danube, at Widdin	60,000
In the quadrilateral of fortresses, Rustchuk, Silistria, Varna, Shumla	50,000
In detachments at minor points along the whole length of the Danube	15,000
South of the Balkans, at Sophia, Philippopolis, Adrianople, and Constantinople.	40,000
Total	250,000

Of these, 165,000 were immediately available for operations in Bulgaria.

During the month of July the Egyptian contingent, 12,000 men, arrived at Varna, and Suleiman's Montenegrin army of about 40,000 men was brought by sea to Enos, and thence to

DECLARATION OF WAR.

Adrianople, thus making a total of 217,000 on the theatre of war in Europe in the month of August. In Asia there was a vast recruiting ground which supplied recruits during the whole war, but the number of them it is not possible to state. But in general terms it may be said that Turkey had 225,000 men on the theatre of operations in Europe; and, until the collapse in the month of January, she replaced her losses by recruits, and maintained her army at about that strength.

From the above statement it will be seen that in artillery the Turks had only something more than half of that possessed by the Russians, and that their regular cavalry was lamentably deficient in numbers. But, on the other hand, they were far superior in the quality of their armament; their artillery was all composed of Krupp's steel breech-loaders, of 8 and 9 centimetres caliber, which, in quality of metal, in range, accuracy, and lightness, were superior to the bronze pieces of the Russians. (See pp. 59 to 63.) In small arms, the great majority of the troops were armed with the Peabody-Martini gun, caliber .45, made by the Providence Tool Company of Rhode Island—an arm which has no superior among modern breech-loaders; there were over 300,000 of these guns on hand at the beginning of the war, and about 200,000 were subsequently received. The rest of the troops were armed with the English Snyder, caliber .58, a gun superior to the Russian Krenk. (See p. 52.) Only the cavalry on the Turkish side was inferior in armament to the cavalry of the Russians; the latter had the short Berdan (see p. 73), while the Turks had the Winchester, which, although a repeating arm, has such a small charge and short range as to make it a very inferior weapon.

In order to make up their deficiency in cavalry, the Turks had recourse to the irregular troops known as Bashi-bozouks.* These were principally composed of the Tcherkesses who were brought from Circassia in 1866 and settled in Bulgaria and Roumelia; they furnished their own horses, and the Government supplied them with arms and ammunition. These troops were insubordinate and unruly, occupied in marauding and pillaging instead of reconnoitring, cowardly and disobedient in battle, and of no military service whatever to the Turks.

* The Turkish words *bashi bozouk* mean simply irregular soldier, or, as we would say, "guerilla," i. e., a man who is a farmer one day and a soldier the next.

The Theatre of Operations.

(See Plate 2.)

The Carpathian Mountains or Transylvanian Alps, coming from Galicia in a southerly direction, form the boundary between Hungary and Moldavia for a distance of about 150 miles; then they suddenly turn due westward for another 150 miles, forming the northern boundary of Wallachia; here they again turn southward, are cut through by the Danube at the Iron Gates, and then lose their identity in the confused mountains of Servia. From these latter runs a small range known as the Etropol Balkans, in a southeasterly direction, until it joins the main chain of the Balkans, which goes due east into the Black Sea. Between the Carpathians and the Balkans is the valley of the Danube, about 200 miles broad. On the northeastern slope of the Carpathians begins a region stretching far away across Russia, known as the "Steppe," and similar in every respect to the plains of Kansas and Colorado. In Galicia rises the Dniester, which flows southeasterly through these plains for 500 miles, and empties into the Black Sea near Odessa. Nearer the Carpathians are two slightly smaller streams, the Pruth and the Sereth, which have a parallel course, and empty into the Danube on either side of Galatz. Along the east-and-west portion of the Carpathians the slopes of the mountains extend southerly for about 50 miles from their crest. The remaining 80 miles to the Danube is made up of the flat, treeless Wallachian plains—the counterpart of those of southern Illinois; the soil is fertile, and well watered by a great number of streams flowing southeasterly from the mountains to the Danube. The northern banks of this river from Widdin to Galatz are nowhere more than 100 feet above the level of the stream, and usually not more than 40 feet. On the other side of the Danube the country is of a totally different character; the Balkans, whose crest is from 3,500 to 5,000 feet above the sea, send their foot-hills to the very bank of the Danube, which is from 500 to 1,000 feet above the river-bed; the country is rolling and hilly, well wooded, and has numerous rich valleys, through which streams flow from the Balkans to the Danube.

The Danube, after breaking through the Carpathians at the Iron Gates, flows in a southerly direction for 70 miles to Widdin, then keeps a generally easterly course for 250 miles, arriving within 35 miles of the Black Sea; then it suddenly turns north, and reaches the sea by going around a right angle, the total length of which is about 175 miles. The country inclosed within this rectangle is known as the Dobrudja; it has a barren and sandy soil, and is remarkable for its scarcity of wood and water; across its narrowest part are still seen the remnants of Trajan's wall, built by that conqueror to protect his newly acquired provinces from the northern hordes.

From Widdin to Silistria the Danube bears a striking resemblance to the Missouri between Bismarck and Omaha; from bluff to bluff the distance is about three miles, and in the bed there are from two to five streams separated by islands of various sizes and constantly varying shapes; the largest stream is usually about 1,000 yards in width, and it has a tortuous channel through which eight feet of draught can usually be carried at all seasons; the current is swift—two and one half to three miles an hour. On the western side of the Dobrudja the bed is over ten miles wide, and consists of an impassable swamp (broken by the bluff at Hirsova), through which the river winds its way in several streams.

In Roumania there is one main line of railway, which comes from Austria over the Galician frontier, and descends the valley of the Sereth to its mouth at Galatz; thence it goes west by a very irregular route to Bucharest; and from there again in a very winding direction it goes on to the west, reaching the Danube at Turn-Severin, near the Iron Gates—the corner of the frontiers of Austria, Roumania, and Servia. Near the Galician frontier a branch line turns off to Yassy, and thence, crossing the Pruth at the little village of Ungheni, goes on past Kishineff, and near Odessa joins the main system of Russian roads. From Bucharest another branch line goes down to the Danube at Giurgevo, and connects with a line on the other side of the Danube which runs from Rustchuk past Shumla to Varna, on the Black Sea coast. The line of Trajan's wall in the Dobrudja is followed by another railway, from Tchernavoda on the Danube to Kustendje on the Black Sea.

These are the only railroads between the Carpathians and

the Balkans.* The Roumanian railroad follows such an irregular course that the distance from Kishineff to Bucharest is 425 miles by rail, though only about 250 by post-road.

In Roumania there are now excellent post-roads connecting all the larger towns; as there was no fighting on that side of the river, it is not necessary to enumerate them. In Bulgaria, on the other hand, there are very few good roads; they will be described in subsequent chapters.

Russian Plan of Campaign.

Between the slopes of the southeastern bend of the Carpathians and the Black Sea the distance is but 120 miles in a straight line, and through this space of course any advance from Russia to Turkey must be made; the Danube divides it into two parts, on one side the Dobrudja, on the other Roumania. By the treaty of Paris in 1856 an artificial boundary line was created, which caused the frontiers of Russia and Turkey to be separated by a narrow strip of territory which was given to the Principalities; and by the same instrument the naval forces of Russia on the Black Sea were destroyed—both measures being aimed to hinder Russia's future operations against Turkey. The former clause proved of no avail, for when the war was declared a convention was at once concluded with Roumania allowing the passage of Russian troops through her territory; the latter clause was wholly revoked by the convention of 1871, but between that time and 1877 Russia had not been able to construct a fleet on the Black Sea which could in any way cope with the powerful ironclads which Turkey had meanwhile been buying in England.

Had Russia had control of the Black Sea, the natural plan of campaign would have been to advance by the Dobrudja, using the ports of the Black Sea as bases of supply; capturing Varna (the only fortified place on the seacoast) by a combined land and sea attack, and masking the other three fortresses, they could have crossed the eastern passes of the Balkans (which are much lower than the western), as Diebitch did in 1829, and thus have reached Adrianople, always basing themselves on the

---

* During the war the Russians built a railroad direct from Bender on the Dniester to Galatz, and also extended the Roumanian railroad from Giurgevo to the bridge at Zimnitza-Sistova.

PLAN OF CAMPAIGN.

Black Sea. But, not having the control of the sea, such a plan was impossible; for they could not have maintained their long, narrow line of communications between the Danube on one side and the sea on the other, both in possession of the enemy's fleet; and the three strongest of the fortresses, Varna, Shumla, and Rustchuk, being connected by a railway, would have constituted a line of defense which it would have been hard to break, for it is well known that the Turks fight well behind fortifications.

The plan therefore adopted was to seize the railway bridge at the mouth of the Sereth, thus securing the line of the Roumanian railway; to send one corps across the Danube at Braila into the Dobrudja in order to protect their rear against any attack by that route, and to march the bulk of the army through Roumania and cross the Danube at Nikopolis or at some point between that and Rustchuk; then to post a strong force along the line of the Yantra or the Lom, in order to mask the quadrilateral; another force on the Vid or Isker to act against the army at Widdin, and, the flanks being thus protected as by two walls, to advance over the Balkans to Adrianople. Had the campaign been begun (as it was ended) by 375,000 instead of 200,000 men, it is quite possible that this plan might have been carried out with very little deviation (until checked by foreign intervention); but, with the insufficient force at hand, having crossed the Danube, seized a pass in the Balkans, and posted the sufficient portions on either flank, there were no troops left to send over the Balkans; and, by the time the reënforcements arrived, affairs had taken quite a different turn.

The campaign, as it resulted, lasted forty-five weeks, and naturally divides itself into three distinct portions, as follows:

1st. Ten weeks, from April 24th to July 3d—the concentration in Roumania, passage of the Danube, and establishment on its southern bank.

2d. Twenty-three weeks, July 4th to December 10th—the operations in Bulgaria up to the fall of Plevna.

3d. Twelve weeks, December 11th to March 3d (Treaty of San Stefano)—the passage of the Balkans and march to Constantinople.

In the first period the line of march (from Kishineff to Sistova) was by the road 370 miles; in the second period, for one column (Sistova to Shipka) 80 miles, for the other column (Sistova to the Orkhanie pass) 150 miles; in the third period, for the Shipka column (Shipka to San Stefano via Adrianople) 300 miles, for the Sophia column (Orkhanie pass via Sophia, Philippopolis, and Adrianople to San Stefano) 450 miles. The total line of direct march was therefore, for the Shipka column 750 miles, for the Sophia column 970 miles.

CHAPTER I.

FIRST PERIOD OF THE WAR.—APRIL 24TH TO JUNE 27TH.—THE CONCENTRATION IN ROUMANIA AND THE PASSAGE OF THE DANUBE.

AT the declaration of war the *Army of the South* was composed as follows : *

	Battalions.	Foot Guns.	Squadrons.	Horse Guns.	
VIII. Corps, Lt.-Gen. *Radetsky.*					Commander-in-Chief,
9th and 14th Infantry Divisions	24	96	..	..	General H. I. H. Grand
8th Cavalry Division	..	..	18	12	Duke *Nicholas.*
IX. Corps, Lt.-Gen. Baron *Krüdener.*					Chief of Staff, General
5th and 31st Infantry Divisions	24	96	..	..	*Nepokoitchitsky.*
9th Cavalry Division	..	..	18	12	Chief of Artillery, Lt.-
XI. Corps, Lt.-Gen. Prince *Shakofskoi.*					Gen. Prince *Massalski.*
11th and 32d Infantry Divisions	24	96	..	..	Chief of Engineers,
11th Cavalry Division	..	..	18	12	Major-Gen. *Depp.*
XII. Corps, Lt.-Gen. *Vannofsky.*					
12th and 33d Infantry Divisions	24	96	..	..	
12th Cavalry Division	..	..	18	12	
3d Rifle Brigade, Major-Gen. *Dobrovolski*	4	..	..	..	
4th Rifle Brigade, Major-Gen. *Zviasinski*	4	..	..	..	
United Cossack Division, Lt. Gen. *Skobeleff I.*					
Caucasian Cossack Brigade	..	..	10	} 6	
Terek Cossack Regiment	..	..	4		
Don Cossack Regiment No. 80	..	..	6		
Unattached Cossacks of the Don.					
Reg'ts Nos. 21, 23, 26, 29, 31, 34, 35, 37, 40	..	..	54	46†	
Total	104	384	144	100	

This force was posted along the Russian frontier, its right flank at the village of Ungheni on the railroad, and its left flank at the village of Kubei, which is situated at the angle of the frontier 50 miles northeast of Galatz.
The headquarters were at Kishineff.

* The VII. and X. Corps also formed part of the Army of the South, but they were formed into a separate detachment for the "defense of the coasts," and were stationed in the Crimea and along the coast near Odessa. A portion of the 7th Cavalry Division joined Zimmermann's Corps in the Dobrudja during the month of July, and one infantry regiment of the same (VII.) corps advanced against Sulina in the month of October. But the rest of them never crossed the Russian frontier, and have therefore been omitted in the above table.

† Including 16 mountain guns.

The auxiliary, or technical troops, were as follows:

1. *Engineers.*

3d Engineer Brigade, Major-General Richter, composed of
  5th Sapper Battalion,
  6th Sapper Battalion,
  5th Pontonier Battalion,
  6th Pontonier Battalion,
  5th Field Telegraph Park,
  6th Field Telegraph Park,
  2d Field Engineer Park.
  2d Siege Engineer Park,
  6th Railroad Battalion;

in all about 5,000 men, with the tools and appliances of their special arms.

Portions of 2d and 4th Engineer Brigades, viz.:
  3d Pontonier Battalion,
  4th Pontonier Battalion,
  7th Sapper Battalion;
about 2,000 men.

With these troops were 4 pontoon trains, each consisting of 26 iron boats and all their appurtenances, making in all 104 boats, or the material for about 900 yards of bridge.

2. *Heavy Artillery.*

A siege artillery park of 400 guns, as follows:
  200 6-inch (24-pdr.) siege guns (bronze),
  80 4-inch (9-pdr.) siege guns, (cast steel), } all breech-loading.
  40 8-inch rifled mortars (bronze),
  40 6-inch rifled mortars (bronze),
  40 4-inch smooth-bore mortars,
and their train, platforms, tools, etc.

The total number of men serving this park was about 10,000. It was divided into 12 divisions, of which Nos. 1 and 2 were for investment, 3 to 10 for bombardment (as at Braila, etc.), 11 and 12 for reserve.

3. *Naval Troops.*

  2 companies of the "Crew of the Guard,"
  2 companies of "Crew No. 1 of the Black Sea."

CONCENTRATION IN ROUMANIA. 149

These men were destined for the service of torpedoes, guards of bridges, etc. Their material included 24 steam torpedo launches, divided into sections for transportation, and the necessary torpedo material.

4. *Hospital Department.*

42 Field Hospitals, each with tents, clothing, medicines, surgical apparatus, train, etc., for from 600 to 1,000 patients.

These were in addition to the Division Hospitals accompanying the troops on the field.

The personnel of these hospitals numbered in all about 5,000 men.

5. *Intendance Department.*

14 Divisions of Intendance Transport, each consisting of 350 wagons.

These were in addition to the Intendants (Chief Quartermaster and Commissary) of the Corps and Divisions, and their clerks, etc.

6. *Gendarmerie* (Provost Marshal's Department).

3d and 4th Squadrons of Field Gendarmes, about 500 men.

The troops which by imperial order of May 6th were added to the "Army of the South," and ordered to the frontier by rail, were as follows:

	Battalions.	Foot Artill'y Guns.	Squadrons.	Horse Artill'y Guns.
XIV. Corps, Lieutenant-General *Zimmermann.*				
17th and 18th Infantry Divisions.................	24	96	..	..
1st Don Cossack Cavalry Division.................	..	..	24	12
IV. Corps, Lieutenant-General *Zotof.*				
16th and 30th Infantry Divisions.................	24	96	..	..
4th Cavalry Division..........................	..	..	18	12
XIII. Corps, Lieutenant-General Prince *Koreakoff.*				
1st and 33d Infantry Divisions.................	24	90	..	..
13th Cavalry Division..........................	..	..	18	12
Total...	72	288	60	36
To this must be added the Bulgarian Militia, formed partly during the previous winter and partly during the month of May, consisting of...	6	..	..	..
GRAND TOTAL of *Army of the South*...............	159	672	204	186

i. e., about 200,000 combatants of all arms.

On the morning of the 24th of April the troops crossed the frontier in four columns, viz.:

Right Wing. (See Plate 4.) Fifty squadrons of cavalry (8th and 12th Divisions, 21st, 26th and 37th Regiments Don Cossacks), under Lieutenant-General Baron Driesen, which crossed the frontier at Ungheni and bivouacked that night at Yassy. Their route thence lay along the base of the mountains to Ploiesti, and thence to Bucharest, the 8th Cavalry Division going on to the Danube opposite Nikopolis.

Center, (XII. Corps, 5th Infantry Division, 34th Regiment Don Cossacks), which crossed a few miles south of Ungheni, and then took a road parallel to the Pruth and about 20 miles from it, as far as Foksani, and thence followed the cavalry column to Bucharest.

Left Wing, composed of (*a*) advance guard under Lieutenant-General Skobeleff, 1st Brigade of Caucasian Cossacks, 23d Regiment Don Cossacks, two sotnias of plastounes, 4th Rifle Brigade and all the mountain artillery; (*b*) 11th Cavalry Division and (*c*) VIII. Corps, the whole under command of Lieutenant-General Radetzky—which crossed the frontier at the village of Bestamak, 50 miles southwest of Kisheneff. Late that evening, after a ride of 65 miles, the cavalry reached the Sereth and took possession of the railroad bridge near Galatz; it subsequently moved on to Bucharest, and the detachment of Skobeleff came down to the Danube opposite Rustchuk; the 11th Cavalry Division took the road arriving on the Danube opposite Silistria; the VIII. Corps followed Skobeleff's detachment as far as Bucharest.

Column of the Lower Danube, composed of the infantry of the XI. Corps, under Lieutenant-General Prince Shakofskoi, which crossed the frontier at Kubei, and proceeded to Galatz and Braila, relieving the cavalry which had previously arrived there, and then sending detachments to occupy all the principal points on the left bank of the Danube as far as Ismail. The 11th Infantry Division of this corps was then sent forward, and reached the Danube at Oltenitza, opposite Turtukai.

The portion of the IX. Corps which had not marched on with General Vannofsky was sent forward as soon as opportunity offered by rail from Ungheni to Slatina, 80 miles west of Bucharest.

On the 24th of May, one month from the date of crossing the frontier, the army was concentrated opposite the portion of the Danube selected for the passage; the bulk of it ($2\frac{1}{2}$ corps) being at Bucharest, with a detachment ($\frac{1}{2}$ corps) on its right flank at Slatina, and a strong line of cavalry pickets with infantry supports along the river bank from Nikopolis to Silistria, where the swampy section of the river begins. The headquarters were at Ploiesti. The date set for the passage was the 6th of June, but this was found to be an impossibility because the bridge materials could not arrive by that time. The spring was an unusually wet one, and on the 1st of June the level of the Danube at Galatz was 15 feet above the ordinary level of that date; and the floods on the smaller streams had carried away several railroad bridges, thus greatly delaying matters. This railroad was totally unequal to the task demanded of it; it was a single track line with a small quantity of rolling stock and insufficient terminal facilities in the way of switches and sidings. Moreover, the Russian railway having a gauge of 5 feet, while the Roumanian had the ordinary gauge of 4 feet $8\frac{1}{2}$ inches, it was not only not possible to supplement the rolling stock by that from Russia, but it necessitated a complete transfer of all freight and passengers at Yassy. In addition to the greater part of the IX. Corps (which might just as well have been marched by road), this single-track railway was required to transport the siege guns and material and ammunition for the batteries at Braila and Galatz, and those opposite Silistria, Rustchuk and Nikopolis, the four pontoon trains attached to the army (104 boats and their wagons and materials), a large number of wooden pontoons built at Galatz, more than 25 steam torpedo-boats and the torpedo materials, and all the hard bread and a few other articles of the rations for the army.

As a result of these various causes of delay, the army remained stationary in the positions previously described for the next month (May 24th to June 24th). The XIV. Corps as it arrived was directed (June 13th) on Galatz, where it relieved the portion of the XI. Corps which was guarding the lower Danube, which portion then proceeded to join the rest of the corps opposite Turtukai. The XIII. Corps was ordered to be at Alexandria (60 miles southwest of Bucharest) by the 27th of June; the IV. Corps to come on by rail to Bucharest and await further orders.

While the army was waiting the arrival of the bridge material, great activity was displayed by the Russians in endeavoring to neutralize the action of the Turkish flotilla by means of torpedoes. At the beginning of the war the Turks had in the Lower Danube below Braila a fleet of 8 large ironclads, with armor of not less than 4 inches in thickness, and carrying altogether about 30 guns. Far from preventing the capture of the bridge over the Sereth or destroying it, these ships retired down the river at the approach of the Russians. Higher up on the river, from Hirsova to Widdin, they had 7 light iron-plated gunboats and 18 wooden ships, carrying in all about 1,000 men and 60 guns. Within a week from the time war was declared the Russians succeeded in placing a line of torpedoes across the river at Reni, which cut off the fleet of large ironclads and restricted them henceforth to the Sulina mouth of the river. A few days later they succeeded in placing another barricade of torpedoes across the river opposite Braila. These two barricades protected the mouths of the Pruth and Sereth, as well as the town of Galatz. They consisted of the ordinary submarine mines, anchored in two rows; their mechanism was so arranged as to explode automatically on contact, as well as by electricity from the shore. They were anchored in the night by means of steam torpedo-boats (ten of which had already arrived by rail), protected by the 9-pdr. field batteries on shore. On the 6th of May a portion of the up-river flotilla, consisting of five monitors and two wooden ships, approached Braila and opened fire upon the Russian batteries and the town; but by this time the Russian batteries at this point were partially armed (viz., with ten 24-pdr. siege guns and four 6-in. rifled mortars); and on the 10th a shell from one of the mortars penetrated the deck of one the largest monitors, the Lufti-Djelil, and exploded in the powder magazine. She blew up and sank instantly, with all her crew of 17 officers and 200 men. The ship was a twin-screw, ironclad, sea-going Monitor, carrying four 150-pdr. Armstrong guns.

On the 25th of May Lieutenant Dubassoff, of the Russian Navy, obtained permission to try to blow up one of the Turkish monitors by means of a torpedo from an open boat, in which he was as completely successful as was Cushing against the Albemarle, and under very similar circumstances. He took four steam launches, carrying in all 6 officers and 40 men, and rigged with spars for torpedoes. Leaving the port of Braila at midnight of a dark rainy night, he arrived about half past two in the morning in the midst of a fleet of two Turkish ironclads and one wooden ship, anchored in the Matchin channel. He was discovered by the sentinel, and all their ships opened fire on him with musketry. He immediately put on full steam and went straight at the largest monitor, and exploded his torpedo under her port quarter. The ship began sinking by the stern, but slowly, and he then called out to Lieutenant Shestakoff, who commanded the launch just behind him, to "come on." This officer then came forward with his launch at full steam, and exploded a second torpedo under the monitor amidships; the ship sank in the course of a few minutes. Meanwhile Dubassoff's launch had been filled with water by the first explosion; Shestakoff's boat had got some of the débris of the monitor tangled in her propeller; the third boat had been pierced by a shell; and only the fourth was not disabled, and was endeavoring to assist the other three. It was a considerable time before the little fleet of boats could repair damages, pump out, and retire. During all this time the Turks kept firing at them with artillery and musketry; but, owing to the darkness and general confusion, the Russians finally managed to escape, *without a single man being hurt.*

The Turkish ship was the Scifé, which is described in the Turkish navy list of 1876 as a light-draught river gunboat, protected with two inches of armor, 115 feet long, armed with two 80-lb. breech-loading Armstrong guns placed in a battery on the fore part of the deck, and two smaller guns near the stern; her crew was about 120 men.

On the 10th of June the Russian steamer Constantine put out from Odessa with six torpedo launches in tow, bound for Sulina. She arrived in that vicinity during the night, and at two o'clock in the morning sent the launches in toward the shore; they found three Turkish ironclads at anchor, and one under steam in the roadstead outside the jetties, which they immediately attacked; but the torpedo of the leading launch exploded before reaching the ship's side (the officer of the boat claimed that the monitor was protected by a wire netting). This gave the alarm to the whole fleet, and the launches were obliged to escape as best they could back to the Constantine and out to sea. One of them was disabled and captured with her crew, including one officer.

On the 20th of June ten steam launches which had been carried overland were launched in the Danube at a point about ten miles above Rustchuk, and at 4 o'clock in the morning Commander Novikoff began placing a barricade of torpedoes across the river at Parapan, in order to isolate the monitors at Rustchuk. He was discovered at 5 o'clock by the Turks, who sent out a monitor, which opened on the launches with shrapnel. Commander Novikoff immediately sent a launch to attack the monitor with a torpedo. The torpedo was disabled before reaching the monitor, owing, as it is claimed, to the wire being cut by bullets; but nevertheless the monitor retreated to Rustchuk, and the operation of placing the torpedoes was successfully finished. Nearly every one in this launch was wounded. Just after the launches had finished their work and regained the shore, a Turkish battery came into position on the opposite bank and opened on them. Five of the launches turned up stream and five down, and after steaming a few miles they reached points where they were hauled out of water and carried overland to Turnu; three of them, however, were so damaged as to be temporarily useless.

On the night of the 23d of June, Commander Novikoff succeeded in placing a barricade of torpedoes at Karabia, five miles above Nikopolis, by means of rowboats; he did not use his steam-launches for fear that they might be injured, and they would be so greatly needed in the passage of the river a few days later. On the same day a Turkish monitor from Nikopolis got up steam and came down the river, and was immediately attacked by two launches, and by four light guns on the shore. There was here, as at Parapan, a failure to explode the torpedo successfully; but the audacity of the attack, combined with the very accurate fire of the guns on shore, compelled the monitor to retire hastily to Nikopolis. On the 24th of June another monitor put out from Nikopolis, and endeavored to escape up stream, but she was turned back by the siege guns of the battery on the Russian shore.

After this date no Turkish gunboats ever left the shelter of their fortresses, and the history of the Turkish fleet on the Danube may be summarized as from first to last a complete failure.

Two of their river ironclads were sunk, two more were captured subsequently at the surrender of Nikopolis, and the other three remained at Rustchuk till the close of the war. Of the large ironclads on the lower river, one was sunk by a stationary torpedo near Sulina in the month of October; the others remained idle in the port of Sulina. The only damage the whole fleet ever did was in wounding five or six men in one boat at Parapan, and in inflicting some slight injuries on three of the launches, which were subsequently repaired. It was not that opportunities were lacking for the flotilla to act. On the breaking out of the war, they could have made an effort to prevent the capture of the bridge over the Sereth, and, failing in this, they might at least have destroyed it, and thereby greatly delayed the Russian operations. Later on, if they had been vigilant and skillful, they might have destroyed a portion at least of the Russian flotilla of small launches; they might have protected their own ships with nettings, and used their small boats to drag for torpedoes, if they could not prevent them from being placed. But they did none of these things; and at the end of two months they found themselves isolated in sections by means of the torpedo barricades, and so alarmed by the loss of two of their ships that the idea of a torpedo became a bugbear to them, and a few launches moving over the water with the motions of planting torpedoes were enough to make them retire under the guns of their forts.

The only means which the Russians used against them were small steam launches and torpedoes, aided somewhat by the batteries on shore. Of these launches the Russians had about 25 at various points on the river at the time of the passage; later on they had 54, engaged in policing the river and guarding the various torpedo barricades. Some of them were of the Thorneycroft pattern, attaining a speed of 15 knots; others were ordinary ship's launches, with the engine covered with bullet-proof boiler-plate iron; the largest of them were not longer than 30 feet, and the most numerous crew 15 men. Their operations were all planned under the general direction of Captain Rogouly of the Russian Navy.

When we remember the brilliant achievements of the gunboat flotillas improvised under the orders of Commodore Foote and Admiral Porter on our Western rivers during the Civil

War, the complete failure of the fine Turkish navy in this instance becomes all the more apparent. The Navy List of Turkey for 1876 gives its strength at 132 vessels and 18,292 officers, seamen, and marines. This force was composed of 15 sea-going ironclads, procured in England at great cost, 5 wooden steam frigates, 11 wooden corvettes, 7 armored river gunboats, and the rest of transport ships, dispatch-boats, yachts, and small wooden craft. The river flotilla accomplished nothing, as just explained, and the sea-going ships did no more; they never penetrated to Odessa or any of the Crimean ports, and their only achievements were the bombardment of a few helpless villages on the Caucasian coast.

The operations of the navy were under the general control of Admiral Hobart Pasha, an ex-officer of the English service.

As previously stated, the Russian plan of campaign involved the passage of the Danube at two points—on the lower river and on its middle course. The first was accomplished without any difficulty whatever (Plate 7). As soon as the river had been cleared of gunboats between Reni and Hirsova, a bridge was thrown across, without opposition, between the 12th and 16th of June, at Braila; but a rise in the water immediately afterward rendered it for the time being useless, as its end on the Turkish shore as well as the opposite country was completely submerged. For this reason General Zimmermann asked permission to delay the passage of his troops until the water was lower; but the Grand Duke replied that it was imperatively necessary for him to pass not later than the 22d. On that day, therefore, two regiments were thrown across the river at Galatz, by means of boats, rafts, and steam-tugs; and after a short struggle, in which the Russians lost 5 officers and 137 men, they gained possession of the opposite heights of Boudjak. Thereupon the Turks abandoned the whole of the lower river, and retired up the Dobrudja, behind the line of Trajan's Wall. As soon as the water was low enough to use his bridge, General Zimmermann crossed his whole force, and advanced slowly in the same direction.

On the middle section of the river the operation was much more difficult. The concentration of the army in front of Bucharest during the last week in May warned the Turks that a passage would be attempted somewhere in that vicinity. They therefore began strengthening the works at Nikopolis, Rustchuk, Turtukai, and Silistria, by the construction of detached earthworks, and they also posted small forces in observation at Sistova and other points, and constructed batteries on the river bank.

The Russians meanwhile had been occupied, as previously explained, in transporting their siege guns and bridge material, and in placing lines of torpedoes across the river, which separated the different parts of the Turkish flotilla from each other, and caused them to retire under the guns of the fortresses. By the 20th of June these operations were nearly completed, and the forward movement was ordered as follows (Plate 4):

IX. Corps to Segartcha.
XII. Corps to Saltcha.
VIII. Corps and 4th Rifle Brigade to Piatra.
XIII. Corps in reserve at Alexandria.
XI. Corps to remain in observation between Giurgevo and Oltenitza, opposite Rustchuk and Turtukai.

The original intention had been to make the passage at Zimnitza-Sistova; but when the army arrived along the Danube, it was reported that the level of the water at Zimnitza was so high that a passage there was impossible. On this information it was determined to cross near Nikopolis, and the forward movement just mentioned was in accordance with that plan, and with the intention of making the passage on the 24th. But just after the order had been issued it was found that a new delay on the railroad would prevent a number of pontoons from reaching the river by the 24th. The army was therefore halted on the line of the river Vede, from Ruse de Vede to Beia, in a position about equidistant from Nikopolis, Sistova, and Rustchuk. While waiting for the pontoons, the Grand Duke and the Chief of Staff made a personal reconnoissance, between the 20th and 24th, of the river bank from Turnu to Sistova, and became convinced that it would be very difficult to force the passage in face of the strong works at Nikopolis; and also that the water had fallen sufficiently at Zimnitza-Sistova to allow the passage. At the last minute, therefore, it was decided to cross at this point; and on the 24th the previous orders were modified as follows:

1. 14th Infantry Division (VIII. Corps), 4th Rifle Brigade, 16 mountain guns, and all the army pontoon trains, to proceed

at once from Beia to Zimnitza, with secret order to pass the river at that point.

2. 9th Infantry Division (VIII. Corps) to continue its march on Piatra; but by special order of the following day it was brought to Zimnitza.

3. XII. Corps to change its march from Saltcha to Piatra.

4. XIII. Corps to move from Alexandria to Piatra.

5. IX. Corps to pass through Segartcha to Siaka, and prepare to pass the river at Flamunda, just below Nikopolis (this latter being a mere feint).

The siege batteries opposite Rustchuk and opposite Nikopolis were ordered to begin the bombardment of these places on the 24th and 25th respectively, and to continue it until further orders.

On the 26th the detachment of General Dragomiroff, consisting of the 14th Division and the troops attached to it, arrived at Zimnitza. At dark that evening the pontons were launched in the creek which runs past the village of Zimnitza, and were then hauled out into the main river and down to the point of embarkation. (See Plate 7.) There were 104 boats of the regular ponton train, 100 boats and rafts which had been constructed in the neighborhood, and four battalions of pontoniers to manœuvre them. The troops numbered in all about 15,000 men, and were divided into six detachments of 2,500 men each, the plan being to cross by detachments in a body; but after the first detachment had crossed this was found to take too much time, and as soon as enough boats returned to take one company they were immediately loaded and sent back.

While the boats were being launched, five batteries (40 guns) of 9-pdrs., supported by regiment No. 35 (of the 9th Division), were established on the northern bank of the main river, to cover the passage, and silence the enemy's batteries on the south bank, as well as the monitors, should they venture down from Nikopolis. The troops began embarking at midnight, and about 1 o'clock in the morning they put out from the shore and began rowing toward the Turkish bank, aiming to reach it at a point about three miles below Sistova, at the mouth of a small stream known as the Tekir-Dere. Just as they were approaching the shore they were discovered by the Turkish outposts, who opened fire upon them and gave the alarm; but the boats, although somewhat dispersed by the wind, reached the shore and landed their men in the vicinity of the point designated. The twelve companies composing this first detachment formed on the bank and climbed up the steep bluff, driving before them the line of Turkish skirmishers. By 2 o'clock they had gained possession of the banks of this little stream, and of a neighboring hill, about three quarters of a mile from the shore and east of the Tekir-Dere. Soon after this the day began to dawn, and the Turks were thoroughly aroused by the noise. They had in this vicinity one camp on the heights southeast of Sistova, counting perhaps 5,000 men, with one battery of 6 guns, and another camp about 6 miles from Sistova on the road to Rustchuk, in which there were probably about the same number of men; but these numbers can not be stated with any accuracy. The little creek Tekir-Dere was about equidistant from these two camps. As soon as the Turks were fully aroused they re-enforced their skirmish line near the river bank between Sistova and the point of landing, and they also took position in front of the Russians on the heights, which rise behind each other in terraces parallel to the river. They also had a battery in Sistova; and from the whole line they opened a very hot fire on the ponton boats which continued to arrive, and they succeeded in sinking five of them and killing and wounding in all about 100 men in the boats.

About 5 A.M. General Dragomiroff, accompanied by Major General Skobeleff II. as a volunteer, arrived on the southern bank and took command. He immediately sent about 15 companies of the 1st brigade of his division on the left of the Tekir-Dere to attack the troops coming from the camp in that direction; meanwhile forming the rest of his troops as they arrived in the valley of this little creek, and then advancing them gradually on both sides of it. By 8 o'clock in the morning the 1st brigade had gained possession of some small heights in its front, which secured the passage from any attack on that side of the little stream. Soon afterward the troops began to arrive more rapidly, thanks to the assistance of a steamboat which had run past the batteries at Nikopolis during the night. By 11 o'clock the 2d brigade of the 14th Division, as well as the 4th Rifle brigade, had arrived and formed on the right of the Tekir-Dere. General Dragomiroff then ordered the principal movement of the day, which was an advance against the heights behind Sistova by the 2d brigade, supported on its right flank by the Rifle brigade, which took the direction of the road toward Sistova, the 1st brigade remaining on the ground it had taken. This advance was covered by the Russian batteries on the other side of the river, which succeeded in silencing the Turkish batteries; the Turks made but a feeble resistance, and at 2 o'clock the Russians gained possession of the heights behind Sistova, and at 3 o'clock entered the town itself. The Turks abandoned all their positions and retreated by the high-road to Tirnova, a portion of those nearest Sistova retreating to Nikopolis. Their losses are not known; those of the Russians were as follows:

	Officers.	Men.
Killed	9	291
Wounded	22	446
Missing	..	53
Total	31	790

of whom over 600 belonged to the two regiments (Volhynia No. 53 and Minsk No. 54) of the 1st brigade, which had done the fighting on the east of the creek early in the morning.

About 3 o'clock in the afternoon General Radetzky, commanding the VIII. Corps, crossed to the Turkish side, and immediately afterward the troops of the 9th Division, which had arrived at Zimnitza during the day, also began coming over. By 9 o'clock in the evening the whole of the VIII. Corps as well as the 4th Rifle brigade, 25,000 men in all, were established in good defensible positions on the Turkish shore. The passage was therefore secured, after 20 hours of labor and a loss of 800 men.

During the next day, June 28th, the 35th Division (XII. Corps) was ferried over on pontons, and at the same time the construction of a bridge was commenced, which was finished on the 2d of July.

In ten weeks from the opening of hostilities, therefore, the Russians had established themselves on the southern bank of the Danube, and with a loss which, in comparison to the importance of the success, was totally insignificant.

The question naturally arises, what were the Turks doing all this time? And it is difficult to give a satisfactory answer to this question, as no official reports or other trustworthy data have ever been published on the Turkish side. It may be said, however, that their defense had been by no means an energetic one. The mobilization of six Russian army corps and their concentration along the Pruth in the months of November and December, 1876, were as well known to the Turks as to the rest of the world; it was also perfectly apparent that if war did break out the Russians had the choice of only two plans, either to cross the lower Danube into the Dobrudja or to advance through the narrow space between the Danube at Galatz and the Carpathians, toward some point on the middle Danube. As they had no navy to cover any operations on the Black Sea, a landing on the coast at Kustendje or Varna, or other point, was not to be feared. If, therefore, the Turks meant to oppose an energetic resistance to the Russian advance, it was very plain that their most advantageous position from which to do so was the Dobrudja. An army of 100,000 men posted behind the river in the northwest corner of this rectangle could oppose the crossing of the lower river, or, if the Russians attempted to march past, could strike them on the flank *en route*. On the declaration of war it could seize the towns of Braila, Galatz, Reni and Ismail, on the northern bank, and fortify them as *têtes-de-pont*, and get possession of the railway bridge at Galatz, over which passes the one railway of Roumania. For their own supplies they had the harbor of Kustendje and the Kustendje-Tchernavoda Railroad, which is only 70 miles from the Danube at Galatz; they also had the Danube itself by which to bring supplies.

But instead of taking positions from which they could strike the Russians as soon as they crossed the frontier, the Turks passed the winter preceding the declaration of war with an army of 50,000 to 60,000 men in the quadrilateral, another of about the same size 200 miles away at Widdin, and a few weak garrisons along the Danube. Whether it was Oriental procrastination, or because, as has been pretended, they had a deep plan of luring the Russians across the Danube and then overwhelming them, or, as is more likely, because they had no very definite plan of campaign beyond simply waiting, according to their traditional mode of warfare, behind fortifications to be attacked, it is hardly possible to state; but the fact is certain that they allowed the Russians to make their preparations for war without taking proper steps to meet them; that when war was declared they opposed only the most feeble resistance to the passage of the lower river; and, when the passage of the middle course was threatened by the concentration of the Russian army to the southwest of Bucharest, they made no movements to oppose it beyond a slight increase of the Danube garrisons and the construction of a few batteries on the river bank. They made no *active* defense. Although the Russians remained near Bucharest for nearly a month waiting for their bridge and siege material, yet the Turks pushed no reconnaissances to develop their strength, position and movements; and more than all, they did not assemble a mobile army at some central point behind the threatened line, ready to move at once to the point where the real passage should begin, and attack the invaders before they got a firm footing on the southern bank.

Von Moltke, in his account of the campaign of 1828 (which was a campaign of sieges), remarks that "the Turks usually began their resistance at that point where in other sieges it usually terminates; i. e., after the crowning of the covered way and the opening of a breach." In the campaign of 1877 there were no regular sieges, but the Turks fought a purely defensive campaign, in which the resistance began only after the Russians were well over the Danube and the first line of Turkish defense was wholly lost.

CHAPTER II.

OPERATIONS OF THE ADVANCE GUARD UNDER GOURKO, JULY 12TH TO AUGUST 6TH.

BETWEEN the Balkans and the Danube there are but two short lines of railway, viz.: that from Rustchuk to Varna, 140 miles, and that along the line of Trajan's wall, 40 miles. Both these roads were in possession of the Turks. In that portion of Bulgaria which became the theatre of the principal military operations, the *chaussées* are as follows:

1. From Rustchuk, via Razgrad, to Shumla and Varna.
2. From Rustchuk, via Razgrad, Eski-Djuma, Osman-Bazar, Kazan (the Kazan Pass), Slivno, and Yeni-Zagra, to Hermanli, and thence to Adrianople.
3. From Sistova, via Tirnova, Gabrova, Shipka Pass, Kazanlyk, and Eski-Zagra, to Trnova, and thence to Adrianople.
4. From Rahova, via Vratza, to Orkhanie and Sophia.
5. From Lom Palanka, via Berkovitza, to Sophia.
6. From Widdin, via Pirot, to Sophia.
7. From Rustchuk, via Biela, Plevna, Lukovitza, and Orkhanie, to Sophia.
8. From Shumla, via Osman-Bazar, Tirnova, Selvi, and Lovtcha, to Plevna.

All these were good, hard, macadamized roads, and were in excellent condition at the beginning of the campaign, and remained so until they had been ruined in some places by the passage of immense artillery and transport trains, and the failure to promptly repair the damages made by them.

Besides these *chaussées* there were common country roads connecting all the larger villages. During the summer, when there was no rain, these roads were always passable, barring slight delays at the small bridges crossing the various streams. When the autumn rains came on in September they soon became wholly impassable.

The bridge at Sistova was finished, as previously stated, on the 2d of July, five days after the passage had been made, and the bulk of the army began passing over in the following order:

1. Advance Guard under Gourko, July 3d.
2. XIII. Corps (except the 35th Infantry Division, which had been ferried over in boats June 28th), July 3d–4th.
3. XII. Corps, July 5th–8th.
4. IX. Corps, July 8th–10th.
5. XI. Corps, July 10th–15th.
6. IV. Corps, July 20th–30th.

In accordance with the general plan of campaign previously explained, Gourko was to push forward rapidly to the Balkans by the main road passing through Tirnova; the VIII. Corps was to follow the same road; the XIII. Corps, followed by the XII., was to take the line of the Yantra on the left flank; the IX. Corps was to attack Nikopolis and the line of the Vid on the right flank; the XI. and IV. Corps were for the present to be held in reserve.

On the 5th of July the cavalry of the XIII. Corps captured the town of Biela, after a short skirmish with some Tcherkesses, and the next day it was occupied by the infantry. On the 7th of July Gourko captured Tirnova. The possession of these two points gave the Russians the control of the two high-roads leading westward from the Quadrilateral, and threw the whole defensive line of the Yantra into their power. The XIII. and XII. Corps were combined into the "Left Wing," under command of the Cesarevitch, and took post on the Yantra, and then gradually moved forward toward the Lom. This was strictly in accordance with the plan of campaign, which contemplated a purely defensive rôle for the left wing; but it is quite probable that a vigorous attack of these two corps upon Rustchuk at any time before the 20th of July might, in the panic which prevailed at that time and in the general unreadiness of the Turks, have been successful. It was not, however, attempted; the left wing moved forward with the utmost caution, and took post along the Lom only about the 1st of August.

The Headquarters of the Army (Grand Duke Nicholas) were

moved forward to Tirnova on July 12th, and of the Emperor to Biela on the 20th. Meanwhile Gourko executed his brilliant move over the Balkans (July 12th–18th), and Krüdener, with the IX. Corps, captured Nikopolis (July 16th) and was defeated at Plevna (July 20th). Each of these movements needs to be described in detail.

OPERATIONS OF THE ADVANCE GUARD UNDER LIEUTENANT-GENERAL GOURKO.

On the 30th of June, three days after the passage of the Danube, the Grand Duke gave orders for the formation of a detachment, under the orders of Lieutenant-General Gourko, which was directed to push forward rapidly to Tirnova·and Selvi, reconnoitre the surrounding country, and be prepared upon the receipt of subsequent orders to gain possession of a pass in the Balkans by which the army could cross; at the same time sending his cavalry south of the mountains to cut the railroads and telegraph, and to do what other damage they could.

This detachment was made up as follows:

Infantry.—4th Rifle Brigade, Bulgarian legion (6 battalions), half battalion of plastounes, and two mountain batteries (14 guns).

Cavalry.—1. 8th and 9th Regiments of Dragoons and 16th horse battery, under Duke Eugene of Leuchtenberg.

2. 9th Regiment Hussars, 30th Regiment Don Cossacks, and 10th (horse) battery of Don Cossacks, under Duke Nicholas of Leuchtenberg.

3. 21st and 26th Regiments Don Cossacks and 15th (horse) battery of Don Cossacks, under Colonel Tchernozouboff.

4. Half squadron of Volunteers from the Guard.

5. Detachment of mounted pioneers, under Colonel Count de Roniquères, composed of Cossacks of the Caucasus, Don and Ural, who had been previously instructed in engineering duties.

In all, $10\frac{1}{2}$ battalions (8,000 men), $31\frac{1}{2}$ squadrons (4,000 men), and 32 guns (18 field and 14 mountain pieces).

The Sistova bridge being completed on the 2d of July, this detachment crossed on the 3d and began its march southward. On the 6th, without having met any opposition, it arrived in the villages just north of the Tirnova-Selvi *chaussée*. Here Gourko made his dispositions for a reconnaissance of Tirnova from the west on the 7th, and and from the east on the 8th, the bulk of his detachment meanwhile remaining near the village of Madrego, 18 miles northwest of Tirnova.

Tirnova has a population of 40,000 to 50,000 people, and is the most important town of northern Bulgaria; from it roads lead to the Shipka, Travna, Elena, and Slivno passes in the Balkans, and to Selvi and Lovtcha on the west, Sistova and Rustchuk on the north, and Osman-Bazar and Shumla on the east. The town is situated in a bend of the river Yantra and on its bank, while perpendicular rocky bluffs over 500 feet high surround it on every side; the roads enter the town from four directions through narrow defiles. Its natural capacity for defense was very great; hence Gourko's caution in approaching it.

For his reconnaissance of the 7th, Gourko took the brigade of dragoons, with which he approached the town from the west over the heights of Kajabunar. Sending two squadrons forward to skirmish with the Turks and make them develop their strength, he soon became convinced that the Turks were not in great force; and he descended from the heights and, about 4 P. M., advanced toward Tirnova with the whole brigade. The Turks retreated before him and crossed to the other side of the river just above the town, where they took up a position commanding the approach by the road. Gourko then brought his light battery into action, and sent back an order directing that the four sotnias of Cossacks, which were acting as his reserve and keeping up communication with the bulk of his detachment at Madrego, should come forward. As soon as they arrived he sent them through the town (on his left and front) with orders to cross the river and threaten the rear of the Turks. Meanwhile, with the brigade of dragoons he advanced directly against the Turks in front of him. The Turks abandoned everything and retreated very hastily by the road to Osman-Bazar. Their strength was five battalions of regular infantry (about 3,000 men), 400 irregular cavalry, and 6 guns. The force with which Gourko converted his reconnaissance into an attack numbered about 1,400 cavalry and 6 guns; his losses were 2 men and 8 horses wounded.

The rest of the detachment came to Tirnova the next day, July 8th, and remained there till the 12th, the bulk of the troops at the edge of the town and small detachments in observation on the principal roads. These four days were occupied in collecting all possible information from the Bulgarians about the various paths over the mountains, in reconnoitering them, and in organizing a pack train and making preparations for the forward movement.

According to the information which Gourko thus gathered, all the Turkish authorities and population had left Tirnova, most of them going to Shumla; the troops had left behind them in their retreat a considerable quantity of forage and wheat (which was confiscated by the Russians). There were no troops in any of the passes except the main one at Shipka, where there were about 3,000 infantry, a few mountain guns, and some bands of bashi-bozouks; some earthworks had been constructed for the defense of this pass, but it was not known whether they had yet been armed with cannon or not.

Upon this information Gourko drew up the following plan, which was approved by the Grand Duke (see Plate 9):

1. To cross the Balkans with the whole of his detachment except one regiment of Cossacks (No. 30) and 2 guns, by a blind trail about half way between the Elena and Travna passes—first sending his pioneers ahead to make the trail passable for his light artillery if possible.

2. The 30th Regiment of Cossacks to leave 4 squadrons at Tirnova, and send the other 2 squadrons and 2 guns to Gabrova to watch the northern outlet of the Shipka Pass. A small detachment of Cossacks at the moment of starting was to reconnoitre the Elena Pass, and be sure at the last moment that there were no Turks there.

3. To leave at Tirnova all the baggage on wheels, and take nothing with the troops but pack-animals, which should carry five days' hard bread and three days' forage; but the men and horses were to live on the country as much as possible, and keep their regular rations and forage till absolutely required.

4. On issuing from the mountains on the south, Gourko would at once proceed to Kazanlyk and attack the Shipka Pass from the south, while the Cossacks of the 30th Regiment should make a demonstration against this pass from the north—this to take place on July 17th.

This plan was approved by the Grand Duke, and the pioneers were sent forward on the 10th of July to clear the road.

On the 12th the whole detachment moved forward; and on the same day the Grand Duke as well the head of column of the VIII. Corps arrived at Tirnova. Of this latter a detachment under Major-General Darozhinsky, composed of the 36th Infantry Regiment, the rest of the 30th Don Cossacks, and 10 guns, was at once sent forward to Gabrova, with orders to attack the Shipka Pass from the north on July 17th (the two squadrons which Gourko had detailed being rather weak for this purpose).

On the night of the 12th Gourko and his detachment bivouacked near the village of Voinis, 18 miles from Tirnova. On the morning of the 13th he moved on 15 miles to the village of Parovtchi, and there halted to rest his troops from 1 to 5 o'clock. During the evening he crossed the divide and bivouacked on the southern slope, at a point about 9 miles from the village of Hainkioi, which is at the mouth of the defile. At 2 o'clock in the morning of the 14th he continued his march, and about 10 o'clock surprised the little garrison (300 regular infantry and some Tcherkesses) at Hainkioi; and captured the place after a slight skirmish, in which he lost six men. Had the outlet of this narrow defile been energetically defended, even by the small force that held it, it would have cost the Russians a very considerable loss. But, as it was, they debouched in the valley of the Tundja, without having met any difficulties except those of the road, which, however, were not slight. The ascent of the mountain began at the village of Parovtchi, elevation about 1,800 feet, and in the next 8 miles the road ascended 1,900 feet, crossing the summit at an elevation of 3,700 feet. On the southern slope in 12 miles the road descended 2,300 feet, the elevation of Hainkioi being about 1,400 feet. Over the greater part of the road from Parovtchi to Hainkioi the guns were dragged by the infantry, the grades being much too steep for the horses to be of any use. Considering that this trail was previously nothing but a foot-path, great credit is due to the pioneers, under Major-General Rauch of the Engineers, for having in two days made a road over which it was possible *by any means* to transport artillery. There was but one accident, in which two guns with their teams rolled down a ravine; they were, however, afterward recovered.

The Turkish garrison of Hainkioi retreated by the road to Slivno, and on arriving at the outlet of the Elena pass (village of

Tvarditza) was joined by the garrison of that place; and the two garrisons, numbering four battalions or about 2,000 men, then turned back during the afternoon (July 14th), and attacked the Russians who were following them, viz., two battalions of the Rifle Brigade; the latter were reënforced by a third battalion, and after a short fight, in which the Russians lost 7 men, the Turks retreated toward Slivno. They were followed till nightfall by part of the Rifle Brigade, which then returned toward Hainkioi. The Russians gained possession of two Turkish camps containing a number of arms, cartridges, rations, etc.

July 15th, Gourko remained at Hainkioi, assembling his troops, which had not at all passed through the defile the previous day. He also sent three squadrons of Cossacks in the direction of Yeni-Zagra. They had a skirmish in the afternoon with some Tcherkesses followed by three battalions of infantry; they called for reënforcements, and the 9th Dragoons were sent to them late in the afternoon, whereupon the Turks retreated in disorder. The Cossacks lost 8 or 10 men, and they as well as the Dragoons returned to Hainkioi during the night. The next day two squadrons of the 26th Don Cossacks succeeded in reaching Yeni-Zagra and cutting the telegraph.

July 16th, Gourko left Hainkioi and began his march toward Shipka, intending to reach the neighborhood of Kazanlyk (20 miles) that afternoon, and attack Shipka Pass the next morning. He took with him $6\frac{1}{2}$ battalions (5,000 men), $19\frac{1}{2}$ squadrons (3,000 men), and 16 guns, and left the balance of his detachment, viz., 4 battalions (3,000 men), 6 squadrons (500 men), and 14 guns, under Major-General Stoletoff at Hainkioi, in order to keep possession of that pass in case of retreat, but with orders to move on toward Kazanlyk on the morning of the 18th.

After Gourko had marched about 8 or 9 miles he came upon a body of Turks about 3,000 strong, posted behind a little stream issuing from the mountains at the village of Uflani. With these he had a sharp fight, in which he lost 2 officers and about 60 men. There were 400 Turkish dead (according to the official report) left upon the field; the number of their wounded was not known. This affair consumed so much time that Gourko could go no farther that day than Maglis, 10 miles east of Kazanlyk. The next morning, July 17th, at daybreak, Gourko moved out with his troops in three columns; that on the right

(1½ battalion) being ordered to follow the mountains and attack Kazanlyk from the northeast, that of the center (5 battalions and 10 guns) to attack the town from the east, and that on the left (all the cavalry and 6 guns) to follow the valley of the Tundja and turn the enemy's right flank. But the Turks were found posted 5 miles in front of Kazanlyk, behind a little stream called Kara Dere; their strength was about 3 battalions and 3 guns, and another column was seen coming from Shipka with the intention of occupying the heights on the Russian right flank. The fight began at 7 o'clock in the morning, but it was a small affair, although it lasted for two or three hours. The cavalry turned the right flank of the Turks, who thereupon began to retreat upon Kazanlyk; the cavalry still outflanking them cut off their retreat from Karlova and turned them toward Shipka, and then converted their retreat into a rout in which they lost 400 prisoners and their 3 guns; the Russian loss was 14 men. The village of Kazanlyk was in possession of the Russians by noon, and Gourko wished to march immediately on to Shipka and attack the pass; but his men were so exhausted (the heat was very great) that he was obliged to give them several hours' rest. Meanwhile with the cavalry he went on in person to Shipka village, where the infantry rejoined him about sunset; it was then too late to attack. In this way it happened that Gourko was one day behindhand for the joint attack which he had ordered from the north and south of Shipka Pass for the 17th of July.

The attack from the north was, however, made on this day, in the following manner:

General Darozhinsky, with his detachment (36th Infantry Regiment, 30th Don Cossacks, and 6 guns), left Tirnova on the 12th and arrived at Gabrova on the 13th. He immediately sent a portion of his Cossacks to Selvi, to drive out some bashi-bozouks that were there, and the rest of them into the mountains east of Shipka Pass to reconnoiter. The latter penetrated as far as the Berdek hill (about 3 miles east of the Shipka) without meeting any resistance; here, however, they came upon a battalion of Turks intrenched in a good position, before whom of course they were obliged to retire, sending back for infantry reënforcements. Two companies were sent to them, and arrived the next day, 16th.

Prince Mirsky (Lieutenant-General, commanding 9th Division) arrived at Gabrova on the evening of July 16th, and superseded Major-General Darozhinsky in command of the troops there. From the vicinity of Gabrova it could plainly be seen that the Turks had several lines of trenches dug across the highroad leading over the Shipka Pass; their numbers were learned to be between 4,000 and 5,000 infantry, with some bashi-bozouks and 12 guns. To attack a mountain position thus defended, with one regiment numbering, perhaps, 2,400 men and 6 guns, would have been simply folly, except that another and stronger attack was to have been made simultaneously from the other side. But, as we have seen, the troops on the other side were one day behindhand; and as a result the isolated attack on the north was a complete failure. It was made in four columns, viz.:

On the right, four companies, with four guns which were to follow a mountain path through the village of Zeleno-Drevo and attack the Bald Mountain two miles west of the main Turkish position, which was at the hill of St. Nicholas on the main road.

In the center, four companies, which were to follow a trail which would bring them in front of the advanced positions on the main road (i. e., near what is marked "Fourth Position," on the Map of Shipka, Plate 13).

On the left, two companies, which were to take a path through the woods leading to the main position at St. Nicholas hill.

On the extreme left, three companies, three sotnias of Cossacks, and two guns, which were to attack the hill of Berdek, three miles from St. Nicholas.

The remaining two companies of the regiment were left to guard the baggage at Gabrova.

The various columns, each conducted by guides, were in motion by 7 o'clock in the morning. The plan of attack shows a considerable ignorance of the Turkish position, for on the Bald Mountain there were no Turks at all, and the weakest column was directed against the strongest position of the Turks (St. Nicholas).

The result of the attack was as follows:

The *column on the right*, after marching all day, arrived at

7 P. M. on the Bald Mountain without having met any Turks; its four guns were left en route at the village of Zeleno-Drevo, with orders to assist the attack of the center column, but they were found to be out of range.

The *column in the center* arrived in front of the Turkish advanced trenches at 3 P. M, and opened fire upon them; but, the position being too strong to assault, it simply remained on its ground till sunset, keeping up a straggling fire with the enemy.

The *column on the left* debouched from the woods at 2 P. M., and round itself only a few hundred yards from the intrenched position of the Turks (at the point marked "Third Position" on map of Shipka Pass); it was very warmly received, but managed to hold its ground till 4 P. M., when it began to retreat, the Turks pursuing till 6 P. M. This column lost 5 out of 6 officers and 115 out of 320 men.

The *column on the extreme left* attacked at 3 o'clock in the morning, and carried the intrenchments on the hill of Berdek, the Turks retreating to St. Nicholas.

This was the only success of the day, and it availed nothing, for it was too far away and the column was too small in numbers to assist the little detachments in the center, one of which had been badly beaten, and in retreating had brought the Turks into a position to threaten the rear of the other. There were no reserves, and nothing had been heard from Gourko; during the night, therefore, all the columns fell back toward Gabrova. The total losses of the day were 6 officers and 205 men.

Gourko meanwhile, as previously stated, had reached the village of Shipka that same evening (July 17th), and made preparations to attack the pass the next morning. Of this he sent word early in the morning by a note taken by a Bulgarian across the mountain to Prince Mirsky, asking him to support his attack by a diversion with the 36th Regiment; but this note did not reach its destination until noon, and then it was too late, so that Gourko's attack from the south (July 18th) was isolated and unsuccessful—just as had been the one from the north the previous day.

Gourko attacked with two battalions of the Rifle Brigade and a half battalion of plastounes. They climbed through the woods on either side of the main road and deployed against the position at the hill of St. Nicholas. Just after the firing had begun the Turks sent out a flag of truce. "Cease firing" was sounded, and a party of officers * advanced to meet the flag, when suddenly the Turkish officers turned and retired hastily to their lines, and at a signal the Turks opened fire upon the Russian party. Fortunately none of them were hit. Excited by this treachery, the rifle battalions rushed forward and gained possession of some of the outer lines of trenches; but they were not strong enough to carry the main works on the St. Nicholas hill, and, hearing nothing of the attack from the north on which they had relied, they retired in good order down the mountain to the village of Shipka. The Turks fired at them with artillery, but did not leave their trenches; the Russian losses were something over 150 men.

Two unconcerted and isolated attacks had therefore been made on the Turkish position in the Shipka Pass, and both had been repulsed. On the morning of the 19th both detachments prepared to renew the attack, but meanwhile the Turks evacuated their positions and dispersed in small bands through the mountains to the west, finally reuniting somewhere near Philippopolis. In order to gain time for this manœuvre, they entered into negotiations with General Gourko looking to a surrender. The Turkish *Parlementaire* came to Gourko's camp at 7 in the morning, bearing a letter from the Pasha offering to surrender, in answer to a summons to that effect sent by Gourko the previous day. It was agreed that the capitulation was to take place at noon, and the Turkish officer departed in order to get the Pasha's answer concerning some details, promising to be back in two hours. Meanwhile Gourko sent some hospital attendants up to the scene of the previous day's fight in order to bring in his wounded. The two hours passed, and finally noon passed, and nothing was seen of the Turkish officer. Then Gourko, suspecting some foul play, sent forward a reconnoitring party, and got two battalions in position to support them. But, before the reconnoitring party had gone far, some of the hospital attendants returned from St. Nicholas hill, saying that Major-General Skobeleff II. was there; and soon after-

* One of these officers was Major Liegnitz, the Military Attaché to the German Embassy in St. Petersburg, who made a very full report of the whole circumstance to his government.

ward arrived a note from that officer saying that he had occupied St. Nicholas hill, and that the Turks had all fled. He had in fact taken nine companies of the 36th Regiment and four guns, and advanced early in the morning to attack the position by the same route as that taken the day before by the column of the center; but he had advanced successively from one line of trenches to another, and finally to the St. Nicholas hill, without finding any defenders. The hospital attendants found but little to do, as the Turks had mutilated all the Russian dead and wounded left on the field. On the road near the Nicholas hill was found one heap which alone contained over twenty human heads which had been cut from their bodies. The Turks left their tents standing, and abandoned their artillery (eight guns) and a large amount of ammunition and supplies, as well as their wounded (whom, in spite of the example set before their eyes, the Russians treated in their own hospitals).

On the 19th of July, therefore, the Shipka Pass was in the hands of the Russians, and the principal objects of Gourko's expedition were accomplished. In eight days from the time of leaving Tirnova, and sixteen days from the Danube, he had gained possession of three passes (Hainkioi, Travna, and Shipka), covering a length of thirty miles in the Balkans, and one of them the great high-road from Bulgaria to Roumelia; he had dispersed various Turkish detachments, numbering in all about 10,000 men, had captured 11 guns and a large quantity of ammunition, clothing, and provisions, and had disarmed the Turkish population throughout a large part of the valley of the Tundja; and all with a loss of less than 500 men. His men and horses had lived off the country and what they captured from the Turks, and on the 19th they still had three days' rations of hard bread (out of the five they had taken with them) untouched.

By this time the whole of the VIII. Corps had arrived at Tirnova and been distributed as follows; Corps Headquarters and 14th Division at Tirnova, watching the road from Shumla; two regiments of the 9th Division in Hainkioi Pass, detachments of Cossacks in Travna Pass, one regiment at Selvi, and of the remaining regiment (No. 36) one battalion at Gabrova and the other two in the Shipka Pass. Gourko's detachment was about equally divided, one half in the village of Shipka and the other half at Kazanlyk. They remained in these positions until the 22d. (See Plate 9.)

It is now necessary to cast a glance at what was transpiring on the Turkish side. The political effect of the passage of the Danube, followed so quickly by the appearance of Gourko's detachment on the south of the Balkans, was tremendous. A panic reigned at Adrianople and at all the larger towns in the valleys of the Tundja and Maritza, the Mohammedan population of which began fleeing toward Constantinople. In that city the panic was hardly less great. Daily councils were held at the palace, and the Sultan wavered between the projects of "displaying the standard of the Prophet," thereby proclaiming a religious war, and of transporting himself and his government to Brusa, in Asia Minor. Then his whole cabinet was overthrown, and the Commander-in-Chief, Abdul-Kerim Pasha, was dismissed in disgrace and banished along with the War Minister to one of the islands in the Ægean. Mehemet Ali Pasha was recalled from Montenegro and appointed Commander-in-Chief, and Suleiman Pasha commander of the troops between Adrianople and the Balkans; and the greatest efforts were made to get together an army to oppose the Russians, who were supposed to be marching in force toward Adrianople. At the same time England sent her fleet to Besika Bay and made other warlike preparations.

In order to follow the movements of the Turkish troops, a few topographical explanations are necessary. The Maritza River rises in the Balkans about 30 miles southeast of Sophia, and follows a course a little south of easterly for 170 miles, and then (at the city of Adrianople) turns and flows south for another 100 miles, emptying into the Ægean Sea near the town of Enos. On the south and west it receives the streams flowing from the Rhodope Mountains, the principal of which, called the Arda, empties at Adrianople; on the north it receives the drainage of a low range of hills known as the Little Balkans, which are parallel to the main range of that name and about 15 miles from it. Between these two is a very fertile valley, long famous for its culture of roses, from which "ottar of roses" is distilled, through which flows the Tundja River past Kazanlyk to Slivno, where it turns south and empties into the Maritza at Adrianople. Between the Tundja and Maritza system and the waters of the

Black Sea there is a range of hills rising in places to the height of 2,000 feet, nearly parallel to the coast and about 12 miles from it. (See Plate 2.)

In this section of the country is the principal railroad of Turkey, which, coming from Constantinople, unites near Adrianople with a branch coming from Enos. From Adrianople the railroad follows the valley of the Maritza to about 30 miles above Philippopolis (the grading of the road is complete as far as Sophia). At the little station of Trnova (which must not be confounded with the large town of Tirnova north of the Balkans) a branch railroad turns off and follows the valley of a stream called Sasli to Yeni-Zagra, and thence turns east to the town of Yamboli in the valley of the Tundja. This road was intended to cross the Balkans and unite near Shumla with the Rustchuk railroad, but it has never been built beyond Yamboli.

The principal high-roads are:
1. Shipka—Kazanlyk—Eski-Zagra—Trnova—Adrianople.
2. Philippopolis—Haskioi—Hermanli (the great road from Sophia to Adrianople).
3. Kazanlyk—Slivno—Yamboli—Adrianople.
4. Philippopolis—Karlova—Kazanlyk.
5. Philippopolis — Tchirpan — Eski-Zagra — Yeni-Zagra — Yamboli.

At the beginning of July the Turks had in the region from Philippopolis to Slivno about 10,000 men and 60 guns, which were then sent forward to the Balkans in the neighborhood of Shipka. Soon after (about July 5th–10th) 10,000 to 12,000 men with 40 guns, under command of Reouf Pasha, were sent from Adrianople by rail to Yamboli, and thence into the Balkan passes about Slivno. It was the western portion of this latter detachment that Gourko drove away in his skirmishes near Hainkioi; the first detachment he destroyed at Kazanlyk and Shipka.

When the news of the passage of the Danube reached Constantinople it was decided to recall the greater part of Suleiman's army from Montenegro, and a fleet of 20 transport ships was sent to bring it. On the 16th of July 49 battalions, 18 guns and 2,000 cavalry (about 30,000 men in all) were embarked at Antivari; they landed at Enos on the 19th, and proceeded by rail to Trnova, where they were assembled July 26th. (At this date the railroad between Trnova and Yeni-Zagra had been cut by Gourko's cavalry.)

By the last week in July, therefore, the Turks had brought together an army of about 50,000 men of regular troops for the defense of Roumelia. It was posted as follows: 35,000 men under Suleiman at Trnova, Karabuna and Gidsal—i. e., at the confluence of the Maritza and Sasli rivers and the junction of the two railways; 15,000 men under Reouf at Slivno, Yamboli, and Yeni-Zagra.

We will now return to the subsequent movements of Gourko's detachment, which was resting at Shipka and Kazanlyk on the 22d of July. On that date, at the request of a deputation of the inhabitants, the town of Eski-Zagra was occupied by the 9th Dragoons, a sotnia of Cossacks and two guns.

On the 23d Gourko began to resume the offensive by sending two raiding parties as follows:

1. Detachment of Colonel Matsioulevitch (8th Dragoons, two sotnias 21st Don Cossacks, section of 16th mounted battery), which was ordered to proceed by Eski-Zagra to the station Karabuna on the Yamboli Railroad, destroy the railroad and telegraph near this point, and gather as much information as possible about the movements of the Turks. This detachment bivouacked for the night at Eski-Zagra, and early the next morning (July 24th) moved forward in three parties, one of which was to strike the railroad above Karabuna, the other below it, while the third as a reserve moved directly on that point. The first party reached the road and destroyed it, the other two were held in check by a Turkish detachment of three or four battalions and several hundred Circassians, which they met before arriving at Karabuna. After skirmishing all day the three parties withdrew, and the united detachment retired to Eski-Zagra at night, having destroyed five bridges, three culverts, several way-stations, and the track and telegraph on a length of several miles.

2. Detachment of Colonel Korevo (9th Dragoons, one sotnia 26th Don Cossacks, section of 16th mounted battery), which was to proceed from Eski-Zagra (July 24th) to the station of Kaiadzik on the Philippopolis Railroad, and destroy the track in that vicinity, as well as gather information about the Turkish forces. They drove off some bashi-bozouks which they found

near the station, and then destroyed the building with all its contents, as well as the track and telegraph line for a considerable distance.

These two detachments, besides destroying the track and telegraph both on the Yamboli and Philippopolis lines, gathered the following information about the Turks, viz.: that there were near Karabuna, on the Yamboli Railroad, from four to six battalions and some cavalry; that troops were beginning to concentrate near the junction of the railroads, and that they were being brought there by rail from Adrianople. The same day by a small reconnaissance in the direction of Yeni-Zagra it was learned that there were Turkish troops at that place, but it could not be discovered in what strength.

Upon these data Gourko divided his detachment into two portions on July 25th, one of which, composed of the Bulgarian Legion (6 Battalions), the two regiments of Dragoons, the 9th Hussars, 3 sotnias of Cossacks (in all 15 squadrons), and 12 guns, he sent to Eski-Zagra under the orders of Duke Nicholas Leuchtenberg; with the other (4th Rifle Brigade, 6 to 8 sotnias of Cossacks, and 22 guns) Gourko proceeded on the 27th eastward along the Tundja, with the intention of crossing the Little Balkans to Yeni-Zagra.

Leuchtenberg's detachment established itself at Eski-Zagra July 25th, with outposts about ten miles out on the roads leading east, south, and west, and on the succeeding days continued to send reconnaissances toward Yeni-Zagra and toward the junction of the railroads. At this latter point the Turkish troops continued to arrive every day by trains, but they had not yet advanced beyond Karabuna, where they had about seven or eight battalions. At Yeni-Zagra was a somewhat larger force.

Gourko then ordered that the Duke of Leuchtenberg with all his detachment should move eastward on July 29th from Eski-Zagra toward Yeni-Zagra (the two towns are twenty-five miles apart), while he himself with his detachment, increased by the 1st Brigade 9th Division from the Hainkioi Pass, would cross the Little Balkans on July 30th and join him, and then move against Yeni-Zagra.

Accordingly, Leuchtenberg moved out at 2 P. M. on the 29th, having sent in the morning of the same day two reconnaissances, one in advance of his own column toward Yeni-Zagra, and the other toward Karabuna. The first of these soon met a column of Turks (6 battalions, 8 guns, and some Tcherkesses) which had advanced the previous day from Yeni-Zagra. The head of Leuchtenberg's column (8th Dragoons and 2 guns) went forward at a trot to support the two squadrons of the reconnoitring party. Thus, the two columns, Leuchtenberg from Eski-Zagra and the Turks from Yeni-Zagra, met on the chaussée midway between these two places in the afternoon of July 29th. The Bulgarian Legion, which formed the infantry of Leuchtenberg's column, did not come up until about 6 in the evening; but meanwhile he held the Turks in check by his cavalry (15 squadrons), one half of which he kept on the chaussée, and sent the other half by a détour to the right to threaten the Turkish left. At nightfall the Turks retired a mile or two to the village of Karabunar. Leuchtenberg bivouacked on the stream which comes out of the hill at Dalbok. During the evening the two squadrons which had been sent in the morning to reconnoitre toward Karabuna (on the railroad) returned, and reported that Suleiman's army was advancing in force direct from Karabuna toward Eski-Zagra, and that it was only 8 miles southeast of the latter place.

This disclosed the plan of the Turks. Suleiman with a large force was moving from the railroad toward Eski-Zagra (and thence probably toward Shipka), while a portion of Reouf's troops were advancing from Yeni-Zagra to meet Suleiman at Eski-Zagra. The Russians, on the other hand, were moving in two columns, one from the valley of the Tundja south of Hainkioi, and the other from Eski-Zagra, with the intention of attacking Yeni-Zagra. On the night of the 29th of July the troops stood as follows: Gourko, with the bulk of the infantry (4th Rifle Brigade and 1st Brigade 9th Division, 10 battalions, 8 squadrons of Cossacks, and 22 guns), was still on the north of the Little Balkans, near the village of Jasiriu. Leuchtenberg, with 4 battalions of the Bulgarian Legion, 14 squadrons, and 12 guns, was bivouacked near the village of Dalbok, facing east, and having in front of him a Turkish detachment of 6 battalions 8 guns, and some Tcherkesses. Suleiman's head of column was 8 miles southeast of Eski-Zagra, at which place were 2 battalions of the Bulgarian Legion and 2 sotnias of Cossacks.

The town of Eski-Zagra was of the greatest importance to the Russians, as it covered their retreat to Kazanlyk and the

Shipka Pass. Leuchtenberg therefore determined to fall back upon this town with his 4 battalions of Bulgarians and 6 guns, and try to hold it for a day against Suleiman, and to direct his cavalry to retreat slowly after him along the chaussée, delaying as much as possible the advance of the Turkish infantry in front of them, and keeping up the connection between Eski-Zagra and Gourko's troops which would come over the Little Balkans during the day.

The cavalry was disposed as follows: in the center, across the chaussée, 3 squadrons in line supported by 2 squadrons in reserve; on the left, 2 squadrons near the foot of the hills; on the right, 3 squadrons in line, with 2 guns, facing southeast near the village of Tchavlikioi. This left a general reserve of 4 squadrons and 4 guns. The Turks opened the attack about 7 o'clock in the morning (July 30th) by a demonstration against the Russian left, before which the 2 squadrons fell back slowly. Skirmishing continued until about noon without much change in the relative positions; but then the Turks began massing their infantry against the Russian right, with the evident intention of breaking past the Russians and effecting a junction with Suleiman. The Russian right was then reënforced by the 6 squadrons in reserve, making 9 in all, while 4 remained on the chaussée and 2 near the mountains. In this way, the Turks continually striving to turn their right flank, the Russians fell back, contesting every step, and about 5 P. M. they reached the village of Aidinli, 3 miles east of Eski-Zagra. Meanwhile, on the left flank several attempts had been made by the Cossacks to break through the line of Circassians and learn something of the whereabouts and movements of Gourko's troops, but they had all been unsuccessful.

Gourko had meanwhile crossed the Little Balkans during the morning (30th), and on the west and north of Yeni-Zagra had found a portion of Reouf's detachment en route toward Eski-Zagra. He fought with this during the greater part of the day, and drove it to the east, thus preventing its junction with the troops near Eski-Zagra. Hearing then of the desperate situation of Leuchtenberg's cavalry, he prepared to return along the chaussée to Dalbok, reunite his detachment, and retreat toward Hainkioi.

On this day (30th) Suleiman had concentrated his force in

front of Eski-Zagra, but he had made no attack. On the evening of that date, therefore, the relative positions were as follows:

Suleiman, with about 40,000 men disposed in a circle of 5 miles radius around Eski-Zagra, from the Tchirpan road on the left to the village of Dzuranli on the right, his right flank being composed of the troops which had come from Yeni-Zagra.

Leuchtenberg, in possession of the chaussée from Eski-Zagra for a distance of about 6 miles east, having the 6 Bulgarian battalions and some Cossacks on his right flank at Eski-Zagra, and the rest of his cavalry at Aidinli and Hirsta.

Gourko, on the chaussée just west of Yeni-Zagra, with 10 battalions ready to march early in the morning to the relief of Leuchtenberg.

On the morning of the 31st, between 6 and 7 o'clock, the Cossacks of Gourko's advance-guard were discovered approaching on the chaussée from the east, but the road was completely under the fire of the Turks from their position at Dzuranli. To make a diversion in favor of these Cossacks, Leuchtenberg sent the 9th Hussars and 4 guns to demonstrate against the left flank of the Turks at Dzuranli; and soon afterward he sent the 8th Dragoons and 4 guns against the right flank of Suleiman's main force south of Eski-Zagra. These two regiments were thus interposed between the Turks at Dzuranli and Suleiman's main force on the south of Eski-Zagra, and prevented their junction for several hours.

Suleiman began his attack about 8 in the morning along the two roads coming into Eski-Zagra from the south and west. There was nothing to oppose him but the 6 battalions of the Bulgarian Legion, which fell back slowly toward the town. About 11 o'clock the bulk of Gourko's forces had arrived and engaged the Turks near Dzuranli. The 9th Dragoons were thereupon sent to Eski-Zagra to aid the Bulgarians, and the rest of Leuchtenberg's cavalry (upon the order of Gourko) was marched along the chaussée under fire of the Turks at Dzuranli to rejoin Gourko's right wing. During the afternoon Gourko succeeded in driving back the Turks in front of him; but by withdrawing his cavalry from Aidinli he had lost all communication with his people at Eski-Zagra. If the Turks had had plenty of good cavalry, they would probably have cut these latter to pieces. As it was, the Bulgarians fell back slowly and in good order, and upon the arrival of the 9th Dragoons to cover their retreat, they made good their escape over the Little Balkans to Kazanlyk.

The main body of Gourko's force retreated that evening (July 31st), in the opposite direction, to the bivouac near Dolbak, the cavalry covering their rear. The next day they crossed the Little Balkans to the neighborhood of Hainkioi.

During the 30th and 31st of July Gourko's detachment of 16,000 men had been fighting with the whole of the newly formed "Balkan Army" under Suleiman, numbering nearly 50,000 men in all. It was impossible, owing to the course of events on the other side of the Balkans, as will be subsequently explained, to send any substantial reënforcements to Gourko and continue the advance in face of this new army. Gourko was therefore ordered to retreat slowly before the Turks, post a portion of his troops in the passes, and bring the rest to the northern side of the mountains. The Bulgarian Legion retired to Shipka; the 9th Dragoons, which had covered its retreat, then made its way past the bashi-bozouks, who had swarmed into the valley of the Tundja, and rejoined Gourko at Hainkioi.

On the 3d and 4th of August a small reconnaissance was made to Eski-Zagra, by which it was learned that Suleiman had reduced the entire town to ashes on account of the "treason" of the inhabitants in asking the Russians to come there, and had then marched his army toward Yeni-Zagra.

On the 5th of August all of Gourko's cavalry retired through the Hainkioi Pass to Tirnova, and on the 8th arrived at the village of Nikup, 18 miles north of Tirnova; there it refitted, cured up lame and sore-backed horses, and generally repaired damages, and was subsequently distributed to the various divisions of which it formed parts. The 1st Brigade 9th Division was posted in the Hainkioi and Elena passes, the 4th Rifle Brigade at Tirnova, and the Bulgarian Legion, as previously stated, in the Shipka Pass. Gourko himself proceeded to Russia to meet and resume his proper command (2d Cavalry Division of the Guard), which had meantime been mobilized and was en route to the seat of war.

The losses of his detachment from the capture of Shipka Pass (July 19th) to their return to the Balkans (August 5th) were about 500 men: their total losses from the time of leaving Tirnova (July 12th) to their return to the same place (August 6th) were as follows:

	Officers.	Men.
Killed	10	181
Wounded	24	709
Missing	..	57
Total	34	947

This expedition of Gourko's was more than a mere cavalry raid: it was an admirably conducted movement of an advance-guard composed of all arms. With 8,000 infantry, 4,000 cavalry, and 32 guns, it had in less than a month gained possession of one of the principal passes of the Balkans, from which the Russians, though terribly attacked, never let go their hold, and which they finally used in January for the passage of a large portion of their army; it had carried a panic throughout the whole of Turkey between the Balkans and Constantinople; and its scouting parties had penetrated to within 70 miles of Adrianople, the second city of the Empire, and had destroyed the railroad and telegraph on the two principal lines; finally, it had gathered accurate information concerning the strength and positions of the large Turkish force advancing toward the Balkans.

In this expedition alone of the whole campaign was the cavalry energetically handled. On several occasions it fought on foot; it was constantly on the move; it subsisted on the country; on the 29th and 30th of July 14 squadrons of it (1,800 men) held their own against 4,000 infantry and several hundred bashibozouks and Tcherkesses; and it finally covered Gourko's retreat before a force more than three times superior to his own. The irregular cavalry of the Turks never waited long enough to come to hand-to-hand blows; on one occasion (July 16th), while fighting on foot against infantry, the dragoons advanced with fixed bayonets, but the Turks retired without accepting a hand-to-hand struggle. The Russian Cavalry, it will be remembered, is armed with the short Berdan rifle, an arm much superior to the Winchester and nearly equal to the Peabody-Martini. In artillery, however, the Turkish superiority was clearly proved, especially during the fight of July 29th on the chaussée near Karabunar; in which the Turks covered the Russian cavalry with shell, while the Russian guns (4-pdrs.), even with their greatest elevation, could not reach the Turkish battery, the distance being something over 4,000 yards. During the fight of the 31st near Aidinli, one well-aimed shell killed and wounded 12 hussars and 10 horses. But the Russian inferiority in armament (as well as in numbers) was more than counterbalanced by the skill and energy with which their squadrons were handled.

CHAPTER III.

OPERATIONS OF THE RIGHT WING UNDER LIEUTENANT-GENERAL
BARON KRÜDENER.

(See Plate 8.)

As previously stated, the IX. Corps crossed the Danube by the Sistova bridge on the 10th of July, and immediately moved eastward toward Nikopolis. Two of the Cavalry regiments (9th Hussars and 9th Dragoons) belonging to this Corps had been taken to form part of Gourko's detachment. To replace them, the brigade of Caucasian Cossacks (12 squadrons), which originally had also been detailed to Gourko's detachment, was relieved from him and ordered to report to Krüdener. One of his infantry regiments (No. 124) was left near Sistova, and another (No. 19) was sent forward toward Bulgareni, on the high-road (Rustchuk-Plevna-Sophia). With the rest of his corps Krüdener advanced along the direct road to Nikopolis. He arrived in front of the Turkish positions on the 13th, reconnoitred and made his dispositions on the 14th, attacked and carried the field works on the 15th, and on the 16th the fortress capitulated.

Nikopolis is a town of some 8,000 or 10,000 inhabitants. Its fortifications consisted of an old masonry fortress situated on a bluff overhanging the river, much out of repair and completely commanded by the hills in rear; the greater part of the town lies outside of this fortress. Behind the town is a plateau, about 700 feet above the river, and from 3 to 8 miles in width, between the Osma River on the west of it and the marshes of the Danube on the east; deep wooded ravines descend abruptly from this plateau to the marshy valleys on either side. About 3 miles west of the Osma River is the Vid River, and between the two is a rolling country, the top of which is about 600 feet above the Danube level. While the Russians had been demonstrating in front of Nikopolis previous to their passage of the river at Sistova, the Turks had placed several batteries in position for firing across the river and had also lined the Danube bank, as well as the bluffs of the Osma and the Ermenli ravine, with rifle-pits; but after the passage of the Danube they hastily began the construction of some work to defend the place in the rear (south). At the time of Krüdener's arrival these works consisted of five redoubts—two of them west of the town on the plateau between the Nikopolis ravine and the Osma, one just south of the town, and two east of it near the Danube—and of three batteries in the form of lunettes on the south and southwest of the town, the most advanced being near the village of Voubla; in front of these batteries were lines of rifle-pits. In these works there were about ten field guns; and there were several siege guns in batteries facing the river. The Turkish forces consisted in all of 10,000 to 12,000 men, the greater part of which were posted in the works just described, and the rest, 3,000 or 4,000 men, were placed on the hills between the Osma and the Vid, in an intrenched position extending from the village of Gradesti to Missilycou.

Krüdener divided his force for the attack into two portions, one of which, under his own orders, was to advance between the Osma and the Ermenli ravine directly against the Turkish works south of the town; and the other, under Lieutenant-General Schilder-Schuldner, commanding 5th Division, was to move down the left bank of the Osma, assault the heights between that river and the Vid, cut off the Turks from Rahova and Plevna, drive them into Nikopolis, and then take the main positions in flank.

The troops were posted as follows at 3 A. M. July 15th:

In the *center*, from Voubla to the Ermenli ravine, 5 batteries of 9-pdrs., supported by the 121st Regiment on their right and the 20th on their left; behind the center of this line was a reserve composed of the 122d Regiment, 3 batteries and 2 sotnias.

On the *right*, 3 sotnias of the 9th Don Cossacks observed the country between Ermenli and the Danube.

On the *left*, Schilder-Schuldner's column, composed of the 17th and 18th Regiments, 3 batteries, the 9th Lancers, and the Caucasian Brigade of Cossacks, was posted in the valley of the

Osma near the village of Debo; communication between them and the main body was kept up by the 123d Regiment, which was in the ravine of Slatina.

At 4 A. M. the batteries near Voubla opened fire, and about the same time Schilder-Schuldner began to advance along the valley of the Osma against the heights on its left bank, having on his right the 18th Regiment, which was to attack these heights forming the right flank of the Turkish position, while the 17th Regiment and the 9th Lancers were to incline to the left toward Gradesti, and thus turn the Turkish right flank—the whole attack being based on the idea of driving the Turks *into* their fortress and then compelling its surrender. The Caucasian Brigade was to cover the left and rear from any reënforcements which might arrive from Rahova or Plevna. At 7 A. M. the 18th Regiment arrived in front of the Turkish heights, and the artillery which accompanied it (one battery) opened fire, to which the Turks replied energetically; not long afterward the regiment moved forward to the assault, and after a struggle gained possession of the heights, driving the Turks back across the Osma toward Nikopolis. Seeing this, the 123d Regiment moved forward toward the Osma, seized the bridge at Missilyeou, sent one battalion across to harass the Turks in retreat, and with the other two battalions moved forward along the road in the valley of the Osma toward the second bridge (at Djournevo). The Turks retreated in good order, delaying the advance of the Russians as much as possible, crossed the Djournevo bridge, and retired to the heights on the right bank of the Osma, between it and the Nikopolis ravine. Two battalions of the 18th Regiment then crossed to the right bank (as also the battalion of the 123d Regiment), and joined the 123d Regiment. These five battalions then began to climb the heights north of Djournevo under a hot fire from the Turks. (See Plate 10.) Seeing them appear and reform on the top of these heights, and having learned of their success on the left bank of the Osma, Krüdener then (about 2 P. M.) gave the order for the 20th Regiment and the five batteries on its right to advance—two battalions against the battery nearest Voubla, and one battalion toward the principal redoubt (No. 3) east of the Nikopolis ravine. The battery was carried, though with heavy loss, about 4 P. M., the Turks losing one gun, but retiring with the other two to battery "*b*." But the battalion advancing against the redoubt was repulsed; the 122d Regiment was brought up to its support, but a second assault was repulsed; a part of the 121st Regiment was then brought up, and a third assault about 6 P. M. was successful, and the redoubt was carried. The 20th and 122d Regiments then advanced along the east side of the ravine in which the town is situated, and arrived in front of the walls of the fortress.

Meanwhile the 18th and 123d Regiments continued to advance along the Rahova road on the heights east of the Osma, and toward evening came in front of a large redoubt (marked No. 2 on the map) forming the principal defense from the direction of the west. The Turks sortied from the redoubt against their left flank, but were repulsed. Soon afterward the 17th Regiment and the remaining battalion of the 18th, which had followed the valley of the Osma through the village of Tcherkovitza, scaled the heights behind that village and opened fire on Redoubt No. 1, near the river. Darkness soon put an end to the fighting. During the night a portion of the Turkish troops tried to break through the Caucasian Brigade and escape toward Plevna, but they were repulsed.

The results of the day were therefore the capture of two of the three principal positions of the Turks on the hills outside the fortress, and the investment of the place. Preparations were made for an open assault the next morning, supported by the 9-pdr. field batteries on the heights overlooking the town, and also by the siege batteries on the opposite bank of the Danube, which had kept up a very lively bombardment throughout the previous day. The troops began to move forward at 4 A. M., but immediately afterward the Turks hoisted a white flag, and during the morning concluded negotiations for an unconditional surrender.

The Turkish losses are not known; 7,000 men, including 300 wounded, surrendered as prisoners of war, and the Russian trophies included 6 flags, 110 guns, over 10,000 small arms, 2 monitors, and a great quantity of ammunition and supplies.

The Russian losses were:

	Officers.	Men.
Killed	3	273
Wounded	28	921
Missing	..	84
Total	31	1,278

FIRST BATTLE AT PLEVNA. 189

While these operations had been going on about Nikopolis, Osman Pasha, with an army of 40,000 men of the best troops in Turkey—those that had defeated the Servians in their campaign of 1876—was on the march from Widdin toward the east; and a force of perhaps 10,000 or 12,000 men had left Sophia and was advancing by the high-road which leads through Plevna (a portion of it having been sent to Lovtcha). The exact date when Osman left Widdin is not known; the order was given by the Commander-in-Chief, Abdul-Kerim Pasha, and probably just after the Russians had effected the crossing of the Danube. The head of Osman's column was first heard of on the 17th of July, when the pickets of the Caucasian Brigade posted along the Vid reported that a strong force coming from the west was marching on the road to Plevna; but neither at the Grand Duke's Headquarters (then at Tirnova) nor at General Krüdener's does much importance appear to have been attached to this report. The Grand Duke simply telegraphed an order to Krüdener to "occupy Plevna as promptly as possible." Krüdener had in fact learned from prisoners even *before* the capture of Nikopolis that reënforcements were expected from the direction of Rahova and Plevna, but he put little confidence in the report; for otherwise he would immediately after the capture of Nikopolis (July 16th) have ordered the Caucasian Brigade, and if possible one other regiment of cavalry, to advance to Plevna (which is only 20 miles south of Nikopolis) and find out what force was there. But instead of this the Caucasian Brigade remained the 16th and 17th on the Vid, and on the 18th was sent off on the left flank to Bulgareni, where the road from Sistova to Plevna comes into the high-road from Rustchuk. In short, Osman Pasha with a large army arrived upon the flank of the Russians without their knowing anything about it. There has been much controversy as to who was responsible for this ignorance, but no satisfactory solution has ever been made public.

On the 18th of July, as just stated, the Grand Duke directed Krüdener to occupy Plevna; and immediately Krüdener ordered Lieutenant-General Schilder-Schuldner, with the 1st Brigade 5th Division (17th and 18th Regiments), four batteries, and the 9th Don Cossacks, to proceed by Bryslan to Plevna and occupy that town; and he placed under his orders to assist him—1, the 19th Regiment, which with one battery and two sotnias was already on the high-road from Rustchuk to Plevna (one battalion with the baggage at Bulgareni and the rest at Poradim); 2, the Caucasian Brigade of Cossacks and its mounted battery, which were also at Bulgareni.

Schilder-Schuldner moved out the same day, and bivouacked about 10 miles from Nikopolis, sending word to the 19th Regiment to move forward to Zgalevitza, and the Caucasian Brigade to Tutchenitza (see map No. 8). On the 19th he continued his march, and about 2 P. M. arrived on the heights south of Verbitza, and was halted by the Turkish artillery from the heights of Grivitza. *Schilder-Schuldner had no cavalry at all with his main column*, and, so to speak, stumbled on the Turks. The 9th Don Cossacks were marching by a road about 5 miles to his right, and at this time (2 P. M. July 19th) were quietly cooking their soup in their bivouac at Riben, 8 miles to the right *and rear* of Schilder-Schuldner. When they heard the noise of the latter's guns they emptied their kettles, mounted, and rode forward at a trot toward Plevna. On the Bukova heights, about $2\frac{1}{2}$ miles north of Plevna, they came upon a detachment of Turkish infantry, with whom they skirmished till nightfall. On the other flank, the 19th Regiment had advanced as ordered to Zgalevitza and bivouacked there, sending meanwhile two sotnias of Cossacks in reconnaissance as far as Grivitza, where they were met and driven back by the Turks. The Caucasian Brigade had marched to Tutchenitza without finding any enemy. On the night of July 19th, therefore, the little force of Schilder-Schuldner (9 battalions, 16 squadrons—6,500 men—and 46 guns) was distributed over a distance of 17 miles, as follows: Near Bukova, 9th Don Cossacks; two miles southwest of Verbitza, 17th and 18th Regiments and 4 batteries; at Zgalevitza, 19th Regiment, 1 battery, and 2 sotnias; at Tutchenitza, Caucasian Brigade and 1 horse battery.

The first portion of Osman's army had arrived a few days previously (the exact day is not known), and up to the present time they had constructed some trenches near Bukova, on the site of the Grivitza redoubt which subsequently became so famous, and on the hills just east and south of the high-road and commanding the approach by the latter.

Schilder-Schuldner ordered an attack on all sides at daylight the next morning (July 20th). But already at 4 A. M. the Turks

FIRST BATTLE AT PLEVNA. 191

came out of Plevna to attack the Don Cossacks on the extreme right near Bukova. Two companies, of the three which formed the guard of the baggage behind Verbitza, and a battery were sent to the aid of the Cossacks, and thus reënforced they held their ground until ordered to retreat about noon.

About 4.30 A. M. the other three batteries were brought into position opposite the Grivitza ridge and about 2,500 yards north of the intrenchments, and opened fire; the 17th Regiment was placed with one battalion on the left, and two battalions on the right of the batteries, in two lines of company columns; on their right the 18th Regiment in two lines of company columns. After an hour's cannonade, at 5.30 A. M. the troops moved forward, crossed the ravine, and assaulted the Grivitza heights. The western extremity of the trenches was carried, and the 18th Regiment and a few companies of the 17th followed the Turks down the south side of the heights to the very outskirts of Plevna, where they were brought to a halt by a very hot fire from behind the hedges and ditches on the edge of the town. This was at 7 A. M., and they remained here till 11.20, when they received the order to retreat. Meanwhile the rest of the 17th Regiment and all the artillery were two miles behind them on their left rear, making unsuccessful efforts to get possession of the main Grivitza position.

On the other flank the 19th Regiment had received at 3 A. M. its orders for the attack, and by 5 A. M. had reached Grivitza; here it brought its battery into action against the trenches south of the chaussée, and after a short cannonade moved forward to the assault in columns of companies; it carried the first two lines of trenches without much difficulty, had a hard struggle for the third, but finally carried it, and followed the Turks to the edge of the town (on the east side), where they were brought to a stand-still by the heavy fire from the gardens and buildings; this was at 9 A. M.

The Caucasian Brigade had moved from Tutchenitza to Radischevo, and thence on to the heights in front of that village. Here it opened fire with its little battery on the right flank of the Turks who were opposed to the 19th Regiment; but finding its guns did not carry half of the distance, it limbered up and moved over toward the 19th Regiment, which it joined when the latter was already in retreat.

At 9 A. M., therefore, the Russian right and left flanks had carried everything before them and reached Plevna itself from the north and from the east; their center had failed to carry the main Grivitza position; the two flanks were not in sight and not in communication except by a détour of about seven miles. Then the Turks formed their troops in the town and sallied forth in great numbers on both sides; the Russians were driven back with great loss, their right flank covered by the 9th Don Cossacks to Bryslan, their left covered by the Caucasian Brigade to Zgalevitza. The Turks pursued them only to their lines of trenches, and the fighting was all over by 5 in the afternoon. The Russians preserved their traditional firmness and did not take a panic, but they left on the field a great part of their dead and wounded, as well as 17 caissons, and all the baggage of the 19th Regiment. Their losses were: 22 officers killed and 52 wounded, and 2,771 men killed and wounded. Nearly two thirds of the officers and over one third of the men were therefore *hors de combat;* of the three Colonels commanding regiments, two were killed; the General commanding the 1st Brigade 5th Division was wounded; of the six field officers present with the 19th Regiment, two were killed and two wounded. The Russians credit the Turks with a loss of 4,000 men in killed and wounded, but this is a mere estimate, and there is no reason to suppose that their loss was any greater than that of the Russians.

The almost criminal faults of this battle on the part of the Russian commander are so apparent that they hardly need to be pointed out. Without having learned anything about the strength or position of the enemy, and without any reserves whatever of his own, his troops were led blindly to the assault in company columns, along two lines which had no communication with each other, and against an enemy which, as the official report says, was *subsequently* discovered to be more than four times their own strength! To crown all, the ammunition parks of the left wing had been left back at Bulgareni, 18 miles in rear of the field, and both the artillery and infantry ran short of cartridges during the retreat.

Immediately after this defeat Krüdener was ordered to bring the 19th Regiment, which had been so roughly handled, to Nikopolis, and leave it there together with some Roumanian troops that had just crossed the river as a garrison, and to proceed at once with the rest of the IX. Corps to the vicinity of Plevna and take command of all the troops there; and to strengthen his command, a detachment was sent to him under the orders of Lieutenant-General Prince Shakofskoi, consisting of the 1st Brigade 32d Division (XI. Corps) the 1st Brigade 11th Cavalry Division from Tirnova, and the 30th Division (IV. Corps), which had just crossed the Danube. These troops were all on the ground by the 25th of July.

The Turks meanwhile were working with the utmost diligence upon their fortifications, confident that they would be again attacked in the course of a few days. They strengthened the Grivitza redoubt and the lines between it and Bukova, and began the construction of the group of redoubts just east of the town. By the 30th of July the Grivitza redoubt and four of those of the "middle group" were more or less completed. (See map of Plevna, Plate 12.)

Between the Lovtcha high-road and the Vid there were no fortifications at this date. Osman's army on the 30th numbered about 40,000 men.

Krüdener reconnoitred carefully the ground in his front, and, on account of the natural strength of the position and the force of the enemy (who was receiving reënforcements every day), he hesitated to assume the responsibility of an assault of which the issue was doubtful. He therefore telegraphed to the Grand Duke, whose Headquarters were at Tirnova, 80 miles off, asking for instructions. The Grand Duke telegraphed somewhat sharply in reply, on the 28th, that he could not understand his hesitation in attacking as he had been previously ordered to do. Krüdener immediately gave orders for the assault, which was to take place on the 30th. On the 29th his troops stood as follows (see Plate 8):

9th Lancers and 9th Don Cossacks, with one horse battery (10 squadrons and 6 guns), at Bryslan;

31st Infantry Division, less 124th Regiment and 1 battery (9 battalions and 40 guns), at Koioulovtsy;

5th Infantry Division, less 19th Regiment and 1 battery (9 battalions and 40 guns), at Tristenik;

2d Brigade 30th Division, with 3 batteries (6 battalions and 24 guns), at Karagatch;

1st Brigade 30th Division, 1st Brigade 32d Division, 1st Brigade 11th Cavalry Division, 6 foot batteries and 1 horse battery (12 battalions, 8 squadrons, and 54 guns), at Poradim;

Caucasian Brigade, with 2 horse batteries (12 squadrons and 12 guns), at Bogot.

Total, 36 battalions, 30 squadrons, and 176 guns (80 9-pdrs., 72 4-pdrs., 18 horse 4-pdrs., 6 mountain guns)—say 30,000 men in all, the losses at Nikopolis and at Plevna on July 20th not yet having been replaced.

The line from Bryslan through Tristenik to Poradim was about 15 miles long, and formed an arc of a circle whose radius was about 10 miles, and whose center was at Plevna. From Poradim to Bogot the distance is about 11 miles.

Krüdener's orders for the 30th were as follows:

1. Cavalry on extreme right, under Major-General Loshkareff, to move forward at 6 A. M., observe the enemy, and protect the right flank.

2. Right flank (31st and 5th Divisions), under Lieutenant-General Wilhelminof, to attack the position north of the highroad (Grivitza redoubt) with the 31st Division followed by the 5th Division in reserve.

3. Left flank (1st Brigade 30th Division and 1st Brigade 32d Division), under Lieutenant-General Prince Shakofskoi, to leave Poradim at 5 A. M. and attack the position between Radischevo and Grivitza.

4. Cavalry on extreme left, under Major-General Skobeleff II., to leave Bogot at 5 A. M. and take position on the Lovtcha high-road near Krishin, and prevent any reënforcements from arriving from Lovtcha.

5. Principal reserve (2d Brigade 30th Division), under direct orders of the Commanding General (Krüdener), to be under arms at Karagatch.

6. The two regiments of cavalry (11th Dragoons and 11th Lancers) were distributed as follows: 4 squadrons to keep up communication between the right and left flanks, and 4 squadrons in the general reserve.

The key of the position was the Grivitza redoubt, which commanded all the others, and against this the largest force was directed (18 battalions and 80 guns); the two flanks were so widely separated that there was no chance that they could lend

SECOND BATTLE AT PLEVNA. 195

each other any aid. Krüdener's headquarters were to be on the left of the right wing, on the heights about 1¼ mile east of Grivitza. (See Plate 12.)

The troops were under way by 7 o'clock in the morning. The right wing advanced in two lines—the first line consisting of 6 battalions and 24 guns, the second of 3 battalions and 16 guns, followed by the 9 battalions and 40 guns of the 5th Division as a reserve, which came into position at 10 o'clock. Soon after 8 o'clock the first line came in range of the Turks, who opened fire. It halted and brought its batteries into position about 3,000 yards east of the Grivitza redoubt. The artillery duel opened about 8:30 A. M. and continued without interruption until 2:30 P. M., the infantry meanwhile not firing a shot.

The left wing marched from Zgalevitza to Radischevo without finding any enemy, and thence to the heights in front of that village, from which the "middle group" of redoubts is in easy range (1,500 to 2,500 yards). These heights were occupied by the 1st Brigade 32d Division, and 28 guns, and an artillery fight was begun which also lasted till 2:30 P. M. The results of this cannonade were about equal : two small Turkish batteries were silenced, and three Russian guns dismounted, causing the whole battery to be withdrawn and replaced.

At half past two the infantry began to advance on both flanks. The right wing was divided into two columns for the assault, one from the north and one from the east. The first column consisted of the 121st Regiment (Penza) and the 2d and 3d Battalions of the 123d (Kozloff), and was followed by the 17th and 18th Regiments as a reserve ; the other column, of the 1st Battalion 123d and the 122d (Tamboff) Regiments, with the 20th Regiment (Galitz) in reserve. The 1st Battalion of the Penza Regiment, which had the lead, carried the first line of trenches, situated about 1,000 yards northeast of the redoubt, but was checked by the second line just behind it. This, however, was carried by the 2d Battalion, and they drove the Turks across the little ravine and began approaching the redoubt itself ; three companies, led by the Major Commanding the 2d Battalion, then rushed for the redoubt, and actually reached the parapet, where the Major was cut down and most of his followers also perished. The rest of this regiment (Penza) tried to advance in face of the terrible fire, but failed, and it fell back to the ravine ; in a few minutes it had lost more than a third of its men and half its officers (29 officers and 1,006 men). The Regiment of Kozloff then moved forward to the assault; as before, a few men reached the redoubt and met their death there, but the rest of them did not reach it. While they were still engaged, the 17th and 18th Regiments arrived somewhat on their right, but they were equally unsuccessful in their efforts to get into the redoubt. The fire which the Turks kept up from the redoubt and the trenches on either side of it was very severe.

Meanwhile the other column (Regiment of Tamboff and 1 Battalion of Kozloff) had moved forward across the ravines just north of the village of Grivitza, with the Regiment of Galitz on its left. The Tamboff Regiment got no farther than a little mound about 400 yards southeast of the redoubt; the Galitz Regiment was stopped abreast of the Tamboff by the fire from the trenches on the slope south of the redoubt. The two regiments remained in place and kept up a lively fusillade.

It had now come to be about 6 o'clock. Of the general reserve, one regiment had been sent to Shakofskoi, and the other was available. One battalion of this latter (No. 120) was then sent, with a squadron of Dragoons and two horse guns, to the right, where the 17th and 18th Regiments were being pressed back. With the aid of these fresh troops they managed to hold on a little longer. Finally, at sunset, Krüdener gave orders for another assault from all sides; it was made with desperation (a general officer being killed within 100 paces of the redoubt), but without success. Then Krüdener gave the order to retire, covering his retreat by the two remaining battalions of the 120th Regiment, by the 20th, which had till then lost comparatively little, and by the 124th, which arrived from Sistova during the evening. The firing continued all night, during which the troops were gradually withdrawn; it was daylight before the last of them retired. At 11 A.M. (July 31) they were all assembled at Tristenik and Kargatch, and took up position there to receive the enemy if he advanced, which however he did not do.

The attack of the right wing had been a total failure.

On the left wing, at half past two the two regiments of the 32d Division (Nos. 125 and 126) began descending the Radischevo ridge; as they came out of the brush at the bottom of the ravine and began climbing the opposite slope, they were received by a murderous fire from the two redoubts marked Nos. 1 and 8 on the accompanying map, and from several lines of trenches in front of them. But, in spite of terrible losses, these two regiments kept pressing on, and carried one after another of the lines of trenches, and by 5 o'clock had gained possession of the two redoubts. From No. 1 the Turks withdrew 10 pieces, leaving 2 in the hands of the Russians; from No. 8 they succeeded in withdrawing all their artillery.

At 5 o'clock, therefore, Shakofskoi had gained possession of the two most southerly redoubts of the "middle group" (the other two remaining still in the hands of the Turks), his left flank had penetrated by a ravine to the edge of the town on the southeast, and his right flank was in Redoubt No. 1. Of the troops forming his second line (1st Brigade 30th Division), one regiment (No. 118) had already been brought into action (one battalion on the left flank and the other two on the right), so that he now had but one regiment in reserve; of his artillery, 8 guns had been advanced to the knoll on which was subsequently built Redoubt No. 10, and 16 guns to a position on the right of Redoubt No. 1. Four guns were with Skobeleff, 3 were disabled, and the remaining 21 were kept in reserve.

It now became a question whether Shakofskoi could hold the ground he had taken. His right flank, in Redoubt No. 1, was separated from Krüdener's troops in front of the Grivitza redoubt by a distance of about two miles in a straight line, and as the Turks occupied the intervening space, at least five miles as the troops must march. All hope of mutual support between the two wings was therefore out of the question. The Turks meanwhile were massing a large force in this interval, and preparing to advance beyond Shakofskoi's right (his line of battle faced nearly north) against his line of retreat. At the same time, 5 P. M., Shakofskoi received word from Krüdener that, of the two regiments forming the general reserve, one (No. 119) was already on the road to him, while the other (No. 120) had been directed toward his own (Krüdener's) position. This regiment (No. 119) never reached Shakofskoi's position, for the following reason: On the march between Grivitza and Radischevo it passed about 1,500 yards in front of the column of Turks which was already advancing through this interval. Seeing the danger which menaced Shakofskoi's right and rear if this column continued its advance, the officer conducting this regiment, a captain on the staff at Krüdener's headquarters, who was familiar with the plan of battle, took the responsibility of halting the regiment and bringing it into action by the right flank against the advancing Turks. This partly filled up the wide interval separating the two wings, and, in conjunction with the firing from the troops near Redoubt No. 1, checked the Turkish advance.

The troops in the ravine near the town (Shakofskoi's left) were meanwhile very hard pressed by fresh Turkish reserves issuing from the town; to sustain them Shakofskoi sent in succession two battalions of the 117th, his only fresh regiment. By 6 o'clock, therefore, every man was engaged, and all hopes of a farther advance were abandoned; and, as their present position was surrounded by the Turks on three sides, it was only a question of holding their ground until dark and then withdrawing back to the Radischevo ridge, which was done in good order. The next morning the troops were marched back to Poradim.

Meanwhile, it will be remembered, there was a small force on the extreme left, under the orders of Major-General Skobeleff II. It was hotly engaged during the whole day, and, although small in numbers, was handled with such skill as to establish beyond doubt the military genius of this brilliant young general. His operations were in brief as follows: With the Caucasian Brigade (12 sotnias and 12 small guns), reënforced by one battalion of the 125th Regiment, he left Bogot at 5 A. M. and moved out to the Lovtcha chaussée, and thence up to the village of Krishin. His orders were to prevent any reënforcements from arriving from Lovtcha, and in general to cover the left flank of the Russians; in case the Turks retreated, to cross the Vid and strike them in flank. At this date, the Turks had not yet built any fortifications between the Lovtcha road and the Vid. Arrived at Krishin, he left there the bulk of his force in a central position, and, taking 2 sotnias and 4 guns, rode forward to the heights about 300 yards southwest of the town of Plevna. From this point he had a complete view of the whole Turkish position, and noticed that besides the troops in the redoubts the Turks had an immense camp of at least 20,000 men in the valley just north of Plevna, and a considerable force of cavalry behind them in the direction of the bridge over the Vid. When Shakofskoi's guns opened fire about 10 A. M. on the Radischevo ridge, Skobeleff also opened fire with his four pieces, and thus diverted about 4,000 Turkish infantry against himself. The Turks made a resolute attack, and Skobeleff with his handful of Cossacks fell back to his main force at Krishin. In this little reconnaissance Skobeleff had taken in at once the whole position of the Turks, and he saw that if they simply moved out about two miles from Plevna on the Lovtcha road, they could occupy a hill (the second knoll of the "Green Hills," on which Turkish Redoubt No. 20 was afterward built), from which at 2,500 yards' range they could enfilade the whole of Shakofskoi's line and take him in reverse as he advanced; Shakofskoi could do nothing against this position, as it was separated from his own by a rocky ravine with perpendicular bluffs. It was of vital consequence to keep the Turks away from this hill; and as the best means to accomplish this result, Skobeleff determined to *attack energetically* with his little detachment. But in order to carry out his instructions about covering the left flank of the whole force, he sent one little detachment of Cossacks to find a ford over the Vid, posted a sotnia between them and Krishin, another sotnia between Krishin and Shakofskoi's position to keep up communication, several strong pickets in the direction of Lovtcha, and finally on the hill near Krishin 3 sotnias and 12 guns. This left him 4 sotnias, and the battalion of infantry with 4 guns; with these Skobeleff moved forward directly against the troops who had attacked him, and who remained on the height just southwest of the town. With them Skobeleff kept up a desperate fight all day and into the night. Until four o'clock he kept 3 companies and 2 sotnias in reserve, leaving the other 2 companies, 2 sotnias (dismounted), and 4 guns to do the fighting; then, just as his men were beginning to give way, he sent in the other 3 companies; and thus he managed to keep up the fight until dark, and also to remove all his wounded. After dark, covered by the remaining 2 sotnias, he made good his retreat to Krishin, and reassembled there the whole of his little force, or what was left of it, for the infantry had lost over 50 per cent. But Skobeleff had gained his object, and had kept the Turks away from this hill, from which, if they had occupied it, they would have cut Shakofskoi's troops to pieces. During the night Skobeleff received orders to return to Bogot and thence to Pelishat.

Thus ended in complete failure the battle of July 30th, the second of the series of assaults upon Plevna.

The Russian loss, out of 30,000 men engaged, was 169 officers and 7,136 men. Of this number, 2,400 men had been killed and were left upon the field. The regiments which suffered the most were the 121st in Krüdener's Corps, and the 126th in Shakofskoi's. These two regiments had led the assaults; the latter lost 725 killed! besides some 1,200 or more wounded—a total loss of about 75 per cent. of its strength.

The Turkish loss, as usual, is not accurately known, but it was estimated at between 5,000 and 6,000 men.

On receiving the news of this defeat, the Grand Duke hastened from Tirnova to Karagatch, and on the 2d of July inspected the troops in the positions which they occupied from Tristenik to Poradim; they were in good spirits notwithstanding their recent rough handling. The trait which more than any other distinguishes the Russian soldier is his steadiness and solidity; he never has taken a panic, and, though he was terribly defeated, there was none now. Some of the wounded carried exaggerated tales to Sistova, and a grand stampede took place among the inhabitants and camp-followers on both sides of the bridge. But there was nothing of this kind among the troops. Had Osman followed them, he would probably have met a very stubborn opposition; the positions about Tristenik and Poradim are favorable to the defense, and the 16th Division, which had just crossed the Danube, was within one day's march, besides the rest of the XI. Corps, which might have been brought from Tirnova (three days' march) if necessary. It would appear at first sight as if Osman made a great mistake in not pursuing the force which he had so signally defeated, especially as he probably had a considerable force of fresh troops which had not been engaged at all, and as the Russians had retreated in two columns on divergent country roads totally independent of each other, leaving the great high-road midway between them perfectly open. Yet it is a fact that every offensive movement of the Turks throughout the war came to naught, and it is more

SECOND BATTLE AT PLEVNA.

than probable that Osman did exactly the wisest thing; he felt sure that the Russians would come at him again as soon as they got a few more men together, and he therefore kept his troops on their own ground, and set them to work as hard as they could with their spades.

The failure of the Russians on this day gave rise to much hard feeling and recrimination. Shakofskoi complained that Krüdener had not supported him, while Krüdener complained that Shakofskoi had not obeyed his orders, which were to advance to the hill midway between Radischevo and Grivitza, and due east of Plevna, and open fire with his artillery, but not to assault without further orders. Krüdener was the senior officer present, but Shakofskoi was also a Corps Commander, though he had only one brigade of his Corps with him. Finally, the Grand Duke had given orders from a distance to attack a position of which he knew nothing, and against a partial remonstrance of the General (Krüdener) in local command.

It is none of our business to follow these controversies or try to fix the responsibility of the failure. It is enough for us foreigners to notice the plain facts:

1. That a strongly fortified position was attacked by an inferior force.

2. That the attack was made by two columns not in supporting distance, but wholly independent of each other.

3. That against the Grivitza Redoubt the regiments were sent to the assault one after the other, not at the critical moment when the regiment already engaged was beginning to waver, but after it had been wholly driven back.

4. That the tactical formation of two lines of company columns was maintained long after the troops came under fire. This close formation partially accounts for the great losses, about 25 per cent. of all the troops on the field.

The redeeming feature of the day was Skobeleff's brilliant manœuvres with a handful of troops on the left flank, whereby he saved Shakofskoi from being knocked to pieces.

CHAPTER IV.

GENERAL CONDITION OF AFFAIRS AT THE BEGINNING OF AUGUST.—BATTLE OF SHIPKA PASS, AUGUST 21ST TO 26TH.—OPERATIONS ON THE LOM IN AUGUST AND SEPTEMBER.

(See Plate 11.)

THE decisive defeat at Plevna on the 30th of July brought the Russian advance to a standstill. The positions of the opposing armies at that time were as follows: The Russians occupied a figure nearly elliptical in shape, and extending from Nikopolis, through Poradim, Selvi, Gabrova, Shipka, Elena, Cesarevo, Katselevo, and the line of the Lom, to the Danube near Rustchuk; from Sistova to the Shipka Pass, i. e., along the major axis of the ellipse, the distance, following the highroad through Tirnova, is about 80 miles; from Poradim to Katselevo, the minor axis, the distance is about 90 miles by the road. The six Corps (IV., VIII., IX., XI., XII., and XIII.) occupying this space had lost about 15,000 men in killed and wounded since the beginning of the campaign. Their total strength was therefore probably about 120,000 infantry, 12,000 cavalry, and 648 guns of all kinds. There was also Zimmermann's detachment off in the Dobrudja, numbering about 25,000 men (XIV. and part of VII. Corps), but this was necessarily limited to the defensive rôle of covering the communications of the army from any attack from the Dobrudja, and it could not be of any assistance to an offensive movement.

The Turks were on the exterior of this ellipse, and occupied in force three points (Plevna, Yeni-Zagra, and Rasgrad) situated nearly at the angles of an equilateral triangle whose sides are

CONDITION OF AFFAIRS IN AUGUST.   203

from 70 to 90 miles long. Osman commanded at Plevna with 50,000 men, Suleiman at Yeni-Zagra with 40,000, Mehemet Ali at Rasgrad with 65,000. They also had strong detachments at Lovtcha and at Osman Bazar, as well as in the Quadrilateral fortresses. Their total force in the field numbered about 195,-000 men of all arms.

Two feasible plans were therefore open to the Russian Commander-in-Chief:

1. To leave small detachments at Shipka and on the Tirnova-Shumla and Biela-Rasgrad roads, and then transfer the VIII., XI., and XIII. Corps with the utmost rapidity to Plevna, and unite them with the IV. and IX. Corps already there, and overwhelm Osman; then move his army rapidly to Tirnova or Biela, according to the movements of the Turks meantime, and attack the other Turkish detachment; the united Russian army was larger than any one of the widely scattered detachments around it, and it had the advantage of short interior lines; or

2. To leave the troops on the defensive in their present positions, and quietly await the arrival of reënforcements from Russia.

All idea of carrying on the original plan of campaign with the troops actually in hand was out of the question; for the two wings posted to cover the flanks—IV. and IX. Corps on the line of the Vid, XII., XIII., and XI. Corps on the Lom—had each an enemy numerically superior in their fronts, and there was nothing left to cross the Balkans with except the VIII. Corps, which was obviously not sufficient in strength. Moreover, the right flank was, properly speaking, not covered at all; for the two most important points along that line, Plevna and Lovtcha, were in the hands of the Turks and strongly occupied. The terrible error of underestimating the enemy and beginning the war with an inadequate force was apparent to every one, and was freely acknowledged. The singular part of it is, that the same mistake was committed in 1828, and again in 1829.

To the first plan, independently of its military difficulties, requiring most active leadership and prompt movements, and resulting if unsuccessful in a retreat across the Danube, there were also the gravest political objections. It was a war which brought out the long pent-up hatreds engendered by difference of race, irreconcilable religions, and centuries of oppression and misrule on one side and suffering on the other. The two classes of the population fled in turn before the approach of the opposing armies, the Mohammedans before the Russians, the Bulgarians before the Turks. Suleiman Pasha had already burned the large town of Eski-Zagra to the ground, and had begun in the valley of the Maritza a wholesale system of hanging at the street corners every Bulgarian who had assisted (as guide, etc.) Gourko's troops during their stay south of the Balkans. As a result the Bulgarians, to the number of nearly 100,000 souls, were fleeing north over the Balkans. If the Russians now withdrew from any of the territory they had occupied, they left the Christian population to the chance of being massacred. In a war undertaken for their liberation, this was not to be thought of.

The second plan was therefore decided upon, and on the 3d of August the Emperor signed the order for the mobilization of the Guard, the Grenadiers, and two divisions of the Line (24th and 26th). Two other divisions of the Line (2d and 3d) had been ordered mobilized just after the outbreak of the war. The strength of these troops was as follows:

	Battalions.	Squadrons.	Foot guns.	Horse guns.
Corps of the Guard	58	24	148	12
2d and 3d Divisions of Grenadiers	24	..	96	..
2d Division of the Line	12	..	48	..
3d " " "	12	..	48	..
24th " " "	13	..	48	..
26th " " "	12	..	48	..
1st Cavalry Division	..	18	..	12
Total	125	42	436	24

or in all about 120,000 men and 460 guns.

In addition to this, the Emperor had a few days previously (July 22d) issued a ukase calling out a portion of the first ban of the militia *—188,000 men—to replace the losses already incurred in battle, and to be ready to replace those of the future. Of the Reserve, three Divisions (36,000 men) were ordered to be mobilized in addition to one division which had been previously mobilized; part of these were destined for garrison duty at home, and part to replace the regular troops on the line of the *étapes* in Russia and Roumania.

* The difference between the Militia and the Reserve is explained at p. 19.

The effect of these measures was to call out 120,000 men for service at the front, and 220,000 more to replace losses and do ordinary duty. They arrived on the Danube as follows: the 2d and 3d Divisions in August, the Guard and the 26th Division in September, the Grenadiers and the 24th Division in October. The 188,000 men of the Militia began to arrive in August, and continued arriving till long after the peace of San Stefano; they came as squads of recruits destined to this or that regiment, and were immediately incorporated with it.

But as only a small portion of all these troops would be available in the course of the next few weeks, an appeal was made to the Prince of Roumania to put his army into the field, to which he promptly responded. The Roumanian Army consisted of 32,000 Infantry, 5,000 Cavalry, and 84 guns, organized into 4 Divisions. They had all been mobilized and ready for active service since the month of May; a portion of the 4th Division had already crossed the Danube and gone into garrison at Nikopolis. Orders were immediately given for the passage of the remainder.

Such were the measures taken by the Russians for carrying on the struggle, and until the arrival of at least a portion of these reënforcements they were restricted to a simply defensive rôle in the positions which they had already gained.

This was the moment therefore for the Turks to strike a vigorous blow. Mehemet Ali had arrived at Shumla on the 22d of July, and relieved the aged Pasha, Abdul Kerim, of the command of the Army of the Lom and the troops in the fortresses. Suleiman, after driving Gourko back into the Balkans, August 1st, had quietly encamped near Yeni-Zagra for the next 15 days. On his movements depended in a large degree the success of the Turkish offensive, and it is not too much to say that he adopted the very worst plan possible under the circumstances. There was no Turkish Commander-in-Chief at this time, the three Commanders, Mehemet Ali, Suleiman, and Osman, being independent of each other and equal in rank; and they were all directed by telegraph from Constantinople, where a "War Council" was in constant session giving orders in the Sultan's name—as bad a system as could possibly be conceived.

Suleiman had the option of joining his army to either one of the other two (a ten days' march), and then striking a vigorous blow at the Russian flank and their communications by the Sistova bridge; or of trying to force his way over the Balkan passes directly in his front. The road to Plevna by the Trojan Pass was not a good one, and it led rather dangerously near the Russian positions at Selvi; moreover, even supposing they gained a victory at Plevna, the Turks could not advance against Sistova without recapturing the fortress of Nikopolis. On the other hand, the road toward Shumla led over the Slivno-Shumla Pass, which is one of the best high-roads over the Balkans, and was nowhere nearer than 30 miles to any of the Russian positions. By taking the garrisons of Shumla and Varna, the united forces of Mehemet Ali and Suleiman would have been more than 125,000 men. By throwing these upon the Russian left wing, they would have compelled the Russians to let go their hold of Shipka in order to get together even 90,000 men (VIII., XI., XII., and XIII. Corps) to resist them; and if they beat the Russians in a decisive battle, there was nothing to prevent their reaching the Sistova Bridge, while if they were beaten they simply fell back upon the fortresses. Such was the plan which it is said Mehemet Ali urged, but Suleiman was determined to attack the Shipka Pass directly in front, and he was sustained by the War Council.

Suleiman moved forward on the 16th, and began his attack on Shipka on the 21st of August, and kept it up with more or less energy for the next four months. Without gaining the least material advantage in so doing, he sacrificed the best part of the fine army he brought with him from Montenegro.

Osman, on the 31st of August, made a lame attempt at the offensive in front of Plevna, but it resulted in nothing; and ten days later (September 11th) he was attacked by the Russians—the third and principal battle of Plevna, unsuccessful like its predecessors, but eventually followed by the investment of Osman's army and its ultimate surrender.

Mehemet Ali, after some preliminary skirmishing, began his attack on the Cesarevitch's army (Russian left wing) on the 30th of August, and drove it back from the Lom to the Yantra. Then he suddenly stopped, and a few days later, toward the end of September, returned to his old positions.

Such in brief was the result of the Turkish offensive. We will now follow these movements somewhat in detail.

BATTLE OF SHIPKA PASS.

SULEIMAN PASHA'S ATTACK ON SHIPKA PASS, AUGUST 20TH–26TH.

(See Plate 13.)

In the vicinity of Shipka the peaks of the Balkans are nearly 5,000 feet above sea-level. The valley of the Tundja, which is parallel to the chain and only a few miles from it on the south, has an altitude of about 1,300 feet; on the north the head waters of the Yantra near Gabrova are at about the same altitude. Near Shipka the chain throws out three long and nearly parallel spurs to the north, and these spurs, although shorter, are also distinguishable on the south; they are separated by deep wooded ravines, and are only united at the top by saddles in the main range of the mountains. The central one of these we may call the Shipka ridge, the easterly one the Berdek, the westerly the Bald Mountain ridge. It is a misnomer to speak of the Shipka Pass as a pass in the ordinary meaning of the word; for the road does not pass through a gorge or ravine between high peaks, but on the contrary it follows the whole length of the central spur and passes over its highest point. From Gabrova the road follows a small stream for about 5 miles to the south and then takes a sudden turn to the east, and in the course of a mile of very steep ascent climbs on to the ridge; it then follows the gradual slope of the ridge for about 3 miles to Mount St. Nicholas, the highest point; from here the road descends rapidly in steep zigzags to the village of Shipka. Near the summit of the central or Shipka spur are three sets of little hills or ridges about 200 feet high, running across the main ridge; the highest and most southerly of these is called Mount St. Nicholas, and for convenience we will call the other two the "Central" and "Northern" hills. The highest points of the western and eastern spurs are known respectively as the Berdek and the Bald Mountain. They dominate the whole position, and are reached by narrow paths along the mountain. The Russian position was on the three sets of little hills just mentioned. On St. Nicholas, the southern side of which is in part a perpendicular rock, the Russians had three batteries, which had originally been built by the Turks for the defense of the pass from the north, and which now, with slight alteration, served the same purpose in an opposite direction; in these the Russians had 25 guns. On the left and rear of St. Nicholas (i. e., to the northeast of it) runs a little spur about 250 yards long, at the end of which the Russians had 7 steel guns, previously captured from the Turks. Connecting this steel battery with Mount St. Nicholas were some trenches hastily thrown up in the rocky soil. On the central hill were the "central" battery and "round" battery, each armed with 4 guns, and some rude trenches.

On the 15th of August the Russian troops in this neighborhood consisted of 34 battalions, or about 27,000 men, with their proportionate artillery and a small force of cavalry, and were posted as follows:

At Tirnova, Headquarters of VIII. Corps and of 14th Division, 55th and 56th Regiments and 4th Rifle Brigade, and 40 guns;

At Selvi, Headquarters 9th Division, 35th, 53d, and 54th Regiments, 3 sotnias of Cossacks, and 24 guns;

In Shipka Pass, 36th Regiment, 5 battalions of Bulgarian Legion, 5 sotnias of Cossacks, and 29 guns;

In Travna Pass, 1 battalion Bulgarian Legion;

In Hainkioi Pass, 33d Regiment, 2 sotnias, and 14 guns;

In Elena Pass, 34th Regiment, 13th Dragoons, and 2 guns.

Tirnova and Selvi are each two days' march from Shipka.

On the 16th of August Suleiman's troops first made their appearance by a demonstration against the Hainkioi Pass, and on the 18th a detachment occupied Bebrova, on the Elena road, at the same time that the head of the main column appeared at Kazanlyk. General Radetzky, commanding the VIII. Corps, immediately ordered the 35th Regiment to proceed in all haste to Shipka, but he was sufficiently deceived by this demonstration against the Elena Pass to proceed thither in person with the 4th Rifle Brigade and the 55th and 56th Regiments. Finding no enemy in force, he returned to Tirnova on the 21st, and there received word from Shipka that the Turks had attacked in great force. In spite of their fatigue, he started the 4th Rifle Brigade and the 55th and 56th Regiments toward Shipka at daylight the next morning, and also telegraphed to the 2d Division (which had just arrived and was in bivouac between Gorni-Studen and Selvi) to proceed to Selvi and relieve the 53d and 54th Regiments, which were then to proceed to Shipka. In other words, all available troops were ordered to Shipka except the two regiments guarding the Hainkioi and Elena Passes. Radetzky himself arrived on the field in the afternoon of August 23d.

Meanwhile Gen. Darozhinsky, who commanded the little force of about 5,000 men at Shipka Pass, and who, on account of the difficulty of procuring water on the mountain, had kept his men in bivouac in the village of Shipka, noticed the approach of the Turks on the 18th, retired to the pass on the 19th, and on the 20th saw the whole force of Suleiman deploy in the plain just below him, and counted 40 battalions, probably 26,000 to 28,000 men, besides a large number of Tcherkesses. He immediately disposed his little force as follows: 1 battalion behind St. Nicholas and the "Steel" battery; 1½ battalion of Russians and 3 of Bulgarians along the Central Hill; and 1½ battalion of Russians and 2 of Bulgarians, as a reserve, on the "isthmus," between the Central and St. Nicholas Hills.

On the morning of the 21st the Turks were visible on the Berdek Mountains, constructing a battery about 2,000 yards from St. Nicholas. In spite of the Russian shells, they finished the construction of it and placed 4 guns in position. After one or two minor attacks, the Turks moved forward about noon from the Sugar-Loaf Hill, and began an assault with 20 battalions against the "Steel" battery, on the left flank of Mount St. Nicholas. They attacked with the utmost desperation, but were as desperately received, and the struggle went on from a little afternoon till 8 o'clock at night. Again and again the Turks came on yelling "Allah," and rushed up the slope to within a few yards of the battery; but they could go no farther. Their last attack was made by moonlight about 9 P. M., and being repulsed they tried no more for that day; but they remained in the positions they had taken—the most advanced of which was not over 100 yards from the Russian battery—and kept up a constant fire throughout the night.

During the day the 35th Regiment had arrived from Selvi and taken position behind the "Round" battery.

The next morning, 22d, the Turks opened a very heavy fire from Berdek, where they now had 10 guns in position; from the Bald Mountain on the opposite flank, whither they had dragged during the night 6 guns; and from the "Woody Mountain," where they had also placed 2 guns. In short, their batteries were in front, on both flanks, and in the rear of the Russian posi-

14

tion; only by reason of intervening woods the battery at Woody Mountain could not reach St. Nicholas, but it completely commanded the "Central" and "Northern" Hills.

Throughout this day (August 22d) a continuous fire of artillery and infantry was kept up, but the Turks made no serious attacks; a few guns were dismounted on both sides, but a far more serious danger was threatening the Russians in the lack of artillery ammunition, which was nearly exhausted. Both parties worked all day at repairing their batteries, and the Turks at covering their advanced positions by shelter-trenches. Meanwhile the Turks were withdrawing a portion of their troops in reserve behind Berdek and sending them over to the western spur (Woody Mountain), with the intention of attacking the right flank of the Russians at the Central Hill (held by the 35th Regiment), and thus cutting off their communications with Gabrova. At the same time a body of Tcherkesses descended the eastern spur and threatened the high-road from that side.

On the morning of the 23d, in fact, the Russian position was well-nigh surrounded on all sides; the narrow ridges, along which ran the high-road, connecting the little hills which formed the Russian position, were wholly exposed to a cross-fire of the Turks at 1,500 to 2,000 yards' range.

At 6 o'clock in the morning Suleiman began his attack, and it soon became general from all sides, one column rushing at the rocks on the south of St. Nicholas, another against the right flank of the Central Hill (where the Russian faced west), and a third against the round battery on the left flank of this hill (where they faced east). A most desperate struggle continued throughout this whole day, 7,500 Russians being engaged to the last man, and trying to hold their own against the 25,000 Turks who came to their assault. During the afternoon the position of the Russians became most critical; their artillery ammunition was exhausted; their losses were enormous, and the men began to lose courage under the demoralizing effect of a cross-fire so long continued, and of the heat and lack of food and water.

About the same time the Turkish column from Woody Mountain reformed and began advancing along the northern slope of the Central Hill, and in rear of it, toward the high-road. There were no reserves left on the Russian side to meet this column. The portion of the 35th Regiment which held the right flank of the Central Hill, having lost nearly all its officers, was broken into little groups, and toward 3 o'clock these groups began to pick up the last of the wounded, turn back to the road behind them, and move off to the rear. The number of wounded going back toward the field hospital was so great that these men, having no officers, thought it was a general retreat. The moment was the most critical of the campaign; if this Turkish column reached the high-road and established itself on the Northern Hill, on the rear of the Russians and upon their one line of communication, a disastrous retreat before a largely superior force, or possibly a surrender, was inevitable. Taking a few non-commissioned officers, Colonel Lipinsky, commanding this part of the field, went back to the road, expostulated, reasoned, threatened, and drove these men back to the positions on the Center Hill. From here they delivered their fire in volleys upon the Turks in their rear, who were just beginning to climb the slope toward the road. Stunned by this sudden reception, the Turks wavered a little; and at this very moment (about 4:30 P. M.) appeared in sight the first of the reënforcements—200 men of the 4th Rifle Brigade, trotting up along the high-road on Cossack horses taken at Gabrova—and with them General Radetzky, commanding the VIII. Corps. The 16th Battalion of this Rifle Brigade came into position on the Northern Hill, and went down the hill at a run against the left flank of this Turkish column. The attack was so bold and spirited that the Turks fell back through the wood, and up on the Woody Mountain, leaving the Russians in possession of their first line of trenches at the foot of the slope. The little valley was filled with the dead of the twelve hours' struggle which had been going on at this point.

Meanwhile, throughout the day, the Russians at St. Nicholas and the "Central Hills" held on to their positions, though at the cost of terrible losses.

During the afternoon and evening the rest of the 4th Rifle Brigade arrived, and was posted along the whole line, partly relieving the men in St. Nicholas, whose physical strength was well-nigh exhausted.

At 5 o'clock on the morning of the 24th arrived General Dragomiroff with the leading regiment (No. 56) of his Division, having marched 38 miles the previous day. One battalion was sent across the ravine to climb the western spur and attack the Bald Mountain position in flank; the other two were moved along the road in reserve of the other troops. While posting his men on the Northern Hill General Dragomiroff was severely wounded in the knee about 10 A. M., and carried off the field, one of his staff officers being also wounded at the same time. A general cannonade and fusillade had been begun by the Turks at sunrise, and was in fact kept up all day, upon every one passing along the road; but it was not until noon that the Turks renewed the attack.

Noticing the arrival of Russian reënforcements, Suleiman now made a last desperate effort to get possession of Mount St. Nicholas. This time the Turks, at least those in the lead, actually got into the Russian trenches on the top of the hill, and were only driven out after a hand-to-hand struggle, in which the bayonet was very freely used. In this affair the leading Turkish battalion (about 500 men) was virtually annihilated. This was the last of the Turkish assaults.

During the day the rest of the regiments of Dragomiroff's Division continued arriving, and on the 25th Radetzky made an effort to get possession of the Woody Mountain, which commanded all the approaches to his own position; but he sent totally inadequate forces to make the attempt. They consisted of the one battalion (56th Regiment) which Dragomiroff had sent across the ravine the previous morning, and of the three battalions which held the right of the Central Hill. The former did not get across the deep wooded ravine and up the Bald Mountain spur till nearly noon on the 25th.

Hearing them engaged, Radetzky then sent the other three battalions against the right of the position, i. e., against Woody Mountain. The Turks were driven out of their advanced trenches during the afternoon, and were followed in hot pursuit by the Russians, who arrived somewhat disorganized at the second line of works on top of the Woody Mountain. Here they met fresh troops of the Turkish reserves, and were in turn driven back. Two battalions of the 53d Regiment were sent to assist them, and a very hot fight went on during the evening and most of the night. But Radetzky did not consider his main force strong enough to detach any more men to reënforce them, and consequently on the morning of the 26th they retreated down the slope and back again to the Central Hill. The Turks followed them as far as their most advanced trenches, but no farther.

Thus ended the first period of this remarkable battle. Desultory firing of both artillery and infantry continued, but no more assaults were made until the 17th of September. After five days of almost uninterrupted fighting, both sides were now substantially where they were at the beginning. Radetzky's report puts his losses at about 100 officers and 3,500 men. That of the Turks was estimated at about 10,000 men; but a British naval officer, who was present with the Turks as correspondent of the "Times," states that they had 8,350 wounded and between 3,000 and 4,000 dead.

For three days (August 21st, 22d, and 23d) less than 8,000 Russians and Bulgarians had held in check the Army of Suleiman, 25,000 to 30,000 strong. During this time their only food was the biscuit (about one day's ration) which they had in their pockets when the affair began; the heat was intense, but the nearest water was at a spring between three and four miles back on the road toward Gabrova, and all that the men had to drink was the little which was brought back in their canteens by the men who carried the wounded to the rear. Whenever the firing ceased for a while, they lay down on the ground they were defending and caught an hour's sleep; for it was the period of full moon, and night brought no cessation to the firing. It was not only during the assaults of the Turks that the men were under fire—it was at all times, dependent only on the pleasure of the Turks; for from behind the woods on the two spurs on either side the *Turks commanded every point of the Russian position*, excepting only a small portion of the reverse slope of the Northern Hill; and even here General Darozhinsky was shot dead on the morning of the 25th by some Turkish pickets in advance of Bald Mountain. The odor of decomposing corpses was sickening and the sight of them demoralizing.

On the afternoon of the 23d the men had just about reached the final limit of human endurance. Then the reënforcements began to arrive, allowing the men to be relieved and have a little rest; the soup kitchens were established back near the spring, and the Bulgarian peasants were impressed at Gabrova and put to carrying water and food up to the men.

For impetuous assaults and tenacious, dogged defense, for long-continued fighting and physical endurance, this five days' battle in the mountains is extremely remarkable; but there were no skillful manœuvres of the troops on either side. Although Suleiman took possession of heights flanking and nearly surrounding the Russians, yet he persisted in dividing his forces and making his strongest attacks upon their strongest position (Mount St. Nicholas), thereby enabling them, although far inferior in numbers, to hold their ground at all points for three days until the arrival of reënforcements. Had Suleiman thrown the whole of his force into either one of his flank attacks, he would in all probability have carried the whole place. On the other hand, the Russians, during the ten days between the time the Bulgarians were driven out of Eski-Zagra and the appearance of the Turks at Kazanlyk, had remained idly at the village of Shipka, and done nothing toward strengthening their position in the pass, except to modify the original Turkish fortifications so as to turn them against the south instead of the north. The Russians in fact felt quite confident that Suleiman would either go through Slivno to Osman-Bazar, or else through the Elena Pass to attack Tirnova. This was a most natural supposition, but it hardly justified the Russians in failing to do their utmost to make the Shipka Pass impregnable. The little force of 5,000 men was not sufficient to occupy the heights on all three of the main spurs, but they might easily have made strong lines of trenches on each of the little hills on the top of the road, and been prepared to make a good defense; whereas, on the third day of the fighting (August 23d) the men on the Northern Hill were firing from behind rocks and piles of blankets; there was a sad deficiency of spades and other implements actually with the troops; and there were no engineer troops anywhere in that vicinity of the theatre of war.

Radetzky's attack on Woody Mountain (August 25th) was a very lame affair. Either he should not have made it at all, or else he should have sent more than 4 battalions to do it. He had on that morning, owing to the arrival of reënforcements, 24 battalions, viz., the 35th, 36th, 53d, 54th, and 56th Regiments, 4th Rifle Brigade, and the Bulgarian Legion; and the 55th Regiment was expected to arrive during the day. If the possession of Woody and Bald Mountains was of great impor-

BATTLE OF SHIPKA PASS. 215

tance (and it would seem that it was so, since it commanded for a long distance the only road over which his ammunition, food, water, and reënforcements could arrive), then he might have risked holding the main position with 14 battalions, since it had been held for three days by 11 battalions, and have sent the remaining 10 to take the hill at any cost. The result of sending 4 battalions was that they were badly defeated and lost over one third of their strength.

Suleiman had, however, exhausted his strength, and was obliged to stop and reorganize his shattered army and bring up the few battalions which he had left at Yeni-Zagra. His troops remained in their positions on the two commanding spurs, and picked off the passing Russians on the high-road to the number of 40 or 50 a day. The latter dug trenches along the road to form a covered way, but still they were more or less exposed in passing.

On the 28th of August the brigade of the XI. Corps (1st Brigade 32d Division), which had fought under Shakofskoi at Plevna on July 30th, and which had subsequently been sent to Selvi, arrived at Gabrova; one regiment of it remained there, and the other was sent to Zelenodrevo, at the foot of the western spur, to prevent a descent of the Turks along the Bald Mountain ridge toward Gabrova. One brigade of the 2d Division was also sent over to Gabrova about August 28th; but, as the Turks failed to renew their attacks, it was a few days later sent back to Selvi, and thence it took part in the battles of Lovtcha and Plevna.

MEHEMET ALI'S ADVANCE ON THE LINE OF THE LOM, AUGUST 22D TO SEPTEMBER 30TH.

(See Plate 14.)

According to the general plan of campaign, as previously explained, immediately after the passage of the Danube the XII. and XIII. Corps were formed into a detachment under command of the Cesarevitch, and posted along the line of the Lom, to cover the left flank of the army from any attacks from the fortresses of the Quadrilateral. The XII. Corps advanced along the Biela-Rustchuk high-road as far as the Lom, and its cavalry penetrated in a reconnaissance (July 21st) as far as the station of Tchernavoda, on the Rustchuk-Varna Railroad, and destroyed a small portion of the track and telegraph there. The XIII. Corps deployed on its right in the direction of Razgrad, and on the 26th of July its scouts were within eight miles of that town. The XI. Corps meanwhile (except the brigade which was sent to Plevna for the attack of July 30th), after crossing the Danube, had been marched to Tirnova, and thence deployed westward along the high-road to Osman-Bazar and Shumla.

In the country between Osman-Bazar and Eski-Djuma are several foot-hills or spurs of the Balkans, which drain toward the Danube by means of the Yantra and Lom Rivers. The affluents of the former flow westward and reach the Yantra not far from Tirnova, and thence the river goes due north past Biela to the Danube. The head waters of the Lom are spread over a wide extent of country; on the east and west respectively of Rasgrad are the Lom and the White Lom; farther west are the Black Lom and Banitchka Lom; the two latter unite at a point about 20 miles southeast of Biela, and a few miles farther on they join the White Lom, and the united river then runs for about 12 miles more and empties into the Danube at Rustchuk.

There are high-roads leading from Rustchuk through Biela to Tirnova, from Rustchuk through Razgrad to Shumla, from Tirnova through Osman-Bazar to Shumla, and from Razgrad through Eski-Djuma to Osman-Bazar, and thence to Slivno. But in the basin of the Lom there are no high-roads; the country is very high and undulating, and the branches of the Lom flow through deep rocky gorges, in the vicinity of which are extensive tracts covered with a short scrub oak; the means of communication are few and widely separated, and it is generally a difficult country for military operations.

On the 15th of August the Cesarevitch's detachment of two corps, numbering in all about 40,000 infantry, 5,000 cavalry, and 200 guns, was scattered over a length of more than 50 miles behind the White Lom, his left flank being at the village of Pirgos on the Danube and his right facing Eski-Djuma.

The position of his troops was as follows:

XII. Corps...
- 12th Division: One brigade at Pirgos; One brigade at Damogila; Picket line from the Danube in front of Rustchuk, along the Lom and Black Lom, to Tabashka.
- 33d Division: At Katzelevo and Ablava.
- 12th Cavalry Division: Along the White Lom, in advance of Katzelevo.

OPERATIONS ON THE LOM. 217

XIII. Corps
- 1st Division .... { At Banitchka, forming the general reserve to the whole line.
- 35th Division .... { One brigade at Karahassankoi; One brigade at Ayazlar.
- 13th Cavalry Division.. At Sarnasuflar.

The XI. Corps was established with the 11th Division on the Osman-Bazar road at Cesarevo, and one brigade (2d Brigade 32d Division) in the direction of the Elena pass. The Cesarevitch's right flank was somewhat in the air, as there was a wide gap (about 20 miles) between the extreme right flank at Ayazlar and the left of the XI. Corps on the Tirnova-Osman-Bazar road.

Mehemet Ali, having taken command of the troops in the Quadrilateral and reconnoitered the ground, concentrated the greater part of his mobile force (independent of the fortress garrisons) in two columns—at Razgrad and Eski-Djuma. He had in the field about 50,000 infantry, 60 guns, and several regiments of regular cavalry, besides a few thousand bashi-bozouks.* Four divisions were at Razgrad, and one Turkish

* In "Der Orientalische Krieg," by Rüstow, pp. 332 and 333, it is stated as follows:
"The field army, which now at the end of August Mehemet Ali actually had at his disposition, consisted of the 3d and 4th Army Corps. The 2d Army Corps, commanded by Achmet Kaiserli in place of Eshreff Pasha, who had been relieved, formed the garrison of Rustchuk, and could not be available for operations in the open field so long as the XII. Russian Corps remained immediately in front of that fortress.

"The two field army corps had, after the reorganization effected by Mehemet Ali, the following effective strength:

3d Army Corps, Achmed Eyoub Pasha. Headquarters, Razgrad.
  1st Division, Fuad Pasha, Brigades Hussein and Mustapha—16 Battalions, 6 Squadrons, 4 Batteries.
  2d Division, Asof Pasha, Brigades Osman and Mehmed, 16 Battalions, 6 Squadrons, 4 Batteries.
  3d Division, Nedjib Pasha, Brigades Ali and Hami—16 Battalions, 6 Squadrons, 4 Batteries.
  Unattached Brigade, Hassan Pasha—6 Battalions, 1 Battery.
  Flying column, Mehmed Bey—3 Battalions Zeibeks, 6 Squadrons, one half Battery.
  Cavalry Brigade, Emir Pasha—18 Squadrons, one half Horse Battery, 2,000 Tcherkesses.
  Total, 57 Battalions, 42 Squadrons, 2,000 mounted Tcherkesses, 14 Batteries.

4th Army Corps, Prince Hassan. Headquarters, Eski-Djuma.
  1st Division, Ismail Pasha—14 Battalions (including 9 Battalions of Egyptians and 2 Battalions of Riflemen) and 4 Batteries in Brigades Safvet and Reshid.

division and the Egyptian Contingent, about equal to a division at Eski-Djuma. Taking advantage of the scattered condition of the Russian force, he planned to strike a hard blow on their right flank and then on their center, and drive them back to the Yantra. Further than that his plans do not seem to have been matured.

The movement was begun on the 22d of August by Sahli Pasha's division, which advanced from Eski Djuma and drove the Russians out of Ayazlar. The next day the Russians retook the position, but were again driven out, and retired in the direction of Popkoi, a few miles to the north. In this affair the Russians lost about 400 men.

The effect of it was to bring the two brigades of the 35th Division a little nearer together, and they stood respectively at Popkoi and Karahassankoi, on opposite sides of the Black Lom and about 8 miles apart. There was a bridge just behind Karahassankoi.

> 2d Division, Salih Pasha, Brigades Sabis and Assim—18 Battalions, 6 Squadrons, and 4 Batteries.
>
> 3d Division, Mehmed Salim Pasha, Brigades Salim and Hassan—16 Battalions, 6 Squadrons, and 3 Batteries.
>
> Reserve Division, Tahir Pasha, Brigades Tahir and Mehmed—15 Battalions and 3 Batteries.
>
> Flying Corps, Baker Pasha—3 Battalions, 1,000 mounted Tcherkesses, one half Battery.
>
> Flying Corps, Ibrahim and Mustapha Beys—2 Batteries of Zeibeks, 8 Squadrons mounted Tcherkesses.
>
> Total, 68 Battalions, 12 Squadrons, 2,000 mounted Tcherkesses, 14½ Batteries.
>
> "The whole field arms of Mehemet Ali, according to the foregoing statement, amounted to 125 battalions, 54 regular squadrons, 4,000 mounted Tcherkesses, and 28½ batteries. Had the organizations been at their regulation strength, the battalion at 800 men and the regular squadron at 150 troopers, then Mehemet Ali would have had 100,000 infantry, and, including the Tcherkesses, 12,100 troopers. But even if we take the battalions as averaging only 600 men each, and the regular squadrons 100, there were still more than 85,000 combatants of infantry and cavalry, and 171 guns."
>
> I have never heard of the publication of any official reports on the Turkish side, and do not know from what source the above detailed statement is drawn. It is stated so exactly as to have the air of coming from a trustworthy authority. The artillery is largely superior in numbers to that given by myself in the text, and the number of men is also greater. My own authority is the correspondence of the London "News" and "Times," dated at Mehemet Ali's headquarters in August and September.
>
> F. V. G.

There were no more movements until the 30th. On that date Nedjib Pasha's division was moved out from in front of Razgrad and threw itself upon the left of the 35th Division, thus cutting it off from the rest of the Russian troops. At the same time Sahli's division and the Egyptians were to advance from Sarnasuflar against the right of the 35th Division at Popkoi. The Russians fought hard all day, but were completely outnumbered, and were driven out of Karahassankoi and across the river, and back upon their principal position behind Popkoi. The Russian losses on this day have never been officially published, but were estimated in the Turkish camp to be about 1,800 men, against 1,000 on the part of the Turks.

Four days more passed in inactivity, and then, on September 3d, the three divisions at Razgrad under Achmed Eyoub Pasha, and Nedjib's division at Karahassankoi, advanced jointly down the White Lom to Solenik, crossed the White Lom near that point on the 4th, and on the 5th attacked the Russian position at Katzelevo from the direction of the north.

The Russian troops, under the command of Lieutenant-General Baron Driesen, consisted of the 12 battalions of the 33d Division, with 40 guns, and 8 squadrons and 6 guns of the 12th Cavalry Division, in all about 10,000 men. Five battalions and 8 guns were posted in front of the river on the heights of Katzelevo, and 7 battalions and 32 guns along the plateau behind the village of Ablava, on the left or south bank of the White Lom. The Turkish force numbered about 30,000 men and 60 guns. They posted their artillery in a semicircle of about 7 miles in length in front of the Russian position, and opened fire about 7 A. M. About 10 the Turks began to advance, and, seeing that they were so far superior in numbers, General Arnoldi, commanding the left flank (Katzelevo), withdrew his force in as good order as possible across the Lom, and fell back about five miles to Orendjik. About 11 A. M., 4 battalions and 1 battery of the 1st Division arrived as reënforcements at Ablava, and General Driesen then sent one regiment (No. 130) to cover the retreat of the left flank. The whole of the left flank had been got across the river by 2 P. M. The Turks, who had kept up a hot artillery fire all day, then (about 3 P. M.) began to advance their infantry; they crossed the Lom by fording, occupied the village of Ablava, and then began to attack the heights behind the village, on which the Russians were posted. But in this they were defeated and driven back again across the Lom. The fight ceased about sunset, the Russian loss being 56 officers and 1,283 men. Driesen's position, however, was totally untenable, threatened as he was on both flanks by greatly superior forces; and the next day he made good his retreat to the left bank of the Banitchka Lom. The Turks followed slowly.

On the same day it appears it was intended that the left wing of the Turkish force, which under the command of Prince Hassan was at Sarnasuflar, should also attack the Russians at Popkoi; but for some reason it was not done. The next day (September 6th) the Russians at that place began their retreat to Cerkovna, and thence behind the Banitchka Lom at Koprivca.

On the 1st of September about 5,000 men of the garrison of Rustchuk moved out to Kadikioi, and crossed the river there to attack the Russian left flank. They made but little progress, however; but on the 4th they were reënforced by another 5,000 men, and then they succeeded in driving the Russians out of their positions along the high-road and back a few miles toward Biela.

By the 8th of September, therefore, 15 days after Mehemet Ali began his advance by the attack at Ayazlar, he had driven the Cesarevitch's detachment back from the line of the White Lom to that of the Banitchka Lom, and had inflicted a loss upon it, in two small battles and several skirmishes, of between 3,000 and 4,000 men in all. Mehemet Ali had, counting the troops that had sortied from Rustchuk, not less than 60,000 men in hand along the right bank of the Banitchka Lom, viz.: 10,000 on the right flank near Kadikioi, 30,000 under Achmed Eyoub at Katzelevo, and 20,000 under Prince Hassan at Popkoi, where were also his own headquarters. From Kadikioi to Popkoi the distance is about 35 miles.

The Russians, meanwhile, had got their detachment into a more compact shape, and took up a position in front of the Yantra, their left flank being on the Danube at Batin and their right at Koprivca on the Banitchka Lom; their length of front was about 25 miles. They also hastened to fill up the gap between the Cesarevitch's right and the XI. Corps on the Tirnova-Osman-Bazar road, by sending the 26th Division, which had just crossed the Danube, to Cerkovna, and the 1st Brigade 32d Division from Gabrova to Cairkioi.

Mehemet Ali, then, on the 10th of September, had under his orders an army composed of excellent fighting material and superior in numbers to the enemy in his front; he had already gained several small successes over the enemy, and driven him back for several miles along his whole line. The question naturally arises, why then did not Mehemet Ali concentrate his whole force and fight a decisive battle about Biela? If successful, there was a fair chance of driving the Russians across the Danube; and if unsuccessful, he had only to retire under shelter of the forts at Rustchuk and Shumla, which now were strong enough to require a regular siege. The only reason which has ever been assigned for the inaction which Mehemet Ali displayed was that his army, though composed of good fighting men, was so badly officered as to greatly diminish its efficiency for offensive purposes; and especially was this incompetence noticeable among the chiefs of regiments and brigades, who desired to conduct their men on their own responsibility, and without subordinating themselves to the general plan of campaign, or even to the orders of the Commander-in-Chief, who on account of his foreign birth never had the confidence of his generals. It appears that Mehemet Ali began his movement simply with the idea of driving the Russians back from the vicinity of Razgrad and Eski-Djuma, which were of the first importance to the Turks, since the capture of the railroad at Razgrad would have enabled the Russians to isolate Rustchuk and invest it with a small force. A general advance formed no part of Mehemet Ali's plan; but having driven the Russians back beyond the Banitchka Lom and arrived himself in the positions explained above on the 7th–10th of September, he then received news of the capture of Lovtcha and the appearance of large bodies of Russian and Roumanian troops in front of Plevna. With the sole object of relieving Osman, whom he believed to be very hard pressed, Mehemet Ali then gave orders for another advance in the direction of Biela, with the hope that the Russians would reënforce the Cesarevitch at the expense of the troops in front of Plevna. His orders for the advance were as follows: Achmed Eyoub's corps to move from Katzelevo and Prince Hassan's corps from Popkoi, and, uniting near Osikova, advance on Biela. Achmed Eyoub was to detach one division under Asof Pasha to cover the right flank in the direction of Sinankoi.

The movement began on the 12th, and on the 14th the troops were in communication with each other on the line from Sinankoi to Voditza. Some skirmishing occurred on the two flanks near each of these points on that day, but without any definite result. The whole force then came to a halt for a week in order to reconnoiter the enemy's position. On the 21st an attack in force was made upon the Russian position near Cerkovna, with the intention of breaking through between the XI. and XIII. Corps. In this the Turks were completely defeated, with considerable loss, and two days later they began to retreat, not only on their left flank, but along the whole line.

This battle of Cerkovna took place as follows: Lieutenant-General Tatisheff, chief of the 11th Cavalry Division, occupied a position facing northeast on the hills just south of the Yordan brook, having his troops on both sides of a road running from Cerkovna through Cairkoi to Cesarevo and thence to Tirnova. He had 2 regiments (Nos. 125 and 126) of the 32d Division (XI. Corps), 1 regiment (No. 1) of the 1st Division (XIII. Corps), and 1 regiment (No. 101) of the 26th Division—in all, 12 battalions, or 10,000 infantry, and the 102d Regiment, on the march from Biela, and only 10 or 12 miles from his left flank. He also had 2 regiments of cavalry (11th Dragoons and 11th Lancers), 5 foot batteries (40 guns), and 1 horse battery (6 guns).

The Turks had 35 battalions—say 20,000 men—of which 20 were Egyptians, and about 50 guns. They were posted on the other side of the Yordan brook, on the heights about Cerkovna. Their plan was to demonstrate against the Russian center and left and strike hard against their right, which was the weakest part of their line. The battle opened about 11 A. M., as usual by an artillery duel between the opposing heights, which continued for four or five hours without doing much harm, in spite of the fact that, owing to the superior range of the Turkish guns, the Russians could not reach a portion of the Turkish batteries. The Turkish detachment on the right and center moved forward about 2 P. M.; they advanced rather too far in making their demonstration, and became very hotly engaged around the little village of Verboka in the valley of the brook; and about 4 o'clock the 102d Regiment arrived, and, striking them in flank, drove the whole line back to Cerkovna in considerable confusion. The turning movement against the Russian right flank was intrusted to the Egyptians, and some idea of the manner in which they executed it may be obtained from the fact that the correspondent of the "Times" with Mehemet Ali states that they lost only 4 men killed and 32 wounded! Their losses were probably larger than that, but the Egyptians certainly fell back the instant the Russians opened fire upon them, and they retreated in great disorder to Cerkovna. The whole affair was over by 5 P. M. It was terribly mismanaged by the Turks; having 35 battalions in hand, the whole fighting was done by the 9 battalions who were on the center and right. The 9 Egyptian battalions which went to attack the Russian right accomplished nothing; the 6 battalions which were in reserve were not brought into action; 10 or 12 Egyptian battalions never left their bivouacs at Voditza; and at Osikova, only 6 miles north of Cerkovna, was a whole division of Achmed Eyoub's corps which did not move a foot all day to help their comrades.

The Russian losses are given in General Tatisheff's report at 25 officers and 436 men; he also states that 800 dead Turks were buried on the field the next day. The Turks acknowledge a total loss of about 1,600 men.

On the 23d there was a truce for the purpose of burying the dead, and on the 24th Prince Hassan's troops retreated to Sarnasuflar with such haste that they abandoned a large amount of material on the road. The conduct of his generals at Cerkovna probably convinced Mehemet Ali that the army under his orders was not one to be led against well-disciplined troops intrenched in good positions. On the 25th Achmet Eyoub's corps began falling back (without having given battle) in the direction of Razgrad, and by the 1st of October the whole of the Turkish force was behind the line of the Lom, and the Russian pickets advanced to their old positions.

Mehemet Ali's offensive movement was over, and, as he had lost more men than his enemy and had not diverted a single Russian from either Plevna or Shipka, it can only be considered a complete *fiasco*—though perhaps from causes beyond his control. On the 2d of October he was relieved from command, and superseded by Suleiman Pasha.

CHAPTER V.

OPERATIONS ON THE RIGHT FLANK IN AUGUST AND SEPTEMBER.—
BATTLES OF LOVTCHA, SEPTEMBER 3D, AND PLEVNA, SEPTEMBER
11TH.

ALTHOUGH attacked at Shipka and threatened on the line of the Lom, the principal attention of the Russians during the month of August was directed to assembling a sufficient force to drive the Turks away from their right flank; as already stated, large reënforcements were ordered from Russia, and the assistance of the Roumanian army was solicited.

The 2d Division was the first of the reënforcements to arrive. It passed through Gorni-Studen on the 20th of August, and was directed on Selvi in order to relieve the detachment of the VIII. Corps which was there and allow it to proceed to Shipka. A few days later one brigade of this division was sent to Gabrova, but when Suleiman ceased his attacks at Shipka on the 26th it returned to Selvi.

The 3d Rifle Brigade and the 2d Brigade 3d Division, which arrived between August 25th and 28th, were also directed on Selvi. The 1st Brigade 3d Division was retained at Gorni-Studen. The Roumanians had already crossed one division at Nikopolis during the month of July; the rest of their force began crossing, by a bridge which they built at Korabia a few miles above Nikopolis, early in August, and were all on the southern bank by the 28th. This force was constituted as follows:

OPERATIONS ON THE RIGHT FLANK. 225

Roumanian Contingent.

			Battalions.	Foot guns.	Squadrons.	Horse guns.
3d Division.	1st Brigade.	8th Regiment Line....	2	..	..	..
		10th Reg't Dorobanz...	2	..	..	..
		12th Reg't Dorobanz...	2	..	..	..
	2d Brigade.	2d Regiment Line.....	2	..	..	..
		9th Reg't Dorobanz...	2	..	..	..
		11th Reg't Dorobanz..	2	..	..	..
	3d Rifle Battalion.................		1	..	..	..
	4th Regiment of Artillery..........		..	36	..	..
Total 3d Division......................			13	36	..	..
4th Division.	1st Brigade.	7th Regiment Line....	2	..	..	..
		14th Reg't Dorobanz...	2	..	..	..
		15th Reg't Dorobanz...	2	..	..	..
	2d Brigade.	5th Regiment Line....	2	..	..	..
		13th Reg't Dorobanz...	2	..	..	..
		16th Reg't Dorobanz...	2	..	..	..
	2d Rifle Battalion.................		1	..	..	..
	3d Regiment of Artillery...........		..	36	..	..
Total 4th Division......................			13	36	..	..
Reserve....	1st Brigade.	1st Regiment Line.....	2	..	..	..
		7th Regiment Dorobanz.	2	..	..	..
		1st Rifle Battalion......	1	..	..	..
	2d Brigade.	4th Regiment Line.....	2	..	..	..
		6th Regiment Line.....	2	..	..	..
		8th Regiment Dorobanz.	2	..	..	..
	3d Brigade.	3d Regiment Line......	2	..	..	..
		5th Regiment Dorobanz	2	..	..	..
		4th Rifle Battalion	1	..	..	..
	2d Regiment of Artillery............		..	36	..	..
Total Reserve....			16	36	..	..
3 Brigades of Cavalry, counting 9 Regiments (2 Line and 7 Kalarash)........................			..	..	36	18
Grand total............................			42	108	36	18

The battalions numbered about 750 and the squadrons 125 men, making the total force 30,000 infantry, 4,500 cavalry, and 126 guns.

By the latter part of August, therefore, the Russian Commander-in-Chief had available for operations on his right flank about 105,000 men, of whom the greater part were on the north and east of Plevna, and the rest between Selvi and Lovtcha. No more Russian troops could be expected to arrive till the latter part of September; the season was advancing, and the Grand Duke determined to attack at once with what troops he had.

On the 31st of August, however, Osman sallied forth from Plevna and attempted the offensive in the following manner (see Plate 8): At 6:30 A. M. word was received from the cavalry outposts between Tutchenitza and Grivitza that the Turks were advancing in the direction of Pelishat, and at 8 they appeared

15

on the open ridge about a mile west of Pelishat. Here they established their artillery (about 40 or 50 pieces), and their infantry moved rapidly forward and drove the Russians out of a lunette which they had constructed about half a mile in front of Pelishat. The Russian troops in this vicinity consisted of the 62d and 63d Regiments, which were in front of Pelishat, and the 20th and 118th* Regiments, with 3 batteries and a company of sappers, in front of Zgalevitza. These two positions, which were fortified with trenches for the infantry and slight epaulments for the artillery, formed the advanced left flank of the Russian defensive line, which extended from Tristenik to Poradim; at the latter place were 3 regiments of the 30th Division (IV. Corps), and on their right were 6 regiments of the IX. Corps.

General Zotof, who by virtue of his seniority commanded all the troops before Plevna at this time, imagined that the attack on Pelishat was a mere demonstration, and that the main attack would be made upon the 4th Roumanian Division, which was upon the road from Plevna to Nikopolis, or upon the right of the IX. Corps; he therefore made no change in the dispositions of his troops until the capture of the Pelishat lunette and the appearance of a dense line of Turks all along the ridge behind it convinced him that the main attack was to be in this neighborhood. He then (about 9 A. M.) gave the following orders:

  a. One brigade of IX. Corps to move forward along the high-road toward Plevna and take the Turks in flank;

  b. Three regiments of IX. Corps to move to a point about two miles north of Poradim, and remain there in reserve ready to move according to further orders;

  c. The Roumanian division to concentrate at Kalysovat;

  d. The 61st Regiment, which was on the march from Zimnitza and had bivouacked at Karagatch, to move forward at once to Poradim.

The Turks meanwhile had been driven out of the Pelishat lunette by the 62d Regiment, but had retaken it; and while their artillery kept up a steady fire upon the Russian line, they were preparing their infantry for the assault. At 1 P. M. they moved forward to the attack across the open ground just west

---

* One battalion of this regiment was in front of Lovtcha.

OPERATIONS ON THE RIGHT FLANK. 227

of the two villages. Their assaults were directed upon three points, viz., Pelishat, the trenches south of Zgalevitza, and the trenches west of that village. The column advancing on Pelishat was received by the concentrated fire of 36 guns in front, and its flank was threatened by 6 squadrons of cavalry; it did not reach the village, and after about an hour it was wholly withdrawn. Around Zgalevitza, however, a very hot fight raged for the next three hours; at one time the Turks had possession of a battery and some trenches on the south of the village, but they were driven out by the 120th Regiment, which arrived from the reserve at Poradim. Soon after they got possession of the trenches north of the village, but here they were again driven out. They then (about 3 P. M.) renewed their attacks upon both these positions, but were repulsed; and they then definitely retired behind the ridge where their artillery was posted. The Russians who followed them were arrested by a third attack made with the Turkish reserves. This fighting about Zgalevitza was remarkable for its duration and for the close quarters at which it was carried on. Several hundred of the Turkish dead lay in and on both sides of the Russian trenches.

About 4:30 P. M. the Turks had regained the ridge, and then, opening a steady fire with their artillery, they began to retreat toward Plevna. The Russians made an effort to follow them, but soon gave it up on account of the fatigue of the troops, and because they had but two regiments of fresh troops available. The Turks therefore withdrew without molestation to the shelter of their works at Plevna. The Russian losses were:

	Officers.	Men.
Killed	3	171
Wounded	27	708
Missing		66
	30	945

Besides carrying off a large number of their dead and all their wounded, the Turks left 400 dead on the field. They advanced over open ground, and one of their columns just before reaching Zgalevitza got into the ravine just southwest of the village, where it was subjected to a cross-fire and was very badly cut up. Their losses were estimated at 3,000 in all, and it is probable that they were little if any under that number.

What purpose Osman had in making this attack has never been made clear. It was too strong for a reconnaissance and too weak for a serious attack, being made with about 25,000 men out of the 50,000 or 60,000 which he then had at Plevna. Whatever its object, it accomplished nothing beyond the loss of 1,000 Russians and 3,000 Turks. The Russians continued undisturbed their preparations for their great effort against Plevna. Their plan was to first gain possession of Lovtcha, and then close in around Plevna with their 100,000 men, and attack it from the north, east, and south.

Lovtcha is the principal village upon the high-road leading from Plevna to Gabrova and the Shipka Pass, and from it also there are smaller roads leading over the Balkans by the Trojan Pass to Philippopolis, and by Mikren to Yablanitza on the Plevna-Sophia high-road. It was therefore a point of considerable strategic importance, Plevna and Lovtcha having the same value for the defense of the right flank as Biela and Tirnova for that of the left flank, in the Russian advance.

On the 17th of July, while Gourko was advancing through the valley of the Tundja toward Shipka, and a detachment of the VIII. Corps, as will be remembered, was operating on the north of that pass, 5 sotnias of Cossacks belonging to this latter detachment advanced east from Selvi, and had a skirmish with several hundred bashi-bozouks, whom they defeated and drove beyond Lovtcha. The town was thus occupied by a small force of cavalry, but there were no infantry troops available to send to their relief in order to occupy the place in force; and a few days later (about July 25th) the Cossacks were driven out by a strong detachment of Turks, under Adil Pasha, which arrived from Sophia.

Immediately after the defeat at Plevna on the 30th of July, Skobeleff was ordered to Selvi with the Caucasian Brigade of Cossacks, and there received in addition one regiment and part of another from the newly arrived IV. Corps. With this command (5 battalions, 10 squadrons, and 2 horse batteries) he made a reconnaissance in force against Lovtcha on the 6th of August. He conducted this with so much boldness and skill that he caused the Turks to develop their whole strength, and meanwhile gained time for his topographers to make a very accurate sketch of the whole of the Turkish position. He found that the Turkish force consisted of about 15,000 men and 25 guns, besides the usual bands of bashi-bozouks; that their position was fortified by a redoubt and some batteries on the left (west) bank of the Osma, by 4 batteries on the right bank, and several lines of trenches in front of each, but that their whole position was commanded by a ridge running across the Selvi road about 4 miles east of the village. Skobeleff, having accomplished his object, with a loss of one or two hundred men, retired behind this ridge, and thence to the village of Kakrina, 10 miles east of Lovtcha.

Lovtcha is about 20 miles from Plevna by the high-road, but between the right of the Turkish position at one point and the left of that of the other the distance is only 12 miles over a good road. Lovtcha was therefore only the right flank—much extended—of the position at Plevna; and the Russians planned to first strike this flank and destroy it, or at least separate it wholly from the main force, and then proceed to the attack of this latter at Plevna. For this purpose troops had been sent to Selvi as already explained, and the command of the forces in that neighborhood confided to Major-General Prince Imeretinsky. On the 1st of September this officer had under his orders: *a*, the detachment of Skobeleff (64th Regiment, 1 battalion 118th Regiment, 1 battery of 16th Division, Brigade of Caucasian Cossacks, and 1 battery of Don Cossack Artillery); *b*, the 2d Division, with its 6 batteries of artillery; *c*, the 2d Brigade 3d Division, with 3 batteries; *d*, the 3d Rifle Brigade; and *e*, the 30th Don Cossacks—in all, 26 battalions, or 20,000 men, with 80 guns, besides the Cossacks and their artillery. On the same day he began to advance, sending Skobeleff's detachment from Kakrina to the heights east of the town, the 2d Brigade 2d Division to Kakrina, the Don Cossacks off on the left flank to observe the Trojan road, and the Caucasian Cossacks on the extreme right to observe the Plevna road. During the night he began the march with the rest of his troops toward Lovtcha. (See Plate 15.)

Skobeleff arrived at the foot of the ridge east of the town at 2 P. M. (September 1st), and drove the Turks out of that portion of it on the north of the road, which they were occupying with only a small force. During the night Skobeleff worked hard at intrenching his own position and constructing epaulments for 24 guns, in which he placed the 8 guns which he had with him. The next morning (September 2d) Skobeleff opened fire at daylight with these guns upon the Turkish battery on the ridge south of the road, by which he compelled the Turks to evacuate this latter during the afternoon. Skobeleff immediately occupied it with the 64th Regiment and again worked all night intrenching his new position and throwing up epaulments for 32 guns. The result of Skobeleff's efforts was that, when Imeretinsky arrived with the bulk of the troops at the foot of the ridge on the evening of September 2d, he had already gained possession of the dominating ridge east of the town, and had epaulments all ready for 56 guns, 24 on the ridge north of the road and 32 on the south. During the night the guns were dragged up into these positions by the infantry.

On the same day General Dobrovolsky, commanding the 3d Rifle Brigade, which formed the right of the line, drove the Turkish pickets out of Prissiaka, and thus came into position on a line with the ridge.

On the morning of September 3d, at 5 o'clock, the Russians opened fire with the 56 pieces established along the heights east of the town, and a short time after with 12 additional pieces (4 of which were siege guns captured at Nikopolis) on the hill just south of Prissiaka.

The line of the Turkish position was along a series of hills just east of the Osma river, the principal and commanding point of which was at its southern extremity, which the Russians called the "Red Hill"; in this line they had batteries containing about 12 guns and a series of lines of intrenchments. Their second line was on a hill behind (west of) the town, where they had a closed redoubt, some batteries containing 10 or 12 guns, and also several lines of trenches.

Besides the guns in position on the ridge, the Russians had 16 guns in reserve; their infantry was massed behind the ridge, the troops on the left under command of General Skobeleff, those on the right under command of General Dobrovolsky. The plan of attack was to bombard the Turkish positions for several hours, then attack the Red Hill, and subsequently the trenches to the north of it. But at 8 A. M. the Turks took the offensive in the vicinity of Prissiaka, and this compelled General Dobrovolsky to attack the northern end of these hills with the 3d Rifle Brigade, supported by the 7th Regiment; he dislodged the Turks and drove them across the Osma.

After about eight hours of cannonading the Turkish batteries were nearly all reduced to silence, and the order was given (2 P. M.) for Skobeleff to attack the Red Hill. This he did with the 64th Regiment, supported by the 11th; at the same time the 1st Brigade 2d Division (5th and 6th Regiments) advanced to the attack of the hills to the north of the Red Hill. The artillery fire had been so well directed that the Turkish lines had been very much injured, and they made but a feeble resistance. The whole of their first line east of the Osma was carried by 3 o'clock.

Placing two batteries (16 guns) on the Red Hill to fire over the town against the redoubt on the hill behind it, Skobeleff followed the retreating Turks through the town, and posted his men in the gardens in the outskirts in front of the second position of the Turks. Skobeleff had the 64th and 1 battalion of the 118th Regiment, the 11th, and the 7th and 8th Regiments (2d Brigade 2d Division); the 5th and 6th Regiments (1st Brigade 2d Division) were on the edge of the river to the north of the town; the Rifle Brigade was on the right; and the remaining regiment (No. 12) was in reserve.

Besides the two batteries on the Red Hill, two more were established on the high-road just beyond the town. While the troops were resting to regain their breath and strength, these four batteries kept up a continuous fire upon the redoubt. At 5:30 P. M., the attack having been sufficiently prepared by the artillery, the whole line moved forward, Skobeleff from the town and the 1st Brigade 2d Division by fording the river, while the Rifle Brigade on the extreme right advanced in the direction of the Plevna road. The Turks withdrew all their artillery, and escaped with it by the Mikren road; but their infantry kept up a very hot fire, inflicting considerable losses on the Russians. The latter continued to advance, however, and soon the Turks abandoned all their trenches, and nothing remained but the main redoubt, which, although surrounded on three sides, kept up its fire to the very last. It was finally carried about 7 P. M. in the midst of a hand-to-hand struggle, in which all its defenders perished. At the close of the fight the bodies of the dead and wounded Russians and Turks together lay piled up in a mass six feet deep around the gorge of the work.

The Russians were thus masters of the whole position, the Turks retreating in scattered bands, which assembled on the road toward Mikren. In view of the necessity of his coöperation in the attack on Plevna, Imeretinsky could not follow them with his infantry, but he sent the brigade of Caucasian Cossacks (which had been observing the Plevna road all day), and they cut down about 3,000 of the fugitives on the road.

Late in the night word was received from the headquarters of the IV. Corps that their pickets at Bogot had seen a strong column advancing from Plevna along the road to Lovtcha. Nothing was heard of it that evening, but the next morning Skobeleff moved out on the Plevna road with an advance guard, and soon began skirmishing with this column, which was apparently making a turning movement round toward the Russian left. Imeretinsky disposed his whole force to meet this, but after some skirmishing the Turks began moving off in the direction of Mikren. Imeretinsky did not follow them, owing to the fatigue of his troops and the necessity of arriving at Plevna. Letting his troops rest during the remainder of this day (September 4th), Imeretinsky marched the next morning by the Plevna high-road toward Bogot, where he arrived in the evening. He left the 2d Brigade 3d Division as a garrison for the works at Lovtcha, and brought the rest of his troops to Bogot.

The losses of the Russians were:

	Officers.	Men.
Killed	6	313
Wounded	33	1,112
Missing	..	52
Total	39	1,477

The losses of the Turks were very great. There were 1,000 buried on the 4th, and 1,200 more after the departure of Imeretinsky; 3,000 were cut down by the Cossacks during their retreat. Very few prisoners were taken, and the number of Turkish wounded does not appear to have been very large. In short Adil Pasha's detachment of 15,000 men was not only defeated, but it was cut to pieces; it made no attempt to retake Lovtcha, and was not again heard of until the month of November, when the Russians began moving toward Tetevan and the Trojan Pass.

On the same day that the battle of Lovtcha took place, Prince Charles of Roumania, to whom had been assigned the command of the allied troops in front of Plevna (with General Zotof as Chief of Staff), arrived at Poradim and took command, and on the same date the orders were issued for the concentration of the troops. This took place the following day (September 4th), the Roumanians between Bryslan and Riben, the IX. Corps at Zgalevitza, and the IV. Corps at Pelishat. (Plate 8.) September 5th was passed in the same positions, and on that evening, Imeretinsky's detachment having arrived at Bogot, the troops were all assembled. On the night of the 6th–7th they moved forward to their positions in front of the Turkish redoubts.

General Levitzsky, Assistant Chief of Staff of the whole army, was temporarily at Prince Charles's headquarters, bearing the dispatches and explaining the plans and wishes of the Commander-in-Chief. The latter moved his headquarters from Gorni-Studen to Poradim on the 7th, and finally on the same day the Emperor of Russia and his suite also came to the village of Radonitza, from which they could drive every morning to the field. Every one knew that this was to be the great struggle, and, if successful, it would probably lead to the complete defeat of the Turks throughout the whole theatre of war. Let us therefore examine in detail the relative forces of the two combatants, and the nature of the position which the Russians were planning to assault.

The troops composing the "Right Wing" of the Russian Army were as follows:

	INFANTRY.		CAVALRY.	
	Battalions.	Guns.	Squadrons.	Guns.
Roumanians, General Cernat..	42	108	86	18
IX. Corps,* General Krüdener..	21	68	16	12
IV. Corps, General Kryloff...	24	90	16	12
2d Division,† } General Imeretinsky........................	12	48	..	..
3d Rifle Brigade,	4	24	..	..
Brigade of Caucasian Cossacks......................................	..	..	12	6
Brigade of Don Cossacks (21st and 26th Regiments)..............	..	..	12	6
Total..	103	864	92	54

* One regiment of Krüdener's corps, No. 19, which had lost all its baggage in the fight of July 20th, was at Nikopolis refitting; and one battery of his corps was also there. A portion of his artillery had also been at Lovtcha, but it was returned before the assault of the 11th.

† Imeretinsky brought with him from Lovtcha the three batteries belonging to

The normal strength of the infantry of a Russian army corps is 24,000 men (1,000 men to a battalion), but the details for detached service, sickness, etc., keep the battalions as low as 800 men when at their fullest. These two corps, however (IV. and IX.), had done all the fighting at Nikopolis and at Plevna up to date, and had lost 13,000 men in killed and wounded.

But this loss counted some of the lightly wounded who had subsequently recovered and joined their regiments; and moreover, the losses had been partially replaced by reënforcements from the reserves in Russia. To what extent these losses had been replaced I do not know; but on the 2d of September General Krüdener told me that his corps numbered 15,000 present for duty, and the IV. Corps 17,000. The Roumanian troops, as already stated, numbered 30,000. The 16 battalions under Prince Imeretinsky had only been engaged at Lovtcha, and their strength was fully 750 to the battalion, or 12,000 in all. This gives a total of 74,000 infantry.

In the artillery, besides the 364 field guns (of which one half were 4.2-in. 9-pdrs. and the other half 3.4-in. 4-pdrs.), there were 20 siege guns—24-pdrs., 6 in. cal.—which arrived at Poradim from Zimnitza on the 4th of September; and also the 4 Turkish siege guns (probably 12-pdrs.) taken from among those captured at Nikopolis, and which were now with Imeretinsky's troops. The number of men in the artillery was about 8,000. With this heavy artillery came 3 battalions of sappers, about 2,500 men.

In the cavalry the squadrons may be taken as numbering 110 men (their maximum strength is 150). This gives the total strength of the cavalry at 10,000 sabres. The 9 mounted batteries which accompanied them were served by about 1,800 men.

The force brought against Plevna therefore numbered over 90,000 men, and was composed of 74,000 infantry, 10,000 cavalry, 24 siege guns, 364 field guns, and 54 horse guns.

As for the Turkish Army, the only means of arriving at a knowledge of its strength is by computing backward as follows:

the brigade of the 3d Division which remained as the garrison of that place. These are the 24 guns credited to the 3d Rifle Brigade above.

THIRD BATTLE AT PLEVNA. 235

Surrendered December 10th, including 2,128 officers	39,000
Killed and wounded December 10th	4,000
Sick and wounded found in the town December 10th	20,000
Killed between September 1st and December 9th (estimated)	5,000
Total	68,000
From this must be subtracted the reënforcements which entered Plevna September 22d	12,000
Strength of Osman Pasha's Army September 1st	56,000

A small number of the wounded of September 11th were transported back to Orkhanie, but the great majority of them remained at Plevna, and died there or were found in the town at the surrender. No account is here taken of the prisoners or killed and wounded at Gorni-Dubrik and Telis, since these troops (although part of the garrison of Plevna) only arrived in October. On the other hand, there were a few regiments of regular cavalry and several hundred bashi-bozouks present in September, who were sent away in the early part of October. At the surrender, 77 field guns were delivered over, and a few were afterward found buried in the ground; but the Turks were at all times deficient in their artillery, and it is not probable that Osman had over 80 pieces. This was also the estimate at the time of the battle in September.

The Turkish Army therefore numbered about 60,000 men, viz., 56,000 infantry and 2,500 cavalry, and 80 guns.

Plevna itself is a little town of 6,000 or 7,000 inhabitants, lying in the midst of a series of hills whose crests are from 200 to 600 feet above the town. Its only military importance lies in the fact of its being the meeting point of roads from Widdin, Sophia, Shipka, Biela, Zimnitza, and Nikopolis. An army posted there was a vital menace to the safety of the Russian communications in any advance.

Osman Pasha, having arrived from Widdin too late to prevent the capture of Nikopolis, occupied Plevna and began throwing up intrenchments to strengthen his position in case of an attack from the Russians. He was attacked on the 20th of July, and having repulsed his assailants he continued to fortify his position, constructing redoubts as well as trenches. Again attacked by the Russians on the 30th of July, and again having beaten them back, he continued unremittingly the work upon his defenses; not following any systematic plan for the fortification of the place against an attack from all sides (because he had not troops enough to occupy the whole extent of the dominating ridge forming the rim of the little Plevna basin, nor time enough to construct works upon so extended a front), but confining his efforts to the hills nearest the town on the north and east, since it was on these sides that the Russians threatened him with the greatest force. At the time of which we are speaking (the first week in September) these works had already reached a development of 18 redoubts, supplemented by several lines of trenches. These works may be divided into three groups (Plate 16):

1. The Grivitza works, consisting of two redoubts situated 2,000 yards northwest of the village of Grivitza, and a line of trenches and batteries running northwest along the Grivitza ridge to the Bukova creek. Beyond these was a large intrenched camp on the heights of Opanetz, overlooking the Vid.

2. The middle group, consisting of 8 redoubts more or less perfectly connected with lines of trenches, on the knolls just east of the town of Plevna.

3. The Krishin group, consisting of the Krishin redoubt on a commanding point 3,000 yards southwest of the town, a redoubt half way between it and the town, and two redoubts connected by a strong trench just outside of the town, commanding the approach by the Lovtcha road.

The Grivitza redoubt was the key of the position on the north, and the Krishin redoubt that on the south; for both of these works were on points commanding the entire country for a range of 3,000 yards on all sides. The middle group, on the contrary, was on a lower level, and was commanded by the Grivitza ridge on the north and the Radischevo ridge on the south. This latter had not yet been fortified by the Turks, for lack of time.

The orders for the advance of September 6th were as follows:

1. The IX. Corps, from Zgalevitza to the vicinity of Grivitza, to take position between the high-road and the Radischevo heights, and to establish the 20 siege guns in two batteries.

2. The IV. Corps, from Pelishat to Radischevo, to establish its 9-pdr. batteries on the ridge in front of the latter place.

3. Imeretinsky's detachment from Bogot to Tutchenitza.

THIRD BATTLE AT PLEVNA. 237

4. Roumanians—4th Division, from Verbitza to the vicinity of Grivitza on the north of the high-road; 3d Division and reserve to Verbitza; cavalry between Verbitza and Riben.

5. The 9th Cavalry Division, on the high-road in rear of the IX. Corps and 4th Roumanian Division.

6. The 4th Cavalry Division, Brigade Caucasian Cossacks, Brigade Don Cossacks, on left flank of IV. Corps.

7. General reserve (2d Brigade 30th Division, Regiment No. 20 of 5th Division, three 4-pdr. batteries, 4th and 9th Hussars, and 1 horse battery), in rear of the left flank of the IX. Corps.

8. Ammunition. Flying Park of IX. Corps at Zgalevitza, of IV. Corps between Tutchenitza and Bogot. Reserve Park of IX. Corps at Bulgareni, of IV. Corps at Leschan. Baggage of IX. Corps at Karagatch, of IV. Corps at Poradim.

9. Field Hospitals. Of IX. Corps at the "three wells" on the Zgalevitza road (2 miles in rear of batteries); of IV. Corps at Tutchenitza; of Roumanians at Verbitza. As many country carts as possible to be collected.

10. The men to take three days' rations (2 lbs. cooked meat and 4 lbs. biscuit) in their haversacks; to take their overcoats slung over the shoulder; to leave their knapsacks and shelter-tents in their bivouacs, under guard of small detachments formed of men fit for light duty.

The troops were all under way at dark on the evening of the 6th. The men in Krüdener's corps carried on their shoulders fascines, gabions, and hewn logs for platforms for the siege guns. Two regiments were thrown forward nearly to Grivitza, to cover the construction of the batteries; but the Turks discovered nothing, and not a shot was fired all night. The construction of the batteries was begun at 9 o'clock and finished at a few minutes past midnight, the infantry battalions working under the direction of the sappers. The first siege battery, containing 8 guns, was built at a point southeast of the Grivitza redoubt and 4,300 yards from it; the second siege battery, 12 guns, was on its left and rear and 5,200 yards from the redoubt. All the field artillery and the infantry of the IX. Corps were massed in the valleys near these batteries, the infantry with three regiments in the first line a little in advance of the batteries, one regiment in reserve on the right and two on the left; the remaining regiment formed part of the general reserve.

The IV. Corps also came into position during the night, placing 5 batteries (40 guns) of 9-pdrs. on the eastern part of the ridge in front of Radischevo. These batteries were due south of the Grivitza redoubt and 5,100 yards from it; and they were 2,700 yards from the nearest of the redoubts of the "middle group." Of the infantry of this corps, three regiments lay behind the batteries in the Radischevo valley, three regiments formed the corps reserve placed about a mile back on the Pelishat road, and two regiments were in the general reserve.

Imeretinsky on the morning of the 7th moved to the west of Tutchenitza, sending Skobeleff with a small force to reconnoiter the position at Krishin.

The Roumanians brought four 9-pdr. batteries (24 guns) into action about 9 A. M. of that day, at a point 4,000 yards due east of the Grivitza redoubt. The infantry of the 4th Roumanian Division lay behind these batteries and on their right.

September 7th.

At 6 A. M. the first shot was fired from the 8-gun siege battery. Several Turks appeared immediately on the parapet of the Grivitza redoubt, and this shot seemed to be the first knowledge they had of the arrival of the Russians; it was not answered for half an hour. The cannonade then became general along the whole line. About 10 A. M. Krüdener sent three 9-pdr. batteries (24 guns) to take position on the hill south of the village of Grivitza, whence they opened fire on the Grivitza redoubt at 3,500 yards. The cannonade continued till after dark, the losses on the Russian side (and probably on the Turkish also) being next to nothing. It will be noticed that the Russians had 20 siege guns and 88 9-pdrs. in action—about one fourth of their artillery—at ranges from 2,700 to 5,200 yards. Most of their fire was concentrated on the Grivitza redoubt, a square earthwork with parapet 18 feet thick; and the firing was reasonably accurate, a cloud of dirt being thrown up from the parapet every few minutes; yet the 8 guns of this redoubt continued to answer all day.

During the afternoon Imeretinsky moved from Tutchenitza to the vicinity of Brestovetz.

THIRD BATTLE AT PLEVNA. 239

September 8th.

The cannonade continued all day.

The three batteries of the IX. Corps were reënforced by two more batteries, and all moved forward to within 2,500 yards of the redoubts of the "middle group," to which they confined their attention.

A portion of the reserve batteries of the IV. Corps were brought into action farther to the left, on the Radischevo ridge, against Redoubt No. 10, at 1,800 yards.

The 3d Roumanian Division advanced to the front of Verbitza and on the right of the 4th Roumanian Division, and brought a portion of its batteries into action on the north of the Grivitza redoubt at 2,500 yards.

General Loshkarieff, with the 9th Cavalry Division and four Roumanian Cavalry Regiments, was sent across the Vid at Riben, and thence to Dolni-Dubnik on the Sophia high-road, to cut the communications of the Turks, and in case of their retreat to fall upon them.

During the afternoon Skobeleff brought on an infantry engagement near the Lovtcha high-road, as will be subsequently explained.

Toward evening the fire of the Grivitza redoubt began to grow very feeble. During the night the 8 guns of the first siege battery were moved over to the Radischevo ridge, whence they could play upon the redoubts of the middle group.

September 9th.

The cannonade continued without abatement, except from the 12-siege-gun battery, whose ammunition was nearly exhausted. The Grivitza redoubt was entirely silent. Noticing this, the Roumanians made a reconnaissance toward it, but were promptly beaten back by a murderous infantry fire. During the afternoon there was a general movement of the IV. Corps to the left, along the Radischevo ridge, as far as the Tutchenitza ravine, and the 123d and 124th Regiments were brought from the right of the IX. Corps to the left, in order to keep up connection with the IV. Corps. The IX. Corps Artillery was advanced to within 1,800 yards of the redoubts of the "middle group," and increased to 8 batteries in action.

September 10th.

The cannonade continued as usual. During these four days of incessant artillery firing the Russian losses were between 300 and 400; those of the Turks are not known. The Grivitza redoubt was silent (as to its artillery only), and was more or less knocked out of shape. Redoubt No. 1 of the central group was also considerably damaged. The rest of the Turkish works were but little injured, though from lack of ammunition their artillery ceased firing altogether.

During the afternoon it began to rain, and during the night there was a succession of violent thunder-storms, in which an immense quantity of water fell, converting the ground everywhere into a pasty black mud, and making it very difficult for the Russians to bring up their ammunition.

September 11th.

Dense fogs and a cold drizzling rain remained over from the last night's storm. The Turks attacked Skobeleff early in the morning, and there was fighting on the left flank all day. The artillery on the center and right fired but little during the morning; but at noon, as the fog lifted a little, they opened with great fury, and kept it up until 3 P. M., when the assaults were made.

Before describing these, it is necessary to explain the course of events on the left flank, beyond the Tutchenitza ravine.

Imeretinsky on the 7th had taken position near Brestovetz, his advance-guard under Skobeleff (5th and 8th Regiments, 9th and 10th Rifle Battalions, four 9-pdr. batteries, 4 siege guns, and the 21st and 26th Don Cossacks) being posted on the "Red Hill" to the right and rear of the village of Brestovetz. From here on the 8th these batteries opened fire on the Krishin redoubt at 4,000 yards. The rest of the detachment with Imeretinsky was about 1½ mile in rear toward Bogot. On the afternoon of the 8th Skobeleff moved forward with the 5th Regiment supported by two battalions of the 8th, drove the Turkish pickets out of the woods on the first knoll of the "Green Hills," and then attacked the second knoll, which was occupied by some battalions of Turks. A very warm skirmish took place with these, but they soon retreated, and following them, Skobe-

left crossed the high-road and took the "third knoll" of the
Green Hills, and was at 5 P. M. only 1,500 yards south of the
town of Plevna. Here, however, he came under the fire of the
Krishin redoubt on his left, and the two redoubts near the
town, which were quickly reënforced by Turkish reserves from
Plevna. Skobeleff was driven back to the second knoll, where
his own reserve (Regiment No. 8) enabled him to halt and stop
the Turks. Here he remained until some time during the
night, when, receiving word that the general assaults which had
originally been intended for the 9th had been postponed to a
later day, he withdrew to the first knoll, and there intrenched
himself. His losses during the 8th were 900 men. At 5 A. M.
on the 9th he was attacked in this position by the Turks, but
drove them back with shrapnel; at 8 A. M. they renewed the
attack with increased strength, and came within 60 yards of the
trenches, but were again driven back. For the rest of the day
the Turks left Skobeleff alone, and remained in their own positions on the second knoll.

On the afternoon of the 9th Imeretinsky's detachment stood
as follows: In the first line, under Skobeleff, the 2d Brigade
2d Division, the 9th and 10th Rifle Battalions, and 2 batteries
of the 3d Division, posted from the "first knoll" of the Green
Hills on the right to the ridge north of Brestovetz on their left.
Behind them, on the Red Hill, were the three 9-pdr. batteries
(24 guns) of the 2d Division, which had been exchanging shots
all day with the Krishin redoubt. Behind these batteries were
the 1st Brigade 2d Division, the other two Rifle Battalions, the
three 4-pdr. batteries of the 2d Division and one 9-pdr. battery
of the 3d Division.

Up to this time Imeretinsky had had the general command
of all the troops on the left flank; Skobeleff, although of the
same rank as himself (Major-General in the Emperor's suite),
was junior to him in date. At Lovtcha Skobeleff had an independent detachment at the time of Imeretinsky's arrival, but
he was then placed under the latter's orders, and had so remained till now. Late in the night of the 9th–10th Imeretinsky received an order from General Zotof, Chief of the Staff,
dividing his troops into two independent portions, assigning
Skobeleff to the command of the first and himself to the second,
and stating that Skobeleff would attack according to instruc-

tions which had already been given him, and that he (Imeretinsky) *was to support Skobeleff in his attack*, as well as protect the extreme left flank with his Cossacks. The effect of this was of course to give Skobeleff the entire control of the operations on the left flank, and virtually to relieve Imeretinsky from command. The order also stated that the 1st Brigade 16th Division would be sent at daylight to report to Skobeleff, taking the road from Radischevo to Brestovetz, which crosses the Tutchenitza ravine at the mill just behind the Green Hills.

At daylight on the 10th Skobeleff sent the 8th Regiment forward, and, almost without fighting, they seized the "second knoll" and immediately fortified themselves there, the men using their copper soup-dishes, bayonets, and naked hands, as the supply of spades was very small. As soon as the 1st Brigade 16th Division arrived, one regiment was placed on the "second knoll" and the other on the "first knoll" in reserve. On the "second knoll," therefore, from west of the high-road to the Tutchenitza Creek, there were 16 9-pounders in position, and the 8th and 61st Regiments on either side; in reserve, the 7th and 63d Regiments and the 9th and 10th Rifle Battalions. Sixteen 9-pounders were sent to the east side of the Tutchenitza Creek, from which they could bring a cross-fire upon the "third knoll" at 2,500 yards' range. Judging a further advance imprudent before the general attack, Skobeleff remained in this position all day.

The Assaults of September 11th.

During the evening of September 10th orders were issued for a general assault the next day at 3 P. M. The assaults were to be directed upon three principal points, the Grivitza redoubt, redoubt No. 10 (2,000 yards southeast of the town), and upon the two redoubts on the Lovtcha road close to the town. The Roumanians and part of the IX. Corps were to make the first, a part of the IV. Corps the second, and Skobeleff's detachment the third. The 31st Division (IX. Corps) was to support the line of batteries from Grivitza to Radischevo, but was not to make an attack.

The orders prescribed a cannonade along the whole line, to commence at daybreak and last till 8 A. M.; then a pause till 11 A. M.; then a heavy cannonade till 1 P. M.; then another pause till 2:30 P. M.; then to fire as rapidly as possible till 3 P. M., when the assaults were to begin. In the morning, however, there was such a dense fog that it was hard to tell when daylight began, and impossible to see anything to aim at, so that this elaborate artillery programme was somewhat disarranged. About 10 A. M. Skobeleff began to move his men forward to the "third knoll," since from there he could more advantageously begin the assault upon the line of redoubts in front of it; but in so doing he had some rather lively skirmishing, the noise of which came through the fog to Radischevo. At the same time the Turks in Redoubt No. 10, thinking perhaps to take advantage of the fog, advanced with the idea of driving the 63d Regiment out of a very advantageous position which they occupied on the extreme left of the Radischevo ridge and near the Tutchenitza ravine. They were repulsed. The 63d Regiment then, in ignorance or disregard of the general plan of assault, or perhaps from the fog and the unexpected firing on the left, thinking that the plan had been changed, or for whatever other reason, but without the order of the Division Commander, followed the retreating Turks; and as they soon became pretty hotly engaged, the 117th Regiment, which was nearest on their right, went to their aid. These two regiments pressed on in the fog and gained the line of trenches running from the redoubt to the Tutchenitza Creek. They then got a terrible fire on their right flank and front from the redoubt, and from some troops in the open to the west of it. The two regiments fell back to their positions on the Radischevo ridge. Their adventure cost them dear, for they lost one half of their men and over two thirds of their officers, and, worse than all, it put these two regiments practically out of the fight for the rest of the day. The programme of the attack was therefore still more disconcerted.

About noon the fog began to rise, so that the redoubts were visible, and then a cannonade opened and kept up furiously till about 2 P. M., when it slackened down again. By the lifting of the fog Skobeleff's position became very critical, for there was but little cover for his men, and they were exposed not only to the fire of the works in front, but also to that of the Krishin redoubt on his left flank. He called upon Imeretinsky for reënforcements, which were sent to him in succession until the latter had not a battalion left under his orders, and at the same time sent to Zotof for permission to attack without waiting till 3 o'clock; his position was an excellent one for beginning his assault, but not one in which he could remain still; the permission was granted, but it did not reach Skobeleff till 2:30 P. M.

About 3 o'clock the artillery recommenced a tremendous thundering on all sides (there were over 250 guns in position), and the infantry began to move forward to the assault. There was a cold drizzling rain at the time, in which the immense quantity of smoke hung low, but was occasionally blown off by the wind; objects could be fairly well seen.

Let us follow the assaults in succession:

1. *Grivitza Redoubt.*

This was to be attacked in four columns, as follows: The 3d Roumanian Division, which was under shelter in the ravine on the north, with its batteries on the hill behind it, 2,800 yards from the redoubt, was to send one brigade to approach through a little ravine on the northwest, and the other brigade on the northeast; the 4th Roumanian Division, whose batteries had gradually crept up to about 1,800 yards on the east of the redoubt, was to send one brigade along the ridge on the east and keep the other in reserve; the 1st Brigade 5th Division (Russians), which was in the valley south of Grivitza, was to advance with two 4-pdr. batteries from the south.

The Roumanians began to move forward at a few minutes past three. Column No. 1 did not get anywhere near the Grivitza redoubt; what had been thought to be a mere auxiliary line of trench was found to be a second redoubt 400 yards north of the main one, and equal to it in size and construction. The approaches on the north were very steep and difficult, and when the Roumanians came within about 80 yards of it they were driven back, and retreated to a secondary ridge about 700 yards to the north, and there intrenched themselves. Column No. 2 was delayed in climbing the slope, but column No. 3, having only an open space of 1,800 to 2,000 yards to pass over, came against the redoubt by half past 3 o'clock; but it was alone of all the columns, and was driven back and sought refuge in the slopes between the redoubt and the village. Column No. 2

then made its appearance from the northeast, but, advancing alone, was in turn driven back, 4 to 4:30 P. M.

Meanwhile the Russian brigade did not pass through Grivitza until 4 P. M.; it then deployed on the west of the village and advanced up the slope northward toward the redoubt, the 17th Regiment in the lead, followed by the 18th, which inclined a little to the left. The two 4-pdr. batteries were brought into action against the trenches on the west and southwest of the redoubt, which were delivering a fire on the left flank of the brigade as it advanced. These two regiments worked their way slowly up the hill, being much annoyed by the fire on the left, against which finally a part of the 18th Regiment advanced and gained possession of a portion of the trenches in that direction. Thus assisted, the leading battalion of the 17th Regiment made a rush for the redoubt on the south, at the same time that a portion of the brigade of the 4th Roumanian Division which had been kept in reserve made a desperate attempt on the east. They were successful, and the troops entered from the two sides about the same time, the commander of the 17th Regiment, as well as that of the Roumanian brigade, being both killed within a short distance from the parapet. But the Turks kept up a terrible fire from the second redoubt, only a few hundred yards off, and from the trenches on the left; and after a half hour they assaulted the allies, and in turn drove them out. It was now growing dark, and a confused fight was kept up at short range and partly hand-to-hand until about 7:30 P. M., when the arrival of the other battalions of the 17th Regiment, as well as a small reënforcement of Roumanians, finally decided the day in favor of the allies.

Their trophies were five guns and one flag. The terreplein of the redoubt as well as its ditch had a complete pavement of dead bodies. Some idea of the closeness of this fight may be gathered from the fact that the Roumanians had more men killed than wounded. Their losses were:

	Officers.	Men.
Killed	15	1,335
Wounded	41	1,176
Total	56	2,511

The Russian brigade lost 22 officers and 1,305 men.

The total force which had been brought into action numbered about 25,000 men.

During the night the Turks made three successive sallies from the second redoubt and from the trenches, but they were each time driven back.

2. *Redoubt No.* 10.

The unfortunate misstep which had been made by the 63d and 117th Regiments in this part of the field just before noon was barely over, and these troops, somewhat disorganized, back in their positions on the left of the Radischevo ridge, by 2 P. M. Desultory picket-firing followed. General Schnidnikoff, chief of the 30th Division, who commanded this part of the line, was anxious to carry out his part of the assault at the hour specified, 3 P. M., and at that hour his two remaining regiments, Nos. 64 and 118, were moved forward. Four batteries of the IV. Corps were posted on the left of the ridge, and were doing their utmost against the redoubt. The 64th and 118th Regiments passed on the right of these batteries down the ridge, and into a little valley where they found shelter; then turning by the left flank, they advanced westward against the redoubt. This was at 4 P. M. The fire became hotter and hotter as they neared the redoubt, but still they kept on. Just then appeared the head of a column of reënforcements for the Turks, taken either from the reserves in the town or from redoubts 7, 8, and 9; they came up the slope and deployed on the left (northeast) flank of the redoubt, and fought there in the open. The Russians, however, still moved on, and at 4:30 P. M. disappeared in the smoke overhanging the ditch, their right flank slightly refused on account of the Turkish reënforcements which had just arrived there. For about three minutes the affair hung in the balance; then the Russians began falling back somewhat hurriedly. The Turks then streamed out of the eastern angle of the redoubt, and joining their comrades, began to follow the Russians at a run; thereupon two battalions stopped, faced about and lay down at about 200 yards from the redoubt, and opened the hottest possible fire. The Turkish pursuit was at once arrested, and the Turks retreated pell-mell into their redoubt again. The Russians then continued their retreat rapidly, but without any running or disorder, although they were losing terribly under the murderous fire which the Turks kept up from the redoubt. One battalion, which formed the only reserve of these two regiments, and which had, during the half hour of their attack, been lying under cover in the little ravine 1,200 yards east of the redoubt, was now brought forward; but it was too late, and one battalion was a mere drop in the bucket —it simply joined in the retreat. The two regiments reached the shelter of the little ravine at 5 P. M.

Meanwhile more or less firing had been going on between the left flank of the Russian position (63d and 117th Regiments) and the trenches between the redoubt and the Tutchenitza creek, but no serious assault had been made there. At Schnidnikoff's request, Zotof had ordered the 123d and 124th Regiments from their position behind the batteries on the right of the Radischevo ridge, to the extreme left of the ridge, to replace the 63d and 117th, which had been so knocked to pieces during the morning. Of the general reserve, the 119th and 120th Regiments were ordered to replace the 123d and 124th behind the batteries, and the 20th as reserve to Schnidnikoff's line. The 123d and 124th Regiments did not arrive on the left till about 5 o'clock, when the attack of the 64th and 118th was already repulsed. From 5 to half past 5 o'clock there was a somewhat oppressive silence over this part of the field; then the guns on the hill began working again, and very quickly there was also heard the musketry of the 123d and 124th. They advanced over the same ground as the 63d and 117th in the morning; the fire was very hot for about 20 or 25 minutes, but the men could not get nearer than 150 or 200 yards from the redoubt. In the darkness which was setting in about 6 o'clock they fell back to the Radischevo ridge. The assault of Redoubt No. 10 was over—and had failed. The Russian losses were in all 110 officers and 5,200 men, nearly half of which were in the two regiments (63d and 117th) which had become engaged during the morning. The dead and a large part of the wounded were left on the field.

3. *Redoubts on the Lovtcha Road.*

Skobeleff's position during the night of the 10th–11th was on the "second knoll" of the Green Hills, 2,000 yards south of the redoubts he was to attack; in front of him was a little valley, then the "third knoll," then another little valley, then the long sloping ridge, extending from Plevna to the Krishin redoubt, on which were the redoubts. The third knoll was occupied by the Turks only with a feeble skirmish line, and at 10 A. M. Skobeleff advanced and drove them out of there in order to have this position in his own possession, from which to launch his troops to the assault during the afternoon. He occupied it without difficulty, but then he was greatly annoyed by the fire from the trenches on the slope in front of the redoubts, which, being something under 1,000 yards away, brought his men in easy range. Skobeleff sheltered his men as much as possible behind the crest of the hill, but still he was losing a good many men, not only in the first line, but in the reserve placed in the little valley between the two knolls. The Turkish fire meanwhile grew warmer and warmer, and about 2 P. M. a strong skirmish line began advancing from their trenches up the slopes of the hill. The 62d Regiment was sent forward to drive back these skirmishers, which they did; there was then for nearly an hour a lull in the fight.

Skobeleff's troops stood as follows:

First line, behind the crest of the third knoll, 61st and 62d Regiments, with the 9th and 10th Rifle Battalions in reserve; between the second and third knolls, 7th Regiment. Second line, on the fortified position of the second knoll, 5th and 8th Regiments and 24 guns.

In reserve, between first and second knolls, 6th Regiment and 11th and 12th Rifle Battalions.

At 2:30 P. M. his batteries opened fire over the heads of the advanced line of troops, and at 3 P. M. he sent these latter forward to the assault. They went down the slope of the third knoll in two lines of company columns, preceded by a strong line of skirmishers and with all the bands playing, cleared the Turks out of their rifle-pits at the foot of the slope, crossed the little stream, and began ascending the hill. Here it got very hot, and the men stopped advancing and began to lie down and open fire upon the trenches connecting the two redoubts in front of them, about 200 yards off. Seeing the line begin to waver a little, *at this instant* Skobeleff sent forward the 7th Regiment to their support, and ordered up the 6th Regiment and 11th and 12th Rifle Battalions to the reverse slope of the third knoll; meanwhile the artillery kept up an incessant fire over

THIRD BATTLE AT PLEVNA. 249

the heads of the men. The arrival of the 7th Regiment gave new courage to the men already so hotly engaged, and they made a renewed effort to advance up the slope, but found it impossible, and again they lay down and opened fire. But it was evident that they could not long remain in such a position, only 200 yards from the redoubts, the Turks behind trenches and the Russians in the open, and exposed not only to the infantry fire in front, but to artillery fire on both flanks—on the left from the Krishin redoubt and on the right from the redoubts of the "middle group." The critical moment had therefore arrived, and Skobeleff sent forward the rest of his troops, viz., the 6th Regiment and the two remaining rifle battalions; and he himself, leaving the second knoll, whence he had been directing the attack, rode forward rapidly, caught up the two rifle battalions, and went forward with them. He was well known to his men as being the only general officer who always rode a white horse and wore a white coat in battle, and there is no doubt that his personal presence encouraged the men; he had the good luck not to be hit, though nearly all his staff fell, and he entered (on foot, his horse being killed) the redoubt with his men. As these reënforcements came forward there was a tremendous enthusiasm and "hurrah" among the men; one more final effort was made to get up the slope; the Turks were driven out of the trenches in front of the redoubt; then for a few minutes, just as at Redoubt No. 10, the affair hung in the balance, but here it succeeded: the Turks began to weaken, a portion of the Russians entered the trenches between the two redoubts, then turned to the left, and finally at half-past 4 the middle redoubt was in the hands of the Russians. The Turks, still firing, retreated to a camp surrounded by a light trench about 600 yards in rear of the line of redoubts.

The Russians had lost 3,000 men in the assault, which lasted little less than an hour.

But the fight did not now in the least abate. The middle redoubt, which the Russians had taken, as well as the eastern one, which was still in the hands of the Turks, were properly speaking not redoubts at all, since they were only built up on three sides; the front side of each was simply an increased height to the strong line of trench connecting the two and extending to the west (left) of the middle one; the other two sides were properly mere traverses to this line; and the fourth side—the rear—was wholly open and exposed to the fire from the trench of the camp only 600 yards off. The ground was hard and rocky, and there were no spades at hand for digging. While the Turks therefore kept up an incessant fire from this camp and from the eastern redoubt, which was still in their possession, a force of one or two battalions sortied from the redoubt (No. 13 of plan) on the left of the Russians, and advanced to the attack of the left flank. Seeing this, Colonel Korupatkin, Chief of Staff to Skobeleff, and the only one of his staff not killed or wounded, took about 300 men and went forward to meet these Turks in the open. A desperate fight at short range took place, in which the Russians lost the greater part of this little force, but drove the Turks back to their redoubt (No. 13). Just at this time some of the artillery which remained in front of Brestovetz increased their fire upon the Krishin redoubt from the other side, and a portion of the Cossacks on the left flank dismounted and advanced on foot against the same redoubt. This created a diversion upon the Russian left flank, and relieved them for a time from further attacks in that quarter. Meanwhile a small force of a few hundred volunteers came out of the middle redoubt and made an effort to get into the eastern one, but they all or nearly all perished. Then Colonel Shestakoff, of Imeretinsky's staff, came across the valley from the third knoll to the line of redoubts, with three companies of the 6th Regiment and portions of the other regiments which had been left in reserve, and, picking up on the way the stragglers and scattered detachments in the valley, made a force of about 1,000 or 1,200 men, with which he made a desperate effort against the front of the eastern redoubt, at the same time that a fresh lot of volunteers sortied from the middle redoubt against its flank. The attack succeeded, and at 5:30 P. M. the eastern redoubt was also in the hands of the Russians. Soon afterward darkness set in, and the fight slackened down to desultory picket-firing, with an occasional shell from the Krishin redoubt.

Skobeleff's precarious position will be at once evident from a glance at the detailed plan of Plevna. (Plate 16.) He occupied, with the 6th, 7th, 61st, and 62d Regiments, and the Rifle Brigade, the line of trench and redoubt shown on this plan just southwest of the town. In his front, at 600 yards, was the intrenched camp of the Turks; on his left flank, at 800 yards, was Redoubt No. 13; and on his left rear, at 2,300 yards, was the Krishin redoubt (No. 14). On his right flank was the "middle group" of redoubts, and on his right rear was Redoubt No. 10, where the Russians had been repulsed during the afternoon. He was entered like a wedge into the midst of the Turkish lines, and on three sides of him were strong works against which either no attack had been made at all or the attack had failed. In his rear, at about 1,800 yards, were still the 24 9-pdrs. supported by two battalions of the 8th and two very weak battalions of the 5th Regiment, which had lost 700 men in the affair of September 8th. The other battalion of the 8th was at Brestovetz, and that of the 5th Regiment was keeping up connection between the two portions of his command. If the Turks in the Krishin redoubt were strong enough to come down upon his rear, there was a good chance that his whole force would be lost. He sent word to Zotof explaining his position, and saying that it was untenable unless he was strongly reënforced, at the same time that other reënforcements were sent against the Krishin redoubt; saying also that he would hold on as long as he could, and asking for further instructions.

Not only was his position most critical, but his men were exhausted and their ammunition was running very short. Skobeleff was indefatigable. He posted himself the battalion of the 8th Regiment between the two positions, with one company facing east across the little valley between the redoubt-line and the third knoll, another company facing west toward the Krishin redoubt, and the other three companies in the center. Some Cossacks who arrived during the night he employed to bring up cartridges; and himself personally visited the left flank of the redoubt-line and set the men to work with their bayonets, soup-dishes, and whatever they had, in throwing up a sort of traverse or trench against the fire from the Redoubt No. 13. Twice during the night he was attacked, once from Krishin and once from the valley on the side of Plevna. The troops making the latter attack were in the darkness mistaken for Russians, supposing that they might be a portion of the IV. Corps coming to their aid from that direction. The Turks thus got within 100 yards of the Russians before it was discovered; the latter fell back upon the three remaining companies of the battalion (8th Regiment), and then fired by volleys on the Turks, and thus drove them back. This was about midnight. About the same time arrived an aide-de-camp (Colonel Orloff) of the Grand Duke, who had been riding since 6 o'clock in the darkness and absence of roads (it was nearly fifteen miles round through the Russian lines from the Grand Duke's headquarters to Skobeleff's position); the critical condition of affairs was explained to him, and he returned to headquarters. A little before daybreak Skobeleff brought 4 9-pdrs. forward and established them in the middle redoubt, to open fire against No. 13.

The morning of the 12th of September dawned bright and clear, after forty hours of continuous rain and fog. At 6 o'clock the Turks opened fire with their artillery from the redoubts surrounding Skobeleff's position, and with musketry from the camp in his front; and not long after appeared a strong column of infantry from the direction of the Krishin redoubt, which advanced to within 300 yards of the Russian position before it was arrested by their fire; it then fell back to Redoubt No. 13. At 8 o'clock they made their second attack in the same direction, but with no better success. Skobeleff had meanwhile brought up 8 4-pdrs. to the third knoll, which did good service with shrapnel against the advancing Turks. At 10:30 A. M. they made a third desperate assault, still upon the left flank of the Russian position; it was repulsed, but now the men in that part of the line, worn out and discouraged with 30 hours' continuous fighting, began to drop out one by one and make their way to the rear. Seeing this, Skobeleff, who was on the third knoll, rode over and expostulated, threatened, ordered, and encouraged the men, and got them back into the redoubt again.

Meanwhile Skobeleff had received two orders from Zotof, the first about 7 A. M. and the second at 10:30 A. M. They were as follows:

1. *To* GENERAL PRINCE IMERETINSKY: By direction of the Commander-in-Chief, I give you and General Skobeleff the order to fortify yourselves in the position which you have taken to-day, and to hold out to the last extremity. We can send you no reenforcements, for we have none.

   (Signed)   ZOTOF, *Lieutenant-General.*

THIRD BATTLE AT PLEVNA. 253

2. *To* GENERAL SKOBELEFF : By order of the Commander-in-Chief. If you can not hold the positions which you have taken, then you must retreat slowly—but, *if such a thing is possible*, not before evening—to Tutchenitza, covering your retreat by the cavalry of General Leontieff. Send a copy of this order—which otherwise keep secret—to General Prince Imeretinsky. The Grivitza redoubt is in our hands, but in spite of this the attack can not be continued ; but the retreat must be slowly begun. 8: 30 A. M.
(Signed) ZOTOF, *Lieutenant-General.*

This latter order was brought by the same Colonel Orloff who had visited Skobeleff during the night, and thence returned to the Grand Duke and Zotof to explain the condition of things in Skobeleff's front.

Skobeleff did what he could to obey these orders—to hold on till evening ; but from the very first his case was hopeless. He always kept hoping, in spite of Zotof's first order, that a portion of the IV. Corps would be sent to help him, or at least that the attack would recommence on some other part of the line, and thus relieve the pressure on him. But this did not happen. There was hardly a shot fired from any other part of the line throughout this day. Zotof and Levitzky were at the Grand Duke's headquarters all the morning, over on the hills east of Grivitza, about $6\frac{1}{2}$ miles in a straight line from Skobeleff's position, watching the fight with their glasses, but unable of course at that distance to make anything out of it. The distance over the route which messengers had to take through the Russian lines was about 12 miles. As to the question of reenforcements, the Roumanians and the 1st Brigade 5th Division were fully occupied in holding the Grivitza redoubt ; from the Grivitza village to the Tutchenitza Creek the line was held by 5 regiments of the IX. Corps and 6 regiments of the IV. Corps ; and of these 11 regiments 5 had not been engaged the previous day at all, viz., the 121st, 122d, 119th, 120th, and 20th. Whether two or three of these regiments might not safely have been sent to Skobeleff—as there was no intention of attacking in any other part of the line—is of course a matter about which opinions will differ. The fact was, however, that at the Russian headquarters it had been determined not to continue the attack (on the ground that their force was not strong enough), and the

Chief of the Staff had *no realization* of what a desperate position Skobeleff was in. Hence the orders cited above.

Skobeleff's position, however, was most desperate. As the morning wore on and there was no sign of a renewal of the attack on the other parts of the line, Osman began to mass a strong force in Plevna to drive Skobeleff out. Whether these troops were drawn from the reserve camp in the valley between the town and the river, or from the Bukova position, or from the middle redoubts, is not known; but it is certain that Osman reënforced the troops in front of Skobeleff to the extent of not less than 12,000 men. Part of them went over the hill and round into the Krishin redoubt, and thence against Skobeleff's left flank, and part of them came out of the town and followed up the Tutchenitza brook for about three quarters of a mile, and then climbing up its bank endeavored to get possession of the third knoll from the rear and thus cut off Skobeleff's retreat. This latter movement began to make itself apparent about 1 P. M., and to meet it Skobeleff brought up the two battalions of the 5th Regiment, which up till now had remained with the batteries on the second knoll. Meanwhile, of the four guns which he had placed in the middle redoubt, two had been dismounted and the other two had lost all their horses and gunners; to replace these guns, Skobeleff sent three of the eight guns which he had kept on the third knoll; they had been in the redoubt but a short time before they were dismounted; and about this time a caisson which had been brought under the shelter of the side of the redoubt for protection was nevertheless found by a shell from the Krishin redoubt, and exploded in the midst of the men, not only creating a fearful loss, but carrying dismay to those who were not hurt. Skobeleff again rushed forward in person to the redoubt, and endeavored to reassure his men; and he was barely in time, for a few minutes later, between 2 and 2:30 P. M., the Turks from the direction of the Krishin redoubt and from No. 13, reënforced now by fresh troops, made their fourth assault. The Russians let them approach to within 400 yards, and then opened on them with well-aimed volley-firing, and with deadly effect. The Turkish line halted and sought shelter, and returned the fire; but every time they endeavored to move forward they met with such terrible losses that they finally gave it up and returned to No. 13.

As Skobeleff was returning from the redoubt to the third knoll, he learned that the 118th Regiment was arriving; it had been sent to him as reënforcement by General Kriloff, commanding IV. Corps, *on his own responsibility*, on account of the heavy firing which he had heard so long on Skobeleff's front. The regiment numbered 1,300 men. At 4:30 P. M. the Turks, greatly reënforced in numbers, began their fifth assault, from the direction of Krishin, and simultaneously from the camp. They kept advancing in spite of the murderous fire of the Russians, and as they neared the redoubt the majority of the latter, worn out with 36 hours of continuous fighting with no appreciable result, began to make off to the rear in small groups; the little band of 200 or more brave men, who remained behind under Major Gortaloff, were cut down to the last man in a fierce hand-to-hand fight.

The middle redoubt was thus lost, but still the men in the eastern redoubt and a part of the trenches between the two remained in their places and kept up the fight. To prevent their being massacred, Skobeleff hastily sent them an order to fall back to the third knoll; and in order that this might be possible, he himself took the 118th Regiment (which had recently arrived as just stated) and led them to the assault of the line between the two redoubts. Under cover of this they returned (what was left of them) to the third knoll. The retreat was then continued under the protection of the 24 guns and 2 battalions (8th Regiment) on the second knoll. Except those who fell in the last affair in front of the redoubts, nearly all the wounded were carried off; the dead were left on the field.

Skobeleff retreated to the "first knoll," and remained there all night, and all of the 13th. The Turks were too much used up to follow or attack him. At night of the 13th he returned to Bogot. His losses were 160 officers and over 8,000 men. About 18,000 men had been engaged. On the 13th, 14th, and 15th the Russian batteries bombarded the town and the Turkish positions, though with what object is not quite apparent. On the evening of the 14th, just before dusk, the Turks sallied out of the second Grivitza redoubt and attacked the first, which was held by the Roumanians and part of the IX. Corps. They attacked with energy, but were repulsed. With this exception the Turks made no attempt to take the offensive. The Russians took up a defensive line from Verbitza to Radischevo, and began fortifying it. The cavalry was between each flank of this position and the Vid.

The third and great assault on Plevna was therefore over, and like the two previous ones it had resulted in a bloody and terrible repulse, the losses reaching the large total of more than 18,000 men out of 75,000 infantry present and 60,000 actually brought into action.

The Turkish losses are unknown, but they were not small. Osman stated after the surrender that he lost more men on the Lovtcha road than Skobeleff did. It is probable that the Turkish losses were in all between 12,000 and 15,000.

The Russian losses were as follows:

			KILLED.		WOUNDED.		TOTAL.	
			Officers.	Men.	Officers.	Men.	Officers.	Men.
In the bombardment, September 7-10th............			....	....	....	....	10	800
In Skobeleff's fight of September 8th.............			....	....	....	....	...	900
September 11th.	Grivitza Redoubt.	{ Roumanians................... { 1st Brigade 5th Division........	15	1,385	41	1,176	56 22	2,511 1,305
	Redoubt No. 10.	{ 2d Brigade 16th Division. { 1st Brigade 80th Division }.. { 2d Brigade 81st Division.	....	....	....	....	110	5,200
Sept. 11th and 12th.	Lovtcha Road.	{ 1st Brigade 16th Division. { 2d Division. { 3d Rifle Brigade......... { 115th Regiment.........	....	....	....	....	103	7,200
Sept. 14th.	Grivitza Redoubt.	{ Roumanians................. { 1st Brigade 5th Division.	....	....	....	....	4 8	550 800
Total...............................			75	7,558	290	10,653	865	18,216

The telegraphic dispatch of the Grand Duke, dated Poradim, September 15th, gives the Russian losses as in all 300 officers (of which 60 killed) and 12,500 men, of which about 3,000 killed; the Roumanian losses at 60 officers and 3,000 men. This dispatch states that 239 officers and 9,482 men (Russian) had passed through their hospitals. At the time this dispatch was written the total losses in Skobeleff's column were not fully known at headquarters. Both Prince Imeretinsky and General Skobeleff personally stated to me a few days after the battle that their losses were over 8,000 men. The 2d Division, while waiting for its reserves to arrive from Russia, was temporarily reorganized *into one regiment* of 4 battalions, each about 1,000 strong.

THIRD BATTLE AT PLEVNA. 257

The figures given above for the losses at the Grivitza and Redoubt No. 10 are taken from Russian official reports. The large proportion of killed is accounted for partly by reason of the fierceness of the fighting, and partly from the fact that all the wounded left in Turkish hands in front of Redoubt No. 10 and the Lovtcha road were never afterward heard of, and must therefore be counted as dead.

That the repulse of the 11th of September was a great disaster for the Russian arms there is no doubt; that it was in no sense an irreparable one, the subsequent course of the campaign abundantly proves. While it is no business of foreigners to attempt to fix the personal responsibility for this failure (which also would be impossible by means of the documents which have as yet been published), yet there are certain facts which will hardly be denied by any one who was present, which largely contributed to the defeat, and which are as much matters of public discussion as the number of men engaged and the losses on either side.

1. There was a certain lack of unity in the command of the army.

The troops assembled at Plevna were under the command of Prince Charles of Roumania, as already stated: but this command was to a certain extent nominal, and the dispositions previous to the battle depended largely upon Lieutenant-General Zotof, who had commanded the troops before Prince Charles's arrival, and who was now his Chief of Staff. General Zotof was unfortunately not a general of the calibre to command 80,000 men; but even had he been a military genius of the first order, it would have been very difficult for him to gain a victory in the circumstances in which he was placed; for a few days before the movement on Plevna began, the assistant chief of the General Staff, Major-General Levitsky, arrived at Poradim to explain to General Zotof the wishes of the Commander-in-Chief. On the day that the bombardment began the Commander-in-Chief arrived in person, and with him his Chief of Staff, General Nepokoitchitsky. He of course confirmed the dispositions already taken, but from this time forward he commanded. Although he rode over the field as far as possible, and even exposed himself imprudently to the enemy's pickets, yet it was impossible for him to be properly familiar

17

with the ground before the assaults were made; so that while he commanded he had to rely upon the information and opinions of others rather than upon his own judgment. Finally, the Emperor was present, with the Minister of War and a large suite. The Emperor came merely as a spectator, to encourage his troops by his presence and in the hope of witnessing their victory. But the Emperor of Russia is regarded by every Russian soldier, from the highest to the lowest grade, with a feeling which it is difficult to explain in other countries; *at all times* his will is law, and his wish a command, and it is not possible for him to be a mere spectator. He took no part, however, in the command, although every report and order was instantly communicated to him, until after the assaults of the 11th and 12th. On the 13th and 14th long councils were held on the field, at which the future "policy," so to speak, of operations against Plevna (i. e., the investment without further assault) was determined upon. The Emperor presided at these councils, at which *all* of the following officers took part, viz., The Grand Duke Nicholas, Commander-in-Chief; General Milutin, Minister of War; Prince Charles, Commander of the troops at Plevna; General Nepokoitchitsky, Chief of Staff of the Army; General Zotof, Chief of Staff of the troops at Plevna; General Levitsky, Assistant Chief of Staff of the Army.

The subject is a somewhat delicate one, and I have no wish to pursue it beyond a statement of the bare facts which were evident to every one present at headquarters who chose to see them; and my only object is to cite enough to show that the ancient and unquestioned maxim of war, that there should be one man in an army to command and all the others to obey, was not fully observed at Plevna.*

---

* It will always be said, in extenuation of McClellan's failure in 1862, that he was improperly interfered with by Mr. Lincoln and Mr. Stanton. On the other hand, when General Grant took command of the armies in 1864, he was never summoned to a council of war, and never asked by either the President or Mr. Stanton to explain his plan of campaign. Full confidence was placed in him and full assistance given him. This I have from General Grant himself; and he has also told me that throughout the war he never called a council of war, though he listened patiently to the volunteer advice of those whose position warranted their offering it. But before every principal movement, and before every battle, he wrote out himself the rough draft of the orders, and as soon as it was finished gave it to

2. As a result of this division of authority, the plan of battle, such as it existed, was a general idea of attacking on all sides, rather than a carefully prepared attack upon the points of greatest importance, or where the enemy was weakest. The importance of the Grivitza redoubt, the key-point on the north, was well known from the previous struggles around it; but *even the existence of the great Krishin redoubt*, the key-point on the south, was not known till the 7th of September. During the month of August the topographers of the IX. Corps had reconnoitered the country in front of Grivitza and Radischevo, and had represented with tolerable accuracy the position of the Grivitza and Bukova lines and the middle group of redoubts upon a reconnaissance sketch, of which several lithographic copies were made. It was on this map that the dispositions for the attack were made. This map shows (in dotted lines, and as a matter of fact in wholly erroneous positions) two redoubts on the Lovtcha road just outside the town of Plevna, but otherwise, west of the Tutchenitza creek, the map is a blank; no reconnaissances had ever been made of that part of the ground, and no one of the chief officers previously named had ever been within sight of it. Their only information concerning it came from a report of Skobeleff, who had fought over this ground on the 30th of July; but at that date the Turks had no fortifications there, and the redoubts and trenches which had since been built had changed the whole condition of affairs. I give these details because they have a bearing upon the great and vital question raised by this war as to the propriety of making direct attacks upon fortified positions defended by breech-loaders; and because they seem to me to warrant the conclusion that *the Russians were defeated at Plevna, not because the position was impregnable, nor because they did not have sufficient forces, but because they were ignorant of the enemy's position, and failed to concentrate their efforts upon the decisive points*. Had they confined their assaults to the Grivitza and Krishin redoubts on the two flanks, and concentrated their forces there, leaving in the center only the troops necessary to support their line of batteries and to make a demonstration, the result of the 11th of

his chief of staff, to be copied at once and immediately sent to its various destinations.

See also Sherman's " Memoirs," vol. i., p. 344.

September might and probably would have been far different; and this both the Grand Duke and General Nepokoitchitsky acknowledged in conversation after the battle, when they were more familiar with the nature of the Krishin position. As it was, in their ignorance of this position, Skobeleff was sent forward almost as into a funnel, leaving commanding positions on either side of him, and attacking a position which if gained led to nothing, and which, as the sequel proved, was totally untenable. As for the attack on Redoubt No. 10, it would have been reasonable in the condition of the fortifications in July; but after the construction of the Krishin works it had no reason whatever.

It only remains to be added, concerning the general dispositions of this battle, that out of 103 battalions present only 72 were actually brought into action. The reserve division of the Roumanians (16 battalions) and the following Russian troops were not actively engaged: 1st Brigade 31st Division, 6 battalions; 2d Brigade 30th Division, 6 battalions; 20th Regiment, 3 battalions. When Zotof wrote to Skobeleff during the night of the 11th–12th that he had no reënforcements to send him, he must have meant (being ignorant of the critical position in which Skobeleff was placed) that he did not consider it judicious to withdraw the troops above mentioned from his center, between Grivitza and Radischevo, where these troops were placed in support of the batteries.

3. If we now come down to the tactics, the manner in which the troops were led to the different assaults, we find that at Grivitza the attack was made by four columns, from the northwest, northeast, east, and south; that these columns endeavored to start at the same hour, 3 P. M.; that, having different distances and different nature of ground to pass over, they arrived one after another, and were all, in their first efforts, beaten in succession. Subsequently a second effort, simultaneous on two sides, was successful, after fearful losses, in gaining possession of half the position, i. e., the southern one of the two redoubts.

At Redoubt No. 10 there was also a succession of assaults on different sides, *all* beaten in detail; in the morning an attack brought on by misapprehension, in the afternoon an attack at the specified hour (3 P. M.), and later an attack by the reënforcements when they arrived, which was after the second attack had been *wholly* repulsed.

In Skobeleff's column, on the contrary, there was none of this lack of *ensemble* and tactical confusion. He held his men well in hand, sent a portion of them forward in reasonably open order, and *at the critical moment when the line began to waver, but before the attack had failed,* sent in his reserves and went in himself with the last of them and carried the place. Once there, he held on to the last extremity, in accordance with his orders, and always in the hope that reënforcements would arrive and enable him to begin an assault against Redoubt No. 13. The reënforcements not arriving, and overwhelmed by numbers, he withdrew his force (as ordered) toward evening of the second day, under cover of artillery and of a small force of infantry which he had kept all the time in a fortified position (second knoll) in his left rear. Skobeleff's extremely reckless courage, while it compels that personal admiration which such qualities always command, is of course open to serious criticism when it is remembered that he was the commanding general on all that part of the line. On the other hand, there is no doubt that without the aid which this display of daring gave to his men the position would not have been carried or held as it was; and the legendary stories of his personal bravery which circulated among the soldiers from this day, especially among the recruits who afterward arrived, constituted a positive military factor of which good use was made at the subsequent assault of the Green Hills (November 15th–17th, 1877) and at the storm of Shenova (January 8, 1878), which compelled the surrender of the Turkish army at Shipka.

CHAPTER VI.

THE INVESTMENT OF PLEVNA—BATTLE OF GORNI DUBNIK, OCTOBER 24TH, 1877.

The Investment of Plevna.

(See Plate 17.)

IN the councils of war which were held as already stated on the 13th and 14th of September, it was decided to make no more assaults upon the works of Plevna, which had already cost the Russians well-nigh 30,000 men, but to fortify their own position on the east from Verbitza to Tutchenitza against any counter-attack, and, upon the arrival of more reënforcements, to proceed regularly to invest the place. Meanwhile the Roumanians were to run a sap forward toward the second Grivitza redoubt and try thus to gain possession of it; and the whole cavalry force was to be united on the other bank of the Vid and cut off the communications of the Turks, and if possible prevent the entry of any supplies, munitions, or reënforcements.

On the other portions of the theatre of war everything was to remain on the defensive, and if possible *in statu quo.*

On the 7th of September, General Loshkarieff, Chief of the 9th Cavalry Division, who was then on the high-road east of Grivitza, between the Roumanians and the IX. Corps, received an order placing the two regular regiments of Roumanian cavalry and two of their militia (Dorobanz) regiments under his orders, making in all 32 squadrons and 3 mounted batteries, and directing him to proceed across the Vid at Riben and act upon the rear of the Turks, and in case of their retreat to pursue and harass them. On the 8th Loshkarieff crossed the river and established a picket line on the other side, about 20 miles long, from Riben through Dolni-Etropol and Dolni-Dubnik to Gorni-

Dubnik, the bulk of the Roumanian cavalry being placed behind this line at Gorni-Etropol (Widdin road), and of his own division at Dolni-Dubnik. On the 8th and 9th the Turks sortied in small numbers from Plevna and skirmished with Loshkarieff, but without any important result. On the afternoon of the 9th the scouting parties beyond Gorni-Dubnik reported a camp of 10,000 Turkish infantry a few miles west and southwest of Gorni-Dubnik. Upon this report Loshkarieff withdrew the bulk of his force to Gorni-Etropol. On the 10th Loshkarieff advanced again the four regiments of his division and took up a position near Dolni-Dubnik, facing south, and sent a few squadrons to his left across the Vid to establish communication with the cavalry of General Leontieff. On the 11th a squadron from General Leontieff's (4th) Division arrived at Dolni-Dubnik, and the communication was thus established. From the 11th to the 18th scouting parties were sent out along the Sophia road as far as Radomirtza, and also westward to and beyond the Isker; they found everywhere plundering parties of Tcherkesses and bashi-bozouks, but otherwise learned nothing. During this time the Turks made no effort to enter Plevna with supplies or reënforcements, and, as already noted, they did not retreat from that place. On the 18th Loshkarieff's division was ordered back across the Vid to take position on the Lovtcha road and form the left flank of the infantry force on that side, and all the rest of the cavalry (except some regiments of Roumanian militia on the right flank) was ordered west of the Vid; the command thus formed was intrusted to Lieutenant-General Kriloff, who had originally commanded the 4th Cavalry Division, and had temporarily replaced General Zotof in command of the IV. Corps when the latter was made Chief of Staff of the "West Army."

Kriloff's command was composed as follows:

4th Dragoons, 4th Hussars, 4th Lancers ....12 squadrons,	2 batteries.
Don Cossack Brigade, Regiments 21 and 26... ....12 "	1 battery.
Caucasian Cossack Brigade, Regiments Kuban and Vladi-	
kavkas.. ....12 "	1 "
Regular (Roschiori) Roumanian Brigade, Regiments 1	
and 2.. 8 "	1 "
Militia (Dorobanz) Roumanian Brigade, Regiments 5	
and 6... 8 "	0 "

In all, 52 squadrons and 30 horse guns.

His instructions were to clear the country between the Vid and the Isker of bashi-bozouks, to seize all the food and forage in that region, to break up Osman's communications, to find out what force lay on the roads to Sophia, Vratza, and Widdin, and above all to prevent the entry of supplies or reënforcements into Plevna.

We thus see that on the 19th of September there was a *quasi* investment of Plevna; but as the infantry stood on but one side, leaving the other three sides to be occupied by cavalry, it was nothing more than a paper investment; and its insufficiency was rendered still more complete by the incompetency of General Kriloff as a cavalry commander.

On the 20th of September Kriloff sent a detachment of four squadrons to reconnoiter in the direction of Telis. Before reaching that village they met some regular Turkish cavalry and skirmished with them, and in so doing discovered that they were the advanced guard of a strong force of infantry; they therefore fell back to Dubnik. On the 21st Kriloff sent the Caucasian Cossacks to make a strong reconnaissance in the same direction. They found Telis occupied by 10,000 infantry, and defended by some earthworks which were partly completed. On the 22d, early in the morning, the pickets reported a strong column of infantry moving on the road from Telis toward Dubnik and Plevna. Kriloff immediately sent word to Loshkarieff across the Vid to advance in the direction of Telis with his division and take this column in rear. Soon afterward he received word that a strong column of Turkish infantry was advancing from the direction of Plevna over the bridge and along the high-road toward his rear. Thereupon Kriloff, almost without firing a shot, withdrew his force 15 miles to the north, to the village of Tristenik in the vicinity of Riben, leaving a small portion of it at the village of Etropol to skirmish with the Turks who had sortied from Plevna. During the night the Turkish convoy quietly continued its road to Plevna. By Turkish reports its strength was 20 battalions (say 12,000 men) of infantry, a regiment of cavalry, 2 batteries, and about 2,000 wagon-loads of provisions and ammunition. Kriloff placidly congratulates himself in his report upon having delayed this column for two days, and states that one of the principal objects of his command was to "spare his men as much as possible, since they constituted the greater part of the cavalry strength of the West Army"!

On the 23d and 24th of September nothing was done, and on the latter date a second small convoy slipped past the Cossacks at Etropol. On the same day Kriloff, according to his report, received an order from Prince Charles to secure the right flank of the West Army (it was not in any way threatened) by a position at Brest, away off near the Danube, "and to base himself in case of necessity upon Riben." Later in the day he received information that the Tcherkesses were recruiting men and horses and obtaining supplies in the district between the Vid and the Isker. On the 25th, therefore, Kriloff, abandoning the care of the Sophia road to the Don Cossack Brigade and the Roumanian militia, took the greater part of his force (32 squadrons and 18 guns) and went off to the west beyond the Isker, to the valley of the Skitt River, which flows into the Danube at Rahova. The bashi-bozouks disappeared before him, and then Kriloff took his cavalrymen down the valley against Rahova (a fortress similar to Nikopolis), and actually began a bombardment of the outlying redoubts with his little 4-pdr. horse-guns! This he kept up for one day (September 27th), and in so doing dismounted one gun in the Turkish works. On the 28th he turned back toward the Vid, and arrived at Tristenik on the 30th. During his absence the Don Cossacks which had been left at Etropol had captured two little convoys, one of 20 and the other of 100 wagons, loaded with flour and barley. Otherwise the Sophia road was now open, and the Turkish communications and telegraph were completely restored.

On the return march to Tristenik Kriloff had detached Colonel Levis-of-Manera, Chief of the Vladikavkas Regiment, with four squadrons of his own regiment, two of Lancers, and two of Hussars, and one battery, to follow up the valley of the Isker to Sumakova, and thence up a small stream which was crossed by the Sophia road over a bridge near Radomirtza. On the 1st of October Colonel Levis struck the road near Radomirtza, routed a party of bashi-bozouks, captured about 1,000 head of cattle and a small train wholly loaded with quinine and salt, and — at last something important — partly destroyed the bridge. Radomirtza is two days' march from Plevna, and therefore too far distant for a convoy arriving from the south to receive prompt aid from that place; the hills on the north of the little stream completely command the bridge and the road for a distance of a mile south of it. Six thousand cavalrymen and 30 guns (which was the strength of Kriloff's force), if properly handled at this point, could make a very stout defense against even a superior force of infantry. But instead of this, Kriloff sent a little detachment of eight squadrons to this place, and with the bulk of his force made a demonstration (October 1st) against the heights of Opanetz, in conjunction with one Roumanian battalion, which was operating a reconnaissance of the fortifications of Opanetz from the north. The Turks sallied out from Plevna across the bridge and attacked Kriloff; an insignificant combat took place, of which the principal result was the setting fire to the village of Etropol; and at evening the Turks retired across the Vid.

On the 2d of October Colonel Levis's detachment at Sumakova was reënforced by the 4th Dragoons and 2 guns, making its total strength 12 squadrons and 8 guns. At the same time little detachments of one squadron each were sent scouting across the Sophia road (of which Osman was already beginning to fortify the villages of Dolni- and Gorni-Dubnik, Telis, and Radomirtza) toward the Vid, where they found portions of Loshkarieff's division—and then returned. Colonel Levis skirmished for three days with the Tcherkesses in the region of Sumakova and Radomirtza, but his detachment was too small to accomplish anything of importance; and on the 5th of October Chefket Pasha, coming from Orkhanie with 5,000 infantry and a swarm of Tcherkesses, rudely brushed Levis aside, and took his troops on to Telis and Gorni-Dubnik, and himself went to Plevna to consult with Osman. Chefket brought with him also a considerable quantity of provisions and munitions; and the Radomirtza bridge had been so slightly injured as to permit its being repaired in a day.

After his demonstration against the heights of Opanetz on the 2d of October, Kriloff remained idle at Tristenik with the bulk of his force until the 8th, on which day he was relieved from his command by General Gourko.

While these events had been in progress considerable change had taken place in the direction of the Russian Army. When it was determined to invest and besiege Plevna, General Todle-

INVESTMENT OF PLEVNA. 267

ben, the famous Engineer of Sevastopol, was ordered from St. Petersburg to the army. He arrived at Gorni-Studen on the 28th of September, and on the 30th accompanied the Grand Duke and a portion of his staff to the position in front of Plevna. General Gourko, who had meanwhile arrived from Russia with his proper command, the 2d Cavalry Division of the Guard, and was in camp near Tirnova, was also ordered to Plevna. On the 4th of October was issued an order of the day assigning Todleben as "Adjunct to the Commander of the West Army," with Imeretinsky as Chief of Staff; Zotof to resume command of the IV. Corps; Gourko to command all the cavalry on the west bank of the Vid, which was to be reënforced by his own division; Kriloff to proceed to Russia as Inspector of Cavalry Remounts. These changes took place within the next few days; the Grand Duke returned to Gorni-Studen, and General Todleben assumed the direction of the siege. At that time the Roumanian works shown on the plan of Plevna (Plate 19) at Kalysovat and Verbitza, and redoubt Alexander, were nearly completed; their approaches on the east of the second Grivitza redoubt were within 70 yards; the Russian batteries from Grivitza to the Tutchenitza ravine were finished and armed. The 20 siege-guns (24-pdrs.) were distributed in three batteries, one just south of the Grivitza brook and the other two on the Radischevo ridge. From these new positions the siege-guns could reach every point in the Turkish lines along the whole length of the Grivitza ridge, and also in the "middle group." They could not reach the Turkish works, which were increasing every day, on the Krishin heights.

The rest of the batteries were armed with 9-pdrs., and in all there were about 250 guns in position. There was no firing except as the Turks were discovered enlarging their works, when the Russians opened upon them with shrapnel; they were thus forced to prosecute their work wholly at night. But little change was evident in the main works of the middle group, except that they were all being connected by trenches serving as covered ways for communication as well as for lines of defense; but along the crest of the ridge between Grivitza and Bukova the works were in course of construction in spite of all the efforts of the Russians to stop them. On the other hand, occasionally the Turks would drop a shell among the men at work on the Russian batteries; immediately more than 100 Russian guns would concentrate their fire upon the Turkish redoubt whence this shot had come, and reduce it to complete silence. The Turks, as already stated, were greatly inferior in artillery, having only about 80 pieces and no siege-guns. These pieces were moved about from one redoubt to another at night, and ventured but rarely to open fire, and always with the result just stated.

While these changes had been taking place on the Russian side, the Turks had been making efforts to reënforce Plevna and secure its communications. Chefket Pasha, who previously commanded a division in Mehemet Ali's army, had been sent to Sophia about September 12th, to take charge of these operations. The troops placed at his disposal were nearly all new recruits from Asia or reserves which had been kept at Sophia, Philippopolis and Adrianople. From Sophia to Plevna the distance is about 135 miles over the high-road, which was then in excellent condition; but as 60 miles of this was over the main chain of the Balkans and up and down over its foot-hills, it was a march of ten days for troops or ox transports. Chefket established his depot of supplies at the town of Orkhanie, at the northern entrance of the defile passing through the main range, and seven days' march from Plevna. From here he sent a force of 12,000 men, accompanying 2,000 wagons loaded with provisions, which entered Plevna on the 22d of September, as already described. After that he sent smaller convoys, of which some were captured and some succeeded in reaching Plevna. He came himself with 5,000 men and a large train, whose exact numbers are not known, on the 5th of October, as we have seen, and, posting his men on the road behind Plevna, went himself to Osman's headquarters and then returned to Radomirtza and commenced fortifying points along the road in order to keep it open. A few days later he sent about 3,000 more men into these works, and had besides a certain force, numbers not known, at Radomirtza and farther back on the road. In all it is probable that he sent into Plevna about 3,000 wagon-loads of provisions, or, estimating the load at a ton, about 60 days' full rations for 60,000 men.

Meanwhile, on the Russian side the troops of the Guard were arriving daily, and were now (October 1st) nearly all on the south bank of the Danube. The Grenadier Corps was following closely behind them. This gave a disposable force of 70,000 infantry and the proportionate cavalry and artillery—all fresh troops; and the question arose as to what disposition to make of them. There was a certain party among the Grand Duke's advisers who warmly urged him to leave matters in their present condition at Plevna and on the Lom (the Russian fortifications in front of Plevna being now quite sufficient to withstand any effort of Osman to break through them, and the force on the Lom having already proved its capacity to repel any attacks from that quarter), to unite the newly arrived troops with those of Radetzky at Shipka, and with this column of 100,000 men to dislodge the Turks at Shipka and advance at once over the Balkans to Adrianople. On the 23d of September an order of the day was issued directing the Cesarevitch to resume command of the Corps of the Guard (his usual command in time of peace); on the 6th of October this order was revoked, and the Cesarevitch was directed to retain command of the troops on the Lom. Between these two dates the plan of advancing had been rejected, and it had been decided to send the Guard and Grenadiers to Plevna, and to capture or destroy Osman's army as a precedent to any farther advance. Had an advance been made the Cesarevitch would have commanded it; but it was not thought becoming for the heir to the throne of Russia to serve under the orders of the Prince of Roumania, as would have been necessary had he accompanied the Guard to Plevna.

On the 19th of October the Roumanians made another effort to gain possession of the second Grivitza redoubt. Their approaches were already within less than 20 yards of the ditch of the Turkish redoubt. At noon four Roumanian battalions jumped out from their trenches and from the first redoubt, and rushed forward toward the Turkish work; they were received by the fire of about 1,000 infantry posted in the work, and that of an equal or greater force which immediately came out from the Turkish trenches and covered ways in the rear of their redoubt to meet them. The Roumanians were obliged to fall back under cover. At 6 o'clock the attempt was renewed by three Roumanian battalions. This time they drove the Turks out of their places along the counterscarp of the ditch, and got possession of the ditch. The Turks then came out on the parapet of the redoubt, and opened fire at arm's length upon the

Roumanians; and as the latter tried to climb up the parapet the Turks received them with the bayonet. Meanwhile the artillery and infantry fire from the Roumanian trenches in rear caused the Turks to leave the parapet and put themselves under cover; but no sooner did the Roumanians appear on the parapet again than the Turks again jumped up to meet them, and drove them back into the ditch. This was kept up for nearly an hour, until darkness had set in; then, finding it impossible to carry the place, the Roumanians returned into their own trenches. Their losses were 2 officers and 200 men killed, 20 officers and 707 men wounded; those of the Turks were probably about equal. This was the last assault ever made upon any of the Turkish redoubts around Plevna east of the river.

On the 20th of October the Guard had all arrived at Plevna, and Todleben prepared to complete the investment. His plan, in brief, was to throw forward his two wings from the Verbitza-Radischevo fortified position, and join them together on the other side of the Vid, thus forming a complete circle. There was nothing to oppose his right wing (which in fact was, with cavalry, already at Etropol), but his left wing would have to dislodge the Turks from their fortified places along the Sophia road, of which there were four within a distance of 35 miles from Plevna, viz., Dolni-Dubnik, Gorni-Dubnik, Telis, and Radomirtza.

The Guard was designated for this purpose, and had already been massed in the villages between the Lovtcha road and the Vid, near the village of Cirakova. The 1st and 2d Infantry Divisions and its Cavalry Divisions were placed under the orders of General Gourko, commanding all the troops on the west bank of the Vid, and were to first attack Gorni-Dubnik, and afterward Telis and Dolni-Dubnik in succession, and then join hands with the large cavalry force, now commanded by General Arnoldi, and reënforced by seven infantry battalions from the 3d Roumanian Division, which was at Gorni-Etropol. Meanwhile the 3d Division of the Guard was to advance parallel to the Vid and seize the heights near Medevan, and continue advancing until they came within close range of the Turkish redoubts, which had lately been constructed all along the Krishin ridge to the bluff overhanging the river. At the same time a detachment which had just been formed under the orders of

General Skobeleff, consisting of his own (16th) Division, the 1st Brigade of the 30th Division, and the 3d Rifle Brigade, was to advance from Tutchenitza to the Lovtcha road and seize the Red Hill (where he had been September 7th) and the heights in front of Brestovetz. This detachment was then gradually to extend to the left, and the 3d Division of the Guard to the right, until they came together. Finally, on the day fixed for this simultaneous movement (October 24th), an energetic bombardment was to be kept up by all the batteries on the east of Plevna, in order if possible to prevent the Turks from sending reënforcements from Plevna to the aid of their works on the Sophia road.

Skobeleff's detachment and the 3d Division of the Guard occupied the position assigned to them almost without resistance; but at Gorni-Dubnik Gourko met with most stubborn opposition, as will presently be seen.

The force acting under Gourko's orders on the 23d of October was as follows:

	Battalions.	Guns.	Squadrons.	Guns.
1st Division of the Guard	16	48	..	..
2d Division of the Guard	15	48	..	..
Rifle Brigade of the Guard	4	..	..	..
Sapper Battalion of the Guard	1	..	..	..
2d Cavalry Division of the Guard	..	..	24	19
Emperor's personal escort	..	..	4	..
1st Brigade 3d Roumanian Division	7	6	..	..
4th Cavalry Division	..	..	18	12
Brigade Don Cossacks	..	..	12	6
Brigade Caucasian Cossacks	..	..	12	6
Regular Roumanian Cavalry Brigade	..	..	9	6
Militia Roumanian Cavalry Brigade	..	..	9	..
Total	44	102	86	48

Or about 35,000 infantry, 10,000 cavalry, and the usual proportion of artillery for each arm.

On the 22d Gourko personally reconnoitered the positions at Telis and Gorni-Dubnik, and on the 23d issued the necessary orders for his advance the next day.

The country on the west of the Vid differs completely from that on the east. As seen from the heights of Medevan, it appears to be a vast plain, but, on descending into it, is found to have long gradual slopes, rising perhaps to the height of 150 feet at the most above the level of the Vid. These slopes are cut through by occasional rivulets flowing to the Vid, and forming what are known on our Western plains as *coulées*. The villages of Telis and Dolni-Dubnik are situated about 7 miles apart, in the same coulée which flows north to Gorni-Etropol, and thence east, emptying into the Vid about three miles north of the Plevna bridge.

The village of Dolni-Dubnik is near the head of another similar coulée. The depth of these coulées varies from 60 to 100 feet, and their width from 200 to 1,000 yards.

The high-road coming from Sophia passes through the village of Telis, and then keeps a straight course to Dolni-Dubnik (and thence to the Plevna bridge), leaving Gorni-Dubnik about half a mile on its left (north).

On the plain around Dolni-Dubnik were six little redoubts, three north and three south of the village. At Telis was a large irregular line of breastwork, northeast of the village, divided in two by the road, and running down on either flank to the stream in the coulée. On the other (southwest) side of the village was a large redoubt.

Near Gorni-Dubnik the fortifications were weakest of all. At the point (about a mile southwest of the village) where the road crosses the coulée was one of those ancient tumuli so frequently found in Turkey, about 40 feet in diameter at the base and 15 feet high. The Turks had leveled off a part of the top of this mound so as to make a *cavalier* holding four guns, and they had then surrounded this with a rudely constructed redoubt upon a polygonal figure about 300 yards in diameter. The parapet of this redoubt was only 4 feet high and 6 feet thick, and the ditch had about the same proportions. In order to partly cover what would otherwise have been a dead space at the bottom of the coulée, there were some trenches on the slope outside of the redoubt. At the edge of the road near the redoubt was a small stone post-road station, and just opposite it, on the southern side of the road, the Turks had built a three-sided lunette of about 50 yards front. Two thousand yards farther to the southeast, their pickets had a few rifle-pits, on a little eminence covered with thick brushwood.

Gourko's plan of attack was as follows:

1. 20 battalions, 6 squadrons, and 48 guns to attack the position at Gorni-Dubnik on three sides, viz., from the north, east, and south.

BATTLE OF GORNI-DUBNIK. 273

2. 12 battalions, 11 squadrons, and 44 guns, to cover the attack on the side of Dolni-Dubnik.

3. 4 battalions, 17 squadrons, and 20 guns, to cover the attack on the side of Telis.

4. 7 battalions, 44 squadrons, and 34 guns, under General Arnoldi, to make a strong demonstration on the north of Dolni-Dubnik, in order to retain the garrison in that place; and at the same time a portion of these troops to operate on the west of Gorni-Dubnik, in order to cut off the retreat of the Turks, and another portion to reconnoiter in the valley of the Isker and toward Lukovitza.

1. *Attack of Gorni-Dubnik.*

The troops designated for this purpose passed the Vid at the Cirakova ford between midnight and daylight of the 24th of October, and were divided into three columns (Plate 15), viz.:

On the right, under Major-General Ellis, the Rifle Brigade (4 battalions), with 3 sotnias and 16 4-pdr. guns.

In the center, under Major-General Zeddeler, the Moscow and Grenadier Regiments, and the Sapper battalion (8 battalions), with 1 sotnia and 16 9-pdr. guns.

On the left, under Major-General Rosenbach, the Paul and Finland Regiments, 8 battalions, with 16 4-pdr. guns.

These columns took up the march soon after 6 A. M., and at 8:30 A. M. they arrived in position: the center column on the little eminence southeast of the redoubt, the right column on the high road northeast of it, the left column on the high-road on the southwest, all at a distance of about 1,800 yards. They deployed their troops in two lines of company columns and a reserve, and placed their batteries in the center of the first line and opened fire. At the same time the brigade of Caucasian Cossacks (coming from the command of General Arnoldi) arrived on the hill northwest of the redoubt, and opened fire with six horse-guns. The redoubt was therefore at 9 A. M. surrounded with 56 guns, which kept up an incessant fire upon it, inflicting considerable losses on the Turks, whose means of shelter in their hastily constructed redoubt were not very good. A little after 10 A. M. Colonel Lioubovitzky, commanding the Grenadier Regiment, led it forward to the assault. They carried the lunette on the southeast of the road, and then followed the

18

retreating Turks and made a vigorous effort against the main work; but they were driven back by a murderous fire and took refuge behind the lunette, the post-house, and in the ditches on either side of the high-road. General Zeddeler then sent the Moscow Regiment and the two batteries to their support; the Regiment found shelter in the ditches of the road on the right of the Grenadiers. The batteries advanced to within 900 yards of the redoubt, but at this distance their horses and gunners were picked off by the Turks with such accuracy that they were obliged to return to their first position. General Zeddeler, Colonel Lioubovitsky, and Colonel Scalon (chief of staff of the division) were all wounded about this time; the troops remained in the ditches of the road, which (see sketch) was nearly parallel to one side of the redoubt and but 60 to 80 yards from it, and from there kept up a fire with the Turks.

Meanwhile the column of the right, upon arriving on the high-road, had come under the fire of the artillery in the works near Dolni-Dubnik. Leaving one battalion to face these works, the other three had turned to the left and advanced to some small mounds about 1,900 yards from the redoubt, and had here opened fire with their artillery. When the Grenadier Regiment assaulted the redoubt from the east, their men remained so close to the redoubt that at that distance it was impossible to tell exactly where they were, and therefore the batteries were advanced to 900 yards and there commenced their fire, but were soon obliged to retire to a greater distance. The place of the battalion which had been left facing Dolni-Dubnik was now taken by the 1st Brigade 1st Division, which arrived on the high-road, and the other regiment (Izmailof) of this column, which was to protect the right flank, was sent to the support of the batteries, while the whole of the Rifle Brigade descended into the coulée near the village, and crept along its slopes until they came under the fire of the trenches on the hillside, northwest of the redoubt.

The column of the left had arrived about the same time as the others (8:30 to 9 A. M.) on the high-road between Gorni-Dubnik and Telis, and then, turning by the right flank, had advanced and opened fire with its batteries. When they saw the Grenadier Regiment advancing to the assault, they also formed on both sides of the high-road, crossed the coulée, and began climbing the hill against the redoubt. But the fire was terribly

BATTLE OF GORNI-DUBNIK.

hot, and they could not stand it; they fell back, the Finland Regiment to the dead angle at the bottom of the coulée, and the Paul Regiment behind a bend in the coulée on the left flank and in rear of the Grenadiers. General Rosenbach, commanding the column, and Colonel Rounoff, commanding the Paul Regiment, were both wounded in this assault.

At noon, therefore, the condition of things was as follows: The Russians had made an assault on the north, east, and southwest, and had been repulsed; the Paul and Finland regiments were in the ravine southwest of the work; the Grenadier and Moscow regiments in the ditches of the high-road a few rods from the redoubt, on the southeast; the Izmailof Regiment between the high-road and the village of Gorni-Dubnik, on the northeast; and the Rifle Brigade in the ravine, north and northwest of the redoubt; the artillery in nearly the same positions as during the morning, but its action much hindered by the fear of hitting their own troops, who were so close to the redoubt. The troops rested in these positions with desultory firing for the next three hours. At 2 P.M. Gourko, who had been during the morning with the column on the right, came in person to the little hill where were the batteries of the column of the center, and here he received word that the four battalions (Jäger Regiment) sent against Telis had met with a terrible repulse, and had fallen back, leaving the road from Telis partly open to an attack by Turkish reënforcements coming from that direction. It was evidently necessary to strike hard and quickly, else his position became a very critical one. Gourko therefore determined to attack from all sides at 3 P.M. For the result I will give his own words, translated literally from his report:

"I gave in person the necessary orders to General Brock, who had taken command of the First Brigade Second Division of the Guard, and I sent a written order to General Ellis.

"In order that the attack might be simultaneously made by all the troops, I decided that, when all the orders had been given, I would have three volleys fired by the batteries on the left; that three volleys should then be fired in succession by those on the center and on the right; and that after the last volley fired by these latter all the troops should rush forward to the assault. I calculated that a simultaneous attack made on all points and at very short distances (100 to 400 paces) would be crowned with success.

"After having given these orders, I went to the column on the left and examined the position of all the troops; I then returned to the battery, where I gave in person the necessary orders to General Count Shouvaloff, commanding the Second Division of the Guard. But before Count Shouvaloff had had time to transmit his orders to the troops, three volleys were fired in succession by the batteries of the column on the right, and this column rushed forward to the assault. The signal agreed upon was thus not observed, and my calculations for a simultaneous attack were baffled.

"It was with a sinking heart (*le cœur défaillant*) that I followed what was about to take place; for in place of a simultaneous assault on all points, there were going to be isolated assaults one after another, of which the success was more than doubtful. To remedy matters as far as possible, and to sustain the column on the right, which had already begun the assault, I sent orderly officers in all directions to give the troops the order not to wait any longer for the signal, but to support the attack of the column on the right. As was to be expected, a series of attacks one after another took place. Received by an extremely murderous fire, no one body of troops could reach the great redoubt. But, with the exception of the Finland Regiment, no one of them fell back; moving forward, they lay down behind shelter of one sort or another, and a few arrived within 40 paces of the redoubt. As for the Finland Regiment, not finding any shelter in front of it, it was obliged to fall back, and establish itself again on the slope of the ridge in the dead space. In this assault Major-General Lavroff, commanding the Finland Regiment, who was marching at the head of his regiment with heroic intrepidity, fell, mortally wounded.

"After this series of assaults, which were over by 4 o'clock in the afternoon, all the batteries ceased firing, for the troops were so close to the redoubt that their fire reached our own troops.

"As for withdrawing the troops in order to continue to cannonade the redoubt, it was absolutely impossible to do it, on account of the losses which they would unquestionably have suffered in this movement, and especially on account of the bad

BATTLE OF GORNI-DUBNIK. 277

impression which this movement in retreat would have produced upon the morale of the troops. I decided then to leave the troops in the positions which they occupied, and to make a new assault at nightfall. After having given the necessary orders, I returned to the eminence opposite the village of Gorni-Dubnik to there await the twilight.

"There was observable a terrible silence, a silence of death. When darkness came, several bodies of troops crept closer to the redoubt. Two battalions of the Izmailoff Regiment, Major-General Ellis II., of the suite of H. M. the Emperor, commanding the regiment, at the head, advanced thus by crawling for about 150 paces, and thus came within 50 paces of the redoubt. Simultaneously the troops rushed forward, and almost from all sides they penetrated into the redoubt. The immense flame of a fire which burst forth in the center of the enemy's work lit up the whole neighborhood, and announced the fall of the redoubt which the Turks had so long and so stubbornly defended."

The Russian trophies were 1 Pasha, 53 officers, and 2,235 men (not wounded) prisoners, 1 standard, 4 guns, and a large number of small arms and ammunition. The Turkish losses were about 1,500 men. Those of the Russians were as follows: 2 brigade commanders and the chief and 3 officers of the Division Staff, wounded; 2 regiment commanders and 1 battalion commander killed; 1 regiment commander and 3 colonels wounded; and the following:

	KILLED.			WOUNDED.		
	Field Officers.	Company Officers.	Men.	Field Officers.	Company Officers.	Men.
Staff................................	..	..	..	1	4	1
Emperor's escort....................	..	..	1	1	1	4
Izmailoff Regiment.................	..	1	57	..	6	219
Moscow Regiment...................	..	3	95	1	12	421
Grenadier Regiment.................	..	3	310	4	22	594
Paul Regiment......................	..	6	164	2	11	500
Finland Regiment...................	1	2	106	4	10	328
Rifle Brigade.......................	..	1	56	1	12	214
Sapper Battalion....................	..	..	5	1	..	58
Artillery............................	..	1	7	2	1	49
Total........................	1	17	811	17	79	2,384

Total, 116 officers and 3,195 men.

2. *Attack of Telis.*

The column whose mission was to protect the Russian left flank against any attack from the direction of Telis, and if possible to gain possession of that place, was composed of the Jäger Regiment (4 battalions), the 1st and 2d Cavalry Brigades, 1 sotnia of the 4th Don Cossacks, and 20 guns. It crossed the river also at the Cirakova ford during the night, and at 6:15 A. M. took up its march toward Telis, leaving the greater part of the cavalry to cover its left flank. The infantry arrived on the high-road in front of the Telis redoubt about 9 A. M., and its artillery (12 pieces) opened fire upon the Turkish work at 1,200 yards. At 10 A. M. the Jäger Regiment, formed in two lines, moved forward and drove the Turks out of some small rifle-pits which they had in front of the main work. But these shallow trenches being wholly open in the rear, i. e., toward the redoubt, and only about 200 yards from it, when the Russians had gained possession of them it was not possible to remain there under the fire of the Turks; it was necessary to retreat or assault the main work. They chose the latter, and rushed at it with great bravery, but without success. They found a little shelter in the irregularities of the ground about 100 paces in front of the parapet, and were lying there keeping up a hot fire with the Turks, when word was received from the cavalry off on the left that considerable Turkish reënforcements were approaching Telis from the South. As his force was evidently unequal to the task of gaining the redoubt, the Colonel of the Jäger Regiment then sounded the retreat, and the regiment fell back about a mile and a half in the direction of Cirakova. The Turks, however, did not make an effort to follow them or to go past them to the relief of Gorni-Dubnik.

In this short affair the Jäger Regiment lost 26 officers and 907 men.

The result of the 24th of October was therefore the capture of the position of Gorni-Dubnik, by which Gourko got a firm footing in the center of the Turkish line of fortifications along the Sophia road. He immediately set to work to fortify his position, facing both ways on the road. The 1st Division was placed in position in front of Dolni-Dubnik, the Rifle Brigade on its left joining hands with the 1st Brigade 3d Roumanian Division, which was on the north and west of that place; the 2d Division was placed in the works at Gorni-Dubnik, with one brigade in advance toward Telis, and the 1st Brigade 3d Division was brought from the vicinity of Medevan toward

Telis on the east. The Cavalry Division was sent in observation on the left (heights of Rahita), threatening the communications of the Turks by the high-road, while the Caucasian Brigade of Cossacks demonstrated from the west against the Turkish works on that side of Telis. On the 28th of October these troops were simply advanced to within 1,500 yards of the Turkish fortifications at Telis, and from there opened fire with 72 guns, firing principally shrapnel. This concentrated artillery fire was kept up from 11 A. M. to 2 P. M., when Gourko sent one of his prisoners with a note summoning the Pasha to surrender, and threatening to attack on all sides if his answer was not received in half an hour. The Pasha (Izmail Hakki) surrendered, with 100 officers, 3,000 men, 4 guns, and an enormous quantity of small-arms ammunition destined for Plevna.

As soon as this surrender took place, the cavalry of the Guard and the Cossacks joined hands on the south of the village, and attacked a large band of Tcherkesses supported by infantry who were posted about half way between Telis and Radomirtza. They drove back the Tcherkesses, but were naturally brought to a halt by the infantry, and after a loss of about 50 men they fell back a short distance toward Telis, establishing a picket-line in observation of the Turks. During the night the latter fell back upon Radomirtza, and, assembling his force there, Chefket Pasha abandoned all his fortifications and took up his retreat to the positions about Pravetz in the foot-hills of the Balkans.

Meanwhile, on the other side of his position—i. e., toward Dolni-Dubnik—Gourko had posted the 1st Division across the high-road, and on its right a portion of the 9th Cavalry Division, keeping up communication with the 2d Brigade 3d Division (Guard), on the heights in front of Medevan, on the east bank of the Vid; on its left was the Rifle Brigade, then the Roumanian Brigade, and then a large force of cavalry near Etropol. The two divisions of the Grenadier Corps which were en route to Bulgaria had meanwhile partly arrived, and the first of them had been directed to the army of the Cesarevitch beyond Biela; but they were recalled by forced marches to Plevna, and, passing around the right flank of the Roumanians, were to cross the river at Riben. Gourko only awaited the arrival of these troops to fill up the space on the north, and then he intended to repeat at Dolni-Dubnik the measures which had gained

Telis—i. e., surround it on three sides with a large force of artillery, supported by infantry four times as numerous as the defenders, then open a concentrated fire with shrapnel, and finally, if the Turks refused to surrender, make a simultaneous assault from all sides. The leading troops of the Grenadiers (2d Brigade 3d Division Grenadiers) arrived at Etropol late in the afternoon of October 31st. Gourko then wrote out his orders for the attack, fixing it at the 2d of November. But the next morning at daylight the Rifle Brigade noticed a lack of defenders in the Turkish work near it, and immediately sent a party of volunteers to reconnoiter, who found the redoubt empty. The Turks had in fact abandoned all their positions at Dolni-Dubnik, and during the night had retreated into Plevna; and as the day became more clear the last of the column could be distinguished just crossing the Plevna bridge. The troops immediately moved forward and took up a position just outside the range of the Turkish guns on the heights north of Medevan. The investment of Plevna was complete. (See Plate 17.)

CHAPTER VII.

EVENTS ON OTHER PORTIONS OF THE THEATRE OF WAR FROM SEPTEMBER TO DECEMBER, 1877—SHIPKA—THE LOM—THE LOWER DANUBE—GOURKO'S ADVANCE TO ORKHANIE.

It is now necessary to refer briefly to the course of events at the other points of the theatre of war.

SHIPKA PASS.

(See Plate 13.)

In a previous chapter we have seen that Suleiman Pasha made a succession of fierce, mad assaults upon the Russians at Shipka from the 21st to the 26th of August, and that, having caused great losses on both sides, but having gained no ground whatever, he was forced to desist and to reorganize his force and call for more reënforcements. The Russians on their side did what they could to repair losses and prepare for a new struggle; they strengthened their own position by fortification, dug trenches and covered ways along that part of the road commanded by the Turkish fire from the Bald Mountain, and brought a few mortars into position; but as they received no reënforcements (all those which arrived in Bulgaria at this time being directed toward Plevna for the great purpose of capturing or defeating Osman's army), they had no troops available for undertaking any operations to dislodge the Turks from their commanding positions; and therefore they (the Russians) remained on the same ground, viz., the three hills on the high-road at the summit of the pass. Their daily losses were from 5 to 10 men. On the 13th of September the Turks increased their fire both in infantry and artillery, and the latter included four large mortars concealed in the woods in front of Mount St. Nicholas, which did great damage to the Russians, whose losses increased to about 40 men per day. At the same time some demonstrations were made on either flank by Tcherkesses, resulting in some skirmishes which accomplished nothing.

This cannonade continued for four days, and then, at 3 A. M. on the 17th of September, Zuleiman sent forward his infantry to the assault on all sides, directing as previously his strongest efforts against Mount St. Nicholas. Here the Turks, under cover of the darkness, climbed up to within about 100 yards of the batteries and trenches on the summit, drove the Russians out of the advanced trenches, and established their own position by means of the gabions and fascines which they had brought with them. At daylight a fierce fight opened for the possession of this hill, and lasted till noon. Radetzky hastened thither in person, taking with him the 56th Regiment to reënforce the 53d, which held this portion of the line. The Turks made several desperate efforts to drive the Russians from the top of the hill, but without success; and the Russians in turn were unable to drive the Turks back beyond the trenches they had taken and constructed before daylight. The struggle went on all the morning, and the bayonet was very freely used on both sides. A part of the 35th and 55th Regiments was brought up to the hill during the morning, and finally about noon portions of the 53d and 56th rushed forward upon the Turks, and succeeded in driving them out. This assault cost the Russians dear, but nevertheless it accomplished the defeat of the Turks.

Upon the Russian right flank (northern hill) the Turks had begun their attack also at daylight; the Russians allowed them to approach within fifty yards, and then opened on them with volley-firing, under which the Turkish lines withered, and the men fell back. Twice more they tried it, and with the same result. At 9 o'clock they withdrew altogether in this quarter.

The loss of the Russians on this day was 31 officers and something over 1,000 men. That of the Turks was naturally much larger, and was estimated by General Radetzky in his report at not less than 3,000 men. The south side of Mount St. Nicholas was a mass of corpses. Suleiman, having gained nothing by this assault, resumed the ordinary mortar and sharpshooter practice, which continued for ten days; when he was nominated to

OPERATIONS AT SHIPKA PASS. 283

the command of the Army in the Quadrilateral, and succeeded at Shipka by Reouf Pasha.

Reouf found it necessary to reorganize the army which Suleiman had turned over to him. Soon afterward bad weather arrived, and, in this high altitude, a considerable quantity of snow. This impeded operations during the month of October, and in November Gourko began advancing toward Sophia, which caused a portion of Reouf's troops to be moved in that direction. Reouf soon afterward was recalled to Constantinople and made Minister of War, and was succeeded by Vessil Pasha, whose force was then increased by troops brought from the Quadrilateral.

But, although desultory firing was kept up during all these months, the Turks undertook no serious assault after the 17th of September; and, on the other hand, the Russians never loosened their grip upon the position which they had captured on the 19th of July. In the first week of January, as will be subsequently explained, they turned the pass on both flanks and captured Vessil Pasha and his army *in toto*.

OPERATIONS ON THE LOM.

(See Plate 14.)

We have already followed in a previous chapter the advance of Mehemet Ali against the detachment of the Cesarevitch during the months of August and September, his successes in the battles of Karahassankoi and Katzelevo, his defeat at Cerkovna, and his subsequent retreat to the line of the White Lom, where on the 2d of October he was replaced by Suleiman.

The detatchment of the Cesarevitch at this time counted, as before, the XII. and XIII. Corps; and the 26th Division on their right, keeping up communication with the XI. Corps on the west of Tirnova; but the dispersion of his force, which had so largely contributed to the necessity for his retreat before the force of Mehemet Ali in September, was now avoided, and his troops were well in hand, in fortified positions between the Danube near Metchka and the mouth of the Banitchka Lom—a distance of only about 18 miles. The country on his right, being most difficult of approach, was occupied only by detachments of the 26th Division in observation. The defense of the road from Osman-Bazar to Tirnova was intrusted to the XI.

Corps under General Dellinghausen, who had replaced Prince Shakofskoi, the latter being broken down by sickness.

Although Suleiman took command of the Army in the Quadrilateral in the first week in October, it was not until the 26th of November that he undertook any serious operations. He first assembled a large force at the village of Kadikoi, eight miles south of Rustchuk, and apparently threatened the Cesarevitch's left flank, and at the same time began building a bridge from Silistria toward the Roumanian bank of the Danube. Against this the Russians simply diverted the 24th Division, which was en route through Bucharest. This demonstration against Roumania was made in conjunction with an intended descent of some Hungarians from the Carpathians upon the line of the Russian communications; but this latter proved wholly abortive, and, the 24th Division being more than ample for the defense of the passage of the river at Silistria, the Turkish bridge was taken up and the whole movement amounted to nothing. Suleiman then moved the bulk of his force to Razgrad, and began reconnoitering in front of that place, at the same time that bands of Tcherkesses and some infantry made demonstrations on the road from Osman-Bazar to Elena. Still, nothing serious was attempted. The troops of the Cesarevitch were kept constantly on the alert and made frequent reconnaissances in order to keep themselves informed of Suleiman's movements. The result was a constant series of skirmishes. Finally, in the latter part of November (Gourko's troops being already in the foot-hills of the Balkans on the Sophia road), Suleiman rapidly assembled a large force near Rustchuk, and on the 19th drove the Russians, with a loss of about 200 men, from their advanced position near Pirgos to their principal position near Metchka; but in the afternoon of the same day the Russians reënforced the point attacked, and drove the Turks out of Pirgos and back across the Lom. On the 26th Suleiman renewed his attack in greater force upon the position of the XII. Corps at Metchka and Tristenik. A very considerable affair took place, in which the whole of the XII. Corps was engaged; the Turks attacked with great energy, but were wholly unsuccessful, and in their retreat were followed by the XII. Corps and driven across the Lom. The Russian official report states that the Turks lost 1,200 men, and that their own losses were 28 officers and 738 men.

On the same day demonstrations were made by the Turks in front of Katzelevo, as well as on the roads leading from Osman-Bazar.

On the 4th of December a large force (reported at 30,000 men), which had advanced by the road leading from Osman-Bazar through Elena to Tirnova, fell upon the two regiments of the 9th Division (VIII. Corps) occupying a fortified position in the ravine of Mahren, two miles east of Elena. The attack was made at daylight, and the Russian commander, Prince Mirsky, seems to have been taken somewhat by surprise; his position was surrounded on three sides, and his troops were driven back to Elena with a loss of 50 officers and 1,800 men, as well as 11 guns, 4 of which had been dismounted and the other 7 had all their horses killed. This affair was also remarkable as being almost the only one in the whole course of the campaign in which the Turks took any prisoners. They here captured about 500 men, who were taken to Constantinople and well cared for.

The Russians fell back in disorder to their fortifications at Elena, and hastily brought up part of the XI. Corps from the vicinity of Tirnova to their aid. The Turks did not follow up their success, and on the 6th, the Russian reënforcements having arrived, Prince Mirsky advanced to his old positions, and the Turks retreated, after some skirmishing, in the direction of Osman-Bazar.

At last, after this long series of indecisive combats, skirmishes, and demonstrations upon both flanks of a line 75 miles long, Suleiman made an attack in force with about 35,000 men (60 battalions) upon the left flank of the Cesarevitch's detachment, i. e., at Metchka and Tristenik, near the Danube. This was on the 12th of December, Plevna having fallen two days before.

At this time the position of the XII. Corps, forming the left of the Cesarevitch's detachment, was as follows (see Plates 14 and 15): at Metchka, near the Danube, 1st Brigade 12th Division; at Tristenik, 4 miles southeast of Metchka, 2d Brigade 12th Division—both in positions well fortified; in reserve to this line, the 2d Brigade 33d Division. The 129th Regiment of the same division was at Damogila, and the 130th at Tabashka, in observation of the Lom. On their right was the XIII.

Corps, of which the 2d Brigade 35th Division was nearest (and was brought into action on the 12th of December). The 12th Cavalry Division was on the right and left of Tristenik, and furnished the cavalry pickets on a line from the Danube to the Lom, about four miles in front of the infantry position. The total strength of these troops was therefore 30 battalions, about 25,000 men, with 16 squadrons and 120 guns. The XII. Corps was commanded by the Grand Duke Vladimir, second son of the Emperor.

The two villages of Tristenik and Metchka lie each in a deep ravine, flowing to the Danube, and the branches of these ravines make the country in front of Tristenik very broken and difficult for manœuvres. On the other side of the high-road are shorter but equally deep ravines flowing into the Lom, whose banks are precipitous, and the bed of its stream fully 350 feet below the level of the plateau between it and the Danube. The position of the Russians was a very favorable one, completely commanding, over an open plateau, the approaches from Rustchuk, either by the high-road which passes near Tristenik, or by the river road near Metchka. Behind their left flank, at the island of Batin, the Russians had a ponton bridge (built in the month of October) over the Danube, and on the Roumanian shore, near Giurgevo, were several siege batteries.

On the afternoon of the 10th of December the Turks drove in the Russian pickets, and appeared in considerable force in front of the Russian positions. The troops of the latter were on the alert, but the Turks retired at sunset without making an attack. The next day the Russians made preparations for an expected attack, and brought the 129th Regiment to Tristenik, replacing it at Damogila by the 2d Brigade 35th Division, and also moved the 130th Regiment a short distance down the Lom. On the morning of the 12th, the Russian batteries at Parapan (5 miles southwest of Giurgevo) signaled that the Turks were moving out of Rustchuk, and at the same time another force of them was discovered by the pickets crossing the Lom just below Kadikoi. Each column contained about 30 battalions and 25 guns. That from Rustchuk immediately advanced along the river road, and at 9 A. M. opened the battle by an attack upon the Russian position at Metchka. Soon afterward the other column came into position on its left (southeast) against the interval

OPERATIONS ON THE LOM. 287

between the works at Metchka and those at Tristenik. A strong line of skirmishers extended on its left all the way to the Lom.

The 2d Brigade 33d Division was immediately moved forward to occupy the small trenches in this interval; but no other change was made in the position of the troops until the Turks should have developed their plan of attack. The Turks made several unsuccessful assaults upon the Russian redoubt at Metchka, and by noon it was evident that their plan was to throw their whole weight upon the left flank of the Russian position, gain possession of the works at Metchka, and then advance against the Batin bridge; the left flank of the Turks, between the high-road and the Lom, seemed to be very weak. As the most efficacious way of meeting this attack, the Russian commander determined to throw forward his right flank against this weak line and thus threaten the Turkish left and rear, and at the same time to attack in force with his center; and also to execute this movement before the enemy should have had time to concentrate too strong a force against Metchka. The 2d Brigade 12th Cavalry Division was therefore moved forward in the space between the high-road and the Lom, and, dismounting a part of its force, gained possession of the plateau about four miles in front of Tristenik; the 2d Brigade 35th Division and the 47th Regiment at the same time followed on its left along the high-road, and coming on the plateau, supported the cavalry, who were just beginning to be forced back. These three regiments then established themselves on this plateau, and, bringing five batteries into action, opened a terrible fire with shrapnel upon the flank of the Turkish reserves, which were still massed in the ravines. At the same time the 2d Brigade 33d Division began to advance through the interval between Metchka and Tristenik. The result of this double attack was not long in doubt; by 2 o'clock the Turks were in full retreat, and then the troops in the works at Metchka in their turn began to advance. The result was a complete rout of the Turks at every point, and a somewhat precipitate retreat to Rustchuk and across the Lom at Krasnoe. They were followed by the Russian cavalry until darkness set in. Their losses were nearly 3,000 (as estimated in the Russian official report), among which were 800 dead left on the field. The Russian losses were 24 officers and 775 men. The Turkish losses were caused in large part by the shrapnel of the Russian artillery.

For more than five months the detachment of the Cesarevitch—which, even counting the 26th Division, had never numbered over 55,000 infantry—had guarded the left flank of the Russian Army and secured its communications against any attack coming from the direction of the Turkish fortresses. During the latter part of August and the first of September, having stretched itself out over a line more than 60 miles in length, and having its right flank within a few miles of Razgrad, it was attacked by Mehemet Ali, who had at his disposal a force of more than 65,000 infantry. It was thus driven back and driven together, but it checked Mehemet Ali's advance by the defeat it inflicted upon him at Cerkovna (September 21st); immediately after which Mehemet Ali returned to his old positions. It then took up a more compact position in front of Rustchuk, and here awaited the further attacks of the Turks. Suleiman, having at his disposal about the same force as Mehemet Ali, and having very thoroughly reconnoitered the whole Russian position, endeavored on the 26th of November to break through the left flank of it near the Danube. Failing in this, he ordered the attack upon Elena (in which Prince Mirsky's detachment of the VIII. Corps was so badly cut up), with the apparent object of diverting a portion of the Russian troops from the vicinity of the Danube to the neighborhood of Tirnova; and a week later Sulciman again attacked (December 12th), this time with the bulk of his force, in the vicinity of the Danube. But his troops were tactically badly handled, and before they were all engaged the Russians took advantage of this and fell upon his exposed flank at the same time that they engaged him in front. Sulciman was badly defeated and driven back across the Lom. Plevna had already fallen, and Gourko was threatening the Balkan defenses near Sophia. Placing a portion of his troops within the fortifications of Rustchuk and Shumla, Sulciman hastened to the south of the Balkans with the remainder.

Thus ended all active operations on the Lom. The achievements of the Cesarevitch's detachment have been somewhat obscured by the more bloody engagements around Plevna, and the subsequent brilliant advance over the Balkans; but it must not be forgotten that throughout the campaign it fulfilled to the letter, and without drawing reënforcements from the other parts of the army, the task which was assigned to it, viz., to assure the safety of the left flank of the Army and to mask the Quadrilateral of Turkish fortresses.

OPERATIONS IN THE DOBRUDJA AND ON THE LOWER DANUBE.

(See Plate 2.)

General Zimmermann, as we have already seen, had crossed the Danube at Galatz on the 22d of June and gained a footing on the south bank of the river, the Turks retreating up the Dobrudja. As soon as the water fell low enough to use his bridge at Braila, Zimmermann crossed the rest of his force at that point and advanced slowly up the Dobrudja. His force consisted of the XIV. Corps, with the 1st Don Cossack Division and part of the 7th Regular Cavalry Division. A portion of the infantry of the VII. Corps took up the line of observation on the lower Danube below Galatz.

Zimmermann reached the line of Trajan's Wall and occupied it without opposition on the 18th of July. His own communications were maintained by the river, which was in possession of the Russians as far as Silistria, and also by the Dobrudja and the Braila bridge. His instructions were to hold the line of Trajan's Wall, from Kustendje on the coast to Tchernavoda on the Danube, against any advance by the Turks, and to observe the Black Sea coast and prevent any landing there. He had about 22,000 infantry; at least half this force would necessarily have to be left to occupy the points above named, leaving him only little over 10,000 men for any offensive movements. The latter were therefore out of the question, as the Turks had about 25,000 men in his front, 10,000 at Bazardjik, and 15,000 at Silistria, besides small forces at Mangalia and Kavarna on the coast. The infantry of Zimmermann's corps therefore remained on the line of Trajan's Wall until after the passage of the Balkans in the following January; his cavalry were occupied with skirmishes and reconnaissances in their front, by which they kept themselves informed of the position of the Turks—who on their part undertook no serious offensive movements. Zimmermann's rôle was purely defensive, and he accomplished the task assigned to him, viz., to cover the Russian line of communications in Roumania from any attacks from the direction of the Dobrudja.

In short, the detachment of the Cesarevitch on one side and that of Zimmermann on the other, with the aid of the Danube on the third, completely masked the fortifications of the Quadrilateral.

On the Lower Danube nothing of consequence took place until the first week in October. The Turkish fleet of three ironclads and as many wooden ships of war remained all the time in the harbor of Sulina, and attempted nothing. On the 8th of October a combined force under Lieutenant-General Verevkine, consisting of one regiment of the VII. Corps on the land, and six small gunboats and six torpedo boats on the river, advanced toward Sulina. At 12 miles from the port they halted and placed a line of torpedoes across the Sulina arm; the Turks kept up a heavy fire from their gunboats, but did not succeed in interrupting the Russian works. During the night the Russians advanced a short distance and placed a second line of torpedoes.

On the morning of the 9th, Commander Dikoff advanced in a gunboat of light draught toward the port of Sulina; the Turkish wooden ship Kartal came out and engaged him. Both of these crafts, having a light draught, passed over the line of torpedoes as Commander Dikoff retreated; but about 9 A. M. a large ship also came out to the attack, struck one of the torpedoes in the first line, and instantly sank with nearly all her crew. The ship was a three-masted, sea-going, broadside ironclad, carrying 5 guns and a crew of about 225 men.

After this affair the Russians erected batteries on the shore, and by means of them and their little flotilla defended their lines of torpedoes. The two Turkish ironclads remained at Sulina. They exchanged shots occasionally with the Russian batteries, but nothing of importance occurred until the following month of January.

GOURKO'S ADVANCE TO ORKHANIE.

With the arrival of the two divisions of Grenadiers at Plevna a few days after Gourko had completed the investment on the west side, the total force of Russians and Roumanians blockading that place amounted to 191 battalions, 120 squadrons, and 650 guns, or about 160,000 men. This was much more than was absolutely necessary for the investment. At the same time

It was known that Mehemet Ali Pasha had been sent to Sophia to relieve Chefket Pasha, and if possible to organize a force sufficient to march to the relief of Plevna and raise the siege. As the most efficacious means of preventing this lay in an offensive movement against Mehemet Ali, and as the troops could be spared, a detachment of about 36,000 men (1st and 2d Infantry Divisions, Rifle Brigade, and 2d Cavalry Division of the Guard, and the Brigade of Caucasian Cossacks) was formed under the orders of General Gourko and sent south along the Sophia road toward the Balkans.

About the same time, or in fact a little before, the 3d Division of the Line, which was posted at Lovtcha, had pushed forward toward the Balkans and occupied the town of Trojan, and then, moving west over the foot-hills, had captured, after a small fight on the 31st of October, the town of Tetevan. The smallness of this force prevented its penetrating farther, and it was to operate in the district west of Tetevan, i. e., in the neighborhood of the high-road to Sophia, that Gourko was sent forward.

Gourko began his march southward on November 15th, the infantry of his command and 20 squadrons of cavalry following the high-road to Sophia, and 20 squadrons of cavalry on his right following up the valley of the Isker and thence over the foot-hills of the Balkans to Vratza—the principal town on the direct road from Sophia to Widdin—which they captured after a skirmish on the 9th of November.

The Cossacks had already occupied Yablonitza on the 5th, and the infantry of Gourko's column arrived there on the 18th, and was joined by the 2d Brigade 3d Division (Regiments No. 11 and 12), coming from Lovtcha and Tetevan. The next two days were occupied in reconnaissances, in addition to those which had already been made by the cavalry. From these it was learned that all the roads leading over the Balkans in this vicinity were fortified and occupied by the Turks. The first of these positions was on the high-road near the village of Pravetz. Here the road, after leaving the village of Osikova, climbs over a high spur of mountain, and then suddenly descends into a narrow gorge through which flows a little stream called the Pravetz into the Isker River. The heights on either side of this gorge were fortified with batteries and trenches, so situated as to command the gorge and to enfilade the road along the portion of it which crossed the spur. On the eastern slope of this spur, and about five miles from Pravetz, was another defile, through which flowed a considerable stream known as the Little Isker, at the head of which lies the town of Etropol. Along the banks of this stream is a road to Etropol, and beyond (south) of that town there is a trail leading over the mountains. To defend this trail the Turks had several small works just in front of the town of Etropol. (See Plate 18.)

After passing through the Pravetz gorge the high-road comes into a little valley and makes a sharp turn to the west, and follows this direction for about eight miles, when it reaches the town of Orkhanie, and then turning sharp to the southeast follows another narrow defile to the crest of the Balkans at Araba-Konak, and over them into the plain of Sophia. At Orkhanie, the entrance of this defile, was a very extensive series of fortifications. On the left of this town and five miles from it were some fortifications covering a trail which led over the mountains past the village of Lutikova. The position of Pravetz, with Etropol on its right flank, was the first line of Turkish defense; that of Orkhanie, with Lutikova on its left flank, their second line; and Araba-Konak (the crest of the Balkans) their third line. The high-road was in good order, although its grades were often as steep as one in ten; the other roads were of the most primitive nature. In all their positions the Turks had about 25,000 men, of whom the greater part were at Orkhanie.

Gourko's plan of operations against this whole series of positions was to make a strong attack upon the Pravetz position, at the same time that demonstrations were made against the two flanks—i. e., Lutikova and Etropol—in order to prevent the Turks from reënforcing Pravetz. The demonstration against Etropol was to be made in considerable force, and might be converted into a serious attack at the discretion of the officer commanding the column. The tactical dispositions for the attack of the Pravetz position were to demonstrate against its front, which was nearly inaccessible, and turn its left flank from the north. In pursuance of this plan, Gourko's field orders, dated Yablonitza, November 21st, prescribed the following movements for the next day:

1. Regiment No. 12, with 8 4-pdrs., and 3 sotnias, to follow

the road leading from Tetevan to Etropol, and arrive in front of the latter place and open fire by 10 A. M.

2. Preobrazhensky Regiment, with 2 9-pdrs., and 2 mountain guns, and 3 sotnias, to follow the road through the gorge of the Little Isker toward Etropol.

3. Grenadier Regiment (of the Guard), 1 battalion of 11th Regiment, 12 field-guns, the 4th Dragoons, and 12 horse-guns, to be on the Tetevan-Etropol road in reserve to the first two columns.

The above troops (12 battalions, 38 guns, and 10 squadrons) to be under command of Major-General Dandeville, who was to confine his movement to a strong demonstration against Etropol, unless the enemy showed signs of weakness; in which case, according to his own discretion, he was to convert it into a serious and energetic attack.

4. Moscow Regiment, 2d and 3d Rifle Battalions, 3 sotnias, and 14 guns, under command of Major-General Ellis, to follow the high-road and attack the front of the Pravetz position.

5. Simeonof Regiment, 1st and 4th Rifle Battalions, 3 sotnias of Cossacks, and 1 squadron of Hussars, and 8 guns, under Major-General Rauch, to follow the small road through Vedrara, Kalugerova, and Lakovitza, and attack the Pravetz position on its left flank, and if possible from its rear.

6. Izmailoff Regiment, 2 battalions of 11th Regiment, 2 squadrons of Hussars, and 8 guns, to remain as reserve to columns 4 and 6, and take position on the high-road near Osikova.

The troops of Nos. 4, 5, and 6 (17 battalions, 9 squadrons, and 30 guns) to be under command of Lieutenant-General Count Shouvaloff.

7. Jäger, Paul, and Finland Regiments, 2 squadrons and 72 guns, to form a general reserve for the whole force, and be posted on the high-road at the intersection of the road to Etropol.

8. Two Regiments of Cavalry to leave Vratza at such time as to arrive in front of Lutikova and open fire upon it with artillery by 10 A. M.

The movement took place very much as ordered, barring a delay due to the impassability of the mountain paths which Rauch's column had to follow. These troops started on the evening of the 21st, and marched the greater part of that night and the next two days, but did not arrive in range of the Turks until the afternoon of the 23d. Meanwhile the troops of General Ellis had advanced along the high-road, driven the Turkish advanced posts out of their trenches on the mountain sides east of the Pravetz defile, and dragged some artillery into position on the eastern side of this defile in range of the Turkish position, and opened fire with them across the deep gorge. Three battalions of the Moscow Regiment had also been sent down the mountain into the valley on the left near the village of Pravetz (their places being filled by the Izmailoff and 11th Regiments from the reserve), thus threatening the right flank of the Turks. Nothing decisive took place, however, until Rauch's column, climbing an extremely steep mountain, appeared on the very back of the Turkish position, about 4 P. M. November 23d. The Turks then made but a slight resistance, and hastily retreated down the other side of the mountain in the direction of Orkhanie. Their retreat was effected under cover of a dense fog which settled in the valleys, and by the darkness of night which soon set in.

The two detachments of the Etropol column arrived in front of the Turkish position near that town on the 22d, and an effort was made to seize the redoubts on either flank of the Turkish line by a *coup-de-main*, but it was unsuccessful at both points. The Russians then concentrated their labors upon dragging artillery on to the high ridges flanking the Turkish line, which ridges the Turks had failed to occupy. During the 23d and the following night they then succeeded in quite reaching around both flanks of the Turks. The latter were greatly outnumbered, and when the Russians opened a vigorous fire about 3 P. M. November 24th, they abandoned all their works and made a hasty retreat through the town of Etropol. There they divided, one portion following a trail leading over the mountains to Slatitza, and the other portion following a trail up to Mount Shandarnik, which formed the right flank of the Turkish position across the Araba-Konak Pass. The latter abandoned 3 Krupp guns, 2 caissons, and over 300 carts loaded with ammunition.

The cavalry column, which, forming part of the general movement, was to threaten the Turkish position at Lutikova and Novatchin, met with misfortune. In the mountain-roads in that region, it got into a *cul-de-sac*, and came near being cut off. It was obliged to retreat, losing two guns, one of which was thrown down a precipice to prevent its falling into the hands of the enemy. In this unfortunate affair 10 officers and 69 men were killed or wounded. The detachment, however, may be said to have accomplished its object, since it diverted the attention of the Turks and caused them to send a considerable force toward Novatchin, and not toward Pravetz, the real point of attack.

As soon as the Pravetz position had been carried, General Rauch crossed over (November 25th) by a mountain-road into the Etropol valley, taking with him the Simeonoff Regiment; this united the whole of the 1st Division of the Guard and the two regiments (Nos. 11 and 12) of the 3d Division of the Line in the Etropol valley, leaving the 2d Division of the Guard and the Rifle Brigade in the Orkhanie-Pravetz valley. The advance guard of the latter, under General Ellis, composed of the Moscow and Finland Regiments and the Rifle Brigade, advanced about six miles west from Pravetz, and brought their artillery into position in front of two large redoubts which guarded the high-road a few miles east of the town of Orkhanie. During the night of the 26th the Turks evacuated these two redoubts, as well as their position at Novatchin and the town of Orkhanie, and fell back to their works near the village of Vratches, which guarded the entrance to the long defile of the Araba-Konak Pass. These works were very extensive and admirably constructed; rising above one another in tiers on the mountain-side, they completely commanded every point of the plan in front of the mouth of the defile. They might fairly be considered as *impregnable* to a front assault. Ellis's troops therefore simply halted in observation in front of them.

But meanwhile a portion of the troops in the Etropol valley, viz., the Izmailoff Regiment of the Guard and the 12th Regiment of the Line, under command of General Dandeville, had been climbing the mountain range which formed the eastern side of the Araba-Konak defile, and on the afternoon of November 28th they drove the Turkish outposts away from a mountain called Greote, in front of Shandarnik. A portion of the 12th Regiment even followed the retreating Turks into the Shandarnik redoubt, but there the Turks rallied in superior numbers and drove them out again. Nevertheless, Dandeville maintained his position on the Greote mountain. The western slope of this mountain is a ridge which has a gently sloping crest for a few miles, when it is abruptly terminated by a steep descent terminating in the high-road at the bottom of the gorge. By simply moving to the western end of this ridge—as he would have done the next day—Dandeville could post his men on inaccessible heights completely enfilading the high-road for a distance of nearly two miles. In short, the Vratches position at the northern entrance of the defile was completely turned, and during the night of the 28th the Turks evacuated it and retreated to the redoubts of Shandarnik. Their retreat was so hasty that, for lack of transportation, they abandoned 3,000,000 rounds of small-arms ammunition, several thousand rounds of artillery ammunition, a complete ponton train of 25 iron boats, about 2,000,000 rations in flour, rice, and hard bread, several thousand bushels of oats, and a large quantity of clothing. In fact, the bulk of the stock of the depot which had been formed at Orkhanie, to be sent to Plevna with the "Relief Army," fell into the hands of the Russians; and very welcome it was in view of the bad weather which had just set in, the length of Gourko's line of communication (130 miles from the Danube at Sistova), and the bad condition of the roads.

Gourko's losses at Pravetz, Etropol, Shandarnik, and Novatchin were in all less than 500 men. There was not much hard fighting, but an almost unprecedented amount of hard marching, climbing, and dragging of guns by hand. Several of the men had died from sheer exhaustion in hauling the guns up the mountains. Gourko's force was not so very much superior to that of the enemy, the numbers being about 35,000 and 25,000; but by his manœuvres of demonstrating against the front of impregnable positions and turning their flanks, he succeeded in eight days in dislodging the Turks from all their fortified points in the foothills, and forcing them back—with the loss of immense quantities of supplies—to their main position on the crest of the Balkans.

All hopes of relieving the beleaguered army of Plevna vanished from this time. For Mehemet Ali it was no longer a question of marching to the aid of Osman, but of defending the line of the Balkans.

Gourko immediately sent the Grenadier Regiment (of the 1st Division of the Guard) to observe the enemy's position at Slatitza, and disposed the rest of his troops in front of the Shandarnik position. General Rauch, with the Preobrazhensky and Simeonoff Regiments, and the 11th in reserve, took position opposite the right flank (east) of the high Shandornik redoubt; but being nearly 1,500 feet lower than it, his artillery could accomplish but little. General Dandeville, with the Izmailoff, Finland, and 12th Regiments, occupied the ridge extending from Mount Greote west to the high-road; while General Ellis, with the Moscow Regiment and the Rifle Brigade, took up a position on a height on the west of the road, and was here somewhat fiercely attacked (December 1st) by the Turks, but held his ground, after a loss of 150 men.

The Turks therefore were on the Shandarnik ridge, i. e., the main crest of the Balkans, with six redoubts, containing 15 guns, forming a fortified position about 7,000 yards in length on both sides of the high-road. Gourko's troops were on the Greote ridge, nearly parallel to the other, and about 4,000 yards from it, and on a height on the other (western) side of the Araba-Konak gorge. Mount Greote is at an altitude of over 4,000 feet above the sea (and the ridge but little less), while the Araba-Konak and Etropol valleys are at an altitude of from 1,500 to 1,800 feet. There were no roads worthy the name leading up the mountain, but nevertheless Gourko's men, assisted by a levy of 200 or 300 Bulgarians, succeeded in the course of four days in hauling up, by drag-ropes, 60 guns (of which half were 9-pdrs.), and placing them in position on these heights. Gourko was therefore greatly superior to the Turks in artillery, but its use was much hindered by the dense fogs and clouds which hung over the ravines separating the two lines; and moreover, it is impossible to destroy earthworks at 4,000 yards, or to render them uninhabitable, by shrapnel. The works were considered too strong for an open assault, and with the force *then* at Gourko's disposal it was deemed imprudent to advance over the Balkans by a turning movement (such as was subsequently executed) and increase the length of his line of communication, which was already very great. Gourko therefore remained simply in observation, keeping up a desultory artillery fire, until the fall of Plevna should give him more troops. The main object of his advance, viz., to prevent the possibility of a relief army coming to break the investment of Plevna, had been most completely accomplished.

Meanwhile the Roumanians had brought a portion of their

reserve force, which had been in observation along the course of the upper Danube throughout the campaign,across the river above Nikopolis, and advancing along the south bank, had attacked the Turkish fortifications at Rahova and carried them by assault on the 19th of November. They then advanced to the next fortified point on the river, viz., the town of Lom-Palanka, which the Turks abandoned after sustaining a bombardment for six days. The large fortress of Widdin is only two days' march from Lom-Palanka, but it was much too strong to be taken by this small force of Roumanians. The latter confined their attention to occupying these points on the Danube, the whole course of which from Lom-Palanka to Rustchuk, a distance of 160 miles, was now in the hands of the Russians and Roumanians; and the entire country between the Danube and the Balkans over this width of 160 miles was cleared of bashi-bozouks and Tcherkesses, as well as of the small Turkish garrisons.

We have now followed the course of events on the other points of the theatre of war up to the 10th of December, on which date Osman made his desperate effort to break through the circle of Russian investment, and in so doing lost his whole army. It is now necessary for us to return once more to Plevna.

CHAPTER VIII.

THE FALL OF PLEVNA.

(See Plate 19.)

AFTER a close investment of Plevna had been effected by the operations of General Gourko on the west bank of the Vid, beginning at Gorni-Dubnik, October 24th, but little had taken place beyond strengthening the lines of works on either side. On the 8th of November Skobeleff's troops, having gradually worked their way with trenches up the slope of the first knoll of the Green Hills (1,000 yards northeast of the village of Brestovetz), made an assault during the night, and drove the Turks out of their trenches on top of the knoll. On the 10th, 11th, 15th, and 19th of November, the Turks made obstinate and determined attacks upon Skobeleff's new position, but in every case they were driven back. This new position of Skobeleff shortened the line of investment by about a mile, and gave the Russians possession of a commanding point from which to observe the Turkish movements. The Roumanians meanwhile kept extending the right flank of their works in front of Bukova; and on the night of the 11th–12th of November they advanced along the valley of the Vid from Riben, seized the heights in front of Bivolar, and began erecting works there facing those of the Turks on the heights of Opanetz.

With these exceptions there was no fighting along the lines —except desultory artillery and picket firing—until the 10th of December. But on both sides the work of fortification continued unabated up to the last minute. The final condition of the works, as they existed on the morning of the 10th of December, is shown on the Plan of Plevna (Plate 19).

On the 13th of November the Grand Duke sent a flag of truce to Osman Pasha with a letter summoning him to surrender in order to prevent the further effusion of blood, as it must be evident to him that his surrender was only a question of time, since he was completely surrounded with superior forces. Osman replied that he recognized the humane motives of the Grand Duke, but that as a soldier the Grand Duke would readily understand that his military honor forbade him to surrender his army until all his means of defense were exhausted —which was not the case at present.

A few days later arrived the news of the brilliant assault of Kars, which fired the imaginations of that same portion of the Grand Duke's staff which had advised a march over the Balkans, without taking Plevna, upon the arrival of the Guard. They now began counseling him to make an assault upon Osman's works; they cited the brilliant example of Kars, they referred to the sufferings of the men in the cold, and rain, and mud of the trenches (the weather had recently become very bad), and argued that if the siege were to last two months longer, more men would be lost by sickness and exposure than in an assault, which, from the positions now occupied by the Russians and their previous experience, could be successfully made. But against any such proposition Todleben protested with the whole weight of his influence, arguing that, although the date of Osman's surrender could not be predicted, owing to lack of positive detailed information concerning the amount of his provisions, yet his ultimate surrender was *a certainty*, and against such a certainty it was most unwise to risk an uncertainty of a most hazardous nature, such as an open assault. Moreover, Todleben reasoned, though you may only lose 10,000 men *hors de combat* in an open assault, you demoralize 50,000, and a considerable time must elapse before they can be reorganized for any ulterior operations; whereas, by pursuing the investment patiently till the end, the troops will then be in good condition for anything. Todleben's advice prevailed, and the assaults were not made.

Meanwhile Osman's provisions had reached their last limit; one third of his army lay sick and wounded without proper medical attendance; alternating rain and snow for the last six weeks had rendered his trenches almost uninhabitable; and desertions were increasing every day. He determined to make an effort to break through the Russian lines on the west of the Vid, either with the hope of reaching Widdin, or of reaching Sophia (since he knew nothing of Gourko's operations), or, as is most probable, since neither of these plans had any chance of success, simply from a preference to surrender his army in the midst of battle rather than without having made any effort to break through the Russian lines. During the night of the 9th-10th of December he abandoned the Krishin and Second Grivitza redoubts and Redoubt No. 10, left about 6,000 men in the redoubts of Opanetz and Blasivatz, built two ponton bridges alongside of the high-road bridge over the Vid, assembled a train of about 1,000 ox-carts near these bridges loaded with ammunition and baggage and the effects of the Turkish inhabitants of the town, distributed what rations of bread and rice he had (about six days' supply) to his army, and then, with about 40,000 men, made a most impetuous attack upon the position held by the Grenadier Corps on the Widdin road. Although he carried the first line of Russian works, his army was by noon completely defeated and himself wounded. He surrendered at discretion.

It is perhaps best to describe this affair by giving a literal translation of the whole of General Todleben's report, addressed, under date of January 9th, 1878, to the Grand Duke Nicholas, Commander-in-Chief, as follows:

"The army of Osman Pasha occupied under the walls of Plevna an intrenched camp very easy to defend, and presenting several lines of formidable positions, which the enemy, during our long sojourn in front of Plevna since the end of July, had rendered still stronger by making good use of all the advantages of the ground, and in adapting his sapping operations skillfully to them. The strength of resistance of these works became all the greater, thanks to the violent fire of quick-loading guns and to the mass of cartridges which the enemy had at his disposal, which enabled him to cover the ground in front of his works as far as a distance of two versts * with a hail of lead. Besides this, the positions of the enemy, by their width and depth, enabled him to keep his reserves out of range of our artillery. Finally, all the ravines came together near the town itself, which allowed

* A mile and one third.

the Turkish reserves, in case of an attack on our part, to come immediately to the threatened point. These conditions, so disadvantageous for us, explain in great part the insuccess of the assault of the 11th and 12th of September against the positions of Plevna, and the decision taken, in order not to shed blood uselessly, to attempt no more to gain possession of them by open assault, but to await the arrival of reënforcements and proceed to the investment of the Turkish army.

" This investment of the intrenched camp of Plevna became complete with the arrival of the Guard, and the capture of Gorni-Dubnik on the Sophia high-road, on the 24th of October, by the troops of this corps. From that date the communications of Osman Pasha were definitely cut, and his army had no longer but to choose between an effort to break through the line of investment or to lay down its arms when all its provisions should be exhausted.

"The length of stay of the Turkish Army at Plevna after its investment depended directly, of course, upon the quantity of provisions which it had at its disposal. It was difficult to state exactly the quantity of provisions which Osman had, but we could conclude, from the information that we had, that the provisions of the Army of Plevna could not allow it to subsist more than about two months at the very utmost. From the moment that, in order to reduce Plevna and its army, we had chosen the method of investment, it only remained to follow strictly this line of action, without making any attempts at assault, which could lead to no definite result, and would only have increased the number of our losses; it was necessary simply to endeavor to make the circle of investment as close as possible, and to take all the necessary measures to prevent the enemy from being able to force it at any point. These measures consisted in strengthening the lines of investment by digging lines of rifle-pits and trenches, in erecting batteries, and in establishing lunettes and redoubts upon the most important points. It was above all necessary to concentrate the fire of our artillery upon the enemy's fortifications, and to carry forward our trenches and ditches to a point near enough to those of the enemy to remove as far as possible from our batteries the fire of the enemy's musketry. It was moreover necessary to build good roads connecting our own positions, and to provide them with sign-posts to facilitate the movements of the troops. It was necessary to construct bridges, establish telegraphic communication around the whole line of investment, and finally to take all the necessary measures to receive the enemy, in case of a sortie, with the greatest possible number of troops concentrated immediately upon the spot that he should choose as a point of attack.

"With this view the positions established around Plevna, and having an extent of 70 versts" (46 miles), "were divided into six sectors,* the defense of which was confided to a number of troops corresponding to the relative extent and importance of each of them. Moreover each Chief of Sector received an approximate summary of the sorties which Osman Pasha might make, and a plan of the concentration of troops which he would have to make upon such or such a point threatened. Finally, a few days before the attempted sortie of Osman Pasha, I had had some manœuvres executed under my own eyes, in the sectors of Generals Ganetzky and Kataley, in order to calculate the exact time necessary for the concentration of the troops in case of an energetic attack on the part of the invested army.

---

* "*First Sector*, between Bivolar and the Grivitza redoubt; the Roumanian troops, under the orders of General Cernat, Commandant of the Roumanian Corps.

"*Second Sector*, from the Grivitza to the Galitz redoubt; the 31st Infantry Division with its artillery, and the 2d Brigade 5th Infantry Division with four batteries, under the orders of Lieutenant-General Baron Krüdener, Commandant of the IX. Corps.

"*Third Sector*, from the Galitz redoubt to the Tutchenitza ravine; 2d Infantry Division with the 30th Artillery Brigade and the 12th Rifle Battalion, under the orders of Lieutenant-General Zotof, Commandant of the IV. Corps.

"*Fourth Sector*, between the Tutchenitza ravine and the Kartushaven ravine; 16th Infantry Division with its artillery, 30th Infantry Division with the 2d Artillery Brigade, 9th, 10th, and 11th Rifle Battalions, and 9th Regiment of Cossacks, under the orders of Lieutenant-General Skobeleff, Commandant of the 16th Infantry Division.

"*Fifth Sector*, between the Kartushaven ravine and the right bank of the Vid at the village of Tyrnen; 3d Infantry Division of the Guard with its artillery, two squadrons of the Guard, and the 10th Don Cossack battery, under the orders of Lieutenant-General Kataley, Commandant of the 3d Infantry Division of the Guard.

"*Sixth Sector*, along the left bank of the Vid, including the positions of Bivolar on the right bank of that river; the Grenadier Corps, the 1st Brigade 5th Infantry Division with two batteries, the 2d Roumanian Division with its artillery, the 9th Dragoons of Kazan, the 9th Lancers of Bug, the 9th Hussars of Kieff, the 4th Cossacks of the Don, the 7th Horse battery, the 2d Don Cossack battery, and a regiment of Kalarash" (Roumanian Militia Cavalry), "under the orders of Lieutenant-General Ganetzky, Commandant of the Grenadiers Corps."

"The eve of the 10th of December found us in the situation which I have just described.

"We could conclude, from all the reports received by the Staff from all the sectors of investment, throughout the whole day of the 9th of December, that Osman Pasha was taking energetic measures to move out his army by seeking to break through our line of investment. Deserters informed us that rations of biscuits and foot-coverings had been distributed to the troops, and their arms had been inspected. A great deal of moving about was noticed near the town on the Sophia high-road, and a great concentration of troops and carts was seen in the camps. The Turks were beginning to construct a bridge over the Vid under the protection of the fortified works of Opanetz. All these indications tended to prove that the enemy was preparing to move out, and that his principal effort would probably be directed against the sector of General Ganetzky.

"In consequence, after having made a report of all these facts to the Commandant of the Army of Investment, His Highness the Prince of Roumania, I gave the following orders by authority of His Highness:

"1. One brigade of the 16th Infantry Division, with three batteries, and a brigade of the 3d Infantry Division of the Guard, will, under the command of Lieutenant-General Skobeleff, proceed, at daylight on the 10th of December, to the left bank of the Vid, and take post as follows: the brigade of the 16th Division, with three batteries, near Dolni-Dubnik, to be ready to support the troops of General Ganetzky; the brigade of the 3d Division of the Guard, until further orders, behind the two redoubts nearest the Vid and on the left bank, in order to be able to support in case of need the troops of General Ganetzky or those of General Kataley.

"2. The other brigade of the 16th Infantry Division, with three batteries, will remain at its post, but will hold itself in readiness to march.

"3. The three battalions of the 3d Rifle Brigade, which used to form part of the garrison of the 4th Sector, will proceed early on the 10th to the village of Grivitza to reënforce the garrison of the 2d Sector, commanded by Lieutenant-General Baron Krüdener.

"4. The advanced position on the Plevna-Lovtcha high-road,

between the Mirkovitch redoubt and the Tutchenitza ravine, will be occupied by one brigade of the 30th Infantry Division. Its other brigade will remain in the camp on the Red Hill, and hold itself in readiness to march. The command of the troops of the 4th Sector is confided to General Schnidnikoff.

"5. Four Roumanian battalions, with three batteries, will be directed, at daylight of the 10th, from Verbitza toward Demirkioi. Four Roumanian battalions and two batteries will be in readiness to march on Verbitza.

"This disposition of the troops, reënforcing the corps of Lieutenant-General Ganetzky, allowed reënforcements to be sent at the same time to the other sectors of investment in case of an attack of the Turks in another direction, with the object of diverting our attention from the real point of attack.

"During the night of the 9th-10th a deserter informed the commandant of the corps on the Plevna-Lovtcha road that the Krishin redoubt had been evacuated by the Turks. General Skobeleff immediately sent a detachment of volunteers to satisfy themselves of the truth of this news. The volunteers found the redoubt deserted, and in consequence of this discovery the great and little Krishin redoubts, as well as the trenches on the Green Hills, were occupied by the troops of the 30th Infantry Division.

"At the same time that I received the news of the occupation of the Krishin redoubts by our troops, I was informed, about 9 A. M., that the Turks had abandoned Redoubt No. 10, and that the redoubt in front of that of Grivitza had been occupied by the Roumanian troops. In presence of these facts I gave orders for all the troops on the right bank of the Vid to move forward. As for the brigade of the 16th Infantry Division, with three batteries, and the 9th, 10th, and 11th Rifle battalions which had not yet reached the village of Grivitza, I sent them to the left bank of the Vid to be placed at the disposition of General Skobeleff, for the purpose of reënforcing the troops of General Ganetzky.

"At noon the Emperor arrived at the Imperial redoubt, between the village of Radischevo and the Tutchenitza ravine, whence His Majesty could observe the forward movement of our troops, as well as the cannonade on the left bank of the Vid.

"At daylight the struggle began between the army of Osman Pasha and the troops of General Ganetzky.

"During the night of the 9th-10th of December, the detail of troops for duty in the positions occupied by the Grenadiers had been made in the 2d Division of Grenadiers by the 5th Regiment of Grenadiers of Kieff; in the 3d Division, by the 9th Grenadiers of Siberia. These troops occupied the trenches of the line of defense. Their nearest supports were the 6th Grenadiers of Taurida and the 10th Grenadiers of Little Russia. All the 9-pdr. guns of the two artillery brigades were in position in the first lines of defense, and the 4-pdrs. in the second line at Gorni-Etropol and Dolni-Dubnik. The trenches and lunette on the north of Gorni-Etropol, as well as the village itself, were occupied by the 17th Regiment of Archangel of the 1st Brigade 5th Infantry Division, and by two Roumanian batteries; the 18th Regiment of Vologda, of the same division, served as reserve to the two batteries.

"During the night the cavalry patrols had already reported that a great concentration of Turkish troops was taking place along the Vid. The attack of the Turks began to show itself about half-past seven in the morning. Our outposts having fallen back before them, Major-General Daniloff, of the suite of the Emperor and Commandant of the 3d Division of Grenadiers, ordered the 2d Battery of the 3d Artillery Brigade of Grenadiers, which occupied the fixed battery No. 3, to open fire, and the 10th Regiment of Grenadiers of Little Russia to march in the direction of Kopany-Moguila. At the same time the 2d Brigade, with its 4-pdr. batteries, had been ordered up from Gorni-Etropol.

"While these orders were being executed, it began to be clear enough to see the Turkish troops which had been concentrated in front of us during the night, and which were followed by a long line of carts of every description. The Turks, having opened fire with their guns established on the heights near the bridge and along the Vid beyond the bridge, rapidly deployed their forces, taking advantage for this purpose of the fog which covered the plain on both sides of the river, and of a long undulation in the ground which exists in front of the bridge, and which afforded shelter for the numerous troops which had been brought there during the night.

THE FALL OF PLEVNA. 307

"The attack of the enemy, directed against the trenches of the 3d Division of Grenadiers, was made with extraordinary impetuosity; thick lines of skirmishers marched in front, followed by battalions deployed in line, behind which came the reserves. The artillery followed the skirmishers, advancing rapidly, only stopping to fire a shell, and hastening to rejoin the skirmishers.

"In spite of the rapidity of the fire of our 9-pdrs., and in spite of the musketry fire of the infantry posted in our intrenchments, the Turks crossed in less than three quarters of an hour the distance which separated them from our position and reached our line of defense, which was occupied near battery No. 3 by a part of the troops of the 3d Division of Grenadiers. The enemy penetrating into the intervals between the trenches, after having killed all those who defended them, found there only a few survivors, who, too weak for resistance, began to fall back. When the trenches of work No. 3 had been occupied by the enemy, and the greater part of the gunners of the 2d Battery had been killed or cut down, our artillerymen only succeeded in withdrawing from the work two guns, carrying off the breech-blocks of the six other pieces.

"Thus at 8:30 A. M. the troops which occupied the center of the position, viz., the 2d battalion and the 2d and 3d Rifle companies of the 9th Grenadiers of Siberia, having lost a great number of men and many officers, began to fall back on Kopany-Maguila and on the lunette to the left. The 3d Battery of the 3d Artillery Brigade of Grenadiers, which occupied work No. 4, held its ground for a little while longer, firing shrapnel upon the Turks, but, seeing itself threatened with being turned on the right, abandoned its position, succeeding moreover in carrying off only six guns, the horses of the other two having been killed.

"The 10th Regiment of Grenadiers of Little Russia, having arrived on the field of battle while the Siberian Regiment was struggling with the enemy, formed in companies and advanced through the interval between lunette No. 4 and Kopany-Moguila. Having rallied the Siberian Regiment, the Little Russians stopped the progress of the enemy, suffering great losses in so doing; in less than a few minutes three chiefs of battalions and half the chiefs of companies were out of the fight.

"The desperate attack of the enemy became more and more threatening. The 1st Brigade of the 3d Division of Grenadiers was exhausted by the efforts it was making to defend the lunettes; eight of our guns were in the hands of the enemy, and the 2d Brigade of the 3d Division of Grenadiers had not yet arrived to the support of the first.

"It arrived about 10 A. M., and at the same moment word was received that the 8th Grenadiers of Moscow and the 7th Grenadiers of Samogitia, of the 2d Division of Grenadiers, were approaching the positions defended by the 3d Division. The arrival of these reënforcements assured us a favorable issue of the struggle, and made it impossible for the enemy to succeed in his attempt to break through. A resounding hurrah which broke forth about 10:30 A. M. informed us that the 2d Brigade of the 3d Division of Grenadiers had just attacked our trenches, which were held by the Turks. Having dislodged the enemy from the two lunettes, the Grenadiers of Astrakhan and Phanagoria, supported by those of Siberia and Little Russia, continued to advance rapidly, and, without paying attention to the losses which the deadly fire of the Turks inflicted upon them, dislodged them from the trenches with the bayonet. Those of our guns which had remained in the hands of the enemy were retaken, and the Grenadiers of Astrakhan gained possession of seven guns and one flag in open fight.

"Two battalions of the 18th Regiment of Vologda, which had some time before approached the lunette to the left and the trenches of the position of the Grenadiers, operated against the flank of the Turks with the aid of a Roumanian battery.

"At the time of the attack of the 2d Brigade of the 3d Division of Grenadiers, the 7th Regiment of Grenadiers of Samogitia, under the orders of Lieutenant-General Svetchin, commandant of the 2d Division of Grenadiers, came forward through the interval between Gorni and Dolni - Etropol. Attacking the enemy with the bayonet, the Grenadiers of Samogitia drove the Turks out of their trenches without firing a single shot, and, having put them to flight, gained possession of three guns.

"After having reoccupied their advanced lines, our troops halted for a while. It was about noon when the Turks began slowly to retreat toward the Vid, all the time keeping up a strong fire against us. The guns taken from the Turks, not having been rendered unserviceable by their gunners, were turned against them and served by the soldiers of the infantry. At the same time all the batteries of the 3d Artillery Brigade of Grenadiers, having been moved forward and brought into action on the same line as our infantry, opened a terrible fire against the enemy and covered him with shrapnel, which gave the retreat of the Turks the character of a general helter-skelter. They came together in disorganized groups near the bridge over the Vid, pell-mell with the carts which were on the edge of the high-road in great numbers.

"In presence of this complete disorganization of his army, and of the enormous losses which it had sustained, Osman Pasha could no longer think of renewing his attempt to break through our lines, especially since the troops of the other sectors of investment had moved forward; and the speedy arrival of the 16th Infantry Division and the 3d Infantry Division of the Guard guaranteed the complete defeat of the enemy.

"Our troops soon moved forward to the attack along the whole line. General Daniloff's Division took the lead, supported on his left flank from the direction of Gorni-Etropol, by the 1st Brigade of the 5th Infantry Division, and on his right flank by the 2d Brigade of the 2d Division of Grenadiers. The 1st Brigade of the 2d Division of Grenadiers, moving out from its trenches, undertook to turn the left flank of the Turks. Moreover, the 2d Battalion of the 5th Grenadiers of Kieff and one battalion of the 6th Grenadiers of Taurida were directed toward the Vid, which they crossed by fording, in order to occupy the heights on the right bank. The Grenadiers, having crossed the river with the water up to their waists, scaled the heights of Blasivatz and rushed upon the Turkish redoubt which crowned them, and whose garrison surrendered without striking a blow.

"The brigade of the 3d Division of the Guard and of the 16th Infantry Division of the Line, sent, in accordance with the orders I had given the night before, to serve as supports to the corps of General Ganetzky, took no part in the battle. It appears from the report of Lieutenant-General Kataley, that at 7 A. M. on the 10th of December he had sent across to the left bank of the Vid, passing over a ponton bridge, six battalions of the 3d Infantry Division of the Guard, under the orders of Major-General Kourloff. At 10 A. M., this detachment, at the request of General Ganetzky, moved toward Dolni-Dubnik, where it received orders to move forward by the Sophia high-road to press the left flank of the enemy. While the detachment was executing this movement, it was joined by Lieutenant-General Skobeleff, who took command of it, ordered General Kourloff to halt his troops, to deploy them in reserve order, and to await the arrival of the brigade of the 16th Infantry Division. Having remained on the spot for two hours, and having received no further orders from General Skobeleff, General Kourloff again moved his detachment forward by the Sophia high-road, and arrived at the stone bridge over the Vid only when the battle was over.

"While the 2d and 3d Divisions of Grenadiers were heroically repelling the attack of the whole Turkish Army, the other troops of the army of investment—under the orders of Lieutenant-Generals Zotof, Baron Krüdener, and Kataley, of Major-General Schnidnikoff, and of General Cernat, who commanded the Roumanian Corps—were advancing against the Turkish fortifications on the east and south fronts. The greater part of these works had already been evacuated, and the troops occupied the town of Plevna in presence of Your Imperial Highness. After having entered the place, the troops, with Your Imperial Highness at the head, received orders to continue to advance in the direction of the Vid upon the rear of the enemy, and they concentrated little by little on the heights to the west of Plevna near the Sophia high-road.

"The Roumanian troops, with whom H. H. Prince Charles had been since thé morning, met some resistance at the redoubts of Opanetz, which the enemy still occupied. After a struggle of short duration, the garrison of these works laid down their arms, and the Roumanians gained possession of 3 guns and 2,000 prisoners.

"General Kataley, having remained on the right bank of the Vid with the rest of the 3d Infantry Division of the Guard, perceived the retreat of the Turks in the direction of the river, and resolved to gain possession of the redoubt fronting the Volhynia hill, in order to cut off every route of retreat for the enemy upon his fortified camp. At 11:30 A. M., the Red redoubt was occupied without striking a blow, and soon afterward that of Fort Mahomet surrendered in its turn, after a short resistance. About 1 P. M., the Black redoubt and the Sugar-Loaf redoubt were also taken after a short musketry fire. In these redoubts* the soldiers of the Guard took prisoners, 1 Pasha, 120 officers, and 3,734 soldiers, and gained possession of four guns. They had on their side 3 men killed, and 15 wounded.

" Hemmed in by superior forces, the Turks could no longer continue the struggle; consequently they sent forward a flag of truce, and the chief of staff of the Turkish Army, who proceeded to General Ganetzky, announced to him that Osman Pasha was wounded, and that he desired to know the conditions of surrender. General Ganetzky demanded the unconditional surrender of the whole army. Osman Pasha consented thereto, and General Ganetzky proceeded in person to his brave wounded adversary.

"There were surrendered on the memorable 10th of December, 10 Pashas, 130 field-officers, 2,000 company-officers, 40,000 foot-soldiers and gunners, and 1,200 horsemen. We took 77 guns, and immense quantities of ammunition, especially of small-arms cartridges. The enemy lost during the battle about 6,000 men.

"On our side, the 2d and 3d Divisions of Grenadiers sustained the following losses: Killed, 2 field-officers, 7 company-officers, and 409 soldiers; wounded, 1 General, 3 field-officers, 47 company-officers, and 1,263 soldiers.

"The 1st Brigade of the 5th Infantry Division had 1 field-officer and 47 soldiers wounded.

"Thus the system adopted under the walls of Plevna, and consisting in observing a complete investment without having recourse to open assault—a sanguinary and risky enterprise—brought about the end which was had in view. The result of this system was the capture of an army of 40,000 men, the best one of the enemy, and the possession of an important strategic point, which closes the principal roads of Western Bulgaria. And during the period of the investment our troops were not only protected, but were able to replace their losses, and now, strong as they are and with the spirit which animates them,

---

* The redoubts here referred to are those lying along the ridge from Krishin to Blasivatz.

they are ready to accomplish new exploits for the glory of our arms.

"In conclusion, I feel it my duty to bring to the notice of your Imperial Highness the services of the chief of staff of the Army of Investment, Prince Imeretinsky, who has been for me a coadjutor whom it would be difficult to replace, throughout the whole period of time which was crowned by the brilliant success of the 10th of December; the former commandants of the sectors of investment, viz., Lieutenant-General Ganetzky, to whom, with the Corps of Grenadiers, belongs the honor of the last day of the investment of Plevna; Lieutenant-Generals Zotof, Baron Krüdener, Kataley, and Skobeleff; General Cernat, commandant of the Roumanian Corps; Major-General Moller, commanding the artillery line of battle; and Major-General Reitlinger, performing the duties of Chief of Engineers of the Army of Investment.

"Having been a witness for two months of the conduct of the troops assembled under the walls of Plevna, of their firmness, their bravery, their self-denial in enduring fatigues and privations, I certify to Your Imperial Highness, with a sentiment of profound respect for these troops, that the conduct of every man of the Army of Investment, from the general to the private soldier, has been above all praise.

[Signed]   "*Aide-de-Camp General* TODLEBEN.

"9th *January*, 1878."

The Turkish defense of Plevna is the one thing which relieves their whole campaign from a charge of complete incompetency. Much high-sounding praise has been lavished upon it in English publications, and perhaps even more by the Russians themselves, who speak of it as the most brilliant defense of the century after Sevastopol. It is well to examine this subject with some care.

It will be remembered that Osman Pasha, commanding an army at Widdin (which had very thoroughly beaten the Servians in the late autumn of 1876), was ordered about the time that the Russians crossed the Danube (June 27; 1877) to march rapidly eastward to the defense of Bulgaria. Further than this the exact nature of his orders has never been made public. It has been supposed that he was ordered to occupy Nikopolis

THE FALL OF PLEVNA. 313

and the line of the Danube in that vicinity. But he approached Nikopolis too late; it had already fallen (July 16th). Osman therefore kept his army at Plevna, a central point 20 miles from Nikopolis and the junction of several roads, probably waiting for further instructions and developments; but he immediately set his men to work, according to the excellent Turkish habit of fortifying every place where they remain forty-eight hours, to construct some trenches and redoubts on the east and north of the town. Hardly were these begun when the Russian brigade under Schilder-Schuldner came stumbling along without reconnoitering the ground in front of them, and attacked Osman's whole army. The latter not only defeated them, but well-nigh annihilated one of the regiments. This was on July 20th. Osman did not need to wait for any further developments; his course was now perfectly plain. He saw (and herein lies the genius of his whole defense) that so long as he could maintain himself with a large force at Plevna close to the flank of the Russians, he *completely paralyzed their farther advance;* and in order to maintain himself there, he renewed work with the utmost energy upon his fortifications.

While therefore the Russians had elaborately planned to mask the fortresses on their left flank during their advance, here was another set of fortifications springing up in the night on their right flank. They hastily concentrated a force (but a totally insufficient one) to dislodge Osman, and again attacked him, July 30th, only to be again repulsed with fearful losses, this time nearly 8,000 men. Osman did not follow up the Russians after their retreat, but devoted his whole energy to elaborating his works of defense. But as the Russians delayed renewing the attack, being obliged to wait for new reënforcements, Osman at last deviated from the controlling idea of his whole defense, viz., to always await an attack. On the 31st of August he assumed the offensive in connection with the advance of Mehemet Ali on the Lom and Suleiman's attack at Shipka. But Osman's attack on Zgalevitza came utterly to naught, and resulted in nothing but the loss of some 2,000 or 3,000 of his men. On the 11th of September the Russians, assisted by the Roumanians, again renewed the assault, and again (barring the capture of one of the Grivitza redoubts) they were everywhere beaten, and now with the appalling loss of 18,000 men.

Osman, while still keeping his men hard at work ever extending and strengthening his lines, now began to be anxious about his communications with Sophia, since he was wholly dependent on them for his supplies, and they were greatly threatened and slightly interrupted by bodies of Russian cavalry. Chefket Pasha finally (September 22d) brought him some reënforcements and numerous supplies, and Osman immediately ordered the fortification of several points on the Sophia road in order to keep it open. But on the 24th of October the Russian Guard, which had just arrived, broke this line of defense completely to pieces, and a few days later Osman found himself tightly and closely invested. The Russians made no more assaults, and finally, when his provisions reached their last ebb, Osman found himself obliged to quietly surrender or to try to cut his way out. Unlike Bazaine, he chose the latter, and made a gallant effort, but it only resulted in defeat and the capture of his whole army.

Certainly that must be called a brilliant defense which arrested the Russian advance, and completely paralyzed their whole plan of campaign and all their movements for five months; which caused them to call forth vast reënforcements from Russia, and, pending their arrival, to supplicate the aid of a petty principality; which killed and wounded and spread disease among nearly 40,000 of his enemies, and caused the affairs of a mighty empire to be directed during half a year from miserable huts in obscure villages of a foreign land.

Yet Osman seems to have failed to comprehend the limitations of his system, and, by overstraining it, broke it, and thereby lost his whole army. Up till the middle of October there seems to be hardly anything in the conduct of his defense (excepting always the foolish attack on Zgalevitza) which is open to criticism. But at that time he knew very well, by the English newspapers, that the whole of the Russian Guard and one or two fresh divisions of the Line had arrived in Bulgaria; he knew that there was a movement of some kind going on in the vicinity of the Vid on his right flank, and had he reconnoitered there he would have found about 35,000 men concentrated for the passage of the river. Although he may not have been familiar with the way in which Pemberton invited capture by shutting himself up in Vicksburg, and Lee postponed it for a whole year by not letting himself be shut up in Richmond, yet it can be taken for granted that he knew something of the history of the siege of Metz, and of the inevitable result which must happen to any army which allows itself to be closely invested in an intrenched camp by a superior force. Therefore Osman should have abandoned Plevna and retreated to Radomirtza, instead of allowing the Guard to cross the Vid and attack Gorni-Dubnik. Radomirtza was only two long days' march (about 45 miles) from Plevna; it was a position of far greater natural strength than Plevna itself, and already its fortifications were further advanced than those at Plevna on the 30th of July. He could well have afforded to risk holding them against open assaults, and if obliged to give them up by a movement of the Russians to surround him, he could again retreat toward the Balkans; everywhere there were good positions for defense, and at every step he came nearer his proper base and increased his strength by taking in small detachments. If he finally had to retreat behind the line of the Balkans, *he still had his army intact.* He could not, of course, have changed the final result of the war, but he could have deferred it, as Lee deferred the fate of the Confederacy; and he might possibly have saved his country from such an annihilating defeat as it finally received after the loss of his army.

But Osman had no such thoughts in his mind, and his own explanation of his ideas is very interesting. While a prisoner at the Grand Duke's headquarters a few days after his capture, he was called upon by General Todleben, and a long conversation ensued upon the events of the siege. Todleben asked Osman precisely this question, why he did not retreat to Radomirtza in October, when the Guard was concentrating on his right flank and threatening him with investment. Osman replied that he had then no thought of retreating—

1. Because he felt sure—at that date and up to the very day of his sortie—that the Russians, and especially the Roumanians near Grivitza, would renew their assaults, and he felt equally sure that he would be able to defeat them with great loss. He longed for these assaults from day to day.

2. Because at that time he had just received a fresh lot of provisions and reënforcements. He could not think of retreating under those circumstances.

There was a third reason which he did not mention in this conversation, but which is abundantly attested from other sources, and which was more imperative than the two just given, viz., that the War Council at the Seraskierate in Constantinople had telegraphed him positive and explicit orders not to retreat under any circumstances.

In this conversation Osman also said that the system of intrenched camps with modern breech-loaders is admirable so long as the enemy has not troops enough to surround them; but it is their fate to be invested, and then they are doomed.

If we compare the two parts of this conversation, we can only reconcile them by supposing Osman to have a contempt for his enemy's tactics, which, as the result proved, was by no means warranted.

There have been in the last twenty-five years six other sieges of a character similar to that of Plevna, viz., Sevastopol, Kars, Vicksburg, Richmond, Metz, and Paris. Of these Kars, Paris, and Metz were fortified places of the first order, consisting of a strong enceinte in masonry and detached forts, supplemented slightly by earthworks built at the last moment. The other four, Sevastopol, Richmond, Vicksburg, and Plevna, were simply places which had been hastily fortified by a series of earthworks, redoubts, batteries, and trenches, constructed only just before the arrival of the enemy, and continually extended and strengthened during the progress of the siege. At Vicksburg and at Plevna the defenders allowed the enemy to attack their rear and closely invest them. Both fell when their provisions were exhausted. At Sevastopol and Richmond, on the contrary, the defenders constantly and incessantly extended their flanks and prevented the enemy from surrounding them. The one place was finally evacuated by its garrison after a portion of the works had been carried in assault. At the other the defensive line became finally so extended that it was too long to be held by the force of the defenders; they were obliged to leave their fortifications in an effort to retreat, and were then almost instantly overwhelmed and destroyed.

The following comparative tabular statement of some of the principal features of these great sieges may be interesting.

THE FALL OF PLEVNA.

	Duration of Siege.	Length of Opposing Lines.	Strength of Opposing Forces at Surrender.				Losses in Assaults, Bombardments, and Sickness.		Expenditure of Ammunition.			
			Assailants.		Defenders.		Assailants.	Defenders.	Assailants.		Defenders.	
	Days	Miles	Infantry	Guns	Infantry	Guns			Artillery Rounds	Infantry Rounds	Artillery Rounds	Infantry Rounds
Sevastopol, October 9, 1854, to September 9, 1855	334	7	229,000	827	115,000	800	95,000	114,000	1,850,000	50,000,000	(?)1,000,000	(?)25,000,000
Kars, June 16 to November 28, 1855	165	49	30,000	18	25,000	172	12,000	10,600				
Vicksburg, May 1 to July 4, 1863	65	12	71,000	248	32,000	178	9,000	17,040				
Richmond, May 4, 1864, to April 9, 1865	340	51	121,000	408	60,000	278	87,000	60,000				
Metz, August 16 to October 27, 1870	73	25	197,000	658	173,000	694	47,000	88,000				
Paris, September 20, 1870, to March 1, 1871	131	53	200,000	738	300,000	744	15,000	25,000				
Plevna, July 20 to December 10, 1877	142	46	110,000	500	40,000	77	40,000	30,000	200,000	10,000,000	80,000	15,000,000

NOTES TO ABOVE TABLE.

1. *Sevastopol.*

1. The trenches were opened October 9, 1854, and the place was evacuated on the night of September 8, 1855.

2. The allied trenches at the time of evacuation measured over 52 miles in length, and those of the Russians about 15, but the allied line along the first parallel, from the Tchernaya to Quarantine Bay, was only 7 miles, and that of the Russians, from Careening Creek to Fort Alexander, 5 miles.

3. Rousset, "Guerre de Crimée" (Vol. II., p. 412), gives the allied force on September 8, 1855, as follows:

French	125,000
English	47,000
Turks	40,000
Sardinians	15,000
Total	229,000

and the Russians in the Crimea at 150,000, of which 115,000 were near Sevastopol.

He also (p. 463, Vol. II.) gives the total losses of the Crimean War, exclusive of the typhoid fever cases after November, 1855, as follows:

French	60,000,	of which 10,240 killed in battle.	
English	22,000	"	2,600 " "
Sardinians	2,200		
Turks	35,000 (?)		
Total	119,200		
Russians	110,000		

Marshal Niel gives the total losses of the French during the siege at 44,497 killed, wounded, and missing, of which 7,627 were killed. The English reports do not give the total losses, but Sir H. Jones (p. 600) gives the killed and mortally wounded at 4,774. In the same proportion their total losses would be about 27,000. The English returns show about 12,000 constantly sick during the winter, and the sick among the allies at the evacuation may be estimated at 20,000. The total losses of the allies will then be as follows:

French	44,500	⎫
English	27,000	⎬ Killed and wounded.
Turks and Italians	6,500	⎭
Sick	20,000	
	98,000	

The Russian losses during the siege, as given in Todleben's "Defense of Sevastopol," are as follows:

Killed	15,553
Wounded	71,312
Missing	2,277
Total	89,142

To which 25,000 may safely be added for sickness, making a grand total of about 114,000.

4. On September 8, 1855, the French batteries numbered 620 guns in position (Marshal Niel's report), and the English 207 (Sir Henry Dacres's report, p. 638).

Marshal Niel gives the total amount of French artillery brought to the Crimea as 1,676 guns of all calibres. Sir Henry Dacres's report (p. 209) gives the total number of English guns in use during the siege as 401. Major Delafield, however ("Art of War in Europe," p. 55), states that the English brought 911 guns to the Crimea. He also states (p. 56) that the total amount of artillery and ordnance brought to Sevastopol was 2,587 guns of all calibres, 2,381,042 shot and shells, and 11,484,804 pounds of powder. Marshal Niel's report states that the French expenditure of artillery ammunition was about 1,100,000 rounds. Sir Henry Dacres (p. 205) gives that of the English as 252,872 rounds. Marshal Niel gives the amount of small-arms ammunition supplied to the French troops at 70,000,000 rounds, but does not state the expenditure. Estimating it at 40,000,000, and that of the English at 10,000,000, we have 50,000,000 for the total.

2. *Kars.*

After the repulse of the Russians in their assault on the west of Kars in September, Mouravieff assembled his infantry on the Erzeroum road, 7 miles south of Kars, and the rest of the long line of investment was kept up by large bodies of cavalry.

The losses are only approximate.

THE FALL OF PLEVNA.

3. *Vicksburg.*

The effective strength of General Grant's command on June 30, 1863, is shown in the following table, compiled in the Adjutant-General's office from the field returns of that date:

DESIGNATION.	INFANTRY.		CAVALRY.		ARTILLERY.		AGGRE-GATE.
	Officers.	Men.	Officers.	Men.	Officers.	Men.	
9th Corps	874	6,632	..	...	9	809	7,824
13th Corps	748	11,500	23	554	84	941	13,805
15th Corps	793	12,444	82	451	23	668	14,411
16th Corps	836	14,318	63	936	21	777	16,956
17th Corps	741	11,846	7	127	85	1,052	13,908
Herron's Division	240	4,286	..	...	11	298	4,837
Total	8,782	61,028	135	2,068	188	4,045	71,141

The other figures are taken from Badeau's "Life of Grant" (Chapters VII. and VIII.), which is unquestionably the best authority on the subject in print. Owing to the difficulty of separating the losses during the campaign from those during the siege proper, the figures given apply to the whole campaign from the crossing of the river to the surrender. The investment proper began on the 22d of May and lasted 35 days, during which the losses were between 4,000 and 5,000 on each side. The losses of the defenders include 7,000 prisoners captured in the various affairs previous to the investment.

4. *Richmond.*

The whole campaign of General Grant from the Wilderness to Appomatox is included in the "siege" of Richmond, in order to make the comparison uniform with the other sieges, which include all the battles immediately preceding the investments. The siege of Petersburg proper lasted 290 days, from June 15, 1864, when Grant crossed the James, to April 2, 1865, when he began his retreat after the battle of Five Forks.

The length of the lines is measured on the engineer map: Lee's lines from the James River above the Iron Works, around Richmond and Petersburg to the end of his line on the White Oak road; Grant's lines from the Topolopotomy across the Peninsula, past Bermuda Hundred, and around Petersburg to his extreme left in front of the White Oak road.

The strength of the armies is taken from the field returns in the archives of the Adjutant-General's office of the War Department. These show that on the 31st of March, 1865, Grant's effective force present for duty numbered 5,288 officers and 115,759 men. Lee's return of February 28, 1865, the last one in the archives, shows his effective force present for duty to be 3,519 officers and 55,575 men.

Grant's losses are computed as follows:

May 4 to June 10, 1864 (Mead's report)	54,500
May 4 to June 10, 1864, 9th Corps	5,000
June 10, 1864, to March 31, 1865, including the attack on the Petersburg mine, on the Weldon road, and other battles and skirmishes	20,000
April 1 to April 9, 1865	8,000
Total	87,500

Lee's losses have never been compiled, and it is doubtful if the returns which have been preserved afford data for an accurate compilation. His return of January 31, 1864, gives 74 officers and 1,374 men prisoners in the hands of the enemy; his return of February 28, 1865, gives 1,707 officers and 26,614 men similarly accounted for. This makes his loss in prisoners alone 26,963. His losses in killed and wounded in the same period may be stated, at the least estimate, as fully one third of those of Grant; this would give 27,000. Between Five Forks and the Appomatox he lost about 6,000. The total of his losses was therefore about 60,000.

5. *Metz.*

The figures are taken from the "German Staff History of the Franco-German War" (French translation, 2d part, pp. 257-297). At the time of the surrender there were 40,000 sick in the German hospitals, mostly light cases of fever arising from exposure in the wet. The French prisoners included 20,000 sick. These are not included in losses on either side in the above table. Only 5,500 of the above losses of the Germans were during the siege proper. The rest were incurred in the bloody battles at Mars-la-Tour and Gravelotte in August, by which Bazaine's army was shut up in Metz.

The French had 876 guns on the walls of the place; these are not counted in the above table, which gives only the field-guns and mitrailleuses.

6. *Paris.*

The figures are taken from the "German Staff History." Of the 400,000 men forming the garrison of Paris, only 100,000 (XIII. and XIV. Corps) were regular soldiers; the rest were National Guard, Mobile Guard, and sailors.

The field artillery of the French numbered 744 pieces (124 batteries), but there were in addition 1,389 guns of various calibres in the outer forts and 805 on the walls of the enceinte.

The principal losses were incurred in the completion of the investment, September 17th and 19th (French 5,000, Germans 4,200), and in the French sorties of November 29th to December 3d (French 12,000, Germans 6,500).

The Germans made no attempts to assault the place, but from the beginning endeavored to starve it out by a close blockade. Their inferiority in numbers was compensated by an admirable system of field works, constructed with great rapidity and with most numerous accessories, such as abattis, inundations, etc., etc., and by the superior quality of their troops.

7. *Plevna.*

The authority for the number of troops, losses, etc., is found in the preceding pages. The expenditure of ammunition is an estimate based upon my own notes made from time to time during the siege. It is probably accurate within 20 to 30 per cent. The official figures have not yet been made public.

CHAPTER IX.

THE PASSAGE OF THE BALKANS NEAR SOPHIA, BY GOURKO'S COLUMN.

ALTHOUGH the fall of Plevna was unquestionably a great disaster for the Turks, since it lost them the best of their armies and possibly the best of their generals, yet it is by no means true, as has been generally assumed, that it rendered the Turks incapable of further resistance to the Russian advance. The Turkish cause was as yet far from being hopeless. They had still 100,000 men in the region of the Quadrilateral, 30,000 at Shipka, 20,000 in the vicinity of Sophia and the Araba-Konak pass, 15,000 at Constantinople, and a certain unknown quantity of reserves in Asia. Of small arms and ammunition they had abundance, although now, as at all times during the campaign, they were short of artillery; they were in a rich country, and the valley of the Maritza was teeming with provisions in spite of all the drains which the war had made upon it. The Turks had, it is true, an enemy in front of them of double their own numbers, and confident of victory; but, on the other hand, that enemy had a line of communications 500 miles long from the Pruth to the Balkans, and this line absolutely cut in two now by the Danube, the ice of which had carried away all the bridges, and in front of him a rugged chain of mountains. It was the middle of December; considerable snow had already fallen, and more was to be expected; the winter climate of Bulgaria is one in which a temperature of 10° Fahr. is frequently encountered; there were but two good roads (Sistova-Shipka and Plevna-Sophia) available for the Russians, and all the rest were now mere quagmires. These various natural difficulties were almost sufficient to neutralize the difference of force, had only the Turks had a leader, a man of the calibre of Amurath I., Mohammed the Conqueror, or Suleiman the Magnificent. But, unfortunately for them, such a man they had not, as they have not had since the 16th century. Their Commander-in-Chief was now that Suleiman who had knocked out the brains of some 15,000 men against the rocks at Shipka during the months of August and September, and who had lately achieved almost equally bad results on the Lom. He was hastily summoned to Constantinople, where he arrived on the 19th of December, and was intrusted by the Sultan with the chief command in Roumelia, and especially the defense of the line of the Balkans. Of the Turkish Army on the Lom, a portion was placed in the fortresses with outposts at Razgrad and Osman-Bazar, and the rest was rapidly withdrawn by Aidos and Slivno to the south side of the Balkans. Work upon the extensive fortifications of Adrianople was pushed forward with great activity, and efforts were made to organize the recruits who were arriving in considerable numbers from Asia.

It is generally conceded that a long line of defense, such as a chain of mountains or a large river, can not successfully be defended by posting isolated bodies of troops, even large in numbers, at various points along it, since the enemy, by demonstrating at several places and concentrating his forces on one point, will overwhelm the defenders at that point before the others can come to his relief. All military writers are agreed that the proper means of defense of such a line is to post small bodies in observation at the various points of passage, and keep the main body of the defenders at some central point in rear, from which, as soon as the enemy's *real* attack is made clear, a force can bear down upon him and strike him before his troops have all crossed the mountains or river. Such a point in this case was Adrianople, in itself a naturally strong position, and now defended by numerous half-finished earthworks, and from which high-roads lead to Sophia, Shipka, Slivno, and Aidos, and railroads to within three days' march of Sophia, two days' of Shipka, and one day's of Slivno. But instead of posting the bulk of his troops there, Suleiman tried to do that very thing which all history condemns, viz., to defend the line of mountains by means of isolated detachments. Leaving only a very small force

—less than 10,000 men—at Adrianople, he increased the Shipka garrison to 40,000, and that around Sophia also to 40,000, and divided the latter into two parts, 25,000 at the Araba-Konak pass and 15,000 at Sophia. With about 20,000 more he was moving to the relief of Sophia when he met the troops from Araba-Konak in full retreat near Philippopolis, where the united force was overwhelmed and driven across the Rhodope mountains to the Ægean.

The mountain chain which separates the Sophia valley from that of the river Maritza is as high and difficult as the main chain of the Balkans; the broad valley of the Maritza is in fact completely shut in by mountains. Could the Turks have had a general capable of assembling the whole of their available force (about 150,000 men) in this valley, and using its interior lines of communication to strike against first one and then the other of the invading columns—which were widely separated—as Napoleon did in 1814, and then as a last resort have fallen back upon the strong fortifications of Adrianople and made a new Plevna of it, the war could at least have been prolonged till the next summer, and Turkey as a military power would not have collapsed in 1878. But such rapid movements require a good force of regular cavalry to keep the commander well informed of the enemy's movements; and in this, as well as in generals and various other military essentials, the Turks were sadly deficient.

Let us now turn to the Russian side. The fall of Plevna set free 110,000 men. The 25,000 Roumanians forming part of this force were to remain near the Danube; but on the other hand, Servia declared war against the Turks immediately after the fall of Plevna, and brought about an equal number of troops into the field. But without taking any account of their small allies, the Russians had 8½ divisions—viz., the IV., IX., and Grenadier Corps, 3d Division of the Guard, 2d Division of the Line, and 3d Rifle Brigade—immediately available for further operations. What should be the plan of operations?

General Todleben, supposing, as was natural, that the Turks would concentrate near Adrianople, and that even after passing the Balkans the Russians would arrive before Adrianople in the dead of winter, with a chain of mountains at their back and a line of supplies impossible to maintain, advised the prudent military course, viz., to put the troops in winter quarters on the main roads at the foot of the Balkans on the north, and to concentrate a large force around Rustchuk and proceed to its regular investment and siege. During the winter this place could be reduced, and then in the spring, the troops having refitted and having a railroad at their back, the army could advance over the Balkans and crush all resistance between it and Constantinople.

But some time before the fall of Plevna the Grand Duke Nicholas had made up his mind, although the idea met with the hearty approval of none of his generals except Gourko and Skobeleff, to cross the Balkans during the winter in spite of all the difficulties of ground, of season, of bad roads, and of insufficient supplies. In this war, as in all others, purely military reasons had to be subordinate to the higher political considerations; and there were the strongest political reasons for an immediate advance, since by postponing active operations until the spring the Turks would have time to reorganize and strengthen their armies, and—more important than all—the war would drift into the hands of diplomacy with all its attendant complications, including the probability of England becoming an active ally of the Turks, in case a peace was not made. At all hazards, the Grand Duke determined to strike before the Turks had had time to recuperate.

Immediately after the fall of Plevna, therefore, he issued orders sending the IX. Corps and the 3d Division of the Guard to Orkhanie, the IV. Corps and 3d Rifle Brigade to Shipka, the 2d Division via Lovtcha and Tirnova to Rustchuk, and the Grenadier Corps in reserve behind Shipka. This gave Gourko 84 battalions, say 65,000 men, of infantry, Radetzky at Shipka 74 battalions or 56,000 men, and the Cesarevitch 72 battalions or 55,000 men, besides the cavalry and artillery with each force. The 3d Division was to advance from Lovtcha over the Trojan pass in connection with Gourko's advance; and in addition there was the XI. Corps in front of Tirnova, available as reserve, and the XIV. Corps under Zimmerman on the line of Trajan's Wall in the Dobrudja. (See Plate 6.)

Gourko's task was to defeat the army in his front at the Araba-Konak Pass, capture Sophia, and then advance by the old Roman road leading from Sophia past Philippopolis to Adrianople; Radetzky was to defeat the Turks at Shipka, advance over that pass, and join hands with Gourko in front of Adrianople; while the Cesarevitch, commanding all the troops left on the north of the Balkans, was to protect the communications from any attack from the direction of the Quadrilateral and prosecute the siege of Rustchuk, with the assistance of Todleben as his Chief Engineer. The distribution of the troops at the beginning of the winter campaign is shown in the table on the following page.

GOURKO'S PASSAGE OF THE BALKANS.

(See Plate 18.)

Plevna fell on the 10th of December, and the troops destined to reënforce General Gourko's detachment began their march as follows: the 3d Division of the Guard on the 14th, and the IX. Corps on the 16th. Up to this date the weather had been rainy with occasional snows, and the roads were in a very bad condition; but on the 18th the veritable winter set in with no little severity. It began with a snow-storm, which continued with but little interruption for five days; and on the night of the 19th–20th the temperature fell to 3° Fahr. The roads then became an alternation of smooth ice and frozen masses of mud ten inches in diameter, and hard enough to resist even the artillery wheels. None of the horses were sharp-shod, and the little Steppe horses of the intendance wagons were not shod at all. The result was that at every hill the wagons had all to be hauled and pushed up by hand.

It was under these difficulties that the reënforcements made their march from Plevna to Orkhanie (75 miles), arriving at the latter place between the 20th and 23d of December.

The force at Gourko's disposal, given in a detail in the previous tabular statement, was then about 65,000 infantry, 6,000 cavalry, and 280 guns of all kinds.

The Turkish force opposed to him consisted in all of about 35,000 infantry, about 2,000 regular cavalry, large numbers of bashi-bozouks, and about 40 guns. It was thus distributed: 25,000 men and 15 guns on the Shandarnik and Araba-Konak positions (see pp. 295–297), where the high-road crossed the mountains; 5,000 men and 4 guns at Lutikova; the same at Slatitza; and 10,000 men and 1,500 guns at Sophia.

Distribution of the Russian Army in Bulgaria, December 25, 1877.

COMMANDERS...	Gourko.		Radetzky.			The Cesarevitch.			Zimmermann, Ganetzky, Dellinghausen, Kartzoff.			Semeka.¶	
ARMY CORPS......	Guard	IX.	VIII.	IV.		XII.	XIII.		XIV.	Grenadier.	XI.	VII.	X.
INFANTRY DIVISIONS	1	5	9	16	24	12	1	32	17	2	11 8§	15	13
	2	31	14	30		33	35	2	18	3	26	36	34
	3												
RIFLE BRIGADES...	1		⎧ Bulgarian	3									
			⎩ Legion.	4									
CAVALRY DIVISIONS	2	4		1		12		8	Cos. No. 1	11	9	7⅔	10
		⎧ Cauc. Cos.						Don Cos.‡	7⅔	13	Don Cos.∥		
		⎩ Don Cos.											
TOTAL.........	84½ battalions = 63,000 men		74 battalions = 56,000 men			72 battalions = 54,000 men			76¼ battalions = 56,000 men			48 battalions = 40,000 men	
	54 squadrons = 6,000 "		18 squadrons = 2,000 "			60 squadrons = 6,500 "			92 squadrons = 10,000 "			28 squadrons = 8,000 "	
	256 foot-guns = 9,000 "		240 foot-guns = 7,500 "			258 foot-guns = 9,000 "			320 foot-guns = 10,000 "			192 foot-guns = 6,000 "	
	24 horse-guns = 1,000 "		12 horse-guns = 500 "			36 horse-guns = 1,500 "			60 horse-guns = 2,500 "			16 horse-guns = 1,900 "	
	80,000 "		66,000 "			71,500 "			60,090 "			60,900 "	

* Regiments Nos. 11 and 12, and 1½ battalion of No. 10.

† This division, consisting of Don Cossack Regiments Nos. 31, 36, 37, and 39, was in the middle of January sent over the Balkans by Shipka Pass, under command of Lieutenant-General Skobeleff I., and joined General Gourko's command at Phillippopolis.

‡ One brigade only.

§ One regiment (No. 9) and half of another (No 10), in all 44 battalions.

∥ One brigade, Regiments Nos. 21 and 30.

¶ The troops under command of this officer constituted the "Coast Army," the greater part of which was stationed at Odessa, with detachments in the Crimea and on the Lower Danube.

Gourko's plan of operations—taking advantage of his superiority in numbers—was to leave a curtain of troops in front of each of these positions, and to send a strong column over the mountains to turn the left flank of the main Turkish position across the high-road. Smaller columns were to pass on either flank and protect the main column from attacks from Sophia, Lutikova, or Slatitza. For this purpose he divided his force of 81¼ battalions (3 battalions being at Vratza) into 9 detachments, and assigned 130 foot- and 20 horse-guns to them, leaving the rest of his artillery in reserve. The men were ordered to take rations of hard bread in haversacks, and beef and mutton on the hoof to last from the 25th to the 30th inclusive. The detachments were as follows:

1. Lieutenant-General Schilder-Schuldner, with 9 battalions with 32 foot-guns, and seven squadrons with 6 horse-guns, on the Lutikova road.

2. Count Shouvaloff, with 12 battalions and 24 foot-guns, on the mountain heights west of the high-road.

3. Prince Oldenburg, with 8 battalions and 28 guns, east of the high-road.

4. Major-General Brock, with 5½ battalions, 2 guns, and 2 sotnias, in front of Slatitza.

These four detachments, something less than half the total force, were placed under the orders of General Krüdener, and were to remain in position, observe the Turks, bombard their positions, and pursue them in case of retreat.

The main turning column was composed of three detachments following each other over the sappers' road, viz.:

5. The advance guard, Major-General Rauch, consisting of 13 battalions with 16 foot-guns, and 11 sotnias with 4 horse-guns, which was to leave Vratches at 5 A. M. December 25th, pass over the mountains, and halt at Curiak until 4 A. M. December 26th, when it was to debouch at Eleznitza and take position on the high-road at Malinne.

6. The "First Echelon," 8 battalions with 16 guns, and 5 squadrons, which was to follow the Advance Guard and take position December 26th on its left at Razdanie.

7. The "Second Echelon," 10 battalions and 8 guns, to follow the First, and take position December 26th at Stolnik as reserve to the detachment in front of it. These two "Echelons"

constituted the 3d Division of the Guard under the command of Lieutenant-General Kataley.

To protect the right flank—

8. Lieutenant-General Wilhelminof, with 6 battalions, 16 squadrons, 8 foot-guns, and 8 horse-guns, was to cross by an old trail over the Umargas Mountain, and debouch at Zilava on the 26th, whence he was immediately to take a defensive position against any troops coming either from Sophia or from the Lutikova road; or in case the Advance Guard was checked at Eleznitza (where the Turks had one or two battalions), then to attack the Turks there in rear. Finally,

9. Major-General Dandeville, with 9 battalions with 8 guns, and 6 squadrons with 6 horse-guns, was to make his way from Etropol over the mountain named Baba, demonstrate on the right and rear of the Turkish position, and debouch into the plain of Kamarlee on the 26th.

Once debouched into the plains of Sophia and Kamarlee, the cavalry of the various detachments was to push forward to the Philipoppolis and other roads, cut the telegraph, and reconnoiter.

The Order of the Day of December 23d, of which the above is the substance, therefore contemplated that the principal column, 31 battalions, 16 squadrons, and 44 guns in all, should in 36 hours march 32 miles, passing over a mountain crest 1,800 feet above the valleys on either side; and these dispositions were made upon the report of the chief of the Sapper Battalion that the road was practicable for artillery, which opinion was shared by the commanding general, who had passed over it in person. This opinion was somewhat sanguine, as the best parts of the road had a slope of one in six, and the worst as steep as one in three, with curves with a radius of 10 yards; and the whole was covered with half-frozen snow or frosted earth.

In the result the horses proved to be totally useless, and were unharnessed; the pieces and caissons were then unlimbered, and the ammunition unloaded and carried by hand; drag-ropes were attached to each limber and each gun; from 100 to 150 men hauled on the ropes and pushed at the wheels and boxes. The first gun reached the summit on the morning of December 26th, and the last on the 30th.

In order to descend the southern slope (where the snow

PASSAGE OF THE BALKANS NEAR SOPHIA. 329

melted each afternoon and froze into smooth ice each night), two drag-ropes were fastened to each side of the carriage and one to the trail; with one rope on each side, a turn was then taken around a stump or bush, the other two ropes were then slacked up, and the piece was let slide the length of the first two ropes; then the operation was repeated. Some effort was made to guide by the trail-rope, but it amounted to little; for on the steep icy slope the men could not stand on their feet without the aid of a stick or a bush. Occasionally the piece got loose, but was brought to a standstill by a stump. There was but one serious accident, caused by the parting of a cable, in which one man was killed and three were seriously injured. Not a carriage was lost or damaged.

The patience and good humor of the men—hauling at the guns twelve hours of the day, sleeping on the snow without tent or blanket, and subsisting on two thirds of a ration of black hard biscuit and meat, which latter was not always on hand—were extraordinary. By examining the map (Plate 18), it will be seen that the sappers' road descends into a valley whose head is not far from the left of the Turkish position at Araba-Konak; thence it follows this valley in a westerly direction to Curiak, where it turns south for two miles, and then, again turning west, passes Potop and arrives at Eleznitza, debouching thence to the south into the plain of Sophia. The greater part of the road between the summit and the Curiak valley was in sight of the Turks along the Shandarnik position; they also had one or two battalions posted at Potop and Eleznitza, with their outposts on a mountain overlooking Curiak and Potop at the bend of the valley.

The Preobrazhensky Regiment, the 1st Regiment of the 1st Division of the Guard, had the advance, and passed over to Curiak during the night of the 24th. On the night of the 25th the Caucasian Cossacks passed over, and on the morning of the 27th the Kozloff Regiment (No. 123) of Rauch's column, with 4 guns. One battalion of this regiment was left in the valley above the point where the sappers' road entered it, and the other two passed through Curiak and over the mountain between it and Potop, at which latter place there was a slight skirmish with the Turks, who retreated into the plain of Sophia.

On the same day, about noon, the Preobrazhensky Regiment took possession of the mountain in front of Curiak, where the Turkish outposts had been, and then, advancing during the night, occupied and fortified a position to the left (east) of the village of Nyagesovo, facing the Turkish position at Taskosen. The Caucasian Cossacks descended into the valley of Taskosen, cut the telegraph to Sophia, and captured a provision train of over 200 wagons en route from Sophia to Araba-Konak. The next two days, the 28th and 29th, were occupied in hauling at the guns. Meanwhile the column on the right, General Wilhelminof, had found its route totally impracticable, and after two days of futile effort had discovered another, by which the guns were brought to Curiak, with labor equal to or greater than that of the main column. The column on the left, General Dandeville, succeeded in getting over the summit of the mountains, but in its descent was overwhelmed by a terrible storm, causing the snow to pile up in great drifts and bury a considerable part of the artillery. All progress was impossible, and after great suffering, this column returned to Etropol, December 29th, having lost 53 men frozen to death and 810 permanently disabled by freezing.

But the main turning column met with better success, and on the 30th all the guns were in the Curiak valley, the pieces assembled and harnessed. On the same day the Turks abandoned their position on the Lutikova road, leaving 4 guns, and escaped to Sophia, with a few losses in their rear guard, which was overtaken by the Caucasian Cossacks. The dispositions were then taken for attack on the 31st.

The plain of Sophia is a shelving oval about 25 by 10 miles in extent, entirely surrounded by mountains from 1,500 to 2,500 feet higher than its own level. Sophia lies in the southwestern corner. As the Plevna high-road, after leaving Sophia, approaches the eastern side of this plain, it meets and passes a spur of the Little Balkans projecting to the north through the villages of Malinne and Razdanie to Nyagesovo. Beyond this spur is a little prairie three miles in diameter, the eastern boundary of which is formed by a spur of the Balkans projecting to the south; over this the road passes near the village of Taskosen, and descends into a second prairie about five miles in diameter—the Kamarlee plain. Here were the principal camps of the Turkish reserves, their stores, munitions, etc. On the north was their position at Araba-Konak, the main range rising abruptly from the plain; on the southeast was the road to Slatitza, and to Petricevo and Ichtimann on the Philippopolis highroad.

At Malinne and Razdanie the Turks had nothing but an outpost, which disappeared on the appearance of the Preobrazhensky Regiment. At Taskosen, however, they seemed prepared to make a defense. They had there ten battalions (about 5,000 men), occupying intrenchments on either side of the highroad back of the village; and on the mountain north of it were three successive lines of earthworks with four guns. To take this position the following dispositions were made:

1. General Rauch, with 10 battalions and 8 guns, to demonstrate against its front and turn the mountain with his left.

2. Major-General Kourloff, with 10 battalions and 8 guns, to make a détour to the right through Cekansevo, and take the mountain behind Taskosen; and two brigades of Cavalry to go still farther to the right and descend into Kamarlee plain.

The reserve, 12 battalions and 20 guns, under General Kataley, was on the high-road about two miles in rear of Rauch.

A small column of three battalions, under Colonel Vasmund, kept up the connection between Rauch and Shouvaloff through the village of Dauskioi.

On the same date, the 30th, General Wilhelminof, with 5 battalions and 8 guns, debouched through Eleznitza to Jana, and the next day took position a few miles in advance in observation of Sophia; and the Caucasian Cossacks were placed under his orders.

The columns were under way before daylight on the 31st, and took the routes above indicated. Rauch's 8 guns got in position at 9 A. M., about 1,800 yards from the Turkish batteries, and an artillery duel opened with shrapnel, at the same time that the Preobrazhensky Regiment and two battalions of the Rifle Brigade began working their way through the deep snow round the mountain to his left.

Kourloff's column on the right met with a warm reception on leaving the village of Cekansevo, and lost over 200 men (including General Mirkovitch, commanding the Volhynia Regiment) in their skirmish line at a distance of *fully 2,000 yards* from the Turkish position. They were obliged to advance very slowly, the men running forward a few yards and then lying down in the snow, as they were entirely exposed in the open plain to the fire of the Turks concealed behind rocks on the mountain. About 2 o'clock their skirmish line got within 500 yards of the Turks, and then the latter fled.

The advance guard of the cavalry column on approaching the Kamarlee plain encountered some infantry intrenchments, and was driven back by their fire; and the cavalry did nothing all day.

The Preobrazhensky Regiment and the Rifle Brigade meantime kept crawling round the left of the mountain out of fire, and approached the Turkish battery from its right rear (north) about 3 P.M. Under cover of heavy clouds which settled on the mountain about this time, the Turks retired their guns to the high-road and then abandoned the whole position. They took up, however, a second position of great natural strength, on a mountain crossing the high-road about a mile in rear. It was now about 4 o'clock, darkness was setting in, and the men were exhausted with the fatigues of the day. They were therefore ordered to bivouac on the heights in rear of Taskosen.

During the night the outposts were somewhat carelessly kept, the men having well-nigh reached the limit of endurance with the terribly fatiguing work of the past seven days; moreover, a dense fog prevailed.

On the next morning, January 1st, the Turks could not be found. The columns began advancing between 8 and 9 A.M., Rauch by the high-road, and Kataley with the 3d Division of the Guard in two columns over the mountain on his right.

As Gourko reached the Kamarlee plain with the advance about 10 o'clock, he saw a column of about 10,000 men, the rear of the Turks, climbing the mountain behind Dolni-Kamarlee on the road to Petricevo. At the same time a reconnoitering party of cavalry advanced over the high-road at Araba-Konak, and met the advance of Krüdener's corps coming from the north. The fortifications at Araba-Konak were all abandoned, and the passage of the Balkans was complete.

Kataley's column came up with the Turks at Dolni-Kamarlee about noon, but the rear guard of 200 or 300 men made a stubborn defense from behind the fences and houses of the village, and the main force secured its retreat.

In the Kamarlee plain the Turks abandoned their hospitals, with about 1,000 sick and wounded under care of the English Surgeons of the Red Cross and Red Crescent Societies, about 600 tents, over five million rounds of small-arms cartridges, and a considerable quantity of hard biscuit. On Shandarnik they abandoned ten guns, being unable to withdraw them under the shrapnel fire of Prince Oldenburg's batteries.

The same day, January 1st, the Turks in Sophia made a sortie with about 5,000 men against the column of General Wilhelminof. The latter disposed his force of 3,500 men along the crest of a low bluff rising from the plain in front of the village of Gorni-Bugaroff, and while the Turks were approaching they constructed hastily a line of little trenches, each large enough for eight or ten men. With wonderful firmness the Russians let the Turks approach within about 100 paces, and then opened fire with well-aimed volleys, succeeded by a hand-to-hand attack with the bayonet. The Turks were completely staggered by the fierceness and suddenness of this attack, and after a few moments lost all cohesion and began to retreat in confusion to Sophia, leaving 800 dead on the field, but carrying off the 1,600 wounded to Sophia. The Russians lost 6 officers and 243 men. The smallness of Wilhelminof's force prevented his following up their retreat.

On the evening of January 1st the following dispositions were ordered : Rauch, with 16 battalions and 26 guns, to leave Taskosen at 2 A. M. and advance by the high-road toward Sophia. Kataley, with the 3d Division of the Guard, 16 battalions and 16 guns, to continue the pursuit of the Turks, joining at Bunova the detachment of General Dandeville, which had succeeded on a second attempt in passing the mountains in that vicinity. The detachments of Shouvaloff and Oldenburg, to withdraw the guns from the mountain positions opposite Shandarnik, and then descend into the plain and bivouac near Malinne. The detachment of Schilder-Schuldner to pass into the plain of Kamarlee and bivouac there. Two brigades of the Guard Cavalry to move to Petricevo in order to take the Turks in flank, and the 3d Brigade to take position on the Philippopolis high-road five miles east of Sophia.

While the movements already described had been in progress, 70,000 pounds of hard bread had been packed across the mountain by the sappers' road on the horses of the artillery left in reserve. This, with the biscuits left by the Turks, furnished the bread ration to the 4th of January inclusive, when the wagons began arriving by the high-road.

Rauch moved forward as ordered, and on the afternoon of the 2d, after a march of 25 miles, came to the Isker bridge, five miles east of Sophia. Here the Turks had posted three battalions of infantry and a regiment of cavalry, which made a defense for about an hour, setting fire to the village of Razdimme and attempting to burn the bridge; but before they could get the fire well under way the Preobrazhensky Regiment crossed the Isker on the ice about a mile to the left, and threatened their rear, whereupon they retreated to the town.

The next day a reconnaissance was made of the Turkish positions, showing that they had five large strong redoubts commanding the approaches by the various roads, and several lines of trenches and batteries recently constructed, a garrison of about 12,000 men, and 15 to 20 guns (estimated). The 8 battalions of Prince Oldenburg and 16 guns were brought up from Malinne, and all the dispositions were made to attack on the 5th. Wilhelminof, with 8 battalions and 12 guns, was to demonstrate on the north, while Rauch, with 20 battalions and 42 guns, was to make the main attack along the Plevna high-road. With the previous experience of the campaign, the result of this assault would have been at least doubtful, and if successful it would have cost over 5,000 men and largely demoralized the whole force. Fortunately, the necessity for it was avoided, as the Turks evacuated the place during the night of the 3d, retreating in the direction of Dubnitza, and abandoning as usual all their tents, an immense quantity of ammunition, and about 1,600 sick and wounded. Here, in addition, they left about 8,000,000 complete rations of flour, hard bread, rice, sugar, coffee, salt, etc., besides oats and barley in great quantities. With this and the abundance of hay, sheep, and cattle in the Sophia Valley, the force under General Gourko's orders was provisioned for over a month.

Gourko's total losses in action during the eleven days of his movement between Orkhanie and Sophia were 32 officers (including 3 generals) and 1,003 men.

The occupation of Sophia completed a military enterprise of no ordinary character, viz., the passage of a high mountain range in the middle of winter. The attacking force was numerically superior to the defenders in about the proportion of three to two; the latter were dispersed at several points, and nearly all their troops occupied positions on the mountain crests, with only a small reserve (at Sophia) in rear. Occupying the attention of each one of these detachments in front, the Russian commander threw a strong column over the mountains between the main mountain position (Araba-Konak) and the reserves (Sophia), and, completely turning the former, caused the hasty retreat of its defenders. Against the road by which they escaped a second turning column had been sent; but, overwhelmed with a snow storm in the mountains, it had been obliged to turn back, and thus the Turkish force escaped capture or complete destruction.

The success of such a movement depends very largely upon the secrecy and celerity with which it is accomplished. Secrecy had in this case been very well observed, since the Turks had no knowledge of the construction of the sappers' road by which the main turning column passed; and its value was augmented by the confident belief of the Turkish commanders that to pass such a range of mountains covered with deep snow at this season of the year, by any but the main road, was *totally impossible.* As for celerity, there was not so much success; for the sappers' road proved so difficult for the passage of cannon that the arrival of the troops in the valleys of the southern slope, which had been fixed in Gourko's orders for the 26th, did not take place until the 30th. For four days—days of no little anxiety—the movement hung fire, half the guns on one side and half on the other side of the mountains, the troops more or less dispersed, and a retreat in case of attack being impossible. There was, moreover, a lateral valley of the mountains which, passing out of range of Shouvaloff's right flank, led directly against the road which the main column was descending. Here was a fine opportunity for the Turks to strike the left flank of Gourko's column as it was descending the mountain, and before the men were well assembled. But the Turks did not take advantage of this opportunity, and what would have happened had they done so it is idle to speculate.

Having compelled the retreat of the Turks from Araba-Konak, Gourko sent one division of infantry and two brigades of cavalry to their pursuit; and without giving his troops any repose, he turned the rest of his force toward Sophia; which the Turks evacuated just as Gourko was preparing to assault it. In the other column the cavalry found such difficulty in traversing the mountains that all their efforts to head off the retreating Turks and strike their flank came to naught; the cavalry arrived too late each time. The infantry followed directly on the heels of the Turks, but in the narrow mountain passes the latter managed to cover their retreat by small bodies of men posted on the heights overlooking the road. They thus from time to time delayed the Russian advance long enough to gain time for their own retreat. In one of these skirmishes, the commander of the division, General Kataley, and one of his brigade commanders, who were riding imprudently in front of the column, were killed.

The Russian troops entered Sophia on the 4th of January, and were granted the few days' rest which was absolutely indispensable to them before undertaking a farther advance. The Turks had abandoned about 8,000,000 rations* of flour, rice, barley, salt, sugar, coffee, and a small quantity of hard bread and salt-beef. They also left all their tents, over 4,000,000 rounds of cartridges, and a large quantity of forage. Sixteen hundred sick remained in the hospitals under care of the surgeons of the various English aid societies. There had been between 7,000 and 9,000 sick and wounded in the hospitals before the Turks abandoned the town, but all those who were capable of walking or crawling, as well as the Turkish population of the town, had been ordered to leave, and had fled in the direction of Dubnitza.

But although a great quantity of supplies had fallen into the hands of the Russians, there was very little hard bread among them; and this article was indispensable to Gourko's farther advance. A supply train loaded with it was brought over the Araba-Konak Pass, from the Russian supplies at Orkhanie. As

---

* Of flour alone there was more than 30,000 tons, according to Gourko's report.

soon as it arrived Gourko distributed six days' rations of it to his men, as well as beef and mutton on the hoof. He then issued orders for his advance toward Philippopolis, which began on the 9th of January.

CHAPTER X.

GOURKO'S ADVANCE TO PHILIPPOPOLIS, AND THE BATTLES NEAR
THAT POINT, JANUARY 15-17, 1878.

(See Plates 2 and 6.)

BEFORE describing Gourko's advance from Sophia to Philippopolis, it is necessary to refer briefly to the topographical features of the intervening country. The plain of Sophia, although south of the main Balkan range, is yet properly a part of the basin of the Danube, for all its drainage is collected into the Isker, which cuts its way through the Balkans in a deep gorge due north of Sophia. The Isker rises near the town of Samakoff, about thirty miles south of Sophia, in a cluster of peaks known as Mount Rilo, which attain an altitude of over 8,000 feet above sea level. From these peaks two ranges of mountains radiate to the northeast and northwest, joining the main Balkans, and along these two ranges is the water-shed between the basin of the Danube and that of the Ægean Sea. A third range, known as the Rhodope Mountains, shoots off to the south of east from Mount Rilo, and between it and the Balkans lies the broad valley of the Maritza, the plains of ancient Thrace, beyond the eastern side of which lies Adrianople. The old Roman high-road, built by Trajan, passes through Sophia and over the water-shed on its east, winding through a deep gorge which still bears the name of Trajan's Gate; descending into the plain of the Maritza above Tatar-Bazardjik, it follows the course of that river for 150 miles to Adrianople.

Having crossed the Balkans to Sophia, Gourko's problem was of course to advance along the direction of this road. By his movement on Taskosen he had separated the Turkish force into two detachments, but they both made good their retreat—that which had defended the Araba-Konak Pass by crossing the divide to the town of Petricevo, which is situated on the Topolnica river, an affluent of the Maritza, and that which had been at Sophia by making a wide détour to the southwest through the town of Radomir and thence east to Samakoff. The eastern detachment numbered about 20,000 men, and the western about 15,000; and they were reënforced by 20,000 men withdrawn from the Quadrilateral and forwarded by rail.

With them arrived Suleiman Pasha, who personally took command about the 5th of January. This force was then distributed along the roads leading over the water-shed, the bulk of the newly arrived troops behind Ichtiman at Trajan's Gate, the detachment of Shakir Pasha on the right at Otlukioi and Petricevo, and the garrison of Sophia at Samakoff on the left. The distance between his extreme right and left flanks was nearly 40 miles, but the communications were good by means of intersecting valleys. This position at the entrance of the defile of Trajan's Gate was one of great natural strength, but it could easily have been turned by either flank by means of the valleys winding in the rear of it. Such was Gourko's plan of operations, and for this purpose he divided his force into four detachments, exclusive of a portion of the 3d Division of the Line, which was sent along the base of the Balkans to Karlovo, there to join the rest of the division, which meanwhile was passing the Balkans through the Trajan Pass.

The four detachments were ordered as follows:

On the right, Lieutenant-General Wilhelminoff, with 8 battalions of the IX. Corps, 12 sotnias of Cossacks, and 12 guns, was to leave Sophia January 7th by the direct Samakoff road, and endeavor, 1, to cut off the retreat of that Turkish detachment which was retreating by way of Radomir (in which he was not successful), and, 2, to advance through Banja against the left flank and rear of the position at Trajan's Gate.

In the center, Lieutenant-General Count Shouvaloff, with 30 battalions, 12 squadrons, and 76 guns, all of the Guard, was to advance along the main high-road, and, arrived at Ichtiman, to act against the front of the position at Trajan's Gate.

On the left, Lieutenant-General Baron Krüdener, with the rest of the Guard and a portion of his own (IX.) corps, in all 24 battalions, 16 squadrons, and 58 guns, was to advance by Petricevo to Otlukioi, whence a good road descends to Tatar-Bazardjik. He was to threaten the Turkish right, and in case of their retreat to endeavor to intercept them.

Finally, the fourth column, a small detachment of 6 battalions and 8 guns under Lieutenant-General Schilder-Schuldner, was to follow the valley of the Topolnica, keep up communications between Shouvaloff and Krüdener, and endeavor to get in rear of the Turkish right. A detachment of 8 battalions, 8 squadrons, and 14 guns was left at Sophia to protect the rear of the advancing columns and guard the stores captured at that place.

The various columns arrived in front of the Turkish positions previously described on the morning of January 11th. Then followed a curious misunderstanding, each of the Turkish detachments sending a *Parlementaire* through the pickets to say that orders had been received from the Minister of War at Constantinople to cease hostilities, as an armistice had been granted by the Russians. Telegrams soon arrived from the Grand Duke, however, saying that proposals for an armistice were expected, but had *not* been received, and that active operations must not in the least be retarded. This misunderstanding on the part of the Turks resulted in delaying the column of Wilhelminoff for twenty-four hours, but otherwise had no effect.

On the 11th Wilhelminoff attacked Samakoff, and gained possession of it after a fight in which he lost 150 men.

On the 10th the Turks received news of the capture of Shipka Pass and the whole army stationed there. This of course rendered a prompt retreat of Suleiman's army imperatively necessary, and on the morning of the 11th his troops evacuated their whole line of defense along the mountains of which Trajan's Gate was the center. Their right flank and a portion of their center united at Tatar-Bazardjik, and at once continued their retreat to Philippopolis.

With the Turkish left flank, however, which had been at Samakoff, the Russians at once began a race, in the hope that Shouvaloff's column, advancing by the high-road through Ichtiman, might first reach the Maritza valley and thus cut off this detachment. But the Turks reached the valley before the Russians, the latter being delayed by their artillery, which again

BATTLE OF PHILIPPOPOLIS. 341

had to be hauled up and down the icy slopes of the road by hand. As the advance guard of Count Shouvaloff debouched from the mountains on the main road at the village of Vetrenova on the afternoon of January 12th, the rear of the Turkish column was in sight a few miles in advance on a parallel road—that from Samakoff to Tatar-Bazardjik. The leading regiment was sent across to that road, but only overtook the baggage—300 ox-carts—which it captured. The next morning, January 13th, it followed on the heels of the Turks, but about five miles behind them, while twelve other battalions of Shouvaloff's column advanced along the main road to about three miles from Tatar-Bazardjik. Here they found a portion of the central column, about 8,000 men, under Fuad Pasha, occupying a strong position behind the Topolnica River, and prepared to defend it in order to gain time for the other Turkish column to enter by the Samakoff road. The Russians were not strong enough as yet to warrant an attack, and therefore nothing was done beyond skirmishing with the outposts. During the afternoon the advance of Krüdener's column was seen debouching from the mountains off on the left; and preparations were made to surround and attack the Turks the next day, provided they remained at Tatar-Bazardjik. But, as was expected, they abandoned their positions during the night, and the pursuit therefore was recommenced early the next morning, January 14th.

Fuad Pasha conducted the retreat of the 20,000 men now united under his orders as a rear guard with no little skill. Instead of marching along the main high-road, where he could have been overtaken and detained by the cavalry long enough for the infantry to come up and overwhelm him, he at once crossed the Maritza, destroying the bridges, and followed the line of railroad with his infantry and the country roads with his artillery, and covered his rear with about 1,500 cavalry, who did excellent service. The Russians were on the march before daylight of January 14th, Shouvaloff on the high-road, Krüdener on a converging road on his left, Wilhelminoff and Schilder-Schuldner on the flanks somewhat in rear. About 5 P. M., after a march of 30 miles without halt, Shouvaloff's advance guard got abreast of the rear of the Turks, about three miles off, on the railroad near the little village of Adakioi. (See Plate 20.) Here his troops forded the Maritza, a stream 200 yards wide and

3 feet deep, and filled with floating ice, and passed through the village. But the Turks, on the run, had got about a mile ahead, and Shouvaloff, having only 8 battalions at hand, was obliged to be prudent, especially as it was already nearly dark. The same night the bulk of the cavalry (28 squadrons) bivouacked between the Karlovo high-road and the Maritza, about four miles from Philippopolis; Krüdener bivouacked at Celapitza on the right flank of the cavalry, with Schilder-Schuldner behind him on the same road; and Wilhelminoff was on the railroad about 12 miles in rear.

The next morning, January 15th, Shouvaloff had 12 battalions in hand and 20 battalions marching toward him by the high-road. He moved out of the village (Adakioi) at daylight, and at once found the Turks, who, overcome with fatigue, had been unable to continue their retreat during the night. They were posted in a good position behind a small but deep rivulet, the ice of which was not passable for artillery, extending from the village of Karatair on their left over a little hill behind Kadikioi toward the village of Airanly, their right resting on the swamps of extensive ice-fields.

Shouvaloff at once deployed his troops and opened fire upon the Turks, and sent word to General Gourko, whose headquarters were on the other side of the Maritza nearly opposite Airanly, that he had a force of about 15,000 men in his front posted in a good position, that he thought he could, if ordered to do so, carry the position in his front, but with considerable loss; and asking for instructions. Gourko sent him back word about 10 A. M., not to attack the Turks, but to keep up a sufficient fire to hold them in place while he sent the rest of his troops around their right flank to cut them off from Philippopolis.

For this purpose Gourko ordered:

1. Krüdener's column, with the 3d Division of the Guard in the lead, to move forward at once to Philippopolis, nine miles in advance (or on the left as the line of battle stood).

2. The Finland Regiment, followed by Schilder-Schuldner's Brigade (17th and 18th Regiments), to cross the Maritza at the village of Airanly, drive the Turks out of that village, and move around the Turkish right flank.

3. The Preobazhensky and Simeonoff Regiments to demonstrate against the center of the Turkish position at Kadikioi.

4. The Grenadier, Paul, and Moscow Regiments and the Rifle Brigade to keep up the fire against the left flank of the Turks, and if possible retain them in place.

5. The column of General Wilhelminoff to move along the railroad and come up on the right of Shouvaloff.

As the Russian cavalry approached the Maritza on the east of Philippopolis early in the morning, the Turks saw that it would be useless to attempt to continue the retreat in that direction, and they were therefore forced to accept battle in the position where they then were, and thus cover their retreat over the Rhodope Mountains to the south.

Suleiman's whole force numbered 100 battalions, or between 50,000 and 60,000 men; but he personally escaped this morning with some 10,000 or 15,000 by Stanimaka and the road leading thence southeast over the mountains; but the rest of his force was cut off by the Russians before reaching Stanimaka, and thereafter formed the right flank of the force under Fuad Pasha, whose troops, with this addition, numbered in all about 35,000 men.

Meanwhile Shouvaloff kept up a sharp fire with the Turks in front of him throughout the day. His right flank, however, was somewhat in the air, but gave him no great anxiety, as the column of Wilhelminoff was expected to arrive every minute along the railroad and join him; but about 4 P. M., Wilheminoff not yet having arrived, and a considerable force of Turkish cavalry having appeared between Karatair and Karadermen, Shouvaloff, not wishing to leave his flank unprotected during the night, resolved to attack the Turkish left at the village of Karatair and drive them out of that position. This attack was executed by the Paul Regiment, which crossed the stream in front of that village by fording, and after a short fight gained possession of the village. Darkness soon afterward set in, and soon arrived Wilhelminoff's column.

On the other flank the Finland Regiment was ferried over the Maritza on cavalry horses about 2 P. M., and drove the Turks out of the village of Airanly. But the column of Schilder-Schuldner did not come up till about 5 P. M.; it was then ferried over in the same manner at a ford about a mile east of the point where the Finland Regiment had crossed. It was unable to advance around the Turkish flank, however, for the country in front of it was a mass of impassable rice-fields. The only fighting of the day was in Shouvaloff's column, whose losses were in all about 300 men.

The 3d Division of the Guard, forming part of Krüdener's column, had meanwhile approached Philippopolis early in the afternoon, and had entered that part of the town on the north of the river; but they found the bridge wholly destroyed, the opposite bank occupied by infantry, and the river not fordable. Beyond preparing some bridge material, they were unable to accomplish anything on that day.

A portion of the cavalry had moved around the town of Philippopolis and reached the Maritza at a point five miles east of the town, but had not crossed.

The force against which Shouvaloff fought during the 15th of January was only the rear guard of the Turkish army, about 15,000 to 20,000 men, under Fuad Pasha. The rest of Suleiman's army, about 35,000 to 40,000 men, with Suleiman himself, had already reached Philippopolis about the 12th or 13th. On the 14th, seeing the Russian cavalry already moving around the south of the town, Suleiman saw that it would be impossible to continue his retreat to Adrianople by the high-road, and he determined to try to escape by the roads on the south of the main road. For this purpose he sent a portion of his troops to the village of Markova (four miles south of Philippopolis), and with the rest he took the road leading to Stanimaka, and thence over the mountains either to Adrianople or due south to some port on the Ægean. This movement he began on the 15th, while the fight was going on around Kadikioi.

During the night of the 15th and 16th Fuad abandoned his position of the previous day, and, passing through the gap between Schilder-Schuldner and the mountains, took up a position along the base of the mountains near the village of Dermendere.

Wilhelminof followed him along the base of the mountains; Schilder-Schuldner moved along the railroad so as to get around his right flank; and Shouvaloff followed along the railroad across the rice-swamps, and then turning by the right flank deployed in his front. But Schilder-Schuldner, after arriving at the village of Komat, halted his troops on account of their fatigue, and did not close around the Turkish right flank. Fuad meanwhile concentrated his troops near the village of Dermendere, and about 3 P. M. made a very savage attack upon Wilhelminof's column, forming the extreme Russian right flank. These were the same troops which had repulsed the Turks so savagely at Gorni-Bugarof (near Sophia) on the 1st of January, and they repeated here the same tactics as on that day, and with almost equally good results—i. e., they lay down behind the rocks on a ridge of the foot-hills and let the Turks approach to within 100 yards, and then received them with carefully aimed volley-firing. The Turks made three attacks, and were each time repulsed, and finally retired, leaving 600 dead on the field, while the Russian loss was only about 60 in all.

Fuad's purpose in this attack was evidently to divert the attention of the Russians, and cause them to send troops to the aid of their right flank by weakening their left, and then to hasten to rejoin the rest of Suleiman's army on the Stanimaka road. But he did not succeed. Two regiments were indeed sent by Shouvaloff to Wilhelminof's aid, but Schilder-Schuldner's column was not weakened, nor that of Krüdener.

But Schilder-Schuldner did fail to get around Fuad's right flank on the 16th, and therefore during the night Fuad again moved along the base of the mountains about four miles, taking up a new position near the village of Beleznitza.

Meanwhile, on the morning of this same day (January 16th), Gourko having gone in person to Philippopolis, and finding that it would be impossible to construct quickly a bridge over the river in place of the one which had been burned by the Turks, immediately sent the 3d Division of the Guard down the river three or four miles to the nearest ford, and there had them ferried over the river on the cavalry horses of the 2d Brigade of the Cavalry Division of the Guard. From there this division advanced at once to the south toward the Stanimaka road, by which Suleiman had retreated the previous day.

About 4 P. M. the 1st Brigade of this division approached this road near the village of Karagatch, five miles from Philippopolis. This village was occupied by a considerable force of Turks, the rear of Suleiman's force, with 18 guns. The Russians immediately moved forward to the attack, and carried the village with a loss of about 260 men, capturing all of the 18 guns. The Turks in turn, reënforced in numbers, attacked the

Russians and tried to regain the position, but without success. The 2d Brigade of this division, however, had been delayed at the crossing of the Maritza, and did not arrive by nightfall. Owing to the weakness of his force and his exposed position (Suleiman's main force being only a few miles farther ahead toward Stanimaka), the chief of this brigade thought it prudent to withdraw his troops and the 18 captured guns during the night a few miles back to the village of Ahlan, where he was rejoined by the 2d Brigade.

Suleiman, however, continued his retreat, leaving Fuad to extricate himself the best way he could. By his retreat to Beleznitza during the night of the 15th and 16th, the latter had joined his troops to that portion of Suleiman's rear guard which had been cut off at Karagatch.

Sending his cavalry to follow Suleiman, Gourko prepared to close in his whole force round Fuad, Wilhelminof on the right near Markova, Shouvaloff and Schilder-Schuldner in the center near Beleznitza, and Dandeville (3d Division Guard) on the left near Karagatch.

Fuad fought with his back to the mountains throughout the whole of this day, January 17th. In the morning he concentrated his troops on the right in one final effort to drive back the Russians in that quarter, and open his way to the Stanimaka road; but his troops were repulsed, and, attacked in turn by the Russians, they lost more of their artillery. About 3 P. M. Schilder-Schuldner's troops moved forward to the attack in front of Tchiftlik, at the same time that Wilhelminof's column advanced along the base of the mountains against the Turkish left flank at Markova. The Turks were incapable of further resistance, and, abandoning everything, they dispersed in small bands, climbing up the mountains through the snow. The Russians followed them till nightfall, and then gave up the pursuit on account of the impracticable nature of the country and the dispersion of the enemy.

The next day Gourko reassembled his troops in the vicinity of Philippopolis, sending in pursuit of the enemy two cavalry columns: 1. The Caucasian Brigade of Cossacks, which followed Fuad's detachment, cutting down more or less of the fugitives, and finally making its way through blind mountain paths to the other side of the mountains, and arriving at De-

BATTLE OF PHILIPPOPOLIS.   347

motika (south of Adrianople) on the 27th; 2. The cavalry of the Guard and a brigade of Don Cossacks, which followed Suleiman's detachment through Stanimaka, and on the 19th captured 40 guns which were halted at a very steep hill under escort of five battalions of infantry, which the cavalry dispersed after a short engagement.

The result of Gourko's movement from Sophia to Philippopolis was the destruction of Suleiman Pasha's army of 50,000 to 60,000 men. The Russians captured 114 guns in all (96 of them in open fight), about 2,000 prisoners, all the baggage, several thousand muskets, great quantities of ammunition, implements, etc., etc. The Turks lost in the series of engagements around Philippopolis very nearly 5,000 men, and retreated in scattered disorganized bands through the wild Rhodope Mountains, their numbers diminishing daily by desertions, freezing, starvation, etc. About the 28th of January this disorganized force began to assemble on the shore of the Ægean near Enos, where a fleet of transports was in waiting for them under command of Manthorpe Bey, an ex-officer of the British navy. About 40,000 men were transported in this fleet to Gallipoli and Constantinople. Suleiman was placed in arrest and ordered for trial by court martial.*

Gourko's losses between Sophia and Philippopolis were in all as follows:

	Officers.	Men.
Killed	7	220
Wounded	34	989
Total	41	1209

We have now followed the first two stages of Gourko's movements during the winter, viz., from Orkhanie to Sophia, and from Sophia to Philippopolis. Direct communications were now opened with the Headquarters and the troops at Shipka; and Gourko's army became simply the right wing of the advancing Russian army, all the parts of which were within supporting distance. Before following this further advance, it is necessary to explain the passage of the Balkans by the other columns, which had meanwhile taken place.

---

* The sentence of the court martial which tried Suleiman was delivered in December, 1878. It was complete degradation and confinement in a fortress for fifteen years.

CHAPTER XI.

CAPTURE OF THE TURKISH ARMY AT SHIPKA PASS.

Gourko's movement over the Balkans by way of Sophia merely formed part, as already explained, of the general plan of advance determined upon just after the fall of Plevna. The other portions of this plan were the forcing of the Shipka Pass and the passage of a small force over the Trojan Pass.

The latter column, under General Kartzoff, consisted only of two regiments of the 3d Division, reënforced by one battalion of the 3d Rifle Brigade and two regiments of Don Cossacks (24th and 30th). The Balkans in the vicinity of the Trojan hill are higher than at almost any other part of them, and there is nothing but rude wood-roads leading over the mountains. The Turks had two or three small redoubts, and perhaps 2,000 men defending these roads—about the same force as at Slatitza. On the 4th of January Kartzoff began the ascent of the mountains, taking only eight guns with him; but each of these was dismounted and placed on a sledge, and required twenty-four yoke of buffaloes, a company of infantry, and a sotnia of Cossacks to draw it up the mountain. His troops were divided into three detachments of about 9 companies, or 1,500 men each. They reached the summit of the mountains on the afternoon of the 5th, and made a reconnaissance of the redoubt. The next two days were passed in reconnoitering a route on the east of the redoubt by which it could be turned, and in hauling at the artillery. On the 7th the redoubt was bombarded in front, while a column of infantry passed around it on the east, and descended the mountain in its rear; at the same time another column of

CAPTURE OF THE TURKISH ARMY AT SHIPKA PASS. 349

infantry attacked it in front. The Turks fled and dispersed in the Little Balkans. The Russian losses were less than 100 men.

Two days later the other portion of this 3d Division, which had crossed the Balkans with Gourko, and had subsequently been sent by Slatitza to rejoin Kartzoff's command, arrived at Slatitza. Finding the Turkish works there abandoned, it moved on and joined Kartzoff near Karlovo, and on the 14th the whole of the 3d Division moved down by the high-road toward Philippopolis, and opened communication with the troops of Gourko, by whom it was directed along the roads north of the Maritza toward Haskioi. (See Plate 6.)

Shipka.

(See Plate 21.)

At Shipka Pass, where the Russians had now for over five months been defending with such gallantry the positions captured in the early part of the campaign, the passage was effected in a very brilliant manner.

The arrival of General Skobeleff with the 16th and 30th Divisions and the 3d and 4th Rifle Brigades at Gabrova, in the first days of January, placed a force of 74 battalions, or about 56,000 infantry, besides artillery and cavalry, at Radetzky's disposition; but of these troops the 24th Division, which had arrived on the heights of Shipka during the latter part of November to relieve for a short time the 14th Division, had in a subsequent snow-storm and cold snap lost a good many hundreds of men from freezing, and had in fact been wholly broken down by the cold. On the 25th of December this division had 6,013 men unfit for duty from frost-bites and sickness brought on by the terrible exposure. It had to be withdrawn to Gabrova to refit, and was for the moment practically *hors de combat*. The rest of his troops, however, were in good order.

Radetzky's plan for forcing the passage was to divide his troops into three columns, one of which, under his own orders, was to remain in the works at the summit of the pass, while the other two were to pass on either flank, cross the mountain, and attack the pass from the rear (south), simultaneously with the attack from the north. Radetzky's detachment consisted of the 14th Infantry Division and the 35th Regiment of the 9th Division. The column of the right, under Skobeleff, consisted of the 16th Division, the 3d Rifle Brigade (3 battalions), 7 Bulgarian battalions, the 9th Don Cossacks, 6 mountain guns, and 6 4-pdrs.—in all, 22 battalions, 6 squadrons, and 12 guns; it was to pass over the trail which leads from the village of Zelenodrevo to the top of the mountains (only about two miles and a half from the left flank of the Turks on the Bald Mountain), and thence descends to the village of Imetli in the Tundja valley; here the detachment was to turn to the left and attack the works defending the village of Shipka. The column of the left, under Prince Mirsky, consisted of the 33d, 34th, and 36th Regiments of the 9th Division, the 30th Division, the 4th Rifle Brigade, one Bulgarian battalion, the 23d Don Cossack Regiment, 6 mountain guns, 8 4-pdrs., and 8 9-pdrs.—in all, 26 battalions, 6 squadrons, and 22 guns. It was to leave the village of Travna and follow the trail over the Selky hill, debouching in the Tundja valley at the village of Gusevo, then turn to the right, and, joining hands with Skobeleff, attack the works defending the village of Shipka.

The movement was fixed to begin on the morning of the 5th of January, and it was calculated that the columns would arrive in the valley on the evening of the 7th, and attack on the morning of the 8th.

In both columns the guns were unlimbered and arranged to be drawn on sledges; but it was soon found impossible to get them up the mountain even in this manner, and they were all left behind except the little mountain guns, one battery of which was with each column. The snow on the paths which the columns had to follow was in many places TEN FEET DEEP.

From Mount St. Nicholas, where Radetzky posted himself, the villages where the two columns were to debouch into the valley could be plainly seen.

The two columns began their march on the 5th, Mirsky in the morning and Skobeleff in the evening, the former having to pass nearly twice the distance of the latter. Mirsky met no opposition in the mountains, and on the 7th descended into the valley at Gusevo, driving the Turkish outposts away from that village, and sent one brigade of the 30th Division to occupy the village of Maglis, four miles east of Gusevo, to protect his left flank and rear. Skobeleff met with resistance in descending the mountain on the 7th, the Turks having hastily occupied a line of trenches on a ridge commanding the trail which Skobeleff was following. In order to dislodge the Turks from this place, he was considerably delayed, and was only able to occupy the village of Imetli with an advance guard on the 7th.

On the morning of the 8th, the day calculated for the attacks, Radetzky watched eagerly on Mount St. Nicholas for the appearance of the other two columns in the valley. About 10 A. M. Mirsky's troops were seen coming out of the mountains near Gusevo; and deploying about noon, they moved forward to the attack in the direction of Shipka village. Skobeleff's troops were not in sight, but a cannonade was heard in the mountains in his direction, where he was, in fact, still fighting with the Turks in the position half way down the slope. About noon also arrived a messenger from Skobeleff explaining the difficulties that he had met. Radetzky sent word back to him to concentrate his column in the valley and attack Shipka from the rear on the morning of the 9th, and if possible to open communications with Mirsky, and attack in conjunction with him. He also informed Skobeleff that the 1st Cavalry Division had been sent over his trail to assist him. Mirsky meanwhile heard the cannonade off on his left, but saw no Russian troops. Finally the cannonade died away, and still no troops were in sight. He was evidently in a bad position to attack alone, with his left flank out in the air; but during the previous night he had received a precise order from Radetzky to attack on this morning. He therefore moved forward with the 4th Rifle Brigade deployed as skirmishers, supported by the little mountain battery and the 33d Regiment. In his second line were the 34th, 36th, and 117th Regiments. The 120th remained with the baggage at Gusevo, and the 118th and 119th, which had occupied Maglis on his left flank the previous night, were ordered to move forward to Kazanlyk.

After a short but hot fight his troops carried the villages of Janina and Haskioi. But beyond Haskioi was a small range of hills stretching across the road, covered with several tiers of rifle-pits. Here Mirsky's troops were brought to a halt by a very hot fire, and, the colonel of the 33d Regiment being severely wounded about this time, the line began to waver.

The 36th Regiment was then sent forward to the support of

the 33d, which held the right of the line, and the 34th to the support of the Rifle Brigade, on its left. One battalion of the 117th was sent off in the direction of Kazanlyk to guard the left flank, and only the other two battalions of the regiment remained in reserve. The little mountain battery advanced to within about 700 yards of the Turkish position, and sent a lucky shot which exploded one of the Turkish caissons. The Russians then moved forward with a rush in spite of the fire of the Turks, and carried the line of trenches, capturing three guns and about 100 prisoners.

They thus came in front of the last line of defense of the Turks, a series of redoubts on the hills just south of Shipka village; but darkness was coming on, the troops were tired out, and their ammunition was almost exhausted. It was impossible to try to carry these redoubts that night. The Turks, however, passed to the attack, and rushed forward upon the Russians with considerable impetuosity, but were driven back by the deliberate volley-firing of the latter.

Although Mirsky was informed early in the evening that the 118th and 119th Regiments had entered Kazanlyk without finding any enemy, yet his position was anything but comfortable. His left flank was in the air, at his back was a high range of mountains over which it would be almost impossible to retreat, and in his front, only 200 yards off, was the enemy in a position which he felt he could not carry. He sent a report to Radetzky explaining his critical situation, stating that he had fought all day with superior numbers, had sustained very great losses, was nearly at the end of his ammunition, and unless he could be reënforced he must begin to retreat. Radetzky sent word back to him to hold on for another twenty-four hours; that Skobeleff would come to his relief on his left flank; and that he (Radetzky) would try to operate a diversion by attacking the Turks in front the next morning. The next morning, unfortunately, there was a tempest of wind, filling the air with blinding snow and a dense fog of particles of frozen mist. Radetzky could see nothing of what was going on in the valley, but through the fog came the sounds of heavy artillery and infantry fire, indicating that the Turks had begun to attack Mirsky. Radetzky at once made his preparations for attack, in the hope of relieving the pressure on Mirsky. He sent for-

CAPTURE OF THE TURKISH ARMY AT SHIPKA PASS. 353

ward the 55th and 56th Regiments and part of the 35th along the high-road and on its right against the Turkish trenches in front of Mount St. Nicholas. The ground was extremely unfavorable for attack, and in the dense fog it was impossible to see what was going on at a distance of ten yards away. Still these troops, between noon and 2 P. M., carried the first two lines of Turkish trenches in open assault, but with enormous losses—over 1,700 men. Having gained these positions, the troops remained there, unable to advance, until news arrived from Skobeleff during the afternoon announcing the surrender of the whole Turkish army.

Meanwhile, in the valley the fog was not so dense. The Turks had early in the morning opened an attack on Mirsky's right flank, but had not made any impression upon it. They then made an attack upon his left flank, without any better success. Mirsky then riposted with his left, and carried a second Turkish redoubt (capturing two guns in it), and also the village of Shipka. This cut off this portion of the Turks from the Kazanlyk road, but they still held a line of redoubts behind Shipka village. While Mirsky's troops were halted in front of this and a lull had succeeded in the battle in their front, they heard loud cheering off on their left at the village of Shenovo. It was the attack of Skobeleff's troops—the most brilliant assault of the whole war, deciding the day and the fate of the entire Turkish army of Shipka.

Skobeleff's column, as already remarked, had met with opposition in descending the southern slope of the mountain, the Turks having hastily occupied on the 7th a ridge northeast of the village of Imetli, from which they took his line of march in flank. This completely stopped the march of his column late in the afternoon, and Skobeleff, arriving in person at its head, found the men lying down and receiving the fire of the enemy, but without replying to it. On asking an explanation, the men replied that it was of no use to fire, for their guns would not reach the position of the Turks—about 1,500 yards off across a ravine. While he was talking his chief of staff was very badly wounded in the shoulder. Skobeleff immediately ordered up a company of the 63d Regiment, which he had armed before leaving Plevna with the Peabody-Martini guns captured from the Turks. They had hardly opened fire before the Turks ceased their fire and retired behind the crest of their ridge. Darkness, however, now set in, and stopped the fighting. The Russians remained in their positions scattered along the trail in the snow during the night.

Early the next morning the two regiments in the lead, the 63d and 64th, resumed their march, and by 9 A. M. had reached the village of Imetli, and found that the Turks had occupied a hill on the southeast of that village. The 64th Regiment attacked this hill and drove them out.

About 11 A. M. Skobeleff received word from the pickets left in observation on the top of the mountain that Mirsky's detachment was moving forward to the attack of Shipka village, and the firing was also heard from that direction; but Skobeleff did not credit the report, thinking that his men had mistaken a column of Turks for Russians, and as for the firing, it seemed to come from the direction of Mount St. Nicholas. Moreover, in reply to his report that he could not get his men together in the valley in time to attack on the 8th, Skobeleff had received orders from Radetzky to attack on the 9th, and *positively not to attack before all his men were assembled in the valley.* Having therefore no direct communication with Mirsky (who had only sent two sotnias of Cossacks to open communication with him, and which had not penetrated beyond Kazanlyk), and having no certain information that Mirsky was actually engaged, Skobeleff stuck strictly to his orders, and kept his two regiments at Imetli until the rest of his troops could arrive. It thus happened that Mirsky had to sustain the fight of the 8th unsupported, as has already been described.

During the afternoon the 61st Regiment got down the mountain to Imetli, and then Skobeleff sent forward the 63d and 64th a short distance toward Shenovo. But all his troops not yet being over the mountains, they were not allowed to attack Shenovo. During the night the Rifle Brigade and the Bulgarian Legion were also assembled at Imetli, but word was received from the 62d Regiment that they could not drag the artillery up the hill. Skobeleff sent word to them to leave the guns behind and march on during the night, so as to be at Imetli at all hazards in the morning.

Before daylight on the 9th his troops at Imetli were under arms, but Skobeleff waited still for the 62d Regiment. As it began to descend the mountain so that he was sure of having it as a reserve, about 10 A. M. Skobeleff sent forward a portion of the 63d Regiment to clear the Turks out of a hill on their right flank (west of Shenovo), which threatened his left; this they accomplished with considerable loss. At the same time Skobeleff sent a portion of his cavalry on his right, and they soon opened communication with Mirsky's detachment.

Everything being at last in readiness, Skobeleff formed his troops for the assault of the Shenovo redoubts. In his first line were the 63d Regiment and the Bulgarian Legion; behind them the 61st and 64th and the Rifle Brigade. With all the bands playing, these troops moved forward to the assault without breaking their line or firing a shot. They lost heavily, even in the bands, but still they moved on, until, on nearing the redoubts, they broke into a run with a wild hurrah and rushed at the Turkish works. There was then a little hesitation in the 63d Regiment, until its colonel arrived among the men in the very front line, and by his personal bravery carried the regiment forward with him.

The Russians entered the redoubts, and then suddenly the hurrahing and noise of the firing were succeeded by a painful, deadly silence, lasting for some minutes, during which a fierce hand-to-hand fight with the bayonet took place. The Russians won, and six Turkish battalions lay down their arms in the redoubts, while the rest began fleeing toward Shipka. Just as Skobeleff was giving the orders for following them, arrived a Turkish officer seeking Skobeleff, and, in the name of Vessil Pasha, commanding the Turkish army at Shipka, surrendered the whole force. Twelve thousand men laid down their arms at Shenovo, and Skobeleff, while sending report of this to Radetzky, immediately set to work to disarm them, since the other half of the Turkish army was still in the positions on the mountains, and might refuse to obey the surrender of their chief, and, coming to the aid of that portion which was at Shipka village, might still make a very serious fight. It was not until midnight that this disarmament was completed and Skobeleff's troops were allowed to rest.

The Turkish army which thus surrendered numbered 41 battalions, containing 36,000 men in all, of whom about 6,000 were sick and wounded; and with it were captured 93 guns (including 12 mortars) and 10 flags. But the Russian losses were not slight, being as follows:

	Officers.	Men.
Killed	19	1,103
Wounded	116	4,246
Total	135	5,349

Of this loss, 1,700 men were in Radetzky's, 1,500 in Skobeleff's, and 2,100 in Mirsky's detachment. Only 37 battalions, or about 25,000 men, had been brought actually under fire; so that the proportion of losses was about 22 per cent.

The capture of this Shipka army surpasses in boldness and brilliancy the advance of Gourko over the Balkans at Araba-Konak. Although Radetzky's attack in front caused him terrible losses and apparently gained no result, yet without this it is possible that the Turks might have withdrawn from the mountains under cover of the fog, and, concentrating about Shipka village, have broken through between Mirsky and Skobeleff, and escaped to the south; and, although Mirsky may be blamed for opening his attack before he had established communication with Skobeleff according to the plan of battle, yet it is possible that, had he remained idle at Gusevo during the 8th, the Turks might have discovered him and begun to retreat. Finally, Skobeleff's energetic attack, as soon as he had got all his men together in the valley, was one of the most splendid assaults ever made, and renders more than doubtful the conclusion which has been hastily drawn from this war (from Plevna particularly), that successful assaults of earthworks defended by modern breech-loaders are impossible. Skobeleff's detachment passed over the Karadja Mountain, which is separated from the Bald Mountain (the left flank of the Turkish position) by a valley (or saddle) less than 1,000 yards wide. One would have supposed that the Turks would have had a picket out on this Karadja Mountain, but such was not the case. Skobeleff's trail passed within two miles of the redoubt on the Woody Mountain, but he was not molested in any way on his march. That the Turks must have seen some portion of his men is probable, since when Skobeleff's advance guard approached Imetli on the 7th they found it strongly occupied by the Turks; but that the latter thought that the movement was anything more than a reconnaissance seems doubtful. The Russians had previously made reconnaissances in the same direction, and it was owing to these reconnaissances that the Turks had some time before constructed the line of redoubts facing southwest and southeast at Shenovo and Shipka villages. The trenches near Haskioi, as well as those at Imetli, had been thrown up in the night after the Russian movement was discovered.

One of the remarkable features of this battle is the fact that Mirsky and Skobeleff both had to leave all their artillery behind (except the little mountain guns, which amounted to nothing), and that both of them carried the enemy's works without any "preparation of the attack by artillery."

CHAPTER XII.

THE ADVANCE TO CONSTANTINOPLE—REMARKS ON THE WINTER CAMPAIGN.

(See Plates 2 and 6.)

In the preceding chapters we have seen that the whole Turkish defense of the Balkans had gone down with a crash; one army of 36,000 men being captured in bulk at Shipka, and the other army of 50,000 men routed at Philippopolis and dispersed over the mountains toward the Ægean.

As soon as the news of the capture of Shipka reached the Grand Duke's headquarters he hastened forward to Gabrova, and, after crossing the mountains, established his headquarters at Kazanlyk. While the prisoners were being sent to the rear under guard of the 24th Division and the Bulgarian Legion, preparations were made for an immediate advance on Adrianople, and orders to this effect were issued on the 13th of January, viz.:

1. *Right Wing*, under General Gourko, consisting of the Guard, IX. Corps, 3d Division, and a special cavalry detachment of 5,000 men under General Skobeleff, Sr., to advance on Adrianople in two columns, the left following the high-road in the valley of the Maritza, and the right crossing the spur of the mountains south of Haskioi, so as to arrive at Demotika, on the south of Adrianople, and cut off the communications between the latter place and the sea.

2. *The Center*, consisting (*a*) of an advance guard under General Skobeleff, Jr., containing the 16th and 30th Divisions and the 3d and 4th Rifle Brigades, preceded (*b*) by the 1st Cavalry Division, under General Stroukoff, and followed (*c*) by the

ADVANCE TO CONSTANTINOPLE. 359

Grenadier Corps under General Ganetzky. Stroukoff was to leave Kazanlyk January 13th, send one regiment to occupy Yeni-Zagra, and with the rest move forward with the greatest rapidity through Eski-Zagra to the railway junction and the Maritza bridge at Trnova, and occupy this most important point. (At the date of this order the battle of Philippopolis had not yet been fought, and it was still possible that Suleiman might be retreating on Adrianople or receive aid from that point.) Skobeleff was to follow Stroukoff as quickly as possible, leaving Kazanlyk on the 15th, and after reaching Trnova to follow the Maritza directly to Adrianople.

Ganetzky's troops were to aid the artillery of the 16th and 30th Divisions and the VIII. Corps, as well as their own, in crossing the Shipka Pass, and then to concentrate around Kazanlyk preparatory to following Skobeleff. They were in fact the reserve of the center.

3. *Left Wing*, VIII. Corps, under General Radetzky, to advance at once by Yeni-Zagra to Yamboli, and thence descend the valley of the Tundja to Adrianople, arriving on its north and east. The 8th Cavalry Division, which had been for some time detached in the army of the Cesarevitch, was to assemble at Tirnova, and, crossing by the Elena-Tvarditza pass, to rejoin its proper corps near Slivno.

4. The XI. Corps; under General Dellinghausen, to be assembled near Tirnova, and cross by the Elena-Tvarditza pass to Yamboli, and thence protect the left flank and rear of Radetzky's column; and also to send reconnaissances along the base of the mountains to Aidos, and there endeavor to join hands with the XIV. Corps under Zimmermann. One regiment of Radetzky's corps to be left at Yamboli until the arrival of the XI. Corps. The 24th Division, as soon as it had returned from escorting the prisoners to the Danube, was to proceed to Yamboli and form part of Dellinghausen's detachment.

5. The Cesarevitch's army, comprising all the troops north of the Balkans except those of General Zimmermann, to move forward against Rustchuk, Razgrad, and Osman-Bazar, to endeavor to gain possession of these latter places, and establish itself on the line of the Rustchuk-Varna railroad.

6. The Dobrudja detachment of General Zimmermann to move forward and endeavor to gain possession of Bazardjik, cut

the railroad between Shumla and Varna at Pravady, and thence try to open communications over the Derbend Pass with Dellinghausen at Aidos. To cover his right flank Zimmermann was to detach a portion of his force to observe Silistria.

Such were the orders of January 13th for the advance; but the armistice of January 31st, for which the Turks were already suing, was signed before the greater part of the troops had made much progress in their movements. The columns of Gourko and Skobeleff, however, were moved forward with the greatest energy and celerity. The cavalry of the latter, under command of General Stroukoff, left Kazanlyk on the 13th and arrived in front of Trnova on the 14th. On the 15th he attacked the detachment guarding this village and the bridge, consisting of a battalion of infantry and about 5,000 armed inhabitants, dispersed them, and gained possession of the bridge, the railway station, etc., and cut the wire and the track. He also captured six Krupp guns abandoned by the Turks in their flight.

Skobeleff left Kazanlyk the same day (January 15th), and, pushing his men forward by forced marches, 55 miles in 40 hours, reached Trnova during the night of the 16th-17th. He immediately sent Stroukoff in advance down the valley of the Maritza as far as Hermanli, which was occupied after driving out some bashi-bozouks. On the 18th Skobeleff moved his infantry to Hermanli and his cavalry to Mustapha Pasha. On the 19th he learned of the approach from Haskioi to Hermanli of an immense train of fugitives escorted by several battalions of Turkish infantry, and he therefore sent the 63d Regiment and the 11th Rifle Battalion to cut them off on the west of Hermanli. This detachment on its approach was attacked by the Turkish escort, as well as by the armed fugitives. A considerable affair took place, causing a loss of over 50 men to the Russians, and resulting in the defeat of the escort and their flight toward the mountains, followed by the able-bodied portion of the immense caravan (over 20,000 wagons, containing 200,000 people), who left the old, the sick, and the babes to perish in the snow. The train was so many miles in length that the Russians could not guard it, and the greater part of it was plundered by the Bulgarians of the neighboring villages, who also massacred the helpless Turks who had not strength enough to flee to the mountains.

On the same day (January 19th) Stroukoff was at Mustapha Pasha, and in the evening received word by Bulgarian messengers from Adrianople that the wildest panic prevailed in that city, and that the Turkish troops had abandoned it and retreated in the direction of Constantinople, after blowing up the powder magazines; and that the Turkish population was also in flight from that city, and from all the surrounding villages. At daylight on the 20th Stroukoff moved forward with his cavalry division, occupied Adrianople, restored order, and installed a temporary government. On the 22d Skobeleff entered Adrianople with his infantry, and immediately sent Stroukoff forward in the direction of Constantinople.

The ancient capital of Turkey and the second city in the empire thus fell without a blow. It was defended by a well-planned and extensive series of earthworks on the surrounding hills, which, however, were not fully completed. Its garrison was about 10,000 men under command of Achmed Eyoub Pasha.

Meanwhile the right wing, under Gourko, had remained at Philippopolis from the 18th to the 21st of January, during which time the troops rested, partly repaired their clothing, and received a fresh supply of rations. On the 22d, leaving a brigade to occupy Philippopolis, Gourko began his march toward Adrianople. That town having been occupied on the same day by the troops of Skobeleff (of which Gourko received news on the 23d), there was no necessity for Gourko's troops to go to Demotika. They therefore simply continued their march by the high-road to Adrianople, and were all concentrated there by the 27th, Gourko himself having entered on the 25th. The Grand Duke and his headquarters also arrived at Adrianople on the 26th.

Negotiations were meanwhile going on for an armistice, but the Turks demurred to the terms, and all the preparations were therefore taken for marching forward at once upon Constantinople. For this purpose the following dispositions were made:

1. The advance guard, under Skobeleff, to advance along the line of the railroad, reconnoiter the line of Turkish defense at Buyuk-Tchekmedje, select its weakest point, and assault it with the utmost energy.

2. The right wing, under Gourko, to advance to Rodosto on the sea-coast, whence it could be used against Gallipoli or Constantinople according to circumstances. The 3d Division to go to Enos, at the mouth of the Maritza, and prevent any landing at that point.

3. The left wing, under Radetzky, to follow the northern road to Constantinople, starting from Kirk-Kilissa, where it had already arrived on the 26th.

4. The Grenadier Corps, under Ganetzky, to remain in the vicinity of Adrianople as reserve until further developments.

On the 31st of January this movement had so far progressed that Stroukoff, with the cavalry, forming the advance guard of Skobeleff's column, was at Tchorlu, which place it had captured after a cavalry skirmish (the last shot of the war) on the 29th. Skobeleff with the bulk of his troops was at Lule-Bourgas (30 miles in rear of Tchorlu), the 3d Division at Enos, Radetzky at Kirk-Kilissa, and Gourko's troops just moving out from Adrianople. Late that night (January 31st) the Turkish commissioners signed the armistice, having received authority for that purpose from Constantinople.

The terms of this instrument are somewhat remarkable, and show that the Turks at last despaired of receiving active assistance from England, without the *hope* of which they would never have undertaken the war, and had determined to throw themselves wholly upon the mercy of the Russians. They accepted definitely the preliminary conditions of peace, as follows: 1. The erection of Bulgaria into "an autonomous tributary principality, with a national Christian Government and a native militia." 2. The independence of Montenegro, with an increase of territory. 3. The independence of Roumania and Servia, with a territorial indemnity. 4. The introduction of administrative reforms into Bosnia and Herzegovina. 5. An indemnity in money to Russia for the expenses of the war.

The armistice then specified that the Turks should immediately surrender the Danube fortresses of Widdin, Rustchuk, and Silistria, with the privilege of withdrawing their material of war, or selling it to the Russians; they should also evacuate Belgradjik, Razgrad, and Bazardjik. The fortifications of the line of Buyuk-Tchekmedje (the last line of defense of Constantinople) should be evacuated by the Turks, but not occupied by the Russians; the Turks should retire behind the line of Kuyuk-Tchekmedje,* and the Russians advance to the line of Tchataldja, and the space between the two forces (about ten miles) should be a neutral zone. The Russians should occupy the towns of Bourgas and Midia on the Black Sea coast, and have the privilege of revictualing their army through these harbors. The Turks were to raise the blockade of the Black Sea ports.

The position of Buyuk-Tchekmedje is as remarkable in natural military strength as is Constantinople itself in geographical situation. The peninsula (between the Black Sea and the Sea of Marmora) is here but twenty miles wide, and twelve miles of this space is occupied by broad lakes extending up inland from either shore. Of the remaining eight miles, at least half is filled with impassable or difficult swamps, and the remaining half with almost impenetrable thickets. Behind this line of lakes, swamps, marshes, and thickets, runs a continuous ridge from sea to sea, from 400 to 700 feet in height; and on this ridge the Turks had in process of construction not less than thirty large redoubts, besides outlying trenches and rifle-pits, the greater part of them concentrated in the center of the line, and disposed irregularly according to the nature of the ground in three lines. These redoubts were only half finished, but they still afforded complete protection for infantry; they would have mounted about 150 siege-guns and as many more field-guns, and their proper garrison would have been 60,000 to 75,000 men. With such a garrison—since the flanks of the line rested on the sea, and could not be turned or invested—these lines might fairly be called impregnable. The force actually in them consisted of about 30,000 men, made up of the wrecks of Suleiman's army, which had been brought by sea from Enos, of Achmed Eyoub's division, which had retreated from Adrianople, and of some reserves which had been at Constantinople during the war—the whole under command of Ghazi Moukhtar Pasha, who had lately returned from Asia, where he had lost his whole army. Yet such was the natural strength of this position, taking into account the shortness of the line, which

* The two villages of Buyuk- and Kuyuk-Tchekmedje are at the mouths of small streams emptying into the Sea of Marmora, and respectively 25 and 10 miles from Constantinople.

allowed the men to be within easy supporting distance of each other, that 30,000 men here constituted a more formidable adversary than 60,000 in the line of works held by Osman at Plevna. But the armistice gave these away with a stroke of the pen to the Russians.

Meanwhile railway communication had been established along the Constantinople-Adrianople railroad, and negotiations were immediately opened at the latter place for the conclusion of a treaty of peace. Skobeleff's whole column was concentrated in front of Tchataldja, on the line marking the "neutral zone" of the armistice; Gourko moved on to Tchorlu and Rodosto; Radetzky was just behind him and on his left flank; Ganetzky's Grenadiers were at Adrianople and Demotika; Dellinghausen's detachment went to occupy the Black Sea ports. On the north of the Balkans, Todleben (who had succeeded the Cesarevitch in his command, the latter having departed for Russia upon the conclusion of the armistice) entered Rustchuk at the head of his troops on the 20th of February without having the trouble of besieging it. Zimmermann occupied Silistria and Bazardjik.

But on the 12th of February the British fleet in the Ægean passed through the Dardanelles and proceeded toward Constantinople, the British Government alleging that this step was necessary to protect the lives and property of their subjects at Constantinople. The British Ambassador had asked, in accordance with the Treaty of Paris, the permission of the Porte for this proceeding, but had been refused; the British then availed themselves of a permission granted under other circumstances some months previously, and their fleet passed through the Straits without regard to the Treaty of Paris. The Turkish Government remonstrated, but did not support their remonstrance by force; which was a prudent proceeding, since the four large ironclads (Alexandra, Devastation, Sultan, and Achilles), forming the main strength of the British fleet, were quite strong enough to have lain alongside the Turkish batteries and demolished them.

As soon as news of this movement on the part of the English was received at St. Petersburg, the Emperor telegraphed to the Grand Duke Nicholas, authorizing him to enter Constantinople with a part of his troops; and at the same time Prince Gortchakoff addressed a note to the Powers explaining to them that the Russian troops entered Constantinople for the same purpose that the British fleet arrived there, viz., the protection of the lives and property of the Christians inhabiting that city. It was however a fact, notorious to every one in Constantinople, that no disturbance either existed or was threatened there, and that life and property were then no more insecure in that city of religious fanatics than at any other time.

Upon the receipt of this telegram the Grand Duke immediately opened negotiations with the Sultan for occupying peacefully a portion of the environs of Constantinople with his troops; and in a few days a verbal agreement (with memorandum) was made, by which the armistice of January 31st was so far modified as to permit the Russians to occupy the village of San Stefano, on the Sea of Marmora, about six miles from the walls of Constantinople, and also to station troops in certain villages on its left (north).

The Turkish troops withdrew therefore to the immediate vicinity of Constantinople, and on the 23d of February the Grand Duke and Staff, accompanied by a regiment of Cossacks and his body-guard, left Adrianople by train and came down to San Stefano, where they arrived on the afternoon of the 24th. On the same day arrived the Preobrazhensky Regiment of the Guard, which had marched down from Rodosto. More troops soon arrived, and during the month of March the headquarters of the 1st and 2d Divisions of the Guard were at San Stefano, of the 3d Division at Kuyuk-Tchekmedje. Skobeleff's headquarters were at St. George, twelve miles north of San Stefano, and Radetzky's at Tchataldja.

At this time (the middle of March) there were but about 30,000 Turks in front of the Russian army, which could have entered Constantinople without any difficulty, from their positions at San Stefano and St. George. Such was, however, far from being the case at the latter part of May, when the Turks had succeeded in assembling an army of 100,000 men, and in erecting a series of strong earth-works around the city, from Makrikioi, on the Sea of Marmora, to the Belgrade forest, between the Bosphorus and the Black Sea.

On the 3d of March, at 5 P. M., was signed the Treaty of San Stefano, upon the basis of the terms of peace above stated.

REMARKS ON THE WINTER CAMPAIGN.

The Russian Campaign of 1877-'78, begun with the plan of crossing the Danube, masking the fortresses in the Quadrilateral, crushing the Turkish force in the field, and marching over the Balkans to Adrianople, was brought to a sudden halt immediately after the first part of the plan—the crossing of the Danube—had been accomplished, by two causes: first, the total inadequacy of the forces with which the campaign was begun; and, second, the opportune arrival of Osman Pasha's army on the right flank of the invaders. Until this obstacle could be removed no further advance was possible, and therefore for five months the campaign was paralyzed, and no forward progress was made.

I have endeavored in the preceding pages to narrate these circumstances as faithfully and accurately as possible; and the mistakes which caused them—and which the Russians most freely acknowledged—are patent to any one who examines the facts. The overweening confidence and contempt for their enemy which induced the Russians to open the campaign with half the force which was found necessary to conclude it; the lack of practical experience at the beginning of the war, which resulted in such ignorant attacks, without reconnaissances, as that of Schilder-Schuldner at Plevna on July 20th; the dispersion of the army into detachments scattered over an enormous extent of territory; the assault of intrenched camps with forces inferior to those of the defenders; the lack of tactical *ensemble* in the assaults—these are some of the faults which characterized the first two stages of the war, and brought delay in the progress of the struggle, and death to many a brave, willing man.

But once this obstacle of Plevna removed by the capture of Osman's army, the whole character of the campaign changed; and among the wars of this century, since those of the great Napoleon, we will seek in vain an instance of a movement more bold in conception, more energetic in execution, more overwhelmingly successful in its results, than the passage of the Balkans during the succeeding winter; and Russia owes a lasting debt of gratitude to the Grand Duke Nicholas, who determined that there *should be* a winter campaign; to Generals Gourko, Radetzky, and Skobeleff, who conducted it; and, above all, to the patience and willing endurance of the Russian soldier, which alone made it possible.

Beginning with the fall of Plevna on the 10th of December, it ended with the conclusion of the Armistice of Adrianople on the 31st of January; and in these fifty-one days the Russian armies had marched over 400 miles; had crossed a lofty range of mountains, where the snow was from three to ten feet deep, and the temperature as low as $-10°$ F.; had fought three series of battles, lasting from two to four days each, and resulting in the complete capture of one Turkish army of nearly 40,000 men, and the dispersion of another of over 50,000; had captured 213 guns, and small arms, baggage, tents, and supplies of all kinds, including cartridges and rations by the millions; and, finally, had been able to dictate such terms of peace to the conquered as to remove them permanently from the list of *independent* military nations. And this the Russians had accomplished with the loss of less than 20,000 men, of whom about half fell in battle, and the other half succumbed to the rigors of the season and climate.

Even after all criticism has been made upon the faults of the Russians at the beginning of the war and around Plevna, still the campaign as a whole must be judged to be the equal in brilliancy and the solidity of its results of any in recent history.

In the Franco-German War of 1870—the military marvel of modern times—the Prussians were as superior in numbers to the French as were the Russians at the close of this to the Turks, and the individual courage of the Turks is not surpassed by that of the French. By their skillful operations the Germans shut up Bazaine in Metz, captured MacMahon at Sedan (the counterparts of Plevna and Shipka), and then marched on Paris, the capital; which surrendered on the 28th of January, 1871, six months and nine days after the declaration of war. In the Russo-Turkish Campaign the Armistice of Adrianople was signed on the 31st of January, nine months and seven days after the declaration of war. In both cases the conquered nation lay absolutely at the mercy of the conqueror. France, owing to her wonderful vitality; to her resources both in agriculture and manufactures; to the skill, frugality, and industry of the great mass of her people, has astonished the world by regaining in the course of a few years her position among the first nations of the earth. Turkey, having none of these resources, and being a heterogeneous collection of conflicting nationalities and creeds, which the dominant race has never been able—if it has attempted —to assimilate, and having her national vitality destroyed by the degeneracy of the ruling class, seems destined never to rise again; but to be protected and propped up for a certain period by other nations having supposed interests in her maintenance, until this outside support shall have been proved wholly and incontestably to be ineffectual, when she will be succeeded by some other form of government for the countries now under her rule. As an *independent* Government, Turkey in Europe has ceased to exist, though the Sultan may yet live for many years on the European side of the Bosphorus. And this is the result of the campaign of 1877–'78.

Of other wars since the long peace, those of 1848 and 1859 are in no way remarkable in a military sense. The Crimean War was mainly a long siege—the most famous perhaps of authentic sieges—which certainly added little to the military fame of the assailants, though it resulted in political humiliation for a certain period to the nation of the defenders.

In the Austrian war of 1866, one great battle sufficed to prove to the Austrians that their wisest course lay in making peace, and the short duration of the campaign prevents any comparison with those of 1870 and 1877–'78.

Our own war from 1861 to 1865 is also difficult to compare with those in Europe, since the two combatants were of the same race, and their fighting qualities were so nearly equal, the theatre of war was so enormously extended and so difficult in general for military operations, and there were at the outset no trained armies of any magnitude. Such rapid and conclusive military movements as those in France and Turkey were therefore not to be expected. Grant's Vicksburg campaign will take its place in history alongside of Napoleon's beautiful campaign of 1796, for its boldness and success; Sherman's Atlanta campaign and march to the sea, and the combined movements of Grant and Sherman in the spring of 1865, will always stand out as magnificent examples of the skillful handling of large bodies of men; while, on the other hand, Lee's long defense of Richmond has placed his name for ever among the list of great soldiers. But it was a war of checkered successes and reverses for both sides, and it was finished, not by one bold movement, but by the absolute crushing of the military strength of the weaker by the stronger party.

It was the winter campaign of the Russians which destroyed the military strength of Turkey, and let us now turn to details and examine the means by which the Russians were able to overcome the difficulties which in this season usually bring military operations to a standstill.

The great and preëminent cause of their success lay in the almost boundless patience and endurance of the Russian soldier. From the time the movement was well under way the men never saw their knapsacks, which remained north of the Balkans, till some time after the armistice. They marched and fought and slept in snow and ice, and forded rivers with the thermometer at zero. They had no blankets, and the frozen ground precluded all idea of tents; the half-worn-out shelter-tents which the men had used during the summer were now cut up to tie around their boots, which were approaching dissolution; and, although an effort was made to shelter the men in the huts in the villages, yet always at least half of them had to sleep out in the open air without shelter. Their clothing at night was the same as in the day, and it differed from that of the summer only in the addition of an overcoat, woolen jacket, and a "bashlik" or woolen muffler for the head. Their food was a pound of hard bread and a pound and a half of tough stringy beef, driven along the road; they were forced to carry six and even eight days' rations on their backs (in addition to an extra supply of cartridges in their pockets); there was more than one instance where the men fought, and fought well, not only without breakfast, but without having tasted food in twenty-four hours. Yet, in face of these unusual privations and hardships, there was not a single case of insubordination; the men were usually in good spirits, and the number of stragglers on the march was far less than during the heat of the preceding summer.

The ordinary, and usually insurmountable, difficulties of a winter campaign may be classed under three heads:

1. The supply of food for men and animals;
2. The supply and transportation of material—ammunition, clothing, camp equipage, etc.;

3. The sickness and suffering among the men and animals.

I will endeavor to explain how all these were overcome or done away in the present instance.

First, as to food. Northern Bulgaria was at the beginning of winter practically exhausted of its supplies of forage and breadstuffs beyond the immediate wants of its inhabitants. Of cattle and sheep, however, there was still a certain quantity available. These were bought by the various colonels from the regimental commissariat fund ("soup money") at whatever price they could bargain for; but the maximum price was fixed at 20 roubles gold ($15.60) per head for cattle of a weight of 300 to 350 lbs., and 1½ silver roubles ($1.10) per head for sheep weighing 30 to 40 lbs. If the peasants refused to sell for less, the colonels were authorized to take by force at these prices, which were from one quarter to one third greater than current prices before the war (many regiments in fact succeeded, especially at first, in buying at much cheaper rates), and the cash was always paid down when the cattle were taken. This inspired great confidence among the peasants, and instead of attempting to conceal their flocks and herds, they brought them to the Russians for sale. Of hard bread and a certain kind of desiccated or "conserved" food for horses, a considerable supply had been accumulated during the summer and autumn in the depot at Sistova. But the Danube bridges were all either carried away in the storm of December 18th-23d, or taken up on account of the ice, and there was then no communication across the river except by a few steam-tugs acting as ferry-boats. Early in January the river froze solid, and carts began to pass on the ice; but this was always more or less dangerous, and it broke up in February. During the time of the active operations, therefore (December 15th to January 25th), it may be said that there was no communication across the Danube, and the only resource of the Russians in the way of base of provisions was therefore the depot at Sistova. But from this they drew their hard bread only; for the rest they lived on the country and on the supplies captured from the Turks. By the celerity and boldness of their movements, war was in truth made to feed war. At Orkhanie was captured 1,000 tons of rations, at Sophia 4,000 tons, at Kazanlyk 1,000 tons. They consisted principally of flour, rice, barley, beans, salt, oats, and a small amount of coffee, sugar, hard bread, and salt meat. But these articles were not portable, and they were enjoyed by the garrisons left behind to guard them; but the troops moving so rapidly in advance must have hard bread, and of this there was unfortunately but a small quantity in the Turkish depots, and it had to be brought, as just stated, from Sistova. For the other articles of the ration—such as tea, sugar, spirits of wine, vinegar, gruel, cabbage, etc.—the men simply had to do without them. The campaign was made on hard bread and the cattle driven along on the hoof—nothing more. Skobeleff's men on the march between Adrianople and Tchataldja were for a part of the time without hard bread even; they were only kept from starving by the extraordinary energy and administrative capacity shown by their young chief in organizing bakeries in every village along the line of his march, and making the peasants bake soft bread enough to last for a day or two days at a time; thus tiding over the difficulty until the armistice brought his march to a halt and enabled him to take other measures.

The country south of the Balkans, particularly the valleys of Sophia and of the Maritza, is *most abundantly* rich in cattle and sheep, grains and rough forage. The Turks had need of this up to the last moment for themselves, and then it was too late to destroy it thoroughly. They set fire to nearly every village on the line of their retreat; but the houses and stacks were covered with snow, and the Russians were so close upon their heels that they arrived in time to put out the fires before they had made much progress. What would have happened had the Turks laid waste their country as the Russians did theirs in 1812, is of course a mere matter of conjecture. The fact as it actually occurred is that the Russians in 1877-'78 overcame the difficulty of food supply by drawing their hard bread from depots previously accumulated on the southern bank of the Danube, and for the rest lived on the country and the supplies captured from the Turks.

Secondly, as to material. All efforts to supply tents or clothing were abandoned, if indeed they were ever contemplated. The men wore the same clothing which they had brought into the campaign and had worn all through the summer and autumn. Their knapsacks were all left behind with the company wagons on the north of the Balkans, and in fact there was not much in them. A little clothing was captured from the Turks at Orkhanie, but not more than enough for one or two regiments. The Turkish dead after every fight were stripped of their clothing for immediate use, but this also afforded very little. Whenever a day's halt was made the men did what they could to patch up their clothing, but at the close of the campaign most of them presented a sorry appearance, with overcoats and trousers burnt by bivouac fires, and gaping boots wrapped up in gunny-sacks and pieces of canvas.

For ammunition the artillery was able to take care of itself without other means of transport. The artillery park nearest the Danube received its ammunition (before the bridges were destroyed) from the railroad which was built up to Zimnitza; it transported this to the next park, and so on until it reached the battery at the front. For Gourko's column, for instance, there were parks at Sistova, Gorni-Dubnik, Orkhanie, and Sophia. Moreover, the artillery was very numerous, its normal strength being 4 guns to 1,000 men; and as the number of men was constantly diminishing, while the number of guns remained the same, it was practically between 6 and 7 pieces to 1,000 men. This was more than necessary; and in Gourko's column half the artillery was left on the north of the Balkans, and did not rejoin the troops until long after they had reached San Stefano.

Skobeleff and Mirsky, as we have seen, crossed the Balkans at Shipka without any artillery, and Skobeleff began his forward march with only about 2 pieces for 1,000 men, leaving the rest to rejoin him when it could.

The infantry ammunition consisted of 48 rounds for the Krenk system, or 60 rounds for the Berdan, carried in two cartridge-boxes; in addition to this, the men carried about 30 to 40 rounds in their pockets, and 100 rounds per man additional accompanied the troops on pack-horses. This gave nearly 200 rounds per man immediately disposable; this was not all used. To provide against emergencies, however, several trains of intendance wagons loaded with cartridges were on the road between Sistova and the Balkans, but the armistice came before they were needed.

Many millions of cartridges were captured from the Turks, but they were of caliber ·45 (Peabody-Martini), whereas the

Russian Berdan was caliber ·42 and the Krenk caliber ·60. They were therefore of no use. Skobeleff got permission on the fall of Plevna to arm one of his regiments with captured Peabody-Martini guns, but there was no time in the midst of the campaign to make any extensive changes of armament of that nature, and it would have been imprudent, at least, to count upon the capture of Turkish ammunition as a certainty.

Lastly, as to the health of the men and horses. Gourko lost about 2,000 men, *hors de combat* from freezing, during the storm of December 18th–23d, before his movement began. During the movement Dandeville's column lost about 1,000 more. At Shipka the 24th Division lost over 6,000 men (80 per cent. of its strength) during the same storm, and was for the moment completely disorganized and useless. After the march was fairly begun there were several hundreds more or less who gave way under the cold or were frozen, but the number was not very great—not so much greater than the sunstroke and diarrhœa cases in the terrible heat of summer, as to be particularly noticeable. Once well in the valley of the Maritza, the climate was not so severe, though still cold enough and accompanied with plenty of snow. But for the moment there was not much sickness. In this march, however, bad food and the lack of change of clothing laid the seeds of the typhus and typhoid fevers which broke out at San Stefano in the following month of May, with such terrible malignity that at one time 50,000 men, 45 per cent. of the whole force stationed thereabout, were in the hospitals.

As for the animals, the cavalry, being always in advance, found plenty of forage, and managed to keep in pretty fair condition; but the artillery horses, than which I never saw a finer looking lot of animals as they passed in review at Gorni-Studen in October, were a sad-looking lot of skeletons when they arrived at San Stefano the next February, even although only the best horses had been selected for the march, the rest having been left with the guns which remained north of the Balkans. Their march had been a very hard one, the roads being almost everywhere covered with smooth ice, on which they fell and hurt themselves a great deal; being always with the infantry, they nearly always found the forage in the various villages eaten up by the cavalry which had preceded them; and it was suspected that no small portion of their desiccated food had found its way into the mouths of the hungry gunners. All the baggage-wagons were left behind the Balkans, the officers' baggage in very limited quantities being taken along on a few pack-horses. The men had no baggage except what they could stow away in the pockets of their overcoats; their rations they carried on their backs.

The only vehicles which kept up with the troops were a few hospital ambulances, in which the wounded of each affair were carried to the nearest village and left there until they could be collected by the sanitary department and transported in country carts to the large hospitals at Sophia, Philippopolis, Adrianople, Kazanlyk, etc.

In brief, then, it may be said that the natural difficulties of a winter campaign were overcome by the extraordinary patience and physical endurance of the men, by the untiring energy of their commanders, Gourko and Skobeleff, and by the fact that all impedimenta were left behind; and that, in spite of the inclement season, the men were deprived of everything but the very minimum of food necessary for life, and of arms and ammunition for warfare.

PART III.

THE CAMPAIGN IN ARMENIA.

THE CAMPAIGN IN ARMENIA.

CHAPTER I.

PROGRESS OF THE CAMPAIGN FROM THE DECLARATION OF WAR TO THE BATTLE OF ALADJA DAGH, OCTOBER 15, 1877.

THE topography of the theatre of war in Asia Minor is of the most complicated nature. (See Plate 3.) The Armenian plateau, of which Erzeroum may be considered the center, is at an altitude of 6,000 feet and more above the sea; on the northwest and northeast it terminates somewhat abruptly in the Black Sea and the Georgian valley south of the Caucasus range; on the east it stretches away through Persia, and ends abruptly in the Caspian; to the southeast it sends off a long spur of mountains which stop only at the Indus; on its southern side are the wide plains of Mesopotamia and the valleys of the Tigris and Euphrates; west of it are the confused mountains of Asia Minor.

This plateau is drained to the Caspian by the Araxes, to the Black Sea by the Joruk, to the Persian Gulf by the Tigris and Euphrates. The head waters of the first two of these streams and of the two arms of the Euphrates are interlocked in the region about Erzeroum; they are separated by parallel chains running northeast and southwest, and attaining an altitude of between 9,000 and 10,000 feet above the sea. In addition to these mountain ranges there are peaks, such as Mount Ararat, 16,000 feet above sea, and minor ranges and groups of mountains, rising from 4,000 to 6,000 feet above the plateau; so that the whole country is a mass of mountains and gorges with only here and there an inclosed valley of 100 to 200 square miles of cultivable ground. The principal of these valleys are those of Erzingan, Erzeroum, Kars, Bayazid, and Musch.

The capital of Armenia is Erzeroum, and from here radiate all its principal routes of travel. These consist of one macadamized high-road, or chaussée, 185 miles long, from Erzeroum to Trebizond, on the Black Sea; and of more or less passable roads to Ardahan, to Kars, to Bayazid (the principal caravan road to Persia), to Van, to Bitlis (in the direction of Mesopotamia), and to Erzingan (on the west). There is also a common road from Batoum on the Black Sea to Ardahan, and a chaussée in process of construction to replace the old road. The ordinary means of transportation throughout the country are pack animals, with an occasional variety of ox-carts; the whole *vilayet* or province of Erzeroum counts but 600,000 inhabitants, and the want of good roads is not much felt; Erzeroum has about 60,000 inhabitants, Kars 30,000; there are half a dozen other towns containing perhaps 10,000 inhabitants each; the rest of the population lives in small villages, and no inconsiderable portion of it is made up of the Kurds and other mounted vagabonds and brigands.

The Russian frontier (as it existed in 1877) begins on the Black Sea between Poti and Batoum, and runs along the mountains in a southeast direction for about 150 miles until it reaches the Arpa Tchai (Arpa river), follows this for 100 miles until it empties into the Araxes, crosses this stream, and then runs east for another 100 miles to Mount Ararat, the corner-stone of the boundaries of Russia, Turkey, and Persia.

For the defense of this frontier the Turks had in 1877 four fortresses, Batoum, Ardahan, Kars, and Bayazid. The last, lying in the valley south of Mount Ararat, and separated from Russia by a high range of mountains, was in a very poor state of defense; the three former, however, had in the twenty years following the Crimean War been strengthened and extended under the direction of foreign engineers, and were formidable places; they consisted each of a stone citadel and a series of eight to twelve detached forts, partly in masonry and partly in earth. Kars mounted about 300 guns, and Ardahan 100.

The principal fortress on the Russian side was at Alexandropol (formerly Gumri), where the road from Tiflis to Erzeroum crosses the Arpa Tchai. From Alexandropol to Kars there are three roads in the Kars valley, and the distance is about 45 miles. From Kars to Erzeroum the distance is about 170 miles; the road follows the Kars River to its source, crosses a range of mountains known as the Soganli, descends into the valley of the Araxes, follows up this stream for some distance, crosses another range called the Deve Boyum, and descends into the Erzeroum valley. In the valley of the Araxes this road is joined by the road from Bayazid, which lies on a branch of the Araxes, beyond the head of the eastern branch of the Euphrates; the distance from Bayazid to Erzeroum is about 200 miles.

Midway between Alexandropol and the Black Sea, the Russians had another fortress at the town of Akhaltsik; from it to Ardahan is a distance of 70 miles by the road; thence there is a road to the southward, winding over mountains and valleys, but parallel in its general course to the Kars Erzeroum road, and reaching after a distance of 120 miles the partially fortified town of Olti, whence one road leads to Erzeroum and the other to Baiburt, midway between Erzeroum and Trebizond.

During the autumn of 1876 and the succeeding winter the Russian troops in the Caucasus had been mobilized for war, under the orders of the Grand Duke Michael (eldest brother of the Emperor), Lord Lieutenant of the Caucasus. The plan of invasion was to advance in four columns, viz. :

1. The *Rion Detachment*, which was to guard the Black Sea coast and endeavor to take Batoum ;

2. The *Akhaltsik Detachment*, which was to advance against Ardahan ;

3. The *Alexandropol Detachment*, which was to advance against Kars ;

4. The *Erivan Detachment*, which was to advance against Bayazid.

Judging from the course of the campaign, their further plan was to gain possession of Ardahan and Bayazid, invest Kars, and with detachments Nos. 2 and 4 and a part of No. 3 to advance on converging roads toward Erzeroum. From the nature of the country, the Rion Detachment was from the very first wholly independent of the others.

These various detachments were made up from five infantry divisions, a rifle brigade, and a horde of Cossacks, distributed as follows:

	Battalions.	Foot-guns.	Squadrons.	Horse-guns.	
41st Infantry Division	16	48	..	..	
19th Infantry Division (2d Brigade)	8	24	..	..	
Caucasian Rifle Brigade (part)	2	..	..	..	Rion Detachment, Lieutenant-General *Oklobjio*.
2d Regiment Kuban Cossacks	..	..	6	12	
Regiment Kutais Cossacks	..	..	6		
Total	26	72	12	12	
39th Infantry Division	16	48	..	..	
Regiment Kuban Cossacks	..	..	6	6	Akhaltsyk Detachment, Lieutenant-General *Devel*.
Regiment Terek Cossacks	..	..	4		
Total	16	48	10	54	
4th (Caucasian) Grenadier Division	16	48	..	..	
19th Infantry Division (1st Brigade)	8	24	..	..	
Division Caucasian Dragoons	..	..	16	12	Alexandropol Detachment, Lieutenant-General *Loris-Melikoff*.
Division Caucasian Cossacks	..	..	22	12	
Regiment Daghestan Cossacks	..	..	6	..	
2 regiments Volga Cossacks	..	..	8	6	
Total	24	72	52	30	
38th Infantry Division	16	48	..	..	Erivan Detachment, Lieutenant-General *Tergukassoff*.
8 regiments Kuban Cossacks	..	..	18	6	
Total	16	48	18	6	
Grand total	82	192	92	102	

A sapper battalion accompanied each column; and there was in the Caucasus a siege train of 336 guns, of various calibres, of which one half was mobilized.

Omitting the Rion Detachment, which had no connection with the main columns, the force with which the Russians began operations in Armenia was about 55,000 infantry, 10,000 cavalry, and 210 field-guns of all kinds.

The Turkish forces in Armenia at the outbreak of the war, under command of Moukhtar Pasha, numbered in all something over 70,000 men and 108 field-guns, distributed as follows:*

	Battalions.	Men.
Batoum		20,000
Ardahan	10	7,500
Kars	34	25,500
Erzeroum	11	8,250
At other points	12	9,000
Total	67	70,250

* The numbers of battalions and guns here given are taken from p. 4 of "The Armenian Campaign," by Charles Williams, correspondent of "The Standard," who states that they were taken from a report made by the British Military Agent (General Kemball) in April, 1877. I have taken the battalions as having an average strength of 750 men. Mr. Williams thinks their strength was much less. On the other hand, the correspondent of the "Daily News" at Moukhtar's headquarters

He was, however, lamentably deficient in cavalry, having less than 1,000 organized troops.

On the 24th of April the troops of all four of the Russian columns crossed the frontier.

Loris-Melikoff's column advanced along the Kars road, capturing some Turkish pickets numbering in all about a hundred men; his cavalry reached that evening the Kars River, and on their approach the Turkish detachment of 5,000 or 6,000 men posted behind that stream retired to Kars. Loris-Melikoff continued his march, and on the 28th established himself about 10 miles northwest of Kars, at the village of Zaim, on the road to Ardahan, thus cutting off all communication between those two places. (See Plate 22.)

On the same day Moukhtar Pasha took 5,000 men and fell back to the Soganli range, 40 miles from Kars, on the road to Erzeroum. He left 15,000 men or more as a garrison for Kars. Loris-Melikoff then began a series of reconnaissances of the forts of Kars on all sides, and at the same time sent strong columns of cavalry to the south as far as Kagisman, which they occupied without resistance, and thence west to the road in rear of Kars, along which they destroyed the telegraph for a long distance. Moukhtar Pasha, supposing the Russian forces to be very much greater than they really were, fell back to Zevin.

On the 8th of May, in one of the reconnaissances on the west of Kars, the Cossacks captured a Turkish messenger making his way along a by-road to Kars. From the dispatches captured on his person Loris Melikoff learned the weak condition of the garrison of Ardahan, and immediately resolved to detach a portion of his force from before Kars to proceed to Ardahan, and make an attack upon that place in conjunction with the column marching from Akhaltsik. This latter column had arrived in front of Ardahan on the 28th of April, and on the 1st of May had established communication by its Cossacks with the troops in front of Kars; the distance between the two places is 45 miles. It had since been engaged in reconnoitering the defenses of Ardahan, and in bringing up siege-guns, mortars, etc. The roads were in a terrible condition; the winter was not yet

states in one of his letters that that Pasha told him he had at the beginning of the campaign 52,000 men under his orders, exclusive of the garrison of Batoum. ("Daily News Correspondence," Vol. I., pp. 102, 348.)

over, snow and rain storms succeeded each other, and the road between Akhaltsik and Ardahan, over which the siege material had to be brought, passed over an ascent of 7,000 feet. The difficulties of this column were not slight.

The troops detached from the camp in front of Kars to march to Ardahan, consisting of the 13th and 15th Grenadiers, 24 guns, a regiment of Dragoons, and 8 sotnias of Cossacks—about 8,000 men in all, under the orders of Lieutenant-General Heimann—left Zaim on the 10th of May, and arrived in front of Ardahan on the 13th. Loris-Melikoff arrived in person on the same day, and on the 14th made a reconnaissance of the place, and gave the necessary orders for the attack. It was found that the town was surrounded with six casemated works of strong profile, and armed with heavy guns, but all of them commanded from heights two to three miles distant. Of these heights the two most important, called Gheliaverde and Ramazan, were occupied, and fortified with strong works. Gheliaverde was on the east, Ramazan on the west of the town; they were some miles apart, and were separated by the Kour River, on which the town is situated. Ramazan was the more difficult and inaccessible of the two, but its fortifications were so constructed that they could only be used against the west. General Heimann's troops were ordered to threaten the town on the south and bombard the heights of Gheliaverde, while those of General Devel were to assault these heights in front, i. e., from the east.

On the 15th the siege artillery arrived, and during the night batteries were constructed, and the guns and mortars brought into position. On the morning of the 16th the bombardment was opened with 40 guns against the Gheliaverde height, besides other batteries directed against the town and its defenses. The artillery appears to have been very well directed, and to have done great damage. It not only seriously injured the fortifications upon this hill, but inflicted great losses upon the defenders. Meanwhile the troops of General Devel (153d and 156th Regiments) were climbing the hill of Gheliaverde on its eastern face, exposed to the fire of the Turks on the hill, and covered by the fire of their own batteries in rear as well as by those of General Heimann on their left flank. They reached the top of the hill about 10 o'clock, and immediately drove the Turks back to the fort (called Emir Ogli), about 600 paces in rear, and separated from them by a deep ravine. After giving his troops a little rest, General Devel sent them forward to the attack of this work, which they finally carried about 1 P. M. It contained 10 guns, besides great quantities of ammunition and stores.

The position thus acquired gave the Russians a foothold from which to conduct their further operations, and they worked all that night and part of the next day in getting their guns into position; the bombardment did not begin until 3 P. M. on the 17th. It had been intended to continue the bombardment during the 17th and 18th, but the effect of the artillery was so destructive upon the enemy's works and upon the enemy himself, who was seen to be withdrawing a portion of his men, that Loris-Melikoff determined to assault that same afternoon (17th) in spite of the lateness of the hour. The attack was made at 6 o'clock by the 13th and 16th Grenadiers and the 153d Regiment, advancing against the works on the southeast of the town. The Turks did not wait to receive them, but abandoned these works, fled through the town, and dispersed in the mountains to the west. They were pursued until after dark by the Cossacks. Fort Ramazan was not defended by them at all. The Russians occupied the whole place by 9 o'clock in the evening. Their losses were 4 officers and 114 men on the 16th, and 11 officers and 410 men on the 17th, or a total loss of less than 550 men. They captured about 1,000 prisoners, 92 guns (two of which were 8-inch, five 6-inch, and the majority of the rest 4-inch Krupp siege-guns), and great quantities of ammunition and stores. There were 1,750 Turkish bodies buried by the Russians, and the total Turkish losses were estimated at 3,000. About half the garrison, therefore, were killed, wounded, or taken prisoners, and the other half escaped into the mountains and disbanded. The losses of the Turks were occasioned almost wholly by the Russian artillery, which seems to have been admirably served.

Leaving a small garrison in Ardahan, Loris-Melikoff sent a detachment in the direction of Olti, and with General Heimann's detachment returned to the vicinity of Kars, arriving there on the 25th of May. Olti was occupied without opposition on the 1st of June, the Turkish garrison retiring to Erzeroum.

Meanwhile the Erivan column, under General Tergukassoff, had crossed the frontier on the 27th of April, and, although delayed somewhat by the difficulties of the road, had arrived in front of Bayazid on the 30th. The Turkish garrison, numbering only 2,000 men, fled at their approach, and dispersed in the Ala Mountains on the south of the town. Leaving a garrison of between 2,000 and 3,000 men in Bayazid, Tergukassoff took up his march (May 8th) to the west, and, descending the valley of the Euphrates, arrived at the village of Kara-Kilissa, from which a detachment of some 3,000 or 4,000 Turks retreated on his approach. On the 10th of May Tergukassoff occupied the town of Alashkert, and advanced westward to the town of Daiar, only 15 miles from the junction of the Bayazid and Kars roads; but here he was obliged to come to a halt in face of large bodies of Turkish troops. He was also considerably worried about his rear, as he received information that the troops which had evacuated Bayazid had reformed in the Ala Mountains and the region of Lake Van, just south of them, and were collecting a large force of Kurds with whom they intended to attack Bayazid from the south. Tergukassoff detached a small portion of his troops to return and make reconnaissances to establish the truth of this report, and with the rest of his troops remained at Daiar, where he was attacked on the 21st of June by the Turks, but held his ground, with a loss of over 400 men.

Loris-Melikoff, having returned to the vicinity of Kars on the 25th of May, immediately began establishing siege batteries on the north, west, and east of the place (about 60 guns and mortars were established by the 25th of June), and at the same time sent his cavalry on both sides of Kars to the south to endeavor to establish communications with Tergukassoff's column and to reconnoiter the position of Moukhtar Pasha at Zevin. On the 15th of June the Turks made a sortie on the northwest of Kars, but were repulsed by the Grenadiers under General Heimann. They left 200 dead on the field, and the Russian losses were about 150 men in all.

Meanwhile the bombardment of Kars continued, with slight losses on both sides.

During the latter part of June Loris-Melikoff, leaving in front of Kars a portion of the Ardahan column and of the 19th Division, advanced west of Kars with the Grenadier Division under General Heimann to the Erzeroum road, and thence along that road over the Soganli range to the position of Moukhtar

Pasha at Zevin. The latter had here 23 battalions (say 15,000 men) in a good position, selected in advance and well fortified. On the 25th of June Heimann assaulted this position, but met with a complete repulse and the loss of 900 men.

Meanwhile the little garrison of Bayazid had in fact been completely surrounded by about 10,000 infantry and a horde of Kurds (said to have numbered over 20,000 men). On the 18th of June the Turkish troops under Faik Pasha and the Kurds entered the town, massacred the greater part of the population, and set fire to the houses. The Russian troops, too feeble in numbers to prevent this massacre, shut themselves up in the citadel and sustained a siege, refusing to surrender, since they knew that if they did so the same fate awaited them as had overtaken the inhabitants of the town. The besiegers had a certain amount of artillery, with which they bombarded the citadel and pretty well knocked it to pieces; but whenever they attempted an assault, the Russians defended themselves with such desperation that they were driven back.

Learning this state of affairs, it became absolutely necessary for Tergukassoff to return to the relief of Bayazid; and as it was impossible for his column and that of Heimann to unite and overcome Moukhtar in his position at Zevin, it was also necessary for Heimann to retreat to the neighborhood of Kars. The two Russian columns therefore returned on divergent roads, Heimann to Kars, and Tergukassoff through Alashkert, and across the Russian frontier to Igdyr, whence he had begun his movement in advance six weeks before. Reorganizing his troops here, and disembarrassing himself of a large number of refugees who had accompanied his retreat, Tergukassoff then moved rapidly by the same road as before from Igdyr to Bayazid, attacked the besieging forces, who made very little resistance—the brigands of Kurds in particular scattering in all directions on his approach—and on the 10th of July relieved the little garrison of 1,600 men, which had sustained a siege of twenty-three days, marked by very great hardship and suffering. They had for several days been living on dead horses and a few spoonfuls of water per day; during the siege they had lost about 500 men in killed and wounded. After destroying what remained of the citadel, Tergukassoff returned with his troops across the frontier to Igdyr. The Turkish force under Ismail Pasha, which had been following Tergukassoff during his retreat, moved so slowly as to arrive at Bayazid too late to prevent the relief of the garrison.

Of the Rion detachment, charged with the defense of the coast and the capture if possible of Batoum, we need only say that it had made no farther progress than the town of Tchikhidsiri, situated on the coast about four miles south of the frontier, and in arriving thus far had lost about 300 men in various combats. Here they attacked on the 23d of June the intrenched camp of about 4,000 Turks under Dervish Pasha, but were repulsed with a loss of 500 men. They saw that they were not strong enough to carry this position, and it was impossible to turn it, for there was an inaccessible range of mountains on one side and the Black Sea on the other, and in the latter were two or three Turkish ironclads which shelled their flank. Their retreat was necessitated partly by these causes, and partly because the Turkish fleet had been bombarding various villages along the coast for a distance of 60 or 70 miles from Poti, and had also landed a force of 1,000 or more Tcherkesses, who had penetrated into the coast districts of Abkhasia and stirred up revolt among the mountain tribes of that locality. The Rion detachment therefore retreated across the frontier into the valley, and was occupied for some months in watching the coast against possible further landings of Turks, and in putting down the insurrections. Before they were able to resume the offensive in proper force, winter had set in; and, in short, Batoum was still in the hands of the Turks when the armistice of January 31st was concluded. It is not necessary, therefore, to refer any more to the Rion detachment; it had no influence whatever upon the campaign.

We thus see that at the beginning of July the offensive campaign of the Russians in Armenia had come to a halt, and for the same reason as in Bulgaria, i. e., lack of sufficient troops. Moukhtar Pasha had conducted his operations very prudently and very successfully. He had about 42,000 men at his disposal, but having no cavalry to keep him posted about the enemy, he believed their forces to be what they were represented to be in the newspapers, i. e., 100,000, whereas in truth they were but very little superior to his own. Leaving a small garrison in Kars, he kept the bulk of his troops near the junction of the roads from Kars and Bayazid, prevented the two Russian columns which were advancing on these roads from uniting, selected a good position (Zevin) for defense, and invited an attack there—which the Russians made on the 25th of June. Meeting with a total repulse, the latter were obliged to retreat, to raise the siege of Kars, if it could be called a siege, and to retire to the line of the Kars River (ten miles in front of Alexandropol), where they arrived about the middle of July. Ardahan was still in their possession, but otherwise the Russians were just where they were at the declaration of war, and minus about 10,000 men.

Moukhtar meanwhile was constantly recruiting his forces, and arming and organizing them. He followed the Russians toward Kars, slowly and without attacking, and then took up a position across the plain of Kars, his left flank resting on the fortress and his right near the Arpa River, the boundary line.

When the news of the retreat of Loris-Melikoff and the general failure of the campaign after the battle of Zevin (June 25th) reached the Emperor's headquarters in Bulgaria, orders were given for the mobilization of the 1st Grenadier Division and the 40th Division of the Line, and their dispatch to the army in Armenia as reënforcements. The 20th and 21st Divisions, quartered in Daghestan and along the Terek, were also mobilized, but they were simply used to put down the insurrections in their neighborhood, and they did not cross the Caucasus. The Grenadier Division had 1,400 miles of railroad travel, from Moscow to Vladikavkas, and nearly 200 miles of march, from the latter point to Alexandropol. The 40th Division, quartered in the neighborhood of Saratoff on the Volga, had 1,000 miles of boat and railroad travel, and also 200 miles of march. The latter began to arrive at Alexandropol about the middle of August, and the last of the Grenadiers reached the same point September 25th.

Meanwhile Loris-Melikoff had the Caucasus Grenadier Division, the 1st Brigade of the 39th Division (previously at Ardahan), the 2d Brigade of the 38th Division, and the 2d Brigade of the 19th Division—about 35,000 men (infantry) in all, besides 5,000 or more Cossacks. He occupied a position in front of the Kars River, facing southwest, his right at Kuruk-Dara, near the road from Alexandropol to Kars, his center at

388   THE CAMPAIGN IN ARMENIA.

Kizil Tepe, and his left at the ruins of Ani, on the river Arpa. (See Plate 22.) The length of his front was about 15 miles.

In front of him were: 1. The garrison of Kars, 16,000 infantry, 30 field-guns, 1,000 cavalry, and over 300 siege-guns; 2. The field army of Moukhtar Pasha, 20,000 infantry, 54 field- and mountain-guns, and 6,000 cavalry. The latter was posted along the northern slope of the Aladja Mountains, with its right flank facing the Russian left at Ani and its left (including part of the Kars garrison) thrown out into the plain at the two hills known as Great and Little Yahni, near the road from Kars to Alexandropol.

The topography of the country in which the two armies were situated is somewhat peculiar. A few miles southeast of the town of Kars begin two ranges of mountains, which run in a southeasterly direction to the river Arpa. The more northern range is about 20 miles long, and is known as the Aladja Dagh * (God's Mountain). In front of the mountain (i. e., north of it) lies the plain of Kars, about 2,000 feet below its summits, through which winds the Kars Tchai, emptying into the Arpa Tchai. This plain is studded with a number of hills, the two Yahni, Kizil Tepe, Uch Tepe, etc., with bluff sides rising from 400 to 600 feet above the plain. These hills had of course considerable tactical importance for the respective armies.

The latter part of July and the early part of August were occupied in numerous reconnaissances on both sides, and the skirmishes resulting from them, but nothing serious occurred.

On the 18th of August, Loris-Melikoff, having a few days previously sent one of his brigades to the assistance of Tergukassoff, who was confronted by a force of over 10,000 men under Ismail Pasha in the region of Erivan and Igdyr, and wishing to divert the attention of the Turks in his front from this movement, made an attack, or possibly a demonstration, against the Turkish left flank at the Yahni hills; he did not carry the hills, and at evening he retired, the losses being about 500 men on each side. For the next few days there was considerable skirmishing in front of both lines, and on the 24th

---

* The following Turkish words are useful to remember in topographical nomenclature:

Dagh, mountain.   *Tchai*, a large river.
Tepe, hill.   *Su*, a small river.

the Russians appeared to be withdrawing from their left to strengthen their right flank, possibly with the intention of renewing the attack of the 18th. Moukhtar thought this a favorable opportunity to strike a blow, and during the night he concentrated about 10,000 men on his right flank, and at daylight sent them forward to the assault of Kizil Tepe. The latter was held by only one or two Russian battalions, owing to their recent concentration on their right flank, and these were easily driven out. The Russians quickly brought up part of their troops from their right, and a severe fight took place, lasting all day, the principal struggle being around the front of the village of Subotan, to the west of Kizil Tepe. Neither side appears to have gained much advantage, and the fight ceased at dark, Kizil Tepe and Subotan, however, remaining in the hands of the Turks. The results of this day's fighting were a loss of about 2,000 men on each side (perhaps more on the Russian), and the doubling up in a measure of their left flank. If Moukhtar ever had any serious intentions of carrying the war into the Russian territory, this was his opportunity; by energetically following up his attack the next day, he might possibly have cut off the Russians from Alexandropol, or have compelled their retreat in that direction. But he did not follow up his success. What were the reasons for his inaction is mere matter of speculation. For his victory on this day the Sultan conferred upon him the title of Ghazi (Victorious), which, in view of the total destruction of his army less than two months later, is somewhat devoid of meaning.

During the month of September nothing whatever of consequence took place on either side of the opposing troops in the valley of Kars. Near Erivan there were some affairs of an unimportant character between the detachment of Ismail Pasha and that of Tergukassoff, the former attacking the latter in the mountain defile southwest of Erivan, but accomplishing nothing except the loss of a few hundred men. Ismail Pasha had under his orders a force of 40 battalions (at least 20,000 men), made up largely of reënforcements recently arrived from Trebizond and from the districts of Mesopotamia, besides a large force of Kurds. Tergukassoff's detachment had been reënforced by some troops sent to him under the orders of Lieutenant-General Devel, so that now he had three regiments of the 19th Division (Nos. 73, 74, and 76), two of the 38th (Nos. 149 and 150), and two of the 39th (Nos. 153 and 154); or in all 28 battalions, numbering about 22,000 men.

Ismail Pasha made no impression upon Tergukassoff; and the latter made no serious movement against the Turks, since he wished to retain them where they were and not drive them back to effect a junction with Moukhtar.

By the latter part of September the whole of the reënforcements (1st Division Grenadiers and 40th Division) had arrived, and the Grand Duke Michael, who had personally assumed command of the army, was ready to resume the offensive.

The troops under his orders in the plain of Kars were as follows:

	Battalions.	Guns.	Squadrons.	Horse-Guns.
1st Division Grenadiers, Lieutenant-General *Roop*.............	12	48	..	..
4th (Caucasian) Division Grenadiers, Lieutenant-General *Heimann*..	16	48	..	..
19th Division (one Regiment, No. 75).............................	4	..	..	..
38th Division (Regiments 151 and 152)............................	8	24	..	..
39th Division (Regiments 153, 155, and 156)....................	12	24	..	..
Caucasian Rifle Brigade (1st and 4th Battalions).................	2	..	..	..
40th Division..	12	48	..	..
Division Caucasian Dragoons	..	..	16	12
Various Cossack Regiments (see p. 880)...........................	..	..	46	24
Total..	66	192	62	36

or about 55,000 infantry, 8,000 cavalry, and 228 guns.

The Turkish army opposed to him (including the garrison of Kars) numbered about 36,000 * infantry, a considerable force of cavalry (of very poor quality), and about 150 guns. They still occupied the position (see Plate 22) extending from the Yahni hills through Kizil Tepe to Uch Tepe, near the Arpa Tchai.

The Russian plan was to overwhelm the Turkish left flank and cut them off from Kars.

On the 2d of October the Russians attacked as follows: *a*,

---

* This number is ascertained as follows:

Taken prisoners October 14th–15th	7,000
" " in Kars November 18th	17,000
Escaped with Moukhtar Pasha after defeat of October 15th......	2,800
Sick and wounded in hospitals at Kars	4,500
Killed and wounded in battles of October 3d and 14th, and November 18th	5,000
Total	36,300

BATTLE OF ALADJA DAGH. 391

1st Grenadier Division against Little Yahni; *b*, portions of 38th and 39th Divisions against Great Yahni; *c*, part of the 4th Grenadier Division against Subotan and Kizil Tepe. Great Yahni was carried, but the other two columns were repulsed. On the 3d Moukhtar riposted with an attack on the Russian left, from between Kizil Tepe and Uch Tepe. He gained no ground, but forced the Russians to strengthen their left and to evacuate Great Yahni, where their right flank was wholly in the air, and where besides it was very difficult to supply the troops with water.

The Russian losses between the 2d and 4th of October were over 3,000 men (1,052 killed, 2,102 wounded). Those of the Turks are not known, but were probably about the same.

Now follows an action upon the part of Moukhtar Pasha which it is difficult to explain. The newspaper correspondents at his headquarters say that he supposed this was to be the last attack of the Russians, and that the campaign would now close for the winter (snow had in fact already fallen). Whatever may have been his reasons, on the night of the 8th-9th of October he abandoned Great Yahni, Kizil Tepe, and Uch Tepe, and concentrated his army in his fortified positions on the heights of Vizinkioi, Avliar, and Aladja Dagh, leaving only a small advance guard in front of his left flank at Little Yahni. He also gave orders to Ismail Pasha to retreat from the frontier near Erivan and join him near Kars.

The Russians, however, had no thoughts of terminating the campaign on account of the winter, but were preparing a blow which resulted in the complete destruction of Moukhtar's army. Their plan in brief was to demonstrate against the heights of Avliar and Aladja Dagh, while a strong column should pass completely around the Turkish right flank and come up on their rear (thus preventing the arrival of Ismail's troops), and, as soon as it should arrive behind the Aladja Dagh, a general attack was to be made on all sides.

To this purpose the following dispositions of the Russian troops were made:

1. Right Wing, Major-General Count Grabbe—3d Grenadiers (3 battalions), 8 guns, and 15 squadrons, which was posted between the Kars Tchai, near Zaim, and the high-road north of Little Yahni.

2. Center, Lieutenant-General Heimann—4th Grenadier Division, 2d Regiment 1st Grenadier Division, Regiment No. 151 (38th Division), 1 battalion of rifles, and 1 sapper battalion; in all, 2¼ battalions, or 20,000 infantry, with 8 squadrons, and 104 guns of different calibres. This detachment was posted from Great Yahni to Hadji Veli.

3. Left Wing, Major-General Kouzminsky—Regiments No. 152 (38th Division) and 154 (39th Division); in all, 8 battalions, or 6,000 infantry, with 24 squadrons, and 24 guns. This detachment was posted in front of Kizil Tepe.

4. Reserve, Major-General Dehn—1st and 4th Regiments 1st Grenadier Division, and a half battalion of sappers; in all, 6½ battalions, or 5,000 infantry, with 8 squadrons and 40 guns. This detachment was posted in front of Kulveran.

The detachments of Grabbe, Kouzminsky, and Dehn were placed under the command of Lieutenant-General Roop.

5. Turning Column, Lieutenant-General Lazareff—40th Division, 75th Regiment (19th Division), one battalion of rifles, and a half battalion of sappers; in all, 17½ battalions, or 15,000 infantry, with 22 squadrons and 70 guns.

Lazareff left the camp at Karajal on the night of the 9th-10th of October, and crossed the Arpa Tchai at the fords behind Uch Tepe; he then moved down the east bank of the river to the village of Kambinsk, where he was joined by the 153d Regiment (39th Division) and a regiment of Cossacks; recrossing the river at this point, he turned westward and marched to Digour, on the rear of the Aladja Dagh, where he was reënforced by the 154th Regiment (39th Division), a few Cossacks, and some artillery, all of which had just arrived from Tergukassoff's detachment in the district of Erivan. This carried the strength of Lazareff's column to something over 20,000 infantry, 3,000 cavalry, and 78 guns. Tergukassoff's main column, about 15,000 men, was ordered to push forward reconnaissances in the direction of Kagisman (about twenty miles on the left or south of Lazareff), and find out the whereabouts of Ismail's troops and prevent their coming to the relief of Moukhtar.

The whole of Lazareff's march was conducted with great secrecy, mostly at night, and the Turks do not seem to have gained any very clear knowledge of it. He unrolled behind him a line of field telegraph—against which the Turks did nothing—which kept him at all times in instant communication with the camp at Karajal, and contributed in no small degree to the final success of the whole movement.

Meanwhile the troops of Heimann and Roop, who had occupied on the 9th and 10th the positions previously mentioned, were to remain quiet until Lazareff should establish himself in the rear of the Turks near Bazardjik, and then Heimann was to throw his whole force upon the heights of Avliar and break through the Turkish center at that point, while Roop was to attack the heights of Aladja Dagh, and, in connection with Lazareff acting on their rear, completely surround the Turkish right wing.

Giving a day's rest to his men at Digour, on the 14th of October Lazareff continued his march in the rear of the Turkish army toward Orlok; but in the afternoon his advance guard found the Turks posted in a strong position to the southeast of the village of Bazardjik. Moukhtar Pasha had in fact on the previous day learned through his spies of Lazareff's presence in his rear, and had thrown back his left flank in order to meet it. For this purpose he had formed a detachment under Reshid Pasha, about 6,000 men strong (including a few battalions which had arrived from Ismail's army), and had sent this detachment to take position between Orlok and Bazardjik and prevent the farther advance of this turning column of the Russians. Reshid Pasha's force, however, was too small for its work, and it was driven out of Bazardjik and forced to retire toward Vizinkioi, leaving the Russians in possession of their positions. The losses on the 14th of October were not great, but the result of the day was to firmly establish General Lazareff's detachment *in rear of the left flank of the Turks*, after having made a complete circuit of their right.

At 2:30 A. M. of the 15th, the Grand Duke Michael received at the camp at Karajal a long telegraphic report from General Lazareff, explaining his own position and the events of the day. The orders for the day were immediately given. Heimann, with the Caucasian Division of Grenadiers and 64 guns, was to storm the heights of Avliar; Roop, with portions of the Grenadier and other Divisions, was to advance on Kerchane, and, if Heimann's attack succeeded, to assault the Aladja Dagh; Lazareff was to continue his movement in the direction of Vizinkioi;

and, finally, one brigade of Heimann's detachment was moved forward from its station on Great Yahni to cover the road from Vizinkioi to Avliar with its artillery, in case the Turks made any movements along it.

The Grand Duke Michael and General Loris-Melikoff arrived on the field near Hadji Veli between 5 and 6 A. M., and the battle opened about daylight. Heimann's 64 guns, which were at first only a short distance in front of Hadji Veli, gradually advanced until they came within 1,500 yards of the Turkish works on the lower slopes of the Avliar hill. From this point, according to all accounts (Russian, Turkish, and English), they did most terrible execution with shrapnel, which they planted on the lines of the Turkish trenches with great accuracy. The Turks had but six guns on this hill, which could accomplish nothing against the greater number of Russian guns. Meanwhile the Grenadier Division lay in front and on both sides of this hill, slightly in advance of their batteries, under cover in the ravines, and waiting the order for the attack. One regiment on the right, between the foot of Avliar and Great Yahni, was so far advanced that Moukhtar sent a force from Vizinkioi to attack it about 10 A. M.; but this force was repulsed, partly by the infantry and partly by the fire of the long-range guns on Great Yahni. It was nearly noon, however, before this affair was wholly over, and then Heimann judged that the moment had come for the assault. The artillery ceased firing, and the columns began climbing the sides of the hill as rapidly as the ground permitted. They were received by a very hot fire from the Turkish trenches, to which they replied, while still moving forward in open order. The Turks did not wait for a hand-to-hand fight, but abandoned their trenches on the slope as the Russians came close to them; the Russians followed on, and then the Turks abandoned their artillery, ammunition, etc., in the position on the crest of the hill, and retreated to Vizinkioi. The whole position was in the hands of the Russians by 1 o'clock. Just at this time Moukhtar Pasha left the western edge of the Aladja Dagh, where he had been viewing the battle, and, passing behind Avliar and just in front of Lazareff's column, escaped to Vizinkioi.

Meanwhile the troops of Reshid Pasha, which had been driven out of Bazardjik the previous day, fell back and took position at the foot of the Vizinkioi hill and northwest of Avliar. Lazareff's leading regiments (Nos. 154 and 75) followed them up, and skirmished with them until about noon, when they moved forward to the assault. The Turks retreated to the crest of the Vizinkioi hill about the same time that those from Avliar began retreating to the village of Vizinkioi; the whole center and left wing of Moukhtar's army then fled in a wild panic to Kars. They were pursued by the cavalry. Heimann's and Lazareff's troops then joined hands near Avliar.

Under these circumstances the Grand Duke Michael, about 2 P. M. gave the following orders: Heimann to occupy Vizinkioi and Avliar with a portion of his troops, and with the other portion to cross the deep ravine between Avliar and Aladja Dagh, and attack the latter from the northwest; Lazareff to direct a portion of his troops to the attack of Aladja Dagh from the southwest, and with the other portion to move back to the vicinity of Bazardjik, and occupy all the roads by which the Turks, who still held firm on the Aladja Dagh, might escape toward Digour or the south; Roop to move forward from Kerchane to the assault of Aladja Dagh from the north. Three columns of superior numbers thus closed in around the right wing of Moukhtar's army, of which the center and left were already in flight.

The troops of General Roop had already occupied the ground in front of the Turkish positions on the northern slope of Aladja Dagh early in the morning, but, pending the result of General Heimann's attack, had confined their efforts to some skirmishing and to the energetic employment of their artillery (24 pieces). But when the heights of Avliar were carried, General Roop noticed that the Turks were beginning to withdraw part of their artillery, and saw that it was necessary to act promptly. He immediately ordered his troops to advance in three columns, the 156th Regiment on the right, the 1st Grenadiers in the center, and the 152d Regiment on the left (i. e., against the extreme right flank of the Turks), the whole supported by 28 pieces of artillery at close range, besides several siege-guns which were established on some heights in their rear. The Turks at first received them warmly, firing in volleys; but, as the Russians continued gradually to advance, their right finally gave way, and began retreating across the Aladja Dagh toward Vizinkioi. But they were not able to escape, for, as they came down the western slopes of the mountain, they were met by the troops of General Lazareff; and, at the same time, Roop's right and Heimann's left compelled the Turks on the left of the Aladja Dagh to give way. The whole of the right wing of the Turkish army was thus, about dark, surrounded, and nothing remained for them but to surrender. Their commander, Omer Pasha, sent a flag of truce to the Grand Duke Michael, and capitulated without conditions.

During the afternoon the small force posted on Little Yahni had profited by the fighting on the opposite flank to make good its escape to Kars, pursued by a few squadrons of Cossacks.

The result of the 15th of October was the crushing defeat of Moukhtar Pasha's army of 35,000 men—nearly half of it being destroyed, and the rest fleeing in a panic to the protection of the forts of Kars. By Omer Pasha's capitulation 7,000 men were made prisoners; 1,000 or 2,000 escaped in dispersed bands to the south of Aladja Dagh, and between 4,000 and 5,000 were killed and wounded in the battle, or cut down in their retreat. The greater part of the Turkish losses were caused by the admirable employment of the Russian artillery with shrapnel.

The Russian losses were very small in comparison with the decisive results of the day; they were as follows:

	Officers.	Men.
Killed	7	223
Wounded	49	1,162
Total	56	1,385

They captured 35 guns, several thousand small arms, a vast amount of ammunition, and such quantities of provisions that for several weeks they were independent of their own supplies at Alexandropol.

CHAPTER II.

ADVANCE OF THE RUSSIANS TO ERZEROUM—THE STORM OF KARS, NOVEMBER 15TH, 1877.

MOUKHTAR PASHA reached Kars in the midst of the disorganized panic-stricken fugitives during the night of the 15th-16th, and remained there one day; on the afternoon of the 16th he confided the defense of Kars to Hussein Pasha, and, taking 2,800 men who were in a reasonable state of organization, and a few guns, started west over the mountains to the Olti valley. Reaching this, he rapidly continued his retreat to Zevin, where he stopped and was joined by some 8,000 or 10,000 men whom he had ordered up from Erzeroum, and where he hoped to be joined by Ismail Pasha. But the latter, upon hearing of the defeat of Moukhtar's army, immediately abandoned all his sick and wounded (about 4,500 men), and began a hasty retreat up the valley of the Araxes, pursued by Tergukassoff. The Kurds then deserted him in a body, and desertions also multiplied among his regular troops, so that he reached the vicinity of Erzeroum with only about 8,000 men. Ismail having thus fallen back behind him, and being threatened in front by Heimann and on his flank by Tergukassoff, Moukhtar had no choice but to continue his retreat in all haste. On the 28th of October he abandoned Zevin and Yenikioi, and during the night of the 29th-30th reached Erzeroum. His chief of staff, a Hungarian named Faizi Pasha, of long service in the Turkish army, had preceded him thither, and hastily selected the site for some fortifications on the heights of Deve Boyum, about seven miles northeast of the town. Joining Ismail's forces to his own—15,000 to 18,000 men altogether—Moukhtar occupied these works.

Meanwhile on the Russian side, immediately after the battle of October 15th, Lazareff was sent to Kagisman with the 40th Division, in the hope of cutting off Ismail's troops; but the latter had received news of the defeat of the 15th by means of the scattered bands which had escaped from the Aladja Dagh, and had already passed Kagisman on the 19th; Lazareff arrived the next morning. Leaving Tergukassoff to follow Ismail, Lazareff was recalled to Kars.

Heimann, with the Caucasian Division of Grenadiers, was then started in direct pursuit of Moukhtar along the main Kars-Erzeroum road. Leaving the vicinity of Kars on the 24th, he crossed the Soganli range, and, passing through Zevin almost on the heels of Moukhtar, came into the valley of the Araxes, arrived in front of the heights of Deve Boyum on the 30th, and began reconnoitering the Turkish position at that place. But before trying an assault he awaited the arrival of Tergukassoff's column, which had not received the news of the defeat on the Aladja Dagh until some days after it had been received by Ismail, and was consequently somewhat behind the Turks. Tergukassoff reached Heimann's camp on the 2d of November, and preparations were immediately made for an assault on the 4th.

The united force under General Heimann consisted of the Caucasian Grenadier Division, the 73d, 150th, 153d, and 156th Regiments—about 24,000 men, with 120 guns—and 4 or 5 Regiments of Cossacks. Moukhtar had about 18,000 men under his orders, and 60 guns. His position was one of great natural strength, being on a high range of hills completely blocking the approach to Erzeroum by the road.

Heimann began his attack early in the morning, and the fight lasted till after dark in the evening. Although at first unsuccessful on their right flank, the Russians finally carried the whole line, capturing 43 guns, a great quantity of cartridges, the whole Turkish camp, and 400 prisoners. Moukhtar Pasha retreated within the line of forts surrounding Erzeroum. The Turkish loss is not known, but from the newspaper accounts was much larger than that of the Russians. The latter lost, according to the official report, a little over 800 men.

On the night of the 9th of November the Russian General intended to make a general assault of the works of Erzeroum;

but several of his columns lost their way in the darkness, and the only result was the capture of Fort Azizieh on the east of the town, where the Russians took 500 prisoners. But when daylight came they were forced to retire (after spiking the 20 guns which they had captured), since the fort was completely commanded by a neighboring work, Fort Medjidieh, and wholly untenable. The Russians lost 400 men in this affair.

On the night of the 12th they made another assault, but also without success. General Heimann then determined to await the arrival of reënforcements before making further efforts to carry the place; and in a very few days the winter set in with a terrible snow-storm, and brought all his operations to a standstill.

We now come to the final act of the campaign in Armenia, one of the most remarkable exploits in military annals, viz., the storming of Kars.

The town of Kars (see Plate 22) lies in the western side of the plain and on the river of the same name. Behind it, on the west and southwest, are volcanic spurs jutting out from the Soganli range; the river follows the base of these spurs to the town, but here cuts through a rent in the mountain and forms a precipitous ravine several hundred feet deep. On the west, north, and northeast of the town are therefore high, rocky, and almost inaccessible hills; on the southeast is an open rocky plain.

The fortifications, as they existed in 1877, had almost all been built since the Crimean war, under the direction, it is said, of Prussian engineers. They consisted of a citadel in masonry, built on a perpendicular rock overhanging the gorge just north of the town, and of twelve detached forts; there was no enceinte except the old Turkish wall built in the 16th century and now partly in ruins. The forts may be divided into four groups, as follows:

1. The defenses of Karadagh (Black Mountain), consisting of Forts Arab and Karadagh, on the high volcanic spur between the river and the Alexandropol road, on the northeast of the town;

2. The defenses of the plain on the southeast of the town, consisting of Forts Hafiz Pasha, Kanly, and Souvari; and of Fort Tchim in the southwestern suburbs of the town, enfilading the Kars River and the Erzeroum road alongside of it;

3. The defenses of Shorak Mountain, on the west of the town, consisting of Forts Tekmass, Tik Tepessi, and Laze Tepessi;

4. The defenses of Tchanak Mountain, on the northwest of the town, consisting of Forts Veli Pasha, Inglis, and Mouklis.

The length of the line of defense was about twelve miles. The forts on the right bank of the river were at an average distance of only 2,600 yards from the citadel; of those on the left bank, the most distant, Laze Tepessi, was 3,000 yards, and the nearest, Veli Pasha, but 1,000 yards from the citadel.

The various forts presented different *tracés* and different constructions. The two forts on the Karadagh were built on the bare rock, with epaulments of earth, which had been transported thither, and were without ditches or traverses. They commanded the neighboring ground in all directions, including the forts on the slopes of Tchanak Mountain on their left. Fort Arab was an irregular hexagon in shape, and had the gorge (on the south) closed by a barrack built of masonry; in advance of its right flank was a simple curtain. The development of the interior crest was 600 yards; the curtain was 300 yards long. Fort Karadagh consisted of a bastion with a curtain on either side of it, and in the space thus inclosed a battery in the form of a cavalier, 21 feet above the crest of the work. It was intended to close the gorge by a stone barrack, but this was not finished at the outbreak of the war. The length of the line of fire was 1,500 yards.

The two forts in the plain southeast of the town were the strongest in construction, and the weakest in situation, of the whole system. Fort Hafiz Pasha was a square redoubt, 400 yards on a side, with bastions at the angles, traverses on the parapet and on the covered way, ditch 12×6 feet, and a casemated barrack in three tiers closing the gorge (on the side of the town). In front of the southeast bastion was a little bonnet, 70 yards long on each face. Fort Kanly consisted of two small square redoubts about 150 yards on a side, and in rear of them a lunette with faces in the form of a bastioned front and closed at the gorge with a casemated barrack. The ditch was 12×6 feet. The development of the line of fire of the whole work was over 2,100 yards.

The two works on the banks of the river, Forts Souvari and Tchim, were simple lunettes without ditches or traverses.

The works on Shorak Mountain were at the altitude of those on Karadagh, or possibly even a little higher. Laze Tepessi was the commanding one of them all, and consisted of three batteries each of 80 yards front, and slightly in front of them an infantry parapet. Tik Tepessi was a square bastioned redoubt of a little more than 100 yards on a side, without traverses, with a ditch 9 × 7 feet. In front of it was a battery 60 yards long. Fort Tekmass was like Fort Kanly on a small scale, but had no outer works, and only an earthen parapet in place of a barrack across the gorge.

Of the works on Tchanak Mountain, Fort Mouklis was built on a sharp rock at the northern edge of a plateau, with the gorge open on the south; it was a simple lunette, with a line of fire of over 400 yards development. Fort Inglis was a small hexagonal work for infantry only; ditch, 21 × 7 feet; line of fire, 250 yards. Fort Veli Pasha was an irregular quadrilateral, with three sides bastioned and the fourth closed by a casemated barrack; ditch, 21 × 7 feet; line of fire, 330 yards.

The counterscarp of all the works having ditches was arranged with a banquette for infantry fire over the glacis.

This was the condition of the works at the beginning of the war. They were but little injured during the quasi investment of the Russians in the months of May and June. When this investment was raised by Loris-Melikoff's retreat during the month of July, the Turks strengthened their works by slightly increasing the size of the ditches, and, under the direction of Hussein Bey, they also ran a line of trenches and little lunettes from the Alexandropol road to Fort Hafiz Pasha, thence to Fort Kanly, and thence to the river near Fort Souvari. On the bare rocks surrounding the other works, trenches were not feasible.

These works presented in general certain qualities advantageous to the defense; i. e., they were (partly) on commanding ground, they were so near together and so constructed that their artillery lent mutual support, and the rocky ground precluded all idea of mining against them. But on the other hand, if the place be considered a fortified place of the first order, they presented many most serious difficulties for the defense and advantages for the attack, viz., 1, their being so near the town as to permit its bombardment; 2, the want of sufficient storehouses or magazines in the works, and of any provision for water, all of which had to be hauled up from the river; 3, the lack of ditches for several of the works; 4, the total lack of flanking defenses, such as caponnières, for such ditches as there were; 5, the lack of traverses, which existed only in Forts Hafiz Pasha and Kanly; 6, the difficulty of repairing the parapets, owing to the lack of earth; 7, the small relief of the parapet, which left the casemated barracks exposed to the fire of the enemy's artillery; 8, the lack of unity in the defense, the whole position being cut in two by the gorge of the Kars River, which was passable only at a few points on narrow paths, and thus prevented rapid movements of reserves from one side to another.

The total armament of the place is about 200 guns (303 were captured at the assault, including a large proportion of field-guns). The total development of the line of fire for infantry is about 6,000 yards, 4,000 in the works on the right bank and 2,000 in those on the left. Allowing 2 men to a yard and 50 per cent. in reserve, the proper garrison would be 18,000 infantry, and, with 25 men to a gun, 5,000 artillery, or in all 23,-000. This was almost exactly the strength of the garrison at the time of the assault.

After the defeat and dispersion of Moukhtar Pasha's army in the battle of Aladja Dagh, October 15th, a portion of the Russian troops were sent, as already stated, in pursuit of the Turks toward Erzeroum; the rest of the troops, consisting of the 1st Grenadier Division, the 40th Division, and portions of the 19th, 38th, and 39th Divisions—in all (counting a small detachment which arrived a few days later from Ardahan) 41 battalions, or 30,000 infantry, with 53 squadrons and 144 guns —were constituted the army of investment of Kars, under the orders of Lieutenant-General Lazareff. They gradually diminished the circle of investment to a diameter of about nine miles, and established their siege-guns in batteries as soon as they arrived; 48 guns arrived on the 4th of November, and were established in 12 batteries on the east and southeast of the town, at a distance of about 3,000 yards from the Turkish works.

The train of reasoning which induced the assault is thus explained in the Grand Duke Michael's report:

"Careful reconnaissances of the ground and of the defenses of the place, and the information gathered concerning the effective strength and morale of the garrison, and concerning its provisions, proved each day more clearly that, although the defeat of Moukhtar Pasha's army may have had a certain demoralizing effect upon the defensive strength of Kars, yet the capture of this town was none the less an extremely difficult enterprise. Large quantities of provisions assured to the 32 battalions of the garrison the means of sustaining a blockade for six months, which during the winter, so rigorous in this locality, would have brought innumerable and inevitable sufferings upon the troops of investment. The excellent armament of the fortifications of Kars, the resolution of the garrison to fight to the last extremity, the well-known firmness of Turkish troops in sieges, and the difficult conditions in which the troops of investment were placed, hardly permitted the idea of sitting down to a siege of which it would have been difficult to foresee the end. Nevertheless, the speedy capture of Kars was of great importance, partly in the light of a military success on this point of the theatre of war, and partly in order to facilitate and develop operations by securing their base against any eventuality, and thus permitting the detachment of a sufficient force in the direction of Erzeroum and the distribution of the troops in a more comfortable manner on the approach of winter.

"The only way to put an end to this state of affairs (*sortir de cette situation*) was to gain possession of Kars in open assault, preparing the assault as far as possible by the bombardment of several forts and of the town, and making the assault under conditions which would insure a certain success, although it might be a partial one, but capable of further development. The line of forts on the southeast, situated on the right bank of the Kars River, Hafiz, Kanly, and Souvari, and the town itself, where all the depots and provisions of the garrison were concentrated, were chosen as the principal objective, partly on account of the conformation of the ground, and partly on account of the situation and relative strength of the defenses commanding the approaches of the place. . . . An energetic sortie made by the garrison on the 5th of November, in order to prevent the construction of our batteries, gave a new proof of the resolution of the garrison, and confirmed the importance of an attack from the side chosen by us. . . . Constructed and armed in the space of six days, the siege batteries opened fire on the 11th of November, and continued it day and night without interruption, increasing their fire toward evening. . . . It was at first thought that it might be possible to reduce the place by bombardment alone, but this was soon seen to be an illusion; the Turks began constructing new batteries. . . . It was all the more necessary to hasten the end; an assault was decided upon. It only remained to fix the time and the means. In front of the line of the forts, which was to be the principal objective of the attack, the ground afforded within musket range of the works hardly any shelter, and not a single favorable position for field artillery. The enormous extent of the line of fire, flanked by several bodies of troops, successive rows of trenches and artificial shelters, the almost incredible range and intensity of the Turkish infantry fire on the defensive, threatened enormous losses in case of an attack by daylight. Moreover, the situation of the other forts upon the tops of mountains, thus permitting the enemy to follow the movements of the columns directed against him, and to reconnoiter their strength and object, deprived a demonstration of all its importance, and made it possible for the Turks to concentrate their defense upon the real point of attack. On the other hand, an attack in the darkness of a night without a moon might lead to a catastrophe. It was necessary to wait the time when the moon, remaining nearly all night above the horizon, would light up the field so that there would be no danger on the one hand of making a mistake in the road, and on the other hand of revealing our movement to the enemy from a distance, and thus giving him time to take his own measures and to direct a murderous infantry fire upon us.

"For these reasons the assault was fixed for the night of the 17th-18th."

It had in fact been ordered for the night of the 15th (November), but postponed on account of a snowstorm and cloudy weather. The greatest secrecy was observed,* and the Turks do not seem to have had the least suspicion of what was going on. They had in fact concentrated over 15,000 men—two thirds of their whole force—in the forts on the Shorak Mountain, on the left bank of the river. This was naturally the

---

* Even as late as the afternoon of the 17th, officers did not hesitate to tell newspaper correspondents with whom they were on reasonably intimate terms that such a thing as an assault was not even thought of. See "Daily News Correspondence," Vol. I., p. 630.

strongest and most commanding point of their line of works, and it was on this side that Mouravieff made his unsuccessful assault on the 21st of September, 1855; but the defenses were (artificially) not as strong on this side as on the other.

The orders of the Grand Duke Michael, giving general directions for the assault, were as follows:

"1. The troops investing Kars are to gain possession of Forts Souvari, Kanly, and Hafiz Pasha.

"2. The attack must be made unexpectedly, and efforts must be made to take prisoner or else to destroy the garrisons of these forts, and to get possession of the guns in them.

"3. At the same time as the attack of these forts, demonstrations will be made against other points of the enemy's line of defense, in order to divert his attention and his troops from the real point of attack.

"4. These demonstrations may be converted into real attacks, taking advantage of the enemy's confusion or other favorable circumstances, but only by small bodies, as experiments (*à titre d'essais*), in order to avoid great losses.

"5. Such attempts may be made also by the troops charged with the principal attack, after this latter has been executed; Fort Tchim and the wall of the town are specially indicated as the objects of these attempts. Under entirely exceptional circumstances, such for example as a case of complete panic on the part of the enemy, such an operation is authorized with reference to Karadagh, but without losing sight of the difficulties of its execution.

"6. After having gained possession of Forts Souvari, Kanly, and Hafiz, the first duty of the troops will be to establish themselves solidly there; they will not evacuate these works except in case it should be absolutely impossible to maintain themselves in them; and in this case they will bring away the prisoners and trophies, and will destroy, as far as possible, all the enemy's means of defense."

In order to carry out these general instructions, five separate columns of assault were formed and two columns of demonstration; about 5,000 men being held in reserve. The artillery was not to follow the troops, but was to remain, ready for action, near the reserves, until daylight or the receipt of further orders. The cavalry was to be stationed at important points on the roads leading to Erzeroum and over the Soganli range, and await orders. The concentration of the troops was to commence at dark, the forward movement at 8 P. M. Profound silence was to be everywhere observed, and no smoking allowed.

The details of these columns were as follows:

First Column, Major-General Komaroff, Regiments No. 151 and 2d Grenadiers, 6 battalions, and 16 guns, to assemble at Tatildja, demonstrate against Fort Tekmass, but with the bulk of his troops follow the Kars ravine and attack Fort Tchim.

Second Column, Lieutenant-Colonel Prince Melikoff, 4th Rifle Battalion and two battalions of 76th Regiment, in all three battalions, to assemble at Kichikkioi, follow the right bank of the river, and attack Fort Souvari.

Third and *Fourth Columns*, Major-General Count Grabbe, Regiments No. 75, 157 (in part), 3d Grenadiers, and 1st Rifle Battalion, in all 10 battalions, and 16 guns, to assemble at Karadjuran, and attack Fort Kanly, in two columns, that on the left commanded by Count Grabbe in person, and that on the right by Colonel Vodjakin.

Fifth Column, Major-General Alkhazoff, portions of 157th and 158th Regiments, in all 5 battalions, and 8 guns, to assemble at the siege batteries east of the town, and attack Fort Hafiz Pasha.

The general command of all the troops on the right bank of the Kars river was entrusted to Lieutenant-General Lazareff, who had also under his orders as reserve 2 battalions of the 152d Regiment and 8 guns.

Sixth Column, Colonel Tcheremissinoff, portions of the 76th Regiment and 4th Grenadiers, in all 5 battalions, and 24 9-pdr. guns, to assemble at Djavra and demonstrate against Forts Laze Tepessi and Mouklis.

Seventh Column, Major-General Rydzevsky, 160th and part of 159th Regiment, in all 6 battalions, and 24 guns, to assemble at Matzra, and demonstrate against Forts Arab and Karadagh.

Both of these columns were to convert their demonstrations into real attacks, in the discretion of their commanders, according to the general instructions previously quoted.

General Reserve at Komatzur, consisting of 1st Grenadiers, 3 battalions and 16 guns.

The Cavalry was stationed as follows:

1. Column of Major-General Sheremetieff, 28 squadrons and 6 guns, at the village of Tchakmaour, to observe the roads leading over the mountains, and to keep up communication between columns 6 and 7.

2. Column of Major-General Prince Sherbatoff, 34 squadrons, between the village of Bozgala and the Erzeroum main road, to observe this road.

3. Column of Lieutenant-Colonel Prince Tchavchavadje, 18 squadrons and 6 guns, to move to the bridge at Kichikkioi, and there wait for orders.

The 3d Engineer battalion was divided up into squads and distributed among the various columns, each squad carrying ladders, dynamite cartridges, and implements of various kinds. With each column was also a squad of artillerymen, with tools for spiking or dismounting the guns.

To resume the Grand Duke Michael's report:

"On the evening of the 17th all the troops assembled at the points indicated, and at 8:30 P. M. the columns moved forward. A perfectly clear sky and the full moon which had just risen gave promise of a clear and calm night; the temperature, which had fallen below zero (32° Fahr.) during the morning, was growing colder and colder. A solemn and cold silence reigned in the air, and the most attentive ear could not have distinguished any noise in the least alarming. The dimly seen line of our skirmishers was advancing prudently, step by step, followed by the troops for the assault, which at first marched in compact columns, then, as they approached the line of attack, formed in deployed order in company column.

"About 9 o'clock some shots were heard at the Turkish outposts, and then, as ours did not reply, they ceased. Only our batteries at Djavra, as a signal, opened a cannonade against the heights of Tekmass, attracting the attention and forces of the enemy toward this point. But not a half hour elapsed before a musketry fire of the Turks burst forth along the whole line of attack, and after a few minutes the works and the trenches of the forts which had been attacked began a continuous firing."

The little column of Prince Melikoff was the first to reach its destination. Advancing without firing a shot and capturing the Turkish pickets, it rushed into Fort Souvari about 9:30 P. M., almost before the Turks knew they were approaching; they then killed the Turkish garrison with the bayonet, spiked or dismounted the guns, and in less than half an hour left the work, broke through some Turkish cavalry which came to attack them, and rushed on to the bridge over the Kars River in order to attack Fort Tchim on its left flank and rear.

Count Grabbe's two columns, assaulting Fort Kanly, had more serious difficulties. They arrived in front of the work about 10 P. M., and crossed, with some difficulty and under a very heavy fire, the obstructions in the shape of pits (*fossés à loup*) in front of the work. On the right (Colonel Vodjakin's column) a few hundred volunteers from the 75th and 157th Regiments swarmed over the parapet of the eastern redoubt, and as quickly as possible killed all its defenders who remained in it; they then rushed on to the eastern flank of the main work, got possession of part of its parapet, and stayed there, awaiting the arrival of the rest of their column, but unable to get any farther forward in face of the superior forces of the garrison. The rest of the column, however, seeing the redoubt occupied, inclined to the right to attack the trenches and a little lunette with four guns situated between Kanly and Hafiz. In this *mêlée* Colonel Vodjakin was wounded and turned over the command to Colonel Karasseff. Having gained possession of these trenches and the lunette, they then began to reform and advance to the relief of their comrades who still held on upon the parapet of the eastern face.

Meanwhile, on the left, Count Grabbe led his column in person and on horseback, and, with the 1st Rifle Battalion in the lead, passed around the flank of the western redoubt and attacked the main work, partly in front against its western face, and partly by turning its extreme western flank and endeavoring to enter the work in rear. Count Grabbe fell dead a few yards from the parapet, receiving two bullets simultaneously in the breast, and was succeeded by Colonel Belinsky. The troops with great difficulty gained possession of the covered way, reformed in the ditch, and at 11 o'clock portions of the 3d Grenadiers and the 75th Regiment rushed over the parapet, at the same time that a part of the Rifle Battalion entered the work from the rear. A fierce hand-to-hand fight then took place in this angle of the work, the traces of which were found in 500 Turkish dead which lay in a small space there the next day. But although a good portion of the garrison was thus exterminated, the rest took refuge in the stone barrack at the gorge, which had two tiers of musketry fire, and several small mortars in barbette on top, and did great damage to the Russians at such close quarters. Colonel Belinsky then took some volunteers, passed round to the rear of the barrack, and tried to break down its doors; but they were of iron, and he made no impression on them, and himself fell dead on the spot. This attempt having failed, it became impossible for the troops to remain in the work under the rain of bullets which the Turks showered on them from the loopholes of the barrack, and they were therefore obliged to return to the ditch, leaving, however, a line of men lying down on the crest of the parapet, who gave the Turks a warm reception whenever they attempted a sortie from the barracks.

Meanwhile the whole space between Kanly, Souvari, and the town was alive with fire, fresh Turkish troops with artillery having arrived from the town. General Lazareff was informed of the condition of affairs at Fort Kanly, and sent part of the reserve of the 152d Regiment to reënforce the troops there. Having no knowledge of what had become of Prince Melikoff's little column after it had left Souvari, General Loris-Melikoff ordered Prince Tchavtchavadje, who was at Kichikkioi bridge with 17 squadrons of Cossacks, to try to clear the enemy out of the space between Kanly and the river, and to send some squadrons to aid the troops at the former point. Loris-Melikoff also sent Colonel Bulmering of the Engineers to take command at Kanly, all the commanding officers there being killed or wounded. It was about midnight when the Cossacks arrived near Kanly. The Turks, encouraged by the lull in the attack, had sortied from the barrack, and were trying to drive the Russians off from the top of the parapet, but without success. At this moment some 250 Cossacks arrived on foot, climbed on the parapet, and, reënforcing the men already there, drove the Turks back to the shelter of the barrack.

The reserves having arrived, Colonel Bulmering formed his troops in two portions for the purpose of turning Kanly by both flanks. The column on the left, commanded by himself in person, and assisted by the Cossacks, drove the enemy out of their trenches between Kanly and Souvari, and, following on their heels, came to the very edge of the town. The column on the right, under Colonel Karasseff, gained possession of the rest of the eastern face of the work. At 1 A. M. the whole of Fort Kanly was in undisputed possession of the Russians, except the barrack at the gorge. Having posted his troops so as to prevent the Turks from again coming out from the town, Colonel Bulmering returned to Kanly, placed his troops in the ditch behind shelter of one kind or another near the barrack, and then summoned the latter to surrender, threatening to knock the whole place to pieces with artillery. The Pasha defied him to do his worst, and said he would defend himself to the last. Alternate firing and negotiations succeeded each other for more than two hours. Finally Colonel Bulmering told the Pasha that if he did not surrender he would blow up his barrack with dynamite, and at the same time proved his ability to do so. To this argument the Pasha (Daoud Pasha) yielded, and at 4 A. M. surrendered. But he had only 300 men! It was all that was left of the garrison of Fort Kanly.

Meanwhile, at Fort Hafiz Pasha a struggle hardly less desperate, although shorter, had been going on. Here General Alkhazoff's troops were also divided into two columns for the attack of the work on its two principal faces. The columns were discovered and fired upon about 9 P. M., not only from the fort itself, but from the trenches between it and the foot of Karadagh and the batteries recently constructed on the southern slope of that hill. It therefore became necessary for the column on the right to get possession of these trenches on their flank. Colonel Fadeyeff, with about 2,500 men in his column, set to work at this, and after a considerable struggle gained possession of some of these trenches; part of the defenders fled toward the town, part along the trenches toward Karadagh, and the rest were bayoneted. Following close upon those who retreated toward Karadagh, Colonel Fadeyeff took advantage of the Turkish confusion and gained possession of the batteries at the foot of this mountain, and immediately followed the Turks, now in considerable disorder and panic, up the paths of the Karadagh to the fort of the same name. While a portion of his men were arranging and placing some dynamite cartridges to blow up the tower at the angle of the outer work, others climbed up on each other's shoulders and penetrated on to the platform from the rear; the defenders then rushed back into the inner work, but were hotly pursued by the Russians, and before they had time to recover from their confusion and disorder about half the garrison had been bayoneted or knocked senseless; the rest fled along the mountain toward Fort Arab. Here at last the Turks got their breath and had time to recover their senses a little before a party of Russian volunteers came on to their attack; this party was practically annihilated. The Turks then returned to the charge, and made several desperate efforts to regain Fort Karadagh. But Colonel Fadeyeff had got a firm footing there, had received the whole of the 158th Regiment as reënforcements (which he had asked for immediately upon reaching the base of the hill), and he held fast in the fort without yielding an inch. The Turkish attacks were all repulsed.

The greater portion of the column assaulting Hafiz had therefore been wholly diverted from its original purpose, but still with most happy results. The rest of the column had meanwhile advanced to take the trenches on the south of Hafiz, in the direction of Kanly, at the same time that the column of Colonel Karasseff, as previously narrated, advanced against the same works from the direction of Kanly. As this attack began to succeed, General Alkhazoff himself took the remaining two battalions of his column and assaulted Fort Hafiz in front, and on the left. The troops poured over the parapet, and the Turks took refuge behind the barrack at the gorge; but this, unlike the one at Kanly, had been nearly demolished by the Russian artillery, and was little better than a heap of ruins. As the Turks retreated behind it the battalion which had gone round by the left appeared in the rear. In the language of the Grand Duke's report, "the garrison was crushed to pieces and annihilated. Fort Hafiz was ours."

At this moment General Alkhazoff received word from Colonel Fadeyeff that he had taken Karadagh, and asking for reënforcements. He immediately sent him what he had of the 158th Regiment, which reached Fadeyeff, as we have seen, in time to repulse the Turkish attacks on Fort Karadagh. He also sent one battalion of the 152d to reënforce the troops attacking Kanly, and with the remaining battalion and a half established himself at Hafiz and sent skirmishers forward toward the small camp between Hafiz and the town, at whose approach the Turks, now pretty well demoralized, fled toward Kars.

It was now about 2 o'clock in the night. All the works on the right bank of the river, from Karadagh to Souvari, were in the possession of the Russians, excepting only the barrack of Fort Kanly, which evidently could not hold out, isolated, much longer. General Lazareff rode along the lines and saw the condition of things, and then united part of the troops of General Alkhazoff and Colonel Bulmering, and sent them forward to occupy the town, to find out what had become of Prince Melikoff's column, and to give it assistance.

While the columns of assault had thus been gaining possession of the forts in front of them on the right bank of the river, the columns of demonstration had also been hotly engaged, with results as follows:

It will be remembered that General Komaroff, having 6 battalions and 24 guns under his orders, was to demonstrate in front of Fort Tekmass, but send the bulk of his troops along the Kars River to attack Fort Tchim in front; while Prince Melikoff's column, having gained possession of Fort Souvari, was immediately to cross the river and attack Fort Tchim in flank and rear.

Komaroff detailed two battalions of the 3d Grenadiers to occupy Mount Moukha, 3,500 yards southwest of Fort Tekmass, and demonstrate against that fort; the other battalion of this regiment and all his artillery were left in reserve; while the three battalions of the 151st, under Colonel Boutchkief, were sent through the Kars ravine to the assault of Fort Tchim. They assembled at 8 o'clock at the Kichikkioi bridge, and as soon as they heard the firing at Souvari, about 9 P. M., moved forward along the ravine. But at the entrance of it the Turks had some outposts posted in trenches very difficult to reach, and the noise of their firing alarmed the camp concentrated between Tekmass and the town; they quickly came forward to the edge of the ravine and attacked Colonel Boutchkieff's column in flank; it was impossible for him to advance under this fire, and he promptly faced his men by the left flank and attacked the heights. In so doing he was exposed to the fire, at about 1,800 yards range, of Fort Tchim; but in spite of the difficulties of his position and of the ground, he continued his attack energetically, and drove the Turks from the heights of the ravine and back toward Fort Tekmass. Following the Turks closely in their retreat, his men arrived in front of this latter work. Retreat was impossible without great losses; a success promised great results. He led his little force forward to the assault; they were received with the musketry fire of three tiers of trenches, with shrapnel, stones, and hand-grenades. Struck with one of the latter, Colonel Boutchkieff was instantly killed; his men lost enormously, and fell back to the Kars ravine. It was about midnight, and these three battalions were so smashed up as to be practically of no further use during the night. The Turks nevertheless did not follow them. Not wishing, however, to give up all idea of an assault upon Fort Tchim, General Komaroff (still leaving the two battalions to demonstrate in front of Tekmass) brought up the one battalion of the 2d Grenadiers which he had in reserve, and his 24 guns, and sent them forward along the river toward Fort Tchim. This little column advanced rapidly, and seized the suburbs on the southwest of the town and the cemetery in front of Fort Tchim, and there opened fire—their artillery at short range, and the infantry scattered about behind the grave-stones of the cemetery. But Fort Tchim gave them the warmest possible reception, and they were moreover exposed to the cross-fire of Forts Tekmass and Veli Pasha, the flashes of their own guns serving as a target. In short, their position was wholly untenable, and about 2 o'clock in the morning the retreat was sounded, and they fell back along the river to the Kichikkioi bridge.

Meanwhile Prince Melikoff's little force, after gaining possession of Fort Souvari early in the evening, as already narrated, had crossed the river partly by fording (the temperature was 10° Fahr. or more below freezing) and partly in boats, had passed through the suburbs of the town, and attacked Fort Tchim in rear. The Turks were completely surprised, and Prince Melikoff thought he might in their confusion be able to carry the work. He led his little force to the assault, but was himself knocked over dangerously wounded, and his men were driven back. They took refuge in the cemetery; but no signs of Komaroff's column appearing (they heard their firing, but knew nothing definite about it), they were obliged to retreat, and made their way back across the river. Just at this time (a little after midnight) the little column sent by Komaroff along the ravine made their attack. They were repulsed, as already stated, but their attack contributed largely to cover the retreat of Melikoff's column and prevent its destruction. The latter fell back along the right bank of the river, and reached the Kichikkioi bridge just at daylight.

The whole attack along the valley of the Kars River therefore failed; the Turks discovered the movement in time, and by attacking one column in flank from Tekmass caused the different assaults to be made one after another without success and with great loss. Nevertheless, the main object of Komaroff's troops was to occupy the attention of the large body of troops concentrated on the heights of Shorak, and thus prevent reënforcements being sent to the aid of Forts Kanly and Hafiz; and this they fully accomplished.

The two other columns, under Colonel Tcheremissinoff and General Ryzdevsky, made their demonstrations with no less vigor, beginning their operations when they heard the firing in the plain southeast of Kars, i. e., about 9 o'clock in the evening. The former attacked Fort Laze Tepessi, carried the trenches in front of the batteries, mounted on the parapet of the latter (although it was covered with a coating of ice), and kept up a fight at close quarters for several hours, until the Turks brought up enough reënforcements to drive them out; but they only retired to the trenches which they had captured, and kept up a fire from them till daylight. The latter opened with their artillery against Forts Arab and Karadagh, contributing largely to the confusion and bewilderment in which Colonel Fadeyeff found the defenders of the latter when he carried it, and sent forward volunteers up to the vicinity of the former work. When he heard of the capture of Fort Karadagh by Colonel Fadeyeff, General Rydzevsky reënforced the volunteers in front of Fort Arab by four battalions (160th Regiment), who made an energetic and successful assault upon the place just after the Turks had returned from their efforts to retake Fort Karadagh. Having entered the work, they killed part of the garrison and took some of them prisoners, and the rest fled along the paths of the ravine toward the town. As for the citadel, it was feebly garrisoned, and surrendered to the 152d Regiment when the latter advanced against it from Fort Hafiz.

As daylight dawned about 5 A. M., the whole series of fortifications on the right bank of the Kars River was in possession of the Russians; but the commanding forts on the heights of Tchanak and Shorak yet held out, and the Turks had still between 12,000 and 15,000 men, somewhat demoralized, but still capable of fighting, on the left bank of the Kars. Massing these between Forts Tekmass and Laze Tepessi, the Pasha determined to make an effort to break through in the direction of the villages of Samovat, Aravartan, and Bozgala, and thence winding through the mountains regain the Erzeroum road. As the day dawned this movement became clearly defined, and Lieutenant-General Roop, commanding on the left bank, took what measures he could to stop it, by disposing the cavalry, stationed near these villages, to take the columns in flank while his infantry retained them in front. The principal column of the Turks, near Bozgala, seeing itself surrounded, laid down its arms; but at Samovat and at Aravartan they broke through the Russian infantry and continued their march toward the mountains. The Cossacks were sent after them with the utmost energy, and attacked them vigorously in flank, causing a loss of several hundreds of men among the Turks, and delaying them while another portion got on their road in front and headed them off. They surrendered here and there by battalions, until finally there remained but one detachment of about 150 mounted men, flying in the direction of the Olti road. The Cossacks put after them, sabred about a hundred of their number whose horses were exhausted, and chased the rest for about 15 miles. Then their own horses gave out, and they had to give it up. Among the 30 or 40 men who thus escaped, thanks to the quality of their horses, were the commandant of Kars, Hussein Pasha, and two or three other principal officers.

Kars was wholly in possession of the Russians. The troops on the left bank returned with their prisoners, occupied the forts on that side, and about 10 or 11 A. M. entered the town, where their comrades from the right bank had already been since early morning.

It was a good night's work—a fortified place of the first order captured in open assault, with 17,000 prisoners, 303 guns of various calibres, 25,000 or more small arms, and an immense quantity of provisions and material of all kinds. Twenty-five hundred Turkish bodies were found dead on the field; there were 4,500 sick and wounded in the hospitals, and several hundreds more were picked up on the field. The Russian losses were:

	Officers.	Men.
Killed	18	470
Wounded	59	1726
Total	77	2,196

It will be noticed that the proportion of officers killed and wounded is about 1 to 28 men, whereas the proportion of officers present was about 1 to 60 men; the commanding officers of Columns 1, 2, 3, and 4 all fell within a few feet of the enemy. One general officer (Count Grabbe) was killed, and one wounded.

After the capture of Kars, a portion of the Turkish prisoners were escorted across the frontier to Tiflis, and a certain portion, about 4,000 in all, not in good health, were granted permission to seek their homes and villages, of which they availed themselves.

During the month of December a part of the garrison (40th Division) was dispatched to Erzeroum, but a severe winter and the difficult nature of the mountainous country hindered their march, delayed the arrival of siege material and provisions, and generally proved a most serious obstacle to General Heimann's siege. It was only on the 12th of January that the Trebizond road was finally and permanently cut, and the investment completed. The place was, however, well provisioned, and the frozen ground and deep snow delayed the establishment of batteries. So the time passed on, and the armistice of January 31st arrived with Erzeroum still in the hands of the Turks. But one of the conditions of that document was the evacuation of Erzeroum. This was accomplished about the 10th of February, when some 15,000 to 20,000 troops marched out under Ismail Pasha, proceeded to Trebizond, and were embarked for Constantinople. Ghazi Moukhtar Pasha had been recalled thither about the end of December, just before the Trebizond road was closed.

The campaign in Armenia, begun by the Russians with insufficient forces, and checked for a while, finally ended in their complete victory and the overwhelming defeat and destruction of the Turkish forces. Its fate was decided by the battle of Aladja Dagh and the storm of Kars, and these are among the most brilliant feats of arms in Russian military annals. The more the latter is studied, and the stubbornness of the defense is considered, the more certain it appears that those who lay down as a proved principle of modern tactical warfare that fortifications defended by breech-loaders can not be carried in open assault, have made a hasty judgment. Moukhtar Pasha, on the night after the battle at Aladja Dagh, attributed his defeat to the wonderful employment of the Russian artillery with shrapnel,* and the same opinion seems to have been shared by the Russian officers; in other words, "the attack was well prepared with artillery." But, on the other hand, Kars was stormed without any artillery preparation (in this sense) at all; its success was due to the skillful dispositions made beforehand, and to the individual courage and endurance of the men. In both cases hand-to-hand fights finally decided the battle.

If troops are led to the assault of trenches and breech-loaders in successive, and not simultaneous assaults, in inferior numbers, over an open country, in a too compact formation, and without reference to the decisive or key points of the defense, then defeat and slaughter will be the result, as happened at Plevna, at Shipka (July 17th), in part at Gorni-Dubnik, at Zevin, at Little Yahni (October 2d), and in our own war at Cold Harbor. But if the points of attack are well chosen, the troops are properly distributed, advance in reasonably open order in successive lines, and make their attacks simultaneously, and in superior numbers at the decisive points, then the assailants will reach the parapet in spite of the breech-loaders, and the strongest party will win—as they did at Nikopolis, at Shenovo, at Kars, and at Five Forks.

Victory lies to-day, as it ever has and ever will, on the side of that general who takes the most skillful measures for the task he has in hand, and who has under him the most patient, brave, and willing soldiers; and though the defense has relatively gained greatly over the attack by the introduction of breech-loaders, yet *that fact alone* will not prevent, any more than a slight superiority in armament, such a general from carrying

* See "Daily News Correspondence," Vol. I., p. 584.

trenches in open assault. It is after all the human factor—the general to think and the men to carry out his thoughts at any sacrifice—and not alone their mere material accompaniments, which gain success in war, as well as in the other affairs of life.

PART IV.

CONCLUSIONS.

THE DEFENSE AND ATTACK OF FORTIFIED
POSITIONS.

CONCLUSIONS.

CHAPTER I.

GENERAL REMARKS—CONSTRUCTION OF THE TURKISH AND RUSSIAN FORTIFICATIONS, AND THEIR DEFENSE.

THE campaign of 1877-'78, like every campaign which was ever fought, furnishes its military lessons for the future—mistakes to be avoided, successful manœuvres to be repeated under similar opportunities. But there is one feature, a question of tactics, in which this war finds no parallel in past history, and which is of the highest importance for the conduct of future wars, particularly to us in America. I refer to the great use which was made of hasty fortifications in connection with modern fire-arms.

Temporary field fortifications were constantly employed by the Romans on the field of battle; they have also been frequently employed and highly commended by all the great masters of war; but it is only within the most recent times that they have attained their great importance, owing wholly to the long range, the precision, and the rapidity of fire of modern rifled muskets. Their first great use was at Sevastopol; in our civil war they attained a development hitherto unknown, not only important points like Washington, Richmond, Vicksburg, etc., being converted into great intrenched camps, capable of sustaining long sieges, but also every bivouac in the presence of the enemy being fortified by a shelter-trench of some kind; in the Prussian wars of 1866 and 1870 they were also used, though not to so great an extent; but in the late war in Turkey the combination of trench and breech-loader attained such a perfection, that the whole campaign may be said to have consisted—tactically—of the attack and defense of more or less hastily fortified positions.

The infantry arm has, in the present century, passed through four essential modifications, viz., from smooth bore to rifle, from flint-lock to percussion-cap, from muzzle-loader to breech-loader, from paper-cartridge to fixed ammunition; and the breech-loaders, by reducing the calibre and increasing the relative length of the bullet, by increasing the twist of the rifling, and augmenting the charge, have doubled their range and general efficiency; so that the Peabody, the Springfield of '73, the Remington, the Berdan, are as much superior to the Needle-gun and Chassepot of 1870, as were these latter to the Enfield or Springfield muzzle-loader of 1861.

A simple calculation will illustrate this point. Four hundred men, garrisoning a little redoubt of 100 yards on a side, and firing both from the parapet and the ditch, can now in twelve minutes easily deliver 24,000 shots, a veritable hail of lead, each pellet of which, if it strikes a vital part, is fatal, *up to a distance of a mile and a quarter;* and if but one in twenty of these bullets find its billet, the defenders will have destroyed 1,200 men during the time that the assailants are passing over this mile and a quarter, i. e., three times their own number; whereas in 1863, the same number of men, in the same position, would have been armed with a gun which could only be fired, at most, three times in two minutes, and which carried but a third of a mile. This the assailants could have crossed in three minutes, and during this time the defenders could have delivered but 1,800 shots, and, if one in twenty of these hit, they would have accomplished a loss among the enemy of only 90 men—less than one twelfth of the destruction possible in 1877. While, therefore, we need not conclude that the attack of a field fortification is now twelve times as dangerous as it was during our civil war (and, in fact, such numerical comparisons have little real value), yet the above illustration is sufficient to call attention to the great fact of modern tactics, viz., that in the *last few years the defense, behind fortifications, has enormously gained upon the attack,* owing to the improvements in small-arms; or, in other words, that any attacking force is now at a very much greater disadvantage than it was fifteen years ago.

DEFENSE OF FORTIFIED POSITIONS. 423

In the following pages I shall endeavor to state the more prominent facts of the recent war which had a bearing upon this important question.

The subject is evidently divided into two parts, viz., the defense and the attack.

DEFENSE.

The Turkish defensive works were of three classes :

1. Large intrenched camps, such as those surrounding Plevna, Rustchuk, Shumla, Sophia, Adrianople, and the Tchekmedje lines.

2. The works for the defense of mountain passes, such as Araba-Konak, Pravetz, Etropol, Trajan's Gate, etc.

3. Hastily constructed trenches and batteries for the defense of a line of battle in open ground.

The Russians, being the invaders, had only one intrenched camp, viz., their line of circumvallation at Plevna, and but one mountain pass, Shipka, to defend; and having failed to occupy in time the commanding ridges of the latter, its defenses were limited to the most meager character; the Russian fortifications, therefore, consisted almost wholly of the third class.

1. INTRENCHED CAMPS.

The general principles upon which the fortifications were located at Plevna, Adrianople, etc., were exactly the same as those upon which Washington and Richmond were fortified, i. e., a series of redoubts upon important points, connected by lines of trenches of more or less strong profile.

Plevna.

The only one of these camps which was assaulted or besieged was Plevna, and therefore this is the only one which needs to be described in detail. In the preceding chapters a full account has been given of the progress and results of the assaults and the siege, and it only remains to briefly describe the technical construction of the works.

In their location (see Plates 12, 16, and 19) but two features are worthy of special mention. *First*, a considerable portion of the works, viz., the "Middle Group," Redoubts Nos. 3 to 10, were placed on low ground, completely commanded by the neighboring ridges on the east and south in easy range; the necessity for this apparently bad location arose from the smallness of the defending force, which did not permit the occupation of these ridges without rendering the whole line too weak for energetic defense. And after all it did not prove so serious a disadvantage, for although the besiegers, in possession of these commanding ridges, were enabled to silence the defenders' artillery, to partially destroy the shape of their works, and to confine them to their bomb-proofs, nevertheless these same works resisted successfully every infantry assault.

Second, the works were built from day to day in the intervals of the Russian attacks and during their siege, without any comprehensive plan and without any maps of the locality. On the 20th of July there were only some trenches along the Grivitza heights, and just east of the town; on the 30th of July the Grivitza redoubt and 4 redoubts of the middle group had been constructed; on the 11th of September there were 18 redoubts (see Plate 16), including two on the key point of Krishin; on the 10th of December (see Plate 19) there were 47 redoubts and batteries and more than 60,000 yards of trenches connecting them.

The works thus grew from day to day under the necessities of the moment; yet, considering the strength of the defenders' forces, it is impossible to criticize their location. Had they been planned after a careful topographical survey, and after weeks of deliberation by a commission of engineers, they could not have been better placed. Their construction was supervised and directed by Tefvik Bey, the Turkish chief of staff, who displayed remarkable skill therein.

In plan the works presented great variety, but they were all of the simplest design possible, consistent with a proper adaptation to the nature of the ground. Not one of the works was bastioned, and usually no measures were taken for a flanking defense of the ditch. There were no accessory means of defense, such as wire entanglements, abattis, fougasses, etc. The prevailing form of tracé was the square or rectangle, of about 75 yards on a side; next in general use was the irregular hexagon, and lastly the pentagon; yet these forms were not rigorously adhered to, but were modified more or less whenever the nature of the ground demanded it.

In Plates 23 and 24 are given four sets of drawings representing the types of these works. On Plate 23 is shown Redoubt No. 1, of the "Middle Group," which was almost identical in shape with the Grivitza Redoubt and Redoubt No. 10; the former of which was carried by assault on September 11th and the latter repulsed its assailants on the same day. (See Chapter V., Part II., *ante*.) Plate 24 gives drawings of Redoubt No. 7 of the middle group, of Redoubt No. 26 of the Blasivatz group, and of Redoubt No. 38 of the Opanetz group.

The dimensions are given in detail in these drawings (the originals of which were given to me by the Russian Engineer Department), and they fully explain their construction. There are three peculiarities worth notice: *First*, there were no flanking defenses for the ditch (as already stated), but, on the other hand, there were (except in No. 26, which is a rare exception in this respect) two tiers of fire and sometimes three. On the counterscarp of the ditch was arranged a shallow, rude sort of covered way, affording ample protection (against infantry) for a single line of men, and thus doubling the defensive strength of the work; in addition, there was often a small trench running in front of the principal side of the work (as in Redoubt No. 1, Plate 23), and affording a third line of infantry fire. *Second*, a very extensive use was made of traverses; in the square redoubts there was usually a large traverse, or more properly a parados in the form of a square, 10 to 15 feet thick and 9 to 12 feet high, placed in the interior of the work, and its ends overlapping in line the rear ends of several traverses of like dimensions placed along the parapet. In the hexagonal and pentagonal redoubts the parados was sometimes straight and sometimes of most irregular form. *Third*, a very extensive use was also made of rude bomb-proofs. These were placed on the unexposed side of the parados, traverses, or parapet. Their shape and construction are shown in the drawings; they were of the same nature as those used during our civil war at Fort Wagner and elsewhere. The Turks employed them very extensively, not only within the redoubts but behind the trenches connecting them, whereas the Russians made no use of them at all. The ordinary dimensions of the Turkish trenches are shown in Profile No. 5, Plate 23; but along the Bukova ridge, which was exposed to fire longitudinally and in front and rear, there was a trench over 5,000 yards long, with traverses at short intervals, and large enough for two men on horseback to ride abreast without exposure. Many of the traverses in the Turkish works also contained rude bomb-proof magazines, but as a rule their ammunition was kept in the caissons (they had nothing but field pieces), and these were concealed and sheltered in the excavations shown by Profile No. 3, Plate 23, and No. 1, Plate 24. On two or three occasions the Russian shells struck these caissons and exploded them.

The steep batir given to their slopes will be noticed in all these drawings. Occasionally (as at Redoubt No. 7) gabions were used to revet the traverses and embrasures, but usually there was no revetment; the soil was a stiff, yellowish clay, admitting a batir of 5 or 6 to 1.

Russian Fortifications at Plevna.

The types of Russian fortifications at Plevna are shown on Plate 25. Fig. 1 represents, *a*, a redoubt for three guns, and *b*, one for infantry alone. There were two tiers of infantry fire, and the ditches were flanked by caponnières. There were two ditches, one in front of each line of fire, in the works represented by Fig. A, which feature does not appear in any of the Turkish works. There were two gorges, protected by a traverse, which at the same time served as a shelter for the reserve from front fire. Fig. 2 shows a lunette, with traverse and trenches on either side for the reserve. Profile No. 7 shows the trench or covered way which ran continuously from the Grivitza works to those on the Radischevo heights. In rear of this at intervals were works for the shelter of the reserve shown in Fig. 3. These afforded no protection to plunging fire, and were in this respect inferior to those of the Turks constructed for a similar purpose (Redoubt 38, Plate 24). The normal form of battery is shown in Fig. 4. These batteries usually contained 8 or 12 guns, and were without traverses, the great superiority of the Russian artillery in numbers and weight to that of their opponents rendering them almost unnecessary.

Adrianople.

The fortified camp surrounding the city of Adrianople, although it was abandoned without assault or siege, was one of

FIELD FORTIFICATIONS. 427

great strength. The terrain resembled that of Plevna in its general features, i. e., a town lying near the banks of a river and surrounded by hills from 300 to 400 feet in height and covered with vineyards, trees, and brush; on the opposite side of the river a flat plain. The works consisted of 24 redoubts, without connecting trenches, of which 19 were on the hills and 5 on the plain; they were constructed comparatively at leisure, upon plans and under the supervision of Blum Pasha, formerly an officer of engineers in the Prussian service; in location they equaled those at Plevna, but were in no way better; but in construction they were far more solid, and the tracés showed great originality and an excellent adaptation to the site. The prevailing type was a circular redoubt (sometimes containing a cavalier or réduit), with traverses containing bomb-proof magazines between each pair of guns, surrounded with a polygonal ditch with banquette for infantry fire; the gorge was closed by an exterior traverse in the form of a semicircle, usually arranged for one gun and for infantry fire. The varieties of this type are shown, in plan and profile, on Plate 23. The soil was a clay, but not so stiff as that at Plevna, and revetments were used, of fascines, timber, and masonry. The finish and workmanship of these works at Adrianople was most excellent. As already stated, they were not brought into action, and a theoretical discussion of the relative value of these tracés and those at Plevna is not within the limits of this chapter.

Buyuk Tchekmedje.

The lines at Buyuk Tchekmedje were planned and constructed by the same engineer (Blum Pasha) who built those at Adrianople, and the tracés and profiles are of the same character. These lines resemble the lines of Torres Vedras, but are far superior to them in natural strength. They are situated about twenty-five miles, by the road, from Constantinople; at this point the peninsula between the Sea of Marmora and the Black Sea is only twenty-four miles wide, and of this space the four miles nearest the Black Sea are occupied by a broad lake (Lake Derkos), and the eight miles nearest the Sea of Marmora are occupied by an arm of that sea, reducing the actual width of the peninsula to twelve miles; and of this space one half is filled with marsh which is impassable for eight months in the year, and the other half with a succession of broken hills covered with brush and interspersed with little valleys filled with ponds and marshes. Behind this line of lakes, swamps, and thickets runs a ridge almost continuous from sea to sea, about 700 feet high, open for the most part and sloping down to the marshes in a gentle glacis. Along this ridge there were at the close of the war thirty-three redoubts, disposed irregularly in three lines and connected by trenches. The works were incomplete and the garrison, about 30,000 men, was insufficient, but they constituted a place of vastly greater strength than Plevna.

Skobeleff's troops arrived in front of these lines just as the armistice was signed. Had it not been signed, his orders were to make an assault, and had it been made it would have furnished most valuable military lessons upon the attack and defense of field works; for on the one hand the position was not only the strongest in Turkey, but probably the strongest of its kind that was ever fortified, and on the other hand, it would have been stormed by that General among the Russians who had the most experience and the best appreciation of the nature of such assaults, and by troops that were the veterans of Lovtcha, Plevna, and Shipka. The assault, however, was not made, and many thousand men who would have lost their lives therein still live; but the question of the impregnability of field works is still an open one.

These works have been increased and completed and (probably) armed by the Turks since the war, and constitute the first line of defense of Constantinople. No other capital in the world possesses such a line of defense, and when completed, armed, and garrisoned in sufficient strength (about 75,000 men) it may fairly be deemed impregnable—except to a nation possessing a navy capable of controlling the Black Sea and Sea of Marmora, and a fleet of transports sufficient to land troops in rear of its flanks.

Shumla and Rustchuk.

The fortifications at Shumla and Rustchuk were not attacked during the war. They were both intrenched camps, one comprising eighteen and the other twenty outlying redoubts, and an old masonry enceinte of very little use at present. The tracés were irregular polygons, the profiles of great strength, and the

FIELD FORTIFICATIONS. 429

revetments largely of masonry. These works, as well as those of Silistria and Varna, are all to be razed, according to the terms of Art. 11 of the treaty of Berlin.

2. DEFENSE OF MOUNTAIN PASSES.

The best constructed works for the defense of the mountain passes were those erected by the Turks along the Balkans in the vicinity of Sophia. As already explained (Chapter VII., Part 2, *ante*) they had three positions or lines of defense along the high-road from Plevna to Sophia as it wound through the mountains, viz., Pravetz-Etropol, Orkhanie-Lukovitza, and Araba Konak. These lines consisted of works of strong profile for artillery and for infantry, constructed on the sides of the mountain in such way as to enfilade the various windings of the road. As a rule, the works were batteries with straight epaulments and small flanks; the ditch being from 4 to 9 feet deep and the parapet 6 feet in relief and 10 feet in thickness, in places where the slope was sufficiently slight to give room for this construction; but on steeper slopes there was no ditch, and the parapet was formed of the material dug out in rear in order to get space for a terreplein.

In the Araba Konak position, however, there was a line of redoubts six in number, running along the main crest of the mountain and about 1,500 yards apart; the two flank redoubts, one of which was on the road, were the strongest, as it was in front of them only that any approach was possible, but all the redoubts could bring their long-range fire to bear along the road. The redoubt which blocked the road was of most solid and excellent construction. It mounted but two guns, one at the front angle of the work and one on a cavalier in the center; in front of each gun the parapet was circular and pierced with three embrasures whose axes were radii of the circle—the advantage of this construction being that both guns had a wide circle of fire without weakening the parapet by giving too great a splay to the embrasures. A few hundred yards in front and lower down the mountain were trenches for infantry in several tiers.

In the position near Orkhanie there was a work of somewhat novel construction, being a straight epaulment for infantry and artillery combined (see Fig. 14, Plate 26); it was about 250 yards long and was pierced for 6 guns, thus leaving a space of over 40 yards between the guns, which space was occupied by the infantry; each gun was protected by a traverse on either side of it carried back about 3 yards from the interior crest, so that the gun fired, so to speak, from a hole protected on the three exposed sides.

In general the characteristic features of all these works in the mountains were a succession of tiers of fire, both for infantry and artillery, rising to a height of 500 feet or more on the mountain side (the various works being connected with good roads), and an abundant use of traverses. There were but few bomb-proofs, and these wholly for ammunition; the other bomb-proofs would probably have grown had the troops remained long in the works.

As narrated in Chapters VII. and IX., all these works near the Sophia road were turned by the flank, causing their evacuation, and none of them were assaulted. They afford therefore very few practical lessons.

The works at Shipka on the other hand were constructed during more than four months of almost incessant combat; but the site was so peculiar and the soil so difficult to work that they afford instances of military curiosity rather than lessons of wide and general application.

The nature of the topography and the position of the batteries at Shipka have already been described in Chapter IV. (See Plate 13.) The Russians, as there stated, occupied a narrow cramped position along the ridge of the high-road, and the Turks nearly surrounded them in a semicircle on the neighboring ridges; the soil on both sides was rocky and there were woods on the ground held by the Turks.

The Russians were thus exposed to fire from three sides, and this, together with their contracted space, necessitated a most curious shape for their batteries.

Fig. 1, Plate 26, represents the "Steel battery" on Mount St. Nicholas; it faced in the direction of Little Berdek Mountain and was commanded from Sugar Loaf Hill and Woody Mountain, on both sides and in the rear; hence the traverses were supplemented by an **L** in the rear, but, as the Turks gradually extended their positions along Bald Mountain Ridge, and the fire in the rear became heavier, an additional longitudinal traverse was added.

Fig. 2 represents the "Central Battery," which was exposed to the fire of the Turkish batteries on both flanks; it consisted of two parallel epaulments connected by one in the form of a semicircle. The piece in front fired in three directions through one of these embrasures; the other pieces fired in opposite directions by moving from one epaulment to the other. The "Round Battery" (Fig. 3) differed from the "Central" in having a longitudinal traverse between and parallel to the two epaulments confining each piece to one direction.

Owing to the rocky nature of the soil, the Russians made their epaulments of gabions filled with stones, or of simple piles of stones, Fig. 6. Fig. 4 represents the "Storm Battery No. 1," which was constructed wholly of gabions filled with stones. They also utilized large trees to construct bomb-proofs.

Fig. 5 represents a rifle-pit, for two men, almost a full circle in shape, affording a protection to the height of 7 feet, and pierced with two holes, or embrasures, lined with stones.

The Turkish works were much more extensive than those of the Russians, owing to the greater extent of position held by them. They displayed very great ingenuity in overcoming the natural obstacles of the soil, and in adapting their batteries to the site. Fig. 7 represents the mortar batteries on the summit of the Sugar Loaf Hill. Three mortars were there placed in two batteries, one above the other, and in front of them were infantry trenches. These batteries, consisting of an epaulment and two flanks, were excavated in solid rock (an argillaceous shale), and the height of the parapet was increased by a hurdle revetment fixed in the cracks of the rocks and filled with gravel (this latter was of more than doubtful utility). The infantry trenches (profiles 11 and 12) were formed in the same way of hurdles and gravel. Fig. 9 represents a battery for two guns on the "Crow's Nest." The battery was wholly excavated in the rocky soil, and as the natural slope was very gentle the sole of the embrasure had a length of 37 *feet*. Between the pieces were bomb-proofs, also excavated in the soil, and a large tree on the flank was ingeniously utilized by digging out a natural bomb-proof under its roots.

Fig. 10 represents a battery of eight pieces on Little Berdek Mountain. Bomb-proofs were placed between the pieces, sometimes horizontal and sometimes inclined, as shown in the profiles. The revetments were of hurdles and the filling was gravel. Figs. 11 and 12 represent the trenches connecting Woody Mountain and Bald Mountain. The trunks of trees were liberally used in these trenches, and occasionally they were disposed (Fig. 13) so as to form loopholes for the muskets.

Fig. 8 represents a battery, in the midst of this line of trenches, constructed in an abnormal but most ingenious manner. It was for two guns which pointed directly on the open part of the road between the Russian works on the Northern Hills and Battery Potiagin. It was screened from the Russian batteries on the Central Hills by traverses on the right flank of each gun, these traverses and the epaulment being constructed of hurdles filled with sand; the embrasure was 8 feet long, *but only 1 foot wide on the interior and 2 feet on the exterior.* The guns could therefore be traversed only a few degrees. But they were designed only to sweep this particular piece of road, on which there were no Russian batteries; and as the long narrow embrasure could only be seen by some one exactly in the direction of the axis, and as the battery was surrounded by trees, it was never discovered by the Russians, who could have demolished its weak high traverses with a few shots. It was in fact a "masked battery"—of which we heard so much in 1861.

The peculiar features of these Turkish works, as is apparent at once from an inspection of the drawings, are the ingenious methods by which the most was made of bad sites and a poor soil, the frequent use of rude but effectual bomb-proofs, and the constant employment of hurdles—the poorest of all revetments—and a filling of gravel and broken stone. That they served their purpose so well is due to the fact that the Russians were weak in artillery, that they had hardly any positions proper for its establishment, and, being surrounded by the Turks, its fire was eccentric and therefore of little effect.

3. FORTIFICATIONS ON AN OPEN FIELD OF BATTLE.

The Russians began the campaign relying on their bayonets and despising the spade.

The Turks, on the other hand, had an evident pride in their fortifications and a full appreciation, from the beginning, of their value. The characteristic feature of the Turkish works was their solidity and the neatness of their finish; those of the Russians (always excepting those built at Plevna after Todleben's arrival) were usually as slight as possible, and their general appearance was "slouchy," as if constructed by men who looked upon such work as servile drudgery.

In the valuable report of General Kiou (referred to in the letter of transmittal) from which copious extracts have been made in this chapter, the following very just observation is made:

"It is the nature of the Russian soldier, when he stops for a month, to instal himself, in the matter of fortifications, as if he would remain but a day; whereas the Turk, stopping for a day, instals himself as if for a month."

Both sides perhaps carried their natural tastes to an extreme; for the Turks constructed more than thirty works which were abandoned without firing a shot to one that was properly defended, and the Russians refused to employ the spade until its lessons had been forced upon them by a very rude experience of the murderous fire of modern breech-loaders from behind trenches. One side erred by excessive prudence and its bad effect upon the morale of the men, and the other by recklessness and its attendant slaughter.

After the bloody repulse of the Russians at Plevna on the 30th of July, they fell back about twelve miles and took up a position extending from Tristenik to Poradim, with their left flank thrown forward to Zgalevitza and Pelishat (see Plate 17), and hastily fortified it. This position was attacked on its left flank by 25,000 men under Osman on the 31st of August (see pp. 226 and 227), and it sustained the attack, repelling the assailants with considerable loss. The character of these fortifications was very slight; the artillery was disposed on the crests of low hills commanding the valleys of approach, usually in batteries of 4, 8, or 12 guns behind a single epaulment without embrasures, but as many as 30 guns being sometimes placed in one group. These epaulments were of a simple nature (see Fig. 17, Plate 26) and presented nothing remarkable. The employment of single guns behind a shelter trench with flanks and bonnets, in the manner laid down in the Austrian and French regulations, was never resorted to. The intervals between the batteries were occupied by lines of shelter trenches for infantry, and on the brows of hills these rose one above another in tiers. The form of these trenches (Figs. 15 and 16) offered nothing remarkable.

The detachment under the Cesarevitch, forming the left wing of the army, after its retreat in September took up a good defensive position behind the line of the Lom, extending from Metchka on the Danube to Tabashka on the Lom (see Plate 14), and in this position defeated all the attacks of Suleiman's army. The position was fortified in the same way as the one just described, i. e., with shallow, sunken batteries, for 4, 8, or 12 pieces of artillery, and lines of shelter trenches for the infantry. The plans and profiles of these trenches closely resembled those in Figs. 15, 16, and 17, Plate 26. There were here, however, two or three redoubts on points of commanding importance.

The cases in which the Russian troops under General Wilhelminof received an attack of the Turks in hastily made trenches and repulsed it with volley firing, inflicting a loss ten times greater than their own, have been fully described in the narrative of the campaign in Bulgaria (Chapters IX. and X.). These trenches were mere scratchings, about a foot deep and twice as wide, the loose earth being thrown up in front; and they are striking examples of what *steady* troops, armed with breech-loaders, can accomplish behind a rude fortification.

The Turks, in constructing their fortifications, aimed usually at works of a stronger character, and capable of a long defense. They would finish one large, strong redoubt and then begin the construction of another, and then a third, according to the time they had available, rather than throw a thin line of shelter trench over the whole position and then gradually strengthen all its parts. Their works, although admirable in construction, required a great deal of time, and the only instances where they fought behind trenches constructed in less than 48 hours were at Plevna, July 20th, and at Taskosen, December 31st.

When they were forced to give battle at Philippopolis in the midst of a retreat, they fought for three days in the open field, taking advantage of rocks, ditches, and hedges, but without constructing any trenches.

The question of equipment of the infantry soldier with implements for fortification is one of the most important ones connected with this general subject, and may properly be considered here.

INTRENCHING IMPLEMENTS.

Concerning the Turkish equipment I am unable to say anything definite. I never saw their soldiers (dead, wounded, or prisoners) provided with any portable spades, and my impression is that the latter were furnished in the same manner as their rations and tents, i. e., by transportation in country wagons obtained by requisition, and like them they were abandoned in large quantities. In the Russian infantry, before the war, every company (numbering about 200 men) was provided with the following tools, viz., 16 axes, 10 shovels, 6 picks and spades, 1 crowbar.

They were all carried in the company wagons.

A company of sappers had the following tools, viz., 103 shovels, 30 picks, 16 crowbars, 71 axes, 8 scythes.

These tools were ordinarily carried in the wagons, but were of such shape that they could be carried on the person if necessary.

It is thus seen that there was almost no provision in the way of tools for hasty field fortification, and that there was also a great lack of instructed men to supervise the construction of trenches, since there were only 3,000 sappers with the army of 200,000 men which began the war (see p. 148). This want was felt more or less keenly throughout the whole campaign, especially during the early days of the fighting at Shipka, and in the battles of Plevna. General Skobeleff, in his report of his attack on the two redoubts near the town of Plevna on September 11th (see pp. 247–255), complains very much of the lack of intrenching tools. When the investment of Plevna was begun a large number of spades and shovels were of course sent forward from Russia and Roumania and distributed to the troops. After the surrender of Plevna General Skobeleff ordered the men in his division to keep these spades and shovels and carry them on their persons; every man carried an implement of some kind, about 85 per cent. being spades or shovels, 10 per cent. picks, and the rest axes, etc. His division marched with these on their backs from Plevna to Constantinople; they were slung over the back, the handle projecting above the left shoulder and the spade below the right hip, and were attached to the shoulder with a piece of string, a strap, a piece of old tent, or anything else that was available; they were heavy (weighing over 5 lbs.), they were uncomfortable, they were in every way inconvenient, but each man had learned by hard experience to feel that his individual life depended upon his musket and his spade—and he took good care to lose neither the one nor the other. When the small "Linneman" spade was issued to these men while they were camped in front of Constantinople, their officers asked them what they thought of it, and they replied laughingly that "it would make a very good soup spoon!"

Other divisions equipped themselves with intrenching tools during the campaign in the same way as Skobeleff's, to a greater or less extent, depending on the Division Commander. At the close of the campaign "the Linneman" spade was issued to the troops.

The propriety of combining an intrenching tool of some kind with a bayonet has been quite as much discussed and experimented upon in Europe as in America. Various devices, such as a trowel bayonet, saw bayonet, etc., as well as using the bayonet and its scabbard as a handle for a spade, which would at ordinary times be carried in a pouch slung from the belt, have all been tried and all uniformly rejected. The question of abandoning the bayonet is at present under discussion, especially in Germany, but no nation has yet made up its mind to it. Concerning this subject I can add nothing to what was contained in the report which I had the honor to make in May, 1878, in reply to a demand therefor from General Sherman, viz., that, although the bayonet may be rarely used, although the percentage of wounds from it to those from the bullet may be very small, although it adds a pound to the 50 lbs. or more which the soldier has to carry on the march, and something less than a dollar to the cost of the musket, *yet in a well conducted assault it still is possible for the assailants to reach the defenders' trench and come to hand-to-hand blows, and then the side which has the bayonet will win if the other side has it not;* and if one battle is won by its aid, the cost of a million bayonets and all the trouble entailed in transporting them have been more than repaid. With us the habitual and so to speak daily use of our army in Indian warfare prevents us from considering the equipment of the troops purely from the standpoint of its effectiveness in great battles. In Indian warfare there is a maximum of marching and a minimum of hard fighting; in a great war it is exactly the reverse. On the plains or in the mountains—in any unsettled country—a sort of universal tool, comprising a saw, a hatchet, etc., is not only always handy, but almost indispensable; the Indian method of warfare is one in which hand-to-hand fights are much more rare than in great battles, in fact they hardly ever occur. The result is that a compromise such as the trowel bayonet is popular with the great majority of officers. This compromise tool injures the bayonet and injures the gun, is most useful as a hatchet, but of no service as an intrenching tool except to throw up the very slightest shelter and that in soft ground. It may be taken for granted that not only ourselves but every other nation will, in considering this subject in time of peace, give more prominence to the inconvenience of a large long-handled spade, which inconvenience exists at all times, than to the necessity for a *thoroughly* efficient intrenching tool, which is only impressed upon the mind by actual individual experience in war itself. We may look then to see every nation adopting in time of peace some half measure, such as the short-handled small spade, the trowel bayonet, etc., but it is more than probable that the next great war on this continent, or in Europe, will bring about the same practical experience as the one in Turkey, viz., that all personal inconvenience must be sacrificed to the vital necessity of having the most efficient intrenching tools, i. e., a common pick and a big spade, and that, once convinced of their great value, the troops will carry them most cheerfully.

At present the "Linneman" spade has been adopted for infantry troops either definitely or as an experiment by Germany, Austria, France, and Russia. This spade as adopted in the Russian service is shown in detail in Plate 26, and alongside of it the long-handled spade of the Russian sappers. The leather pouches in which they are carried are also shown; the Linneman spade hangs from the waist-belt behind the right hip, with the handle down; the long-handled spade has the handle up, the pouch hanging from the back of the waist-belt and the handle projecting above the shoulder and steadied by a strap fastened to a shoulder-belt.

The Linneman spade has a blade 7 × 5½ inches, and a handle 12½ inches long; its weight is from 1.5 to 1.7 lbs. (.70 to .77 kilogramme) without the pouch, or 2.1 to 2.3 lbs. with it. Two sides have a fine edge, and the third is a saw. Its total length, being about half a meter, forms a convenient unit for laying off measures in working.

The sapper spade has a blade 10 × 7⅜ inches, and a handle 34 inches long; its weight is 4 lbs. without the pouch and 4.86 lbs. with it.

As General Brialmont* says: "The Linneman spade has many good qualities, but it has also all the defects of an implement intended for several uses."

After weighing its merits and defects, however, he decides unqualifiedly in favor of it as against the long-handled spade, on account of the inconvenience attending the transportation of the latter by the men.

The principal objections to the Linneman spade are that the blade is small; the saw and hatchet edges will be of no use after they have been used in the ground; the handle is so short that the men have to work in a cramped position on their knees and can not get a proper purchase upon it to develop their whole strength, and can only throw the earth a short distance. Great numbers of experiments have been made to determine the relative amount of work which the two spades can accomplish in the same time, and the relative amount of time required to construct the same works; in these experiments the Austrians took the lead prior to their adoption of the Linneman spade in 1874, the Germans have followed, and the Russians also since the war. The result of the Russian experiments made in the summer of 1878 is shown in the following table:

	Cross section of excavation in square feet.	TIME.	
		Linneman spade.	Sapper spade.
		h. m.	h. m.
Shelter trench..................	1.5	0 8	0 10
Shelter trench..................	4.5	0 30	0 30
Intrenchment...................	9	0 54	0 40
Redoubt........................	66.5	8 46	2 35
Battery.........................	74	2 19	1 56

For the shelter trenches and intrenchment the men were in one row, for the redoubt in three rows, and for the battery in five rows; in each row the men were one pace (28 inches) apart, and in all cases they were divided into two reliefs, changing every 20 minutes.

* For a very full discussion of this subject see chapter 3 of "La Fortification du Champ de Bataille," by Lieutenant-General A. Brialmont, Chief of Engineers in the Belgian army, and author of several works on fortification.

These experiments, which give the same general results as those made in Austria and elsewhere, show that for the shallow shelter trench the small spade is more convenient than the large one, and accomplishes the work in less time; but for larger works, where the earth needs to be broken up in as large shovelfuls as possible and thrown to some distance, the large spade is decidedly superior to the small one, and performs the same work in two thirds of the time.

In regard to the number of implements to be carried, the Austrians and Russians have adopted the principle that every file shall carry one spade (or 1 to every 2 men), the Germans every second file (or 1 to every 4 men), and that picks, in the proportion of about 10 per cent. and large spades in the proportion of 25 per cent. of the portable spades, and a certain number of axes, shall be carried in the company wagons. On the basis of the Austrian and Russian regulations, since the soldier occupies 22 inches in line and 28 inches when at work with the spade, three half platoons of each company would do the intrenching, the front and rear ranks relieving each other, and the fourth half platoon would be in reserve, guard the muskets, or be thrown forward as skirmishers.

Each of the three nations above mentioned has also adopted a regulation prescribing that a certain number of picks, large spades, and axes shall be carried in the company wagons by the cavalry. But, during the campaign, in several Russian cavalry divisions there were formed detachments of mounted sappers and pioneers, which carried portable intrenching tools on their saddles, and it is probable that the same plan will be adopted in every future war. The utility of such detachments is beyond question in clearing roads, in destroying railroads, in seizing some commanding point and hastily fortifying it until the arrival of the infantry, etc., etc.

To sum up this matter of equipment of infantry with intrenching tools, it may be stated that, as the result of our civil war and of the European wars of 1866, 1870, and 1877, every great military nation on the Continent has now adopted the short-handled Linneman spade, to be constantly carried by a certain portion of the infantry, and a number of long-handled spades and picks, to be carried in reserve in the company wagons.

CHAPTER II.

ATTACK OF FORTIFIED POSITIONS.

THE first essential to success in an assault upon a fortified position is, of course, a numerical superiority of forces on the part of the assailants. The rapidity of fire of breech-loaders has so increased the relative strength of troops defending a line of works, that this superiority must at least be 50 per cent., in order to warrant any hope of success. In every case in which the Russians were successful in their assaults, their superiority was as great or greater than this. If the weaker side wishes to gain a battle, it can only hope to do so by choosing a position favorable for defense, fortifying it, and compelling an attack by the enemy.

The Russian regulations, as well as those of other countries, prescribe that the assault shall "be prepared by artillery," i. e., that the defender's position shall be bombarded for several hours, the duration of this cannonade to depend on circumstances. Its objects are—1. To silence the defender's artillery; 2. To destroy or injure his works; 3. To inflict such a loss upon him as to demoralize his men.

The first object can be attained sooner or later, depending on the defender's strength in artillery; the second, as was abundantly proved in our civil war no less than in Turkey, can not be attained; after months of bombardment, field-works will still afford ample protection for infantry fire, and the injury of a day can always be practically repaired in a night. The third object may or may not be possible of attainment, depending upon the extent of the defender's works and the number of bomb-proofs with which they are provided.

The old question, whether this bombardment accomplishes

any good purpose, or whether it is preferable to make the attack during the night or at early dawn, without giving any warning by the use of artillery, has received very little elucidation in the recent war. At Plevna, after three days' bombardment by artillery four times superior in number to that of the Turks, the Russians were defeated in an assault with terrible losses. On the other hand, at Lovtcha a nine hours' bombardment of the Turkish lines (much weaker than those of Plevna, and without bomb-proofs) did greatly demoralize the defenders, and pave the way for a completely successful assault. Still, again, Kars, a place equal or superior to Plevna in natural and artificial strength, was carried by infantry in an open assault during the night—an assault as heroic as it is unusual in military annals. And at Shipka, Skobeleff's troops stormed the Shenovo lines in daylight, without any artillery at all, and compelled the surrender of an army of nearly 40,000 men as the result of a single battle. It should be remembered, also, that at the assault of Plevna (September 11th), Skobeleff did carry the works in his front (Redoubts Nos. 11 and 12), and that he was driven out the next day because these works were open to the rear, and were commanded on every side by other Turkish works. His attack succeeded; but as it had not been directed upon a commanding point, he was obliged to relinquish all the ground that he had acquired. (See pp. 247–255, *ante.*)

The only conclusion to be drawn from these discordant results would seem to be that for weak lines without bomb-proofs, artillery may serve a very useful purpose in preparing the attack; for strong lines with bomb-proofs it is of very little if of any use; and that it *may* be possible for a skillful, energetic commander to make a successful assault without any artillery at all.

Before speaking of the infantry formation for the assault it must be premised that the traditions of the Russians are for the tactics of the "shock" followed by the bayonet; and such traditions die hard. But the shock of heavy columns is powerless before the rain of bullets poured out by breech-loading muskets. A modification of the Russian tactics of the Crimean war was therefore made after the war of 1870. Although the lessons of our civil war have been but little regarded by European armies (partly due to the lack of authoritative reports on the subject from our own War Department and partly due to other causes), yet the campaigns of 1866 and 1870 made a profound impression and induced a change in the tactics of every European nation. Fighting in dispersed lines became the order of the day, and the Prussian company column * was adopted as the formation previous to actual firing, in place of the deeper columns of battalions or regiments. The state of the Russian regulations on this subject, as they existed in 1875, has been given in the chapter on Tactics (see pp. 128 to 132, *ante*).

These regulations prescribe that the attack shall be made in open order, the battalion being formed in two lines of company columns (the companies of the first line being deployed in line or formed in column by platoons, and those of the second line in column by platoons or half platoons); at the signal "deploy," the companies of the first line send forward each a half platoon (one eighth of a company) as skirmishers, in groups or "swarms" of fours; the first line of companies follows the swarms at a distance of 300 paces, and if necessary sends forward additional sections to replace losses in the skirmish line; the second line of companies follows at a distance of 300 to 400 paces from the first line; the fifth or rifle company of each battalion remains in reserve, and at the proper moment is deployed around the flanks to follow up the retreat of the enemy, in case of success, or to receive his counter attack, in case of failure. The "swarms" in the skirmish line run forward with rushes of 50 paces at a time, then lie down under cover if possible, begin firing, regain their breath, and run forward again.

This formation therefore prescribes three lines for the battalion, viz., the skirmish line, or "swarms," the supports, consisting of the first line of companies, and the reserve, consisting of the second line of companies. The tactics also permitted another formation, viz., the battalion in simple line preceded by its rifle company deployed as skirmishers. These formations are shown in the following figures :

* For a thorough analysis of the Prussian company column, see an article on the subject by General Emory Upton in the "International Review" for May, 1875 (Vol. II., p. 302); also his report on "The Armies of Asia and Europe," p. 270, *et seq.*

ATTACK OF FORTIFIED POSITIONS. 443

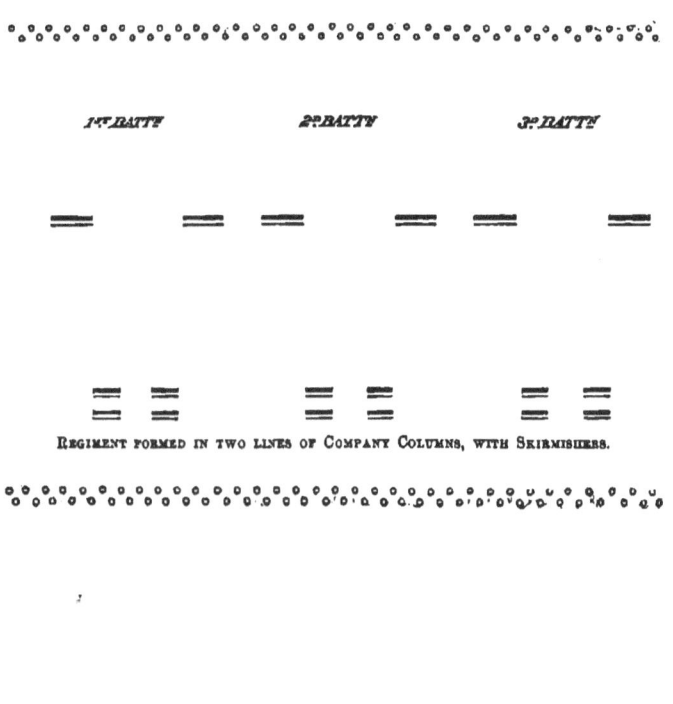

When large bodies of troops are assembled in battle there are three main lines; the first composed of one or more battalions of each regiment disposed as just described; the second composed of the remaining battalions of the regiment in compact column, under shelter as near as possible to the troops engaged; the third composed of the general reserve, one third to one fourth of the whole force, in compact battalion columns (usually double column on the center), at such points in rear of the line as the Commander-in-Chief may designate, and under his sole orders.

For the manœuvres near St. Petersburg in the summer of 1876, a slight change was introduced in the tactics; the division of the company into 2 platoons, 4 half platoons, and 8 sections, was changed to 2 half companies, 4 platoons, and 16 sections. The battalion of 4 companies was formed for the attack in two lines of company columns (with platoon front) at 300 yards distance. At the signal "deploy," each company of the first line sent a half company forward 200 paces, and then the half company sent forward 2 sections (one fourth of its strength) as skirmishers, and reënforced the skirmishers by other sections as necessary.

This formation was afterward adopted for all the 4-battalion regiments of the army; it is a modification in detail only of the formation previously given, and it had but little bearing on the campaign in Europe, since nearly all the troops there engaged were 3-battalion regiments.

Such were the regulations and the tactics in which the Russian troops were drilled at the outbreak of the war.

At the first battle in which they were engaged, viz., the passage of the Danube at Sistova on the night of June 26th–27th, a regular formation was not possible. General Dragomirof, commanding the 14th Division, which made the passage, makes the following remarks in his report: "The characteristic feature of the combat of the 15th (27th) was that the first troops engaged did not form whole battalions, nor companies, nor even platoons; on landing the troops formed themselves into improvised groups; . . . each group observed attentively what its' neighbors were doing, each regulating its movements by those of the others, and lending each other a mutual support.

"It was not possible to think of forming a general reserve until after the passage of the last detachments of the 14th Division, i. e., about 9:30 A. M., nearly eight hours after the beginning of the action."

It will be remembered that the passage of the Danube cost the Russians only about 800 men; and one of the chief causes of the smallness of the loss and of the success of the action may be found in the individuality displayed in the manner of fighting.

At the next battle, viz., the assault of the works surrounding Nikopolis, and the capture of that place and its garrison by the IX. Corps under General Krüdener, on July 15th and 16th, a more compact order was observed. In General Krüdener's report it is stated that the 18th Regiment, which attacked the Turks on the west side of the Osma, advanced with two battalions in line, two batteries being in the interval, and one battalion in reserve. The regiment moved forward to the as-

ATTACK OF FORTIFIED POSITIONS. 445

sault after a short fusillade, and drove the Turks from five successive positions, although covered on their front, and afterward on their right flank, by shells from the Turkish batteries. The troops which assaulted the works on the east bank of the Osma and near the town, moved forward approximately in the order prescribed by the regulations, i. e., a line of skirmishers followed by a line of companies, and finally by the reserve. Two attacks were defeated, and only the third, in which nearly all the reserve was engaged, was successful. The Turkish resistance in this instance, however, was not very stubborn. Among the 7,000 men who surrendered there were only 300 wounded; the total losses of the Russians were about 1,300.

In Gourko's first expedition over the Balkans in July, there was no serious fighting until he was obliged to retreat before the army of Suleiman Pasha. Previous to that time his troops had been engaged mainly in cavalry raids for cutting the telegraphs and railroads and in the skirmishes incident to that service; when this retreat began it was principally remarkable for the good use made of the cavalry in defending a position on foot, and then retreating rapidly to another position, and for the stubbornness shown by the Bulgarians in disputing the advance of the Turks.

The defense of the Shipka position involved no tactical manœuvres; the Russians merely stood their ground on a line of rocky hills and tried to keep the Turks from gaining possession of them.

At the first battle of Plevna, July 20th, the troops were formed in the prescribed manner, i. e., two lines of company columns—the first of which sent forward its skirmishers—and a reserve, the artillery being posted in the intervals.

This battle, however, is not worth considering as an illustration of tactical formations, for in it 7,500 men attacked 25,000 without reconnoitering their strength or position; such an attack was doomed to utter failure and great loss, no matter in what formation the troops were placed.

At the second battle of Plevna, July 30th, about 30,000 men attacked a force of over 40,000. The battle began with a bombardment lasting from 8:15 A. M. to 2:40 P. M. The troops were formed in the usual manner. There were two attacks against the Grivitza redoubt, one on the right, or north of the redoubt, and the other on the left, or southeast of it; in the first the skirmishers reached the parapet of the redoubt and engaged in a hand-to-hand fight; their supports, consisting of three battalions, marched forward, says the official account, deployed in line "in perfect order and singing." But before they had had time to reach the redoubt they lost considerably over a third of their strength, and they stopped and fell back—what was left of the skirmishers joining in their retreat. A battalion was then sent forward from the reserve, and subsequently a second; this constituted an entirely new attack, having no direct relation to the first, which was wholly finished and defeated; the troops reached the ditch and kept up a fight with the defenders at a few paces distance until nightfall, when, being unsuccessful in their efforts to get over the parapet, they were obliged to withdraw. The troops attacking this redoubt on the left or southeast met "such a deadly fire that they could not reach the redoubt; the men fell in such numbers that the bodies of the dead and wounded interfered with any movement."

The attack on the left flank against the redoubts of the middle group was made in a similar manner, but with somewhat more of tactical unity; it succeeded in gaining possession of two redoubts, but there were no reënforcements available, and at nightfall the order was given to retreat.

At the battle of Lovtcha, September 3d, 22,000 Russians attacked about 15,000 Turks. The artillery cannonade lasted from 5 A. M. to 2:30 P. M. The assault was then made by the infantry, formed in two lines of company columns preceded by skirmishers; it was completely successful, and by nightfall it had destroyed one fourth of the defenders and put the rest to a disorderly flight. The following order of the day, given by General Skobeleff to his troops the evening before the battle, contains many useful hints:

"In the first part of the action which is about to take place the preponderating rôle belongs to the artillery. The order of attack will be communicated to the chiefs of batteries, who are recommended not to scatter their artillery fire. When the infantry moves forward to the attack the artillery will support it with all its efforts. Special vigilance is then necessary; the fire will be accelerated if the enemy should unmask any reserves, and pushed to its utmost limit if the attacking column meets

ATTACK OF FORTIFIED POSITIONS. 447

any unforeseen obstacles. When the distance permits, shrapnel will be used against the enemy's trenches and troops. The infantry must avoid disorder in the struggle, and make a careful distinction between the forward movement and the attack. Do not forget the necessity of aiding your comrades at any sacrifice. Do not waste your cartridges. Remember that the nature of the country renders it very difficult to supply ammunition. I mention once more to the infantry the necessity of order and silence in fighting. Do not cry 'hurrah' until you are close to the enemy and are preparing to charge him with the bayonet. I call the attention of all the soldiers to the fact that in an intrepid attack the losses are a minimum, and that a retreat, especially a retreat in disorder, results in great losses and in shame.

"This order will be read in every company in so far as it concerns the infantry."

At the third battle of Plevna, September 11th, the Russians were at last numerically superior, the relative forces of infantry being about 74,000 to 56,000. The assault was preceded by an artillery cannonade of more than three days' duration; it began at 6:30 A. M. September 8th, and was kept up without intermission during daylight, and at intervals during the night, until 3 P. M. September 11th, when the assaults were made. The Roumanians and part of the Russian IX. Corps, which assaulted the Grivitza redoubts from three sides, were formed in the same manner as on July 30th; the attack was made in the same disconnected fashion as on that day, and met with nearly the same result, except that just at nightfall a simultaneous rush from two sides carried the assailants into one of the redoubts, where they got the best of the Turks in a hand-to-hand fight.

The assault in the center against Redoubt No. 10 was made in two distinct efforts at intervals of more than three hours; the second one was made by six battalions, of which four were deployed in line, with skirmishers about two hundred paces in front, the fifth in company columns at the center of the line, and the sixth in reserve under shelter at about 1,200 yards from the redoubt. When the line arrived within about 300 yards of the redoubt it halted and lay down to fire, the center battalion deploying into line; after a few minutes it got up and moved forward again in solid line and came very close to the redoubt, the skirmishers reaching the ditch. But the fire was too strong for such a line, and the men were obliged to fall back, one battalion halting and checking a counter attack of the Turks. The battalion in reserve was brought forward to their assistance, but was altogether too feeble to do anything but join in the retreat to its place of shelter.

At the battle of Gorni-Dubnik, October 24th, 18,000 Russians attacked 4,000 Turks occupying a redoubt of small profile with an outlying lunette and a few trenches. The artillery cannonade lasted only from 9 to 10 A. M. The infantry was formed on three sides of the redoubt, in two lines of company columns and a reserve. It moved forward to the assault in this order, preceded by a line of skirmishers. The lunette and trenches were carried, but the men could not reach the redoubt; they lay down in the ditch of the road and under other slight shelter, at distances varying from only 100 to 400 paces from the redoubt, and remained there, keeping up their fire whenever the defenders were visible. During the afternoon a second disjointed attack was made without success (see p. 275, *et seq*.). Finally, about dark, a simultaneous rush was made from three sides, which gained possession of the work. The Turks had inflicted on the Russians a loss nearly equal to the total strength of their own force, and had themselves lost about 35 per cent.

The instances which have been given are the principal assaults in the first half of the war; they have been cited somewhat at length, and in repetition of what has already been narrated in the accounts of the battles themselves, in order that the salient features of their tactics may be compared; and they present many points of resemblance. In nearly every case the troops were drawn up in two lines of company columns and a reserve. The skirmishers were sent forward, the first line followed at 150 or 200 paces distance, and then the second line. In no instance, however, does it appear that there was more than one line of skirmishers; behind them the troops marched with dogged bravery, in solid line of two ranks, shoulder to shoulder, or in company columns with platoon fronts, far inside the line of rapid effective fire; and they continued this march until the fire caused a break in their lines and a retreat, or until they reached the work after enormous losses, and held it as the result of a hand-to-hand fight. The skirmish line was so small in

ATTACK OF FORTIFIED POSITIONS. 449

comparison with the main force that it really amounted to nothing, and the attack was in fact made in solid line. The attack and the forward movement were *not* distinguished. This defective formation was the principal cause of the heavy losses.

We next observe that, where attacks were made on two or more sides of a work, they were frequently made not simultaneously, but one after the other; so that the defenders were able to move from one side of their work to another and repulse the attacks in detail. We also notice that the reserve was often sent forward, not just before the line began to waver, but after it was already in retreat. The effect of these dispositions was the same as if the attack had been made with only a portion of the force instead of the whole, since the new attack had to gain all over again what had been gained (and lost) in the first.

In the latter part of the war (and also in Skobeleff's attack at Plevna on September 11th) these faults, which experience had demonstrated, were not repeated. In all of Gourko's operations, during and after the passage of the Balkans, there was no instance in which a fortified position was assaulted in front; having a superiority of force, he threatened the enemy's front (occupying their attention with the fire of a skirmish line, with strong supports posted in the nearest shelter), and turned their flanks, compelling their retreat—the tactics, in short, of Sherman's Atlanta campaign. The counter attacks of the Turks were received with careful, cool volley-firing by half companies, delivered when the Turks were within 150 yards, and in every case attended with success.

The two direct front assaults made by Skobeleff's troops, at Plevna, September 11th, and in rear of Shipka, January 8th, were conducted in the following manner. The troops were formed under shelter, between 2,000 and 3,000 yards from the Turkish lines, in battalion masses (double column of half companies on the center). In beginning the action the rifle company of each battalion was sent forward as a thin line of skirmishers, half the company as skirmishers, and one platoon (quarter company) in column of half platoon behind the line, at a distance of not more than fifty paces, and constantly replacing its losses. About 200 paces behind the skirmishers came the first battalion, which moved forward in line, not touching elbows, but with intervals of about two paces (or less) between the men

—a strong skirmish line in fact—each company having three fourths of its strength in line and one fourth just behind it, in half platoon column, to replace its losses. The men moved forward preserving a general alignment, but each man taking advantage of any shelter that lay in his path, and firing from behind it, and then moving forward again. Another battalion followed in precisely the same order, at a distance of about 300 paces, so that the men could feel that there were supports coming behind them.

The remaining battalion of the regiment was held in hand by the division commander until the fight developed itself, and it could be seen where the most resistance was met, whether the enemy was bringing any troops on the flank, etc.; the battalion was then directed on the point where it was most needed.

The regiments on either side were sent forward in the same manner.

Meanwhile the reserve regiment of the division, always under the control of the division commander, was kept under shelter as near as possible to the line; as the troops already engaged, which had now merged into two lines (and at points where the resistance was greatest into one), began to move slowly, to halt, to waver, the reserve regiment or a portion of it was sent forward rapidly to the point where the fighting was hottest.

In the course of a long conversation on this subject, General Skobeleff expressed himself as follows (I quote from the rough notes made at the time): " The only formation in which troops can successfully assault intrenched positions is in successive lines of skirmishers. The division general must be perfectly thoughtless of his own comfort or safety, and put himself between the skirmishers and the reserves where he can feel the pulse of the battle and have his troops in his own hand, and judge himself of the moment when the successive battalions in reserve should be sent forward. There are in every command a small percentage of cowards who will slink away at the first opportunity, a certain number of men of rash bravery who will go too far forward and get killed, and the great majority of men of ordinary courage, but liable to waver as the fight gets hot. The reserves must be sent in at the moment when the reasonably brave men have been long enough engaged and met with enough resist-

ATTACK OF FORTIFIED POSITIONS. 451

ance to begin to feel nervous, but before they have actually begun to retreat; and it is in deciding upon the opportune moment for sending forward his reserves that the art of a division commander consists."

Such are the opinions of the General who made more open assaults than any other in this war, and who never failed in any one of them to carry the works which he was ordered to attack. They are very different from the "shock" tactics of Suwarof and the deep columns of Napoleon at Wagram, but they suit the requirements and spirit of this age as those of Suwarof and Napoleon suited theirs. They only amplify but do not change in any way the lessons of our civil war; and had these lessons been more carefully studied in Russia there would have been far less slaughter around Plevna.

Concerning the company column, which is the adopted formation for attack in every continental army, a few words may not be out of place.

In all civilized armies the tactical unit is the battalion, numbering about 1,000 men. The continental nations, having large armies in time of peace as well as in war, unite four (or sometimes three) battalions into a regiment, for purposes of economy in administering their affairs in common; from the same motive of economy the number of officers is reduced by dividing the battalion into as few companies as possible, viz., four (or sometimes five). The companies thus number 250 or 200 men; and it is necessary to have a formation sufficiently compact for the whole company to be in reach of the captain and not so deep as to be cut to pieces by artillery fire; this necessity has given rise to the "company column," i. e., the formation of the company in column of platoons (one fourth of its strength) at half distance. The front of the platoon (for a company of 250 men) is about 18 yards, and the depth of the column about 32 yards. The 4 companies formed in such column and placed with the heads of the columns in line and at deploying intervals, form the battalion in company column—a most convenient formation under the circumstances.

If now we examine our own service, we find that none of these circumstances exist. Our army is so small in time of peace that 4,000 men never have been brought together, and it may be safely said that they never will. According to the returns of the Adjutant-General of February 28th, 1879, the army of 25,000 men was scattered at 140 garrisoned posts (exclusive of arsenals), which therefore averaged 178 men at each. The largest post (Fort Clark, Texas) had 18 companies, or about 1,000 men, being parts of one artillery, two cavalry, and two infantry regiments. Only one regiment in the whole service (5th Infantry) was united.

The administration of our service in time of peace is by posts rather than by regiments, and the necessity of combining several battalions into one regiment for purposes of economy in administration has no existence whatever. The propriety of forming an organization of several battalions in one regiment—which organization will exist only on paper in time of peace, and in time of war will be as new as if it had never existed at all—is at least open to question.

The large companies and small proportion of officers is also not in accordance with the necessities of our service. In time of peace, small detachments of ten or fifteen men are constantly being sent on scouts and other duty requiring the presence of an officer; in time of war we have always relied upon calling out large numbers of volunteers, and these require a greater proportion of officers than regularly drilled troops.

For actual use in battle, the tactical unit (whether called a regiment or a battalion is immaterial) is 1,000 men all over the world. This our present regimental organization gives.

In battle, also, the smaller companies, numbering 100 men each, are easier to handle than the larger ones which all Europe has copied from the economical Germans. The formation of each company into double column of fours on the center puts the regiment in a shape as convenient for handling as that of the battalion in company columns; from this the regiment can be developed into line and the number ones sent forward as the first line of skirmishers, to be reënforced by the number twos or threes; or, without deploying the column, the numbers one of odd companies and four of even companies (the outside men of each column) could be deployed as skirmishers. The company column and its method of forming skirmishers by one platoon followed by another, by which the men of different platoons and even of companies and battalions become mingled together in line, is at best a clumsy contrivance. Our present

ATTACK OF FORTIFIED POSITIONS.   453

tactics for skirmishing, in which one or more men of each set of fours are sent forward according to the strength of line required, is the simplest and most effective which has ever been devised; it admits a great variety of manœuvres without complication, and it meets more fully than any other the conditions of attack imposed by the rapid fire and long range of the modern breech-loader; it is the legitimate outgrowth of the tactics on this continent, where fighting in open order first originated and where the tactics of the "shock" and deep columns never had an existence, and have left no traditions to be overcome in order to meet modern requirements.

Concerning the use and the tactics of artillery and cavalry, there is little to be said as the result of the war in Turkey.

The cavalry never fought in any great battle. In Gourko's first expedition over the Balkans it accomplished some purpose in cutting the railroads and telegraphs, and in covering Gourko's retreat; during the latter it fought on foot on several occasions. After this the Russian cavalry accomplished but little, and even failed on several occasions in its essential duty of keeping a constant touch of the enemy and a knowledge of his whereabouts. The lamentable failure of the large cavalry force assembled behind Plevna, under General Kriloff, for the purpose of intercepting supplies en route to that place, has been fully explained in the previous pages (263–267). There were also fine opportunities throughout the campaign for cutting the Varna-Rustchuk railroad, whereby great annoyance might have been caused to the Turks; but they were not utilized. The employment of large bodies of cavalry (mounted) on the field of battle belongs to the order of "shock" tactics, whose day is wholly past. There has been but one instance of it in the last twenty years, viz., at the battle of Gravelotte, where, under very peculiar circumstances, the Prussians sacrificed a division of cavalry in order to obtain a result which could be gained in no other way, the infantry not yet having arrived on the field. The true use of cavalry in modern warfare was developed in our civil war, viz., in scouting and reconnaissances, in independent raids against lines of communication and supply, in following up a retreat, and in doing its heavy fighting always on foot. Since 1865 there has been nothing new on the subject.

The Russian artillery was numerous, being in the propor-

INDEX.

Academies, Military.............. 122
Administration, Methods of.... 82, 125
Adrianople, Capture of............ 361
   Fortifications at................ 427
Aladja Dagh, Battle of............ 391
Alexander, Emperor of Russia, Commander-in-Chief of Russian forces...................... 82
   Declares war................... 139
   Establishes Headquarters at Biela. 165
   Orders reënforcements.......... 204
   Arrival at Plevna.......... 233, 258
Allowances in the Russian Army, 104, 109
Araba Konak Pass, Capture of.. 295, 334
   Fortifications at 429
Ardahan, Capture of............. 383
Armenia, Campaign in 377–418
Armistice, Signature of........... 362
Army, Administration in time of War....................... 97
Army Corps, Strength of.......... 31
Army of the South, Organization of. 147
   Concentration in Roumania...... 150
   Naval operations on the Danube. 152
   Passage of the Danube......... 156
   Plan of Campaign.............. 144
Artillery, Strength and Organization of........................ 27
   Classes of..................... 58
   Dimension, Range, etc.......... 61
   Projectiles.................... 64
   Carriages..................... 68
Attack of Fortified Positions..440 et seq.
Ayazlar, Battle of................ 218

Bayazid, Defense of............. 385
Berdan Musket................ 54, 58

Breech-loaders—Effect of their fire. 422
Bulgaria, Campaign in........ 137–374
   Theatre of Operations in.... 142, 163
Buyuk Tchekmedje, Lines of...... 427

Cavalry, Strength and Organization of......................... 24
   Armament of.................. 72
Cerkovna, Battle of............. 222
Charles, Prince of Roumania, orders his troops to cross the Danube. 205, 224
   Arrives at Plevna, and assigned to command of "West Army". 233
Circumscriptions, Military......... 88
Company, Methods of Administration in a............................ 96
Company Column, Formation of the........................ 451
Constantinople, Advance to... 358, 365
   Defenses of................... 428
Cossacks, Strength and Organization of..................... 46, 49

Danube, Passage of the.......... 156
Dardanelles, Passage of, by the English Fleet.................... 364
Defense of Fortified Positions..424 et seq.
Deve Boyum, Battle of........... 398
Discipline, Methods of enforcing... 100
Dobrudja, Line of Advance.....156, 161
   Operations in the...289, 324, 326, 359

Education, Military.............. 118
Egyptian Troops at Battle of Cerkovna...................... 223
Elena, Battle of................. 285

INDEX.

	PAGE
Engineers, Strength and Organization of	28
Equipments used in the Russian Army	74
Ersatz Troops, Organization of	40
Erzeroum, Operations near	397
Eski Zagra, Combat of	181
Etropol, Capture of	294
Field Troops, Strength and Organization of	20, 32
Fortifications, at Plevna	423
at Shipka Pass	430
at Orkhanie	429
at Adrianople	427
at Buyuk Tchekmedje	427
at Shumla and Rustchuk	428
Galatz, Passage of the Danube at	156
Gorni Dubnik, Battle of	272
Gourko, General, First Expedition over the Balkans	163–184
Ordered to Plevna	267
Advance to Orkhanie	290
Passage of the Balkans near Sophia	321
Advance to Philippopolis	338
Advance to Constantinople	358
Grivitza Redoubt, Assault of,	195, 244, 269
Infantry, Strength and Organization of	21
Armament of	52
Intrenching Implements	434, 437
Irregular troops, Strength and Organization of	46
Karabassankioi, Battle of	219
Kars, Assault of	399–416
Siege of in 1855	317
Katzelevo, Battle of	219
Krenk Musket	52, 58
Krilof, General, Cavalry Operation near Plevna	263
Krüdener, General, Capture of Nikopolis	185
Attack at Plevna	193
Land Forces of Russia, Summary of	51
Linneman Spade	437

	PAGE
Local Troops, Strength and Organization of	36
Lom, Operations on the	215, 283, 288
Lovtcha, Battle of	229
Maritza, Valley of the	338
Mehemet Ali Pasha, Advance on the Lom	215
Relieved from command	223
Ordered to Sophia	291
Metchka, Battle of	286
Military Circumscriptions	88
Military Laws, Codification of	84
Military Schools	118
Military Service, Laws of	3
Duration of	6
Exemption from	8
Militia, Laws of Service in	7
Minister of War, Duties of	82
Naval Operations on the Danube,	152, 290
Nicholas, Grand Duke, Commanding the Russian Army, crosses the frontier	150
Passage of the Danube	157
Orders the Attack of Plevna,	189, 193
Commands in person at Plevna,	233, 257
Gives orders for the winter campaign	324
Arrives at San Stefano	365
Nikopolis, Capture of	186
Orkhanie, Capture of	295
Osman Pasha arrives at Plevna	190
Defeats the Russian Attacks,	191, 193, 235
Attacks the Russians	226, 301
Defeated and captured	311
Remarks on the Siege of Plevna.	315
Paris, Siege of	317, 320
Pay in the Russian Army	104, 109
Pelishat, Battle of	226
Philippopolis, Battle of	342
Plevna, Battle of, July 20	190
Battle of July 30	193
Battle of September 11	235
Investment of	264, 280
Fall of	299, 316

INDEX. 459

Plevna, Russian Fortifications at... 426
 Turkish Fortifications at........ 423
Pravetz, Battle of................ 293
Radetzky, General, Defense of Shipka Pass............ 208, 281, 349
 Advance to Constantinople...... 359
Recruiting, Laws and Methods of, 3, 10, 18
Reënforcements, Arrival of in Bulgaria...................... 204
Regiment, Methods of Administration in a...................... 93
Remounts in Cavalry and Artillery.. 115
Reserve, Organization of the....... 40
Richmond, Siege of.......... 317, 319
Rifle Brigades, Strength and Organization of..................... 24
Roumanian Troops, Strength of.... 225
 Attack at Plevna by....... 244, 269
 Capture of Rahova by.......... 298
Russian Army, Organization of the. 20
Rustchuk surrendered to the Russians....................... 364
 Fortifications of............. 428

San Stefano, Arrival of Russian Troops at................... 365
 Treaty of.................... 365
Schools, Military................. 118
Sevastopol, Siege of.......... 317, 318
Sieges, Tabular Statement of...... 317
Shipka Pass, Capture of.......... 173
 Battles at................ 207, 282
 Capture of Turkish Army at..349, 355
Shumla, Fortifications at.......... 428
Skobeleff, General, Attacks at Plevna............ 198, 247, 297
 Attack at Lovtcha............ 231
 Attack at Shenova............ 354
 Advance to Constantinople.. 360, 365
 Remarks on Tactics........... 450
Sophia, Capture of............... 334

Suleiman Pasha, Arrival in Roumelia 176
 Attacks Shipka Pass....... 207, 282
 Ordered to command on the Lom. 283
 Attacks the Russians at Metchka. 286
 Ordered to Roumelia....... 322, 339
 Escapes from Philippopolis.. 343, 346
 Relieved from command........ 347

Tactics of Artillery............... 128
 of Cavalry.................... 132
 of Infantry................... 132
 of assault during the campaign, 444–450
Taskosen, Battle of.............. 331
Tatar-Bazardjik, Capture of....... 341
Tellis, Attack of............ 277, 279
Tetevan, Capture of.............. 291
Tirnova, Capture of.............. 166
Todleben, General, Arrival at Plevna 267
 Orders investment of Plevna..... 270
 Report of the Capture of Plevna.. 301
 Enters Rustchuk............... 364
Trajan's Gate, Capture of......... 340
Trojan Pass, Capture of.......... 348
Treaty of Peace signed at San Stefano 365
 Conditions of................. 362
Tristenik, Battle of.............. 286

Uniform worn in the Russian Army. 97

Vicksburg, Siege of.......... 317, 319
Volunteers, Enlisted.............. 14
Vratza, Capture of............... 291

War, Declaration of.............. 139
War Council at Constantinople.... 205
War Ministry, Organization of..... 83
Winter Campaign, Remarks on the.
366, 369, 374

Yeni Zagra, Combat of........... 180

Zgalevitza, Battle of............. 226

INDEX.

Engineers, Strength and Organization of.................... 28
Equipments used in the Russian Army....................... 74
Ersatz Troops, Organization of..... 40
Erzeroum, Operations near........ 397
Eski Zagra, Combat of............ 181
Etropol, Capture of............... 294

Field Troops, Strength and Organization of................. 20, 32
Fortifications, at Plevna.......... 423
  at Shipka Pass............... 430
  at Orkhanie................... 429
  at Adrianople................. 427
  at Buyuk Tchekmedje.......... 427
  at Shumla and Rustchuk....... 428

Galatz, Passage of the Danube at... 156
Gorni Dubnik, Battle of........... 272
Gourko, General, First Expedition over the Balkans........ 163-184
  Ordered to Plevna............. 267
  Advance to Orkhanie........... 290
  Passage of the Balkans near Sophia 321
  Advance to Philippopolis....... 338
  Advance to Constantinople...... 358
Grivitza Redoubt, Assault of, 195, 244, 269

Infantry, Strength and Organization of........................ 21
  Armament of.................. 52
Intrenching Implements...... 434, 437
Irregular troops, Strength and Organization of............... 46

Karabassankioi, Battle of......... 219
Kars, Assault of............. 399-416
  Siege of in 1855.............. 317
Katzelevo, Battle of.............. 219
Krenk Musket................. 52, 58
Krilof, General, Cavalry Operation near Plevna................. 263
Krüdener, General, Capture of Nikopolis....................... 185
  Attack at Plevna.............. 193

Land Forces of Russia, Summary of. 51
Linneman Spade.................. 437

Local Troops, Strength and Organization of..................... 36
Lom, Operations on the... 215, 283, 288
Lovtcha, Battle of................ 229

Maritza, Valley of the............ 338
Mehcmet Ali Pasha, Advance on the Lom........................ 215
  Relieved from command........ 223
  Ordered to Sophia............. 291
Metchka, Battle of................ 286
Military Circumscriptions......... 88
Military Laws, Codification of..... 84
Military Schools................. 118
Military Service, Laws of.......... 3
  Duration of................... 6
  Exemption from............... 8
Militia, Laws of Service in........ 7
Minister of War, Duties of........ 82

Naval Operations on the Danube, 152, 290
Nicholas, Grand Duke, Commanding the Russian Army, crosses the frontier..................... 150
  Passage of the Danube......... 157
  Orders the Attack of Plevna, 189, 193
  Commands in person at Plevna, 233, 257
  Gives orders for the winter campaign....................... 324
  Arrives at San Stefano......... 365
Nikopolis, Capture of............. 186

Orkhanie, Capture of............. 295
Osman Pasha arrives at Plevna.... 190
  Defeats the Russian Attacks, 191, 193, 235
  Attacks the Russians....... 226, 301
  Defeated and captured......... 311
  Remarks on the Siege of Plevna. 315

Paris, Siege of.............. 317, 320
Pay in the Russian Army..... 104, 109
Pelishat, Battle of................ 226
Philippopolis, Battle of........... 342
Plevna, Battle of, July 20......... 190
  Battle of July 30.............. 193
  Battle of September 11........ 235
  Investment of............ 264, 280
  Fall of................... 299, 316

INDEX. 459

Plevna, Russian Fortifications at... 426
Turkish Fortifications at........ 423
Pravetz, Battle of................ 293
Radetzky, General, Defense of Shipka Pass............ 208, 281, 349
Advance to Constantinople...... 359
Recruiting, Laws and Methods of, 3, 10, 18
Reënforcements, Arrival of in Bulgaria...................... 204
Regiment, Methods of Administration in a.................... 93
Remounts in Cavalry and Artillery.. 115
Reserve, Organization of the....... 40
Richmond, Siege of.......... 317, 319
Rifle Brigades, Strength and Organization of.................... 24
Roumanian Troops, Strength of.... 225
Attack at Plevna by....... 244, 269
Capture of Rahova by.......... 298
Russian Army, Organization of the. 20
Rustchuk surrendered to the Russians., ... 364
Fortifications of................ 428

San Stefano, Arrival of Russian Troops at.................... 365
Treaty of..................... 365
Schools, Military.................. 118
Sevastopol, Siege of.......... 317, 318
Sieges, Tabular Statement of...... 317
Shipka Pass, Capture of.......... 173
Battles at................ 207, 282
Capture of Turkish Army at.. 349, 355
Shumla, Fortifications at.......... 428
Skobeleff, General, Attacks at Plevna................. 198, 247, 297
Attack at Lovtcha............. 231
Attack at Shenova.......... 354
Advance to Constantinople.. 360, 365
Remarks on Tactics............ 450
Sophia, Capture of............... 334

Suleiman Pasha, Arrival in Roumelia 176
Attacks Shipka Pass....... 207, 282
Ordered to command on the Lom. 283
Attacks the Russians at Metchka. 286
Ordered to Roumelia........ 322, 339
Escapes from Philippopolis.. 343, 346
Relieved from command........ 347

Tactics of Artillery............... 128
of Cavalry................... 132
of Infantry.................. 132
of assault during the campaign, 444-450
Taskosen, Battle of.............. 331
Tatar-Bazardjik, Capture of....... 341
Telis, Attack of............. 277, 279
Tetevan, Capture of.............. 291
Tirnova, Capture of.............. 166
Todleben, General, Arrival at Plevna 267
Orders investment of Plevna...... 270
Report of the Capture of Plevna.. 301
Enters Rustchuk............... 364
Trajan's Gate, Capture of.,....... 340
Trojan Pass, Capture of.......... 348
Treaty of Peace signed at San Stefano 365
Conditions of.................. 362
Tristenik, Battle of.............. 236

Uniform worn in the Russian Army. 97

Vicksburg, Siege of.......... 317, 319
Volunteers, Enlisted............. 14
Vratza, Capture of............... 291

War, Declaration of............. 139
War Council at Constantinople.... 205
War Ministry, Organization of..... 83
Winter Campaign, Remarks on the.
366, 369, 374

Yeni Zagra, Combat of........... 180

Zgalevitza, Battle of............. 226

RECENT PUBLICATIONS.

I.
The Data of Ethics.
Being the First Part of the "Principles of Morality." By HERBERT SPENCER. 1 vol., 12mo. Cloth. Price, $1.50.

Mr. Spencer's main purpose is to ascertain and describe the objective qualities of right conduct, the external signs of the highest virtue, and to show their coincidence with the results of progressive evolution. This he has done in the course of the profound and exhaustive analysis, of which he is so consummate a master, of vigorous but singularly lucid reasonings, and of ample and impressive illustrations from every department of Nature." —*N. Y. Tribune.*

II.
Early Christian Literature Primers.
Edited by Professor GEORGE PARK FISHER, D. D.

I. The Apostolic Fathers, and the Apologists, A. D. 95-180. By the Rev. GEORGE A. JACKSON. 16mo. Cloth. Price, 60 cents.

The "Early Christian Literature Primers" will embody, in a few small and inexpensive volumes, the substance of the characteristic works of the great Fathers of the Church. The plan recognizes four groups of works:
1. The Apostolic Fathers and the Apologists, A. D. 95-180. (*Now ready.*)
2. The Fathers of the Third Century, A. D. 180-325.
3. The Post-Nicene Greek Fathers, A. D. 325-750.
4. The Post-Nicene Latin Fathers, A. D. 325-590.

These groups are to be embraced in four books. In the first book are given exact translations of the principal works of the Apostolic Fathers and the Apologists, preceded by introductions upon the writings of the period, and by sketches of the several authors. Nearly every known author of the period is mentioned, and his place pointed out.

III.
The Development of English Literature.
The Old English Period. By Brother AZARIAS, Professor of English Literature in Rock Hill College, Maryland. 1 vol., 12mo, 214 pages. Cloth. Price, $1.25.

IV.
The Life of His Royal Highness the Prince Consort.
By THEODORE MARTIN. With Portraits. Vol. IV. 1 vol., 12mo. Cloth. Price, $2.00.

V.
Essays from the "North American Review."
Edited by ALLEN THORNDIKE RICE. One vol., 12mo, 482 pages. Cloth, price, $2.00.

"The Essays collected in this volume may, without pretension, be truly said to represent the growth of native thought and scholarship in the United States from the close of the second war with Great Britain down to the close of the great Civil War. In few libraries, public or private, can complete sets of the 'North American Review' be found, and the best thoughts and the freshest activity of two generations of conspicuous American writers have thus remained inaccessible to the great mass of the American reading public."—*Extract from Preface.*

VI.
The Spectator.
A new edition carefully revised. With Prefaces Historical and Biographical, by ALEXANDER CHALMERS, A. M.

This is an *édition de luxe* of "The Spectator," being printed in large type, on choice paper, in perfect style, and bound in vellum cloth with gilt top, after the manner now so popular with standard books. In six volumes, 8vo. Cloth. Price, $12.00.

For sale by all booksellers. Any work sent post or carriage free, to any address in the United States, on receipt of price.

D. APPLETON & CO., Publishers, 549 & 551 Broadway, N. Y.

HISTORICAL AND BIOGRAPHICAL WORKS.

The Life of the Prince Consort.
By THEODORE MARTIN. With Portraits. Vols. I., II., III., IV. 12mo. Cloth, $2.00 each volume.

The English Reformation:
How it came about, and why we should uphold it. By CUNNINGHAM GEIKIE, D. D., author of "The Life and Words of Christ." With a Preface by the author for the American edition. 1 vol., 12mo. Cloth. Price, $2.00.

A History of England in the Eighteenth Century.
By WILLIAM E. H. LECKY. 2 vols., 8vo. Cloth, $6.00.

Prehistoric Times,
As illustrated by Ancient Remains and the Manners and Customs of Modern Savages. Illustrated. By Sir JOHN LUBBOCK, Bart., author of "Origin of Civilization, and the Primitive Condition of Man." Entirely new edition. 8vo. Cloth. Price, $5.00.

The French Revolutionary Epoch.
Being a History of France from the Beginning of the First French Revolution to the End of the Second Empire. By HENRI VAN LAUN, author of "History of French Literature," etc. 2 vols., 12mo. Cloth, $3.50.

The Historical Poetry of the Ancient Hebrews.
Translated and carefully examined by MICHAEL HEILPRIN. Vol. I. Crown 8vo. Cloth. Price, $2.00.

History of New York
During the Revolutionary War, and of the Leading Events in the other Colonies at that Period. By THOMAS JONES, Justice of the Supreme Court of the Province. Edited by EDWARD FLOYD DE LANCEY. With Notes, Contemporary Documents, Maps, and Portraits. In two vols., 8vo, 748 pp., 713 pp. Cloth, gilt top, price, $15.00. Printed for the New York Historical Society, in "The John D. Jones Fund Series of Histories and Memoirs."

The Last Years of Daniel Webster.
A Monograph. By GEORGE TICKNOR CURTIS. 8vo. Paper, 50 cents.

For sale by all booksellers. Any volume mailed, post-paid, to any address in the United States, on receipt of price.

D. APPLETON & CO., PUBLISHERS, 549 & 551 BROADWAY, NEW YORK.

RECENT AMERICAN HISTORY AND BIOGRAPHY.

Destruction and Reconstruction:
Personal Experiences of the Late War. By RICHARD TAYLOR, Lieutenant-General in the Confederate Army. 1 vol., 8vo. Cloth. Price, $2.00.

Four Years with General Lee:
Being a Summary of the more Important Events touching the Career of General Robert E. Lee, in the War between the States; together with an Authoritative Statement of the Strength of the Army which he commanded in the Field. By WILLIAM H. TAYLOR, of his Staff, and late Adjutant-General of the Army of Northern Virginia. 8vo. Cloth, $2.00.

Military Operations of Joseph E. Johnston.
Narrative of Military Operations directed during the Late War between the States. By JOSEPH E. JOHNSTON, General C. S. A. Illustrated by Steel Plates and Maps. 1 vol., 8vo. Cloth, $5.00; sheep, $6.00; half morocco, $7.50.

The Life of General Albert Sidney Johnston.
By his Son, Colonel WILLIAM PRESTON JOHNSTON. One large octavo volume, 774 pages. With Maps, a fine Portrait on Steel, and 8 full-page Illustrations. Cloth, $5.00; sheep, $6.00; half turkey, $7.00.

The Autobiography of William H. Seward (1801–1834).
With a later Memoir by his Son, FREDERICK W. SEWARD, late Assistant Secretary of State. Per volume, over 800 pages, cloth, $4.25; sheep, $5.25; half turkey, $6.25; full turkey, $8.25.

Military History of General U. S. Grant.
From April, 1861, to April, 1865. By ADAM BADEAU, Colonel and Aide-de-Camp to the General-in-Chief, Brevet Brigadier-General U. S. A. With Portrait, and numerous Maps. Vol. I. 8vo. Cloth, $4.00; half calf, extra, $6.50.

Memoirs of W. T. Sherman.
By Himself. (With a Military Map showing the Marches of the United States Forces under General Sherman's command.) Two handsome vols., 8vo. Blue cloth, $5.50; sheep, $7.00; half morocco, $8.50; full morocco, $12.00.

CHEAP EDITION. 1 vol. Cloth, $3.50.

D. APPLETON & CO., PUBLISHERS, 549 & 551 BROADWAY, NEW YORK.

D. APPLETON & CO.'S PUBLICATIONS.

Tactics for Non-Military Bodies:

Adapted for the Instruction of Political Associations, Police Forces, Fire Organizations, Masonic, Odd-Fellows', and other Civic Societies. By Major-General UPTON, U. S. A. 12mo. Cloth, $1.00; paper, 50 cents.

A New System of Infantry Tactics.

Double and Single Rank. Adapted to American Topography and Improved Fire-Arms. By Major-General UPTON, U. S. A. Revised edition. 1 vol. Bound in leather, with clasp, $2.00.

Artillery Tactics, U. S. A.

Assimilated to the Tactics of Infantry and Cavalry. 1 vol. Bound in leather, with clasp, $2.00.

HEADQUARTERS OF THE ARMY, WASHINGTON, *July* 17, 1873.

GENERAL ORDERS No. 6.

The following order, received from the War Department, is published for the information and guidance of the Army:

WAR DEPARTMENT, WASHINGTON CITY, *July* 17, 1873.

The revision of Upton's Infantry Tactics by the author, and the Tactics for Artillery and Cavalry [including the proceedings of the board—Major-General Schofield, President—instituted by General Orders No. 60, Headquarters of the Army, Adjutant-General's Office, series of 1869], assimilated to the Tactics for Infantry, pursuant to instructions from the General of the Army, by Lieutenant-Colonel Emory Upton, 1st Artillery, Instructor of Tactics, U. S. Military Academy; Captain Henry A. Du Pont, 5th Artillery, commanding Battery "F," 5th Artillery; Captain John E. Tourtellotte, 7th Cavalry, Colonel and Aide-de-Camp to the General; Captain Alfred E. Bates, 2d Cavalry, Assistant Instructor of Cavalry Tactics, U. S. Military Academy—having been approved by the President, are adopted for the instruction of the Army and Militia of the United States.

To insure uniformity, all exercises, evolutions, and ceremonies, not embraced in these Tactics are prohibited, and those therein prescribed will be strictly observed.

WM. W. BELKNAP, Secretary of War.

By command of General SHERMAN:

WILLIAM D. WHIPPLE, Assistant Adjutant-General.

The Armies of Asia and Europe:

Embracing Official Reports on the Armies of Japan, China, India, Persia, Italy, Russia, Austria, Germany, France, and England. By Major-General EMORY UPTON, U. S. A.

D. APPLETON & CO., 549 & 551 Broadway, New York.

www.ingramcontent.com/pod-product-compliance
Lightning Source LLC
Chambersburg PA
CBHW051856300426
44117CB00006B/414